IMAGERY
Its Many Dimensions and Applications

IMAGERY
Its Many Dimensions and Applications

Edited by

Joseph E. Shorr, Gail E. Sobel, Pennee Robin, and Jack A. Connella

American Association of Mental Imagery
Los Angeles, California

Plenum Press · New York and London

Library of Congress Cataloging in Publication Data

American Association for the Study of Mental Imagery.
    Imagery, its many dimensions and applications.

    "Proceedings of the first annual conference of the American Association for the
Study of Mental Imagery, held in Los Angeles, California, June 22–24, 1979."
    Inlcudes index.
    1. Imagery (Psychology) – Congresses. 2. Psychotherapy – Congresses. I. Shorr,
Joseph E. II. Title. [DNLM: 1. Imagination – Congresses. 2. Psychotherapy –
Congresses. WM420 A511i 1979]
RC489.F35A43 1980   616.8'914   80-15723
ISBN 0-306-40456-7

Proceedings of the First Annual Conference of the American Association for
the Study of Mental Imagery, held in Los Angeles, California, June 22–24, 1979.

©1980 Plenum Press, New York
A Division of Plenum Publishing Corporation
227 West 17th Street, New York, N.Y. 10011

Printed in the United States of America

PREFACE

Imagery--the miraculous quality that human beings use to
re-evoke and reorganize perceptions--is no longer considered idiosyncratic. It is an absolutely integral part of human development
and motivation which gives substance to subjective meaning and
realistic abstract thought. A necessary ingredient of the trans-
mission and development of human life, imagery must be understood
and carefully studied to enhance our knowledge and our lives.

The imaginations people have of one another and the imagination one has of oneself are composed of the stuff that we call
imagery. To my way of thinking, there is waking imagery (consisting of our stream of images while we are awake) and dream, or sleep
imagery (consisting of all that goes on in our minds while asleep).
Daydreaming, reverie, fantasy, hallucinations and unbidden images
are forms of waking imagery. Dreams, nightmares, hypnogogic and
hypnopompic images are all part of sleep imagery.

To be aware of and to study the manifestations and complexity
of waking imagery--which appears to function in an effortless,
instantaneous and ubiquitous manner--is now considered a fit subject for study after a half century of denial.

The interest in and study of imagery has been far more emphasized in Europe than in America. In Sweden, for example, all
clinical training for psychologists includes major emphasis on the
works of Hanscarl Leuner and my own work in imagery.

Only in the last decade has there been a blossoming of imagery
theories and imagery techniques for therapy in America. Emphasis
on the clinical use of imagery has shown a steady increase from its
former insignificance. Thus, it is not strange that an American
society for the study of mental imagery was not organized until
1976, after I had returned from the International Congress of Mental
Imagery in Paris. At that time I was the only American on the program, and I found it difficult to explain to Dr. Andre Virel, the
French leader, why America did not have its own group dedicated to
the study of imagery. But there have been recent increases in

interest. Witness the 350 members of AASMI. Witness the 50 pre-
senters at the first convention of the Study of Mental Imagery.

This volume of the proceedings of the convention held in Los
Angeles in June of 1979 contains emphasis on the theoretical dimensions of imagery and its many applications.

The book is organized into several sections. The first section contains papers related to the theoretical understanding of
the nature of imagery. The second section is devoted to studies
and explorations in Psycho-Imagination Therapy. The third section
relates to studies of the use of imagery in movement and art
therapy, and the fourth section deals with studies of guided imagery
and fantasy. The last section deals with the applications of imagery to various aspects of psychological life.

I wish to thank my co-editors, Gail Sobel, Pennee Robin, and
Jack Connella, for their diligent and tireless work in preparing
this volume. I wish to offer my gratitude to Jane Stewart for her
valuable work in editing, and especially to Anita Matthews for her
major effort in secretarial preparation of this volume.

Most of all I wish to thank the staff of the Institute for
Psycho-Imagination Therapy, who sponsored the meeting, and all those
persons who helped plan and develop into fruition a fine convention
that brought with it excitement, erudition, novelty, and finally
this book of imagery and its many dimensions and applications.

Joseph E. Shorr, Ph.D.,
President
American Association for the
   Study of Mental Imagery
Spring, 1980

CONTENTS

I: THEORETICAL ASPECTS OF IMAGERY

THERAPY AND THE FLOW OF THOUGHT

Eric Klinger, Ph.D.

University of Minnesota

Morris, Minnesota

It is uncannily fitting that the first annual meeting of the American Association for the Study of Mental Imagery took place on the centennial of Wilhelm Wundt's founding of his Leipzig laboratory; but at the same time it is somewhat eerie that this meeting was only the first gathering of an American association for the study of mental imagery. There appeared to be a faintly festive spirit--even a somewhat triumphant spirit--about this occasion, a sense that within a framework of historic dimensions something with which the members of AASMI identify was being vindicated.

Perhaps one reason for the sense of vindication is that so many different kinds of practitioners and investigators have moved into this area of imagery, which was not so long ago beyond the pale of respectability in American psychology. Suddenly we have behavior therapists, electrophysiologists, information-processing cognitivists, verbal learning theorists, biofeedback researchers, hypnosis researchers, and psychotherapists discovering their shared interest in imagery and other phenomena of consciousness (e.g., Anderson, in press).

How did all this come about? If 1920 can serve as a rough marker for the triumph of the behaviorist revolution over the older American psychologies, 1960 witnessed the opening guns of the mentalistic counter-revolution. The 1960s and early 1970s saw a succession of books and articles whose effect can only be described as liberating. I recall my own sense of thrill at Silvan Tomkins' 1962 book, and I remember regarding its title--Affect, Imagery, Consciousness--as an act of courage on his part. Today, it would be merely another catchy title. There followed books such as Neisser's Cognitive Psychology and Singer's Daydreaming that

3

launched a science of thought flow about whose vigor there can now
be little question.

Revolutions do not, of course, materialize out of nowhere. The
psychological scene even in this country continued to harbor mental-
ists before 1960, although they were not encouraged. People interested in imagery often identified themselves with the projective test
area or with psychoanalysis. However, electrophysiological investigators of sleep became concerned with dream imagery, and sensory
deprivation people with hallucinations. Particularly in other parts
of the world, interest in imagery remained publicly vigorous:
Australasia, with the work of McKellar and Richardson; European
phenomenology; and the various Europeans who pioneered the use of
imaginal techniques in therapy, such as Jung, Desoille, Leuner,
Virel, Fretigny, and Assagioli. By the 1960s, in parallel with the
emerging science of conscious flow, a second vigorous movement was
thus getting established in this country, a movement toward the
clinical application of imaginal techniques in therapy, including
such figures as Perls, Rehyer, and Shorr.

Together, these movements have accumulated a considerable mass
of data and clinical experience. Many of the findings, perhaps
especially some of the clinical accounts, are tantalizing in their
dramatic portrayals of--to borrow Singer and Pope's (1978) title--
the power of human imagination. In recognition of the diversity
and richness of these experiences, the purpose of this chapter is
to look for order, to systematize, to integrate.

The imaginal therapies have emerged mostly out of Pavlovian,
Skinnerian, Freudian, and Jungian frameworks. None of these frameworks adequately encompass the rich phenomena the imaginal therapists have encountered; and none of them brings those clincal findings into communication with contemporary experimental work.
Nevertheless, the outlines of a set of principles seem to be emerging out of the growing body of data--principles that govern the
flow of thought (by which I mean to include imagery) and that have
a direct bearing on clinical application. What I propose to do here
is to outline these principles, or at least to outline the issues
whose clarification might yield principles.

THE NATURE AND DETERMINANTS OF
  IMAGINAL CONTENT

[1]Imaginal activity is an efferent process. It is more akin to
previous conceptions of motoric action than it is to earlier con-
ceptions--which were probably misconceptions--of sensory activity.
Imagining is a constructive activity, in the sense that the imager
actively constructs his or her own images. This point has been
argued at length elsewhere (Klinger, 1971) and need therefore not

be argued here. It is in substantial agreement with Tomkins' (1962) argument that perception and recall require that we model the world perceived or recalled, Festinger's theories of perception as efferent activity (Festinger, Ono, Burnham and Bamber, 1967), Neisser's (1967) conception of perception and memory as construction, Sokolov's (1969) similar notion that when we perceive we construct a neural model of the thing perceived, and Weimer's (in press) cogent arguments in behalf of "motor theories of the mind." Taken together, the evidence strongly suggests that imaginal activity obeys similar laws of conditioning, skill learning, organization, and motivation as other efferent activity.

This may all seem to be a bit too abstract and removed from practical reality to be very useful or interesting, but the principle actually serves as a theoretical basis for each of the further principles described below. For one thing, it indicates that whatever we know about the modification or use of other forms of behavior provides knowledge that can be applied judiciously to imaginal activity as well. For another, it suggests that what we do in imagery reflects the same general schemata with which we approach things in general--the perceptual schemata with which we construe our worlds, the expectations we hold for what will happen to us in given situations, and the responses that we muster for coping.

In other words, imagining things is in a real way our doing those things except that the doing is confined to the mental arena with only minimal leakage into the peripheral motor system that moves our bodies around.

It seems quite likely that imagery represents the functioning of important parts of the same psychological apparatus that we exercise in all our activities. That is, imagery represents the central core of perceptual, retrieval, and response mechanisms. There are a number of reasons for believing this. First, people are not always able to distinguish between their nonperceptual images and their perception, as Perky (1910) showed in a laboratory setting with presumably normal subjects. Second, imagery carries with it low-level electromyographic activity in the appropriate muscle groups. Third, there is considerable evidence that practicing motor skills mentally can improve motor performance.

If imagery indeed constitutes activity in the central parts of the usual psychological apparatus, experiencing something in imagery can be considered to be in many essential ways psychologically equivalent to experiencing the thing in actuality. After all, actuality is psychologically a cipher except insofar as it is reflected in psychological functioning. Therefore, to the extent that we set the psychological apparatus to moving in the absence of the usual external context, we produce an equivalent psychological reality. Insofar as we can produce experiences in imagery, we approximate psychological effects equivalent to those that would accompany the corresponding external reality.

Of course, waking imagery is for most people rarely so powerful as to deceive them into treating it as a transaction with the environment. There are, fortunately, clues that enable people to keep imagery and reality separate. When people imagine, their experience is usually more completely under voluntary control, is more subject to interference from sensory activity, produces fewer changes in sensory activity, and brings different feedback from the motor apparatus. Furthermore, insofar as people can distinguish imagery from real transaction with their environments, they can learn to do things in imagery that they would not do otherwise. Thus, efferent activity in imagery is not restricted to what people are willing or able to do in motoric transactions. Nevertheless, they are bound to be closely related. We can conclude that imagery not only contains rich diagnostic information about people, but also that it is a way of getting under the hood, so to speak, for purposes of modifying behavior.

One highly specific consequence of this efferent view of imagery was recently demonstrated by Peter Lang (1977). He induced subjects to imagine particular emotionally arousing scenes. In one condition he described the scene to subjects in largely sensory terms--what they would see or hear, for instance. In another condition he added "response propositions"--descriptions of what subjects would do in the scene. The second of these conditions, which provided subjects directly with efferent properties of the image, produced significantly more emotional response as measured psychophysiologically. This, then, brings us to the next principle:

[2]The imaginal stream carries with it affective responses to cues operating in the situation, including the internal cues of the imaginal stream itself. It would be unnecessary to make a special principle out of this if it were generally recognized that affect forms an integral part of all behavioral organization (Klinger, 1971, 1977a). In any case, the truth of the principle cannot be in doubt. Such well-known techniques as systematic desensitization and implosion depend on it. Anyone who has worked with imaginal techniques or has merely been sensitive to his or her own inner experience is aware of it. Its implications merely strengthen assertions made above regarding the value of imagery for both diagnostic and intervention purposes. It might be worth pointing out, however, the implications of one particular view of affect, that affect constitutes an evaluative feedback system and therefore forms the psychological basis for value and hence for decision-making (Klinger, 1977a). If this view is correct, imaginal techniques provide diagnostic information concerning value and hence the bases for the client's decision-making; and, in accordance with other principles, imaginal techniques then also provide ways to

modify these.

[3]The imaginal stream shifts in thematic content in a lawful way
described by the Induction Principle and its refinements, as moderated by operant elements. It will take some filling in of background to make this principle comprehensible. To understand the
Induction Principle requires understanding a motivational concept
that has become quite basic to our work, the concept of current
concern. This is a construct that emerged to take into account the
mass of data that had accumulated up to 1970 in work on play and
dreams and, especially, on TAT need scores. "Current concern"
refers to the state of a person between two rough points in time.
The first point is the moment at which the person becomes committed
to pursuing a goal. The second point is the time at which the person consummates the goal or the point at which the person gives up
pursuing the goal. In this framework, a person has a current concern about every goal he or she has become committed to pursuing
and has not yet reached or given up on. One might have simultaneous current concerns about eating dinner tonight, going skiing,
making up after an argument with a friend, writing one's next
article, and so on--all at the same time. This construct and many
of its far-reaching implications are described fully elsewhere
(Klinger, 1977a).

The original TAT evidence available up to 1970 seemed to lend
itself to the following interpretation: while people are in a
state of current concern about something--that is, after they have
become committed to pursuing the thing but before they have reached
or given up on it--they are more likely to have thoughts about it
than they otherwise would have had. After one has become committed
to writing an article, one is more likely to have stray thoughts
about that article. This is not a particularly startling conclusion, but it does accommodate the old TAT evidence better than all
the less obvious explanations then in use. On the other hand, in
itself it does not tell us much about what governs shifts in moment-
to moment content: shifts in what a person thinks about at given
moments in time. Indications in the experimental literature suggested an answer to this question, however, which we have since
been able to confirm experimentally (Klinger, 1978a): thought content, along with attention and storage in memory, shift to focus on
those cues in the person's immediate surroundings (and probably
internal cues as well) that are in some way related to the person's
current concerns. This is true even though the cues occur in ways
that make them unusable for actually advancing toward reaching the
goal in question, and even though the thoughts they evoked are not
problem-solving thoughts. In our experimental tests of this relationship, we sat people down in a laboratory and asked them to
listen to story narratives through stereo headphones dichotically--
that is, to two different passages played simultaneously, one to
each ear. For instance, they might have been listening

simultaneously to two different passages from Aldous Huxley's Doors of Perception. They were free to listen to whichever channel they wished at any time. These were subjects who had been carefully trained to report their thoughts according to a predetermined format and who had given us extensive interview and questionnaire information on the basis of which we could determine their current concerns. The passages to which they listened had been modified intermittently to allude indirectly to one of their individual current concerns on one channel of the tape and to something comparable on the other channel of the tape that we believed was not a current concern of the particular subject. These pairs of modifications always occurred at the same time on two channels. Ten seconds after the end of the modified portions, the tape stopped with a tone to signal the subject to report his or her latest presignal thoughts. Many more thoughts were found to be related to the cues that represented current concerns of a subject than to the other cues. Analyses established that it was the cues that set off these thoughts, rather than the results simply reflecting different base rates for these thought classes (Klinger, 1978a).

These observations led to the conclusion that, for want of a label, was dubbed the "Induction Principle": at any moment, concerns and cues jointly induce relevant thoughts that best bridge them. In other words, as people travel through their world of stimulation they ignore most of it and process those features of it that fit into one or more of their current concerns. Where one's mind goes from one moment to the next depends on which cues one encounters that relate to one's various current concerns.

We have not, of course, been able to vary subjects' internal, self-generated cues experimentally. However, it seems highly likely that they function in somewhat the same way. After all, imagery constitutes a large part of what goes on in responding to external cues. If someone produces a piece of imagery, that fragment may be associated with a number of different current concerns and give rise to a number of different kinds of affect, just as the perceptual process that meets an external stimulus would. There is no a priori reason to suppose that the Induction Principle functions very differently in the imaginal stream.

The results of the experiment described above were the same for thoughts that occurred to subjects spontaneously (respondent thoughts) as they were for thoughts that subjects experienced as deliberate, problem-solving (operant) thoughts. Operant thoughts do have some features not shared to an equal degree by respondent thoughts. Particularly, operant thoughts contain more attempts to control the direction of the subject's attention and more evaluations for how useful the thought was in advancing the subject toward a goal (Klinger, 1974). One might suppose that the tendency to control attention by focusing it on a problem would alter the functioning of the Induction Principle. At this time, however, it appears likely that the chief effect is to reduce sensitivity to external cues unrelated to the problem at hand.

Given that the Induction Principle probably works over a wide range of conditions, it is nevertheless true that it needs fleshing out in a number of respects. For instance, not all current concerns exert equal influence on the stream of thought. Given the many concerns each person carries around at particular moments in time, some preoccupy the person much more than others. We have, therefore, tried to specify the characteristics of different current concerns that make some more influential in cognitive processing than others, characteristics we are calling "concern influence variables."

The principal method used to look for these variables has been a series of "Concern Dimensions Questionnaires" (CDQs) (Klinger, Barta and Maxeiner, in preparation a and b). The latest-generation CDQ, the CDQ III, asks untrained subjects to list five "things" they have thought about most "today and yesterday," and then to list five more things significant in the subject's life that he or she had not thought about, or had thought about little, during the same period. Subjects next rank these 10 things according to the amount of time they had spent thinking about them and they estimate the percent of their "thinking time" they had devoted to each thing. They then characterize each thing on a long list of variables that are potentially concern influence variables. The amount of time people report thinking about their 10 things ("Thought Content Frequency") can then be correlated with the ratings of those things on the other variables. These correlations are obtained within subjects and pooled across subjects, so as to eliminate influences of individual differences that might distort relationships.

One might question how well subjects' reports of thought content frequency reflect the actual frequency with which they thought about the various things. We were able to perform a test of the validity of this CDQ measure in the following way. Seventeen subjects who filled out CDQs were asked to carry pocket programmers, or "beepers," that emitted soft tones at quasirandom intervals averaging about 40 minutes. These subjects had been trained in thought reporting procedures, and every time they heard a tone they stopped and wrote down their latest presignal thoughts. Since they carried the beepers during the 24 hours just following their taking of the CDQ, it seemed reasonable to compare the frequency with which they reported thoughts of different kinds of the CDQ with the frequency of thought reports about the same things during the next 24 hours. There were some problems in doing this, of course. First, since we were measuring thought frequency for different time periods, discrepancies might reflect real changes in content. Second, since there were only a few thought samples per

subject that related to any of the CDQ things, it was not feasible
to obtain very stable correlations for individual subjects. To
circumvent the latter problem, the data for the 17 subjects were
aggregated to see whether the number of times first-ranked CDQ
things emerged more often in the thought samples than second-ranked
CDQ things, and so on down the ranks for the things listed as most
thought about. The correlation between CDQ Thought Content Frequency ranks and thought frequency in the thought samples was .65
(p < .05). (Median individual-subject correlations were in the
.30s.) One can conclude that the CDQ Thought Content Frequency
measure is reasonably valid. It follows that CDQ kinds of procedures, as well as the thought-sampling procedures they were compared with, might both make useful tools for monitoring thoughts
and evaluating progress in cognitive and cognitive-behavior
therapies.

     To return to the question of concern influence variables, how-
ever, what did the CDQ data suggest? Within the CDQ, the best
single-variable predictor of Thought Content Frequency listed is a
measure of the subject's sense of commitment to the thing. Among
the CDQ things most thought about, Commitment correlates with
Thought Content Frequency at about .40. Across all 10 things on
the CDQ III, the correlation is in the .30s (p < .001). Clearly,
people spend more time thinking about the things they feel most
strongly committed to than about other things. However, Commitment
ratings are themselves highly predicted by the incentive value of
the thing for a subject and by the subjective probability of success, and both of these variables also predict Thought Content
Frequency (p < .001).

     The way in which the CDQ III measures incentive value might be
of interest here. Incentive value actually comprises a set of
variables, each of which represents the subject's scaling of affect
experienced in imagery. For instance, the Positivity scale asks
subjects to imagine that they have succeeded in attaining the thing
they listed (or succeeded in keeping it, or whatever else they
wanted to do with it), and then to rate how much joy or relief they
imagine feeling. The Loss scale asks subjects to imagine that they
are unable to consummate the thing and to rate how much sorrow they
imagine feeling. And so on.

     On the CDQ, then, the best predictors of thought frequency
about something are the subject's sense of commitment to pursuing
the goal and, by the same token, the incentive value of the goal
and the subject's belief in the accessibility of the goal. A further correlate of Thought Content Frequency is the imminence of
the goal: people think most about the things they have to do something about the soonest (p < .001).

     There is another cluster of variables that correlate with

Thought Content Frequency. They were predicted by the theory of incentive-disengagement (Klinger, 1977a), but we found them originally by a close inspection of the laboratory data described earlier, and then built them into the CDQ III. These "incentive-disengagement" variables all relate to disruptions in goal-striving--disruptions that, if continued, would presumably end with the person abandoning the goal. They include such variables as being in the process of disengaging from the thing, the thing representing a threatened personal relationship, pursuing the thing is presenting unexpected difficulties, or the thing representing a special challenge to the person. In each of these instances, the thing is more likely than chance to be among the things subjects report thinking about most. Conversely, if the thing represents a fairly routine part of the subject's life--something that may be highly valued but is presenting no special challenges or problems--it is much more likely than chance to be among the things thought about little.

People are also more likely to think about things if just thinking about them makes the person feel good, and also if the things occurred in the recent past.

One might object that even though the CDQ finds these relationships consistently, they might merely represent the obvious fact that people surround themselves with the cues for important, imminent, or troubled goal pursuits, and that the thought frequencies reported simply reflect the incidence of cues in the subjects' environments. However, this is probably not the appropriate explanation. We were able to test this hypothesis directly using the same data described earlier for subjects who carried beepers around through their daily lives. When the signal tones sounded and the subjects wrote down their latest thoughts, they also wrote down descriptions of the situations in which they found themselves. Thus, it was possible to tabulate the frequency with which the situations described were probably related to the things subjects had listed on their CDQs. We were unable to find any consistent relationships between the CDQ value, imminence, or accessibility of the things and the frequency with which subjects reported being in situations related to those goals during the next 24 hours.

Ideally, it would now be possible to present laboratory evidence that when subjects are presented with cues for goal pursuits that are important, imminent, accessible, or troubled, they respond to these cues with more thought and other cognitive processing than they do to other cues. However, we have so far been unable to confirm these relationships in the laboratory, perhaps because the sole attempt to do so employed variables less refined than those of CDQ III. A great deal of laboratory work obviously remains to discover just how the concern influence variables established in the CDQ studies exert their effects.

In the meantime, purely on the basis of the CDQ results, one might qualify the Induction Principle to state that the current concerns whose cues most evoke cognitive processing are those involving highly valued, reasonably accessible, and imminent goals, and goals whose pursuit entails difficulties beyond the ordinary routine of coping.

One immediate implication of this revised Induction Principle is that the stream of imagery observed in imaginal therapies is most likely to overrepresent the client's problem area. Unlike polite social discourse, imaginal techniques invite material that is likely to move selectively into the troubled areas of the client's life.

THE FORMS OF IMAGERY

The discussion has so far made no distinctions between the flow of ordinary waking thought and the flow of imagery in other circumstances, such as dreaming while asleep, "waking dreams," drug-induced hallucinatory experience, and so on. The reason for avoiding such distinctions up to this point is that the principles so far enunciated are intended quite generally to pertain to all of these states. Furthermore, even "ordinary" states vary along a number of important dimensions (Klinger, 1978a, 1978b). Nevertheless, there are obviously some important changes in the properties of conscious flow according to the person's state.

Many of the differences between imagery in the non-ordinary waking states and in ordinary waking thought flow can be summed up in qualities designated elsewhere as fusions and conceived within a response-organizational framework (Klinger, 1971). These fusions are intended to include the kinds of phenomena Freud (1900/1961) drew attention to under the names condensation, symbolization, and displacement and conceived within the conceptual scheme he revealed in his Project (1895/1966). Freud's work and that of his successors have provided intriguing tools for drawing inferences on the basis of the fusions in dreams and other imagery. However, the fact remains that no presently available system allows us to predict the forms that particular fusions will take. No system suggests specific conditions of the person, specific properties of the ingredients of the images, or properties of the current concerns the images represent that would enable us to predict what fused images will occur at a given moment in time. To achieve this kind of prediction is a great challenge, of course; but until some measure of predictability has been achieved we cannot say that we properly understand the process by which fused images occur.

In the meantime, we are left with some gross empirical generalizations to the effect that [4]fusions occur more commonly during sleep, and especially during Stage 1-REM sleep, or during specifiable drug states, sleep deprivation, self-induced waking dreams, and certain psychotic states. We are also, of course, left with Freud's and others' rich speculations regarding the so-called drive connections between ideational representations and form compatibilities that dispose toward fusion. None of this should suggest, however, that fusions in ordinary waking states are especially rare. Foulkes and Fleisher (1975) found that over a fifth of the thoughts reported by relaxed but awake subjects contained "regressive" features, a figure that accords well with our own thought-sampling data (Klinger, 1978a).

Not only do fusions occur, but images move in and out of various kinds of fused states in the course of imagining. Rossi's (1971) inspections of many dream reports led him to the following conclusion about changes in imagery: [5]transformations in dream imagery can probably be described within no more than five categories:

1. Creation de novo--that is, new images can appear apparently out of nowhere.

2. Division: one image can divide into two or more figures.

3. Transformation: one image can be transformed into another.

4. Parallel processes: similar psychological changes can occur in different dream sequences employing somewhat different content while preserving a basic thematic parallelism.

5. Unification: two or more dream figures may merge to form a single figure.

Rossi's taxonomy gives us something to work with. The challenge will be to determine whether the taxonomy can be operationalized and to discover the conditions that govern the choice of transformation in particular instances.

In reviewing numerous descriptions of waking dreams produced by clients in therapy, one kind of condition appears to emerge that tends to produce transformations:

[6]Asking a client to focus on some part of the imagery often results in a transformation of the thing. The literature suggests at least three kinds of changes when clients are, for example, asked to look more closely:

1. The image may become more detailed. The imager may notice features of the thing imaged that were not apparent before.

2. The thing imaged may change in form. For instance, a
monster may change into an uncle.

3. There may be a change in affect. Apparently, this change
may take the form of increased affect, reduced affect, or a change
from one affect to a qualitatively different affect, presumably
depending on the particulars of the scene imagined, including its
duration. Again, it is a challenge for research to discover the
conditions under which each kind of transformation takes place.

There is also another kind of transformation described by
Beck (1970) as a function of asking clients to repeat daydreams:
on repetition, the daydreams become progressively more realistic.

Principle 6 seems to hold for many reported instances of asking clients to focus on particular images. However, there is no
present basis for offering even an informed guess as to the proportion of requests to focus on an image that lead to each kind of
transformation. It is furthermore almost certain that transformations do not always occur, and there appears to be a class of images
described by Ahsen (1977) that resist even intentional efforts to
change them.

Ahsen has, in fact, made the resistance to change of certain
images an operational criterion for what he calls "eidetic images"--
images for which people have a species-specific predisposition
(somewhat in the manner of Jungian archetypes) but which become
concretized in particular, emotionally laden personal experiences.
One very common instance of unchanging images is a person's image
of one's parents standing before one. Ahsen has devised a diagnostic "Parents Test" in which clients are asked to imagine their
parents standing before them and are then asked to perform certain
operations on this image, such as having the parents change places
with each other. Many people--perhaps most--find this a difficult
thing to do. Some simply report that the images seemed to resist
the change. If the father started out standing to the client's
right, the father image would resist moving to the client's left.
Other clients report having to go through various maneuvers. For
instance, the image could be changed only if the father walked to
the other place.

The theory of eidetic images, in Ahsen's use of that term, is
still a largely clinical construction without rigorous, systematic
evidence to support it; but the observation that some images resist
change is nevertheless of fundamental importance. Ahsen's explanation is intriguing but far from established. It presents a challenge to imagery researchers to specify the conditions under which
images resist change, change at an accelerated pace, and undergo
the various transformations that have been observed to occur.

SOCIAL AND PHYSICAL CONDITIONS

Clinical wisdom suggests that imagery is richer when the imager is relaxed with eyes closed. Following previous experimental work by Bakan and associates, Pope (1978) has recently provided experimental work that sheds light on a number of related factors. Pope had college students think aloud or indicate with a keypress when their thoughts moved from one thematic focus to another. In one thinking aloud condition, the subjects themselves said "shift" at each shift in content that they themselves detected. In another condition, raters read through thinking-aloud transcripts to determine the presence of shifts. These various methods produced largely parallel effects of the main experimental conditions, which were the subject's posture (lying down, sitting up, and walking), and social context (alone or with an experimenter who either could or could not hear what the subject was saying). The results permit the following generalization:

[7]Thought flow shifts faster and dwells more on the immediate environment the more active (or upright?) the person is and (for males) in the presence of others. The fact that the social condition did not exert a similar effect on the women in Pope's study is hard to interpret. Perhaps social conditions are perceived as less different from being alone by women than by men; but another explanation might reside in the fact that all of Pope's experimenters were male, thus confounding a same-sex social condition with the sex-of-subject condition.

Pope also found that the number of shifts in thought content reported when subjects were thinking aloud was far fewer than the number of shifts subjects signaled with the keypress when they were thinking silently. Pope's figures agree roughly with our own findings using thought-sampling methods and thinking aloud. This pattern of findings then enables a further conclusion:

[8]When people think aloud, their thought content segments are longer than during normal silent thought. One possible cause of this difference is that subjects regard thinking aloud as a communicative process, which requires a certain level of detailed articulation and coherence not necessary in silent thought (Klinger, 1971). However, other factors may also be operating, including, for instance, the fact that self-generated cues are more prominent when they are spoken than when silent. In any event, therapists who asked their subjects to think aloud during directed fantasy should be aware that they may be retarding the flow of imagery in so doing. Whether a rapid or slow flow is more desirable for therapeutic purposes is an issue that seems not to have been broached, and the answer may well depend on the circumstances, which have yet to be systematized.

THERAPEUTIC EFFECTS

The literature on imaginal techniques in therapy provides repeated case evidence that guided waking dreams can have a therapeutic effect on clients without the therapist interpreting anything and even without the client gaining any apparent intellectual insights. The imaginal therapies area has so far not come up with controlled outcome studies that would allow one to determine confidently that guided imagery techniques lead to improvement of any kind, let alone without interpretation or insight; but until such studies are performed, the case evidence seems fairly compelling. Consider, for instance, a case described by Leuner (1977). A chemistry student has flunked a test given by a professor as a result of "inner tensions." Leuner has the student imagine meeting the instructor on a meadow, where, with Leuner's repeated encouragement, the student strikes up a conversation with the instructor and eventually begins feeding him a picnic supper of roast chicken, French bread, and red wine. Leuner instructs the student to continue the feeding imagery at home that evening. The next day, the student came back to report having passed the test calmly and without difficulty.

The treatment of this case did not employ any of the usual methods for desensitization or relaxation training. It did not seek to achieve insights. One might guess that some degree of sheer desensitization probably did occur, and perhaps even some insight. It is impossible to evaluate case evidence such as this in rigorous fashion, and what we clearly need here is some hard-headed research. But in the meantime, based on the intuitive appraisals of experienced clinicians, it seems reasonable to arrive at a tentative conclusion:

[9]Guided waking dreams can often have therapeutic effects without interpretations by the therapist or intellectual insight by the client. In Leuner's term, one can solve pressing problems through an "operation on the symbol." This is not to suggest that the therapist takes a passive role in the therapy. Leuner's role in the example was very active indeed, both in suggesting the starting imagery and directing the action thereafter; but he did not attempt an intellectual formulation and did not attempt to modify the student's behavior directly. One might hypothesize that by "operating on the symbol," he was producing changes in the psychological substructures that mediate both imaginal expression and overt behavior.

A review of the imaginal therapies literature suggests a further feature:

[10]The imaginal stream tends to circumvent resistances, self-deceptions, and defenses, but the circumventions are often shrouded

in metaphor. Verbal free association is often a process of verbal
communication about oneself--not reports of what is going on here
and now but generalizations about oneself, recollections about past
scenes, and so on. This kind of discourse necessarily relies
heavily on the client's construing processes (Fiske, 1978) and on
highly selective recall. In contrast, imaginal therapies require
the client to engage in imaginal activities here and now and to
report them as they occur. Assuming that they are subject to the
Induction Principle, we would expect them to reflect current concerns about problematic goals, including avoidant, defensive goals;
and we would expect the imaginal stream to contain the affects
appropriate to the imagery. Therefore, resistances to therapy--
which are ways to protect goals threatened by the therapy--can be
expected to emerge.

For example, Starker (1971) reported a case treated by hypnotic
serial fantasy. At a session rife with resistances, the client
first imagined a whirlpool "going round and round" and then being
in a spotlight surrounded by a large audience, after which she
imagined departing by floating away like a big balloon. Subsequently, this client related these images to feeling trapped and being
in the spotlight during her therapy, and to her wish to escape. It
would be easy to multiply this kind of example.

By representing resistances and defenses actively, rather than
through omission, the imaginal stream may provide better information about them and may make it easier for clients to achieve
insight than is true of other methods. Whether this is really true,
only much further work can establish. At the moment, this is at
least a good working hypothesis. The catch, of course, is that the
active representation of resistances is often metaphoric. Until we
understand the process by which current concerns become encoded in
imagery, detecting resistances will continue to depend on the raw
humanistic skill of the therapist.

Finally, it might be well to spell out one final point that
is already implied above:

[11]Fantasy solutions, perhaps especially when rehearsed, seem to
generalize outside of therapy. If the psychological processes
brought into play in fantasy indeed form a substantial part of the
psychological apparatus that enters into all human activity, there
is no a priori reason to doubt the truth of Principle 11. Until
we have well-controlled outcome studies, there will be no firm
assurance that it is true in general. In the meantime, however,
there are some specific indirect reasons to be optimistic (Klinger,
1977b). First, there is the evidence obtained from behavior
therapy uses of imagery.

Although decisive outcome studies still need to be performed

for most methods, and even though the fantasy approaches may in a
behavior therapy context be less effective than in vivo approaches
(Marks, 1978), systematic desensitization, covert sensitization,
covert reinforcement, covert modeling (e.g., Cautela and McCullough,
1978; Kazdin, 1978), and related methods have accumulated a sufficiently good record to stand as favorable indicators for the ability
of fantasy solutions to generalize. Second, there is the evidence
that mental practice of motor skills improves motor performance.
There are some obviously important parameters that govern the effectiveness of mental practice. For instance, the person must already
possess the rudiments of the skill and must practice motor imagery,
not simply visual or auditory imagery. Failure to observe these
constraints has tended to muddy the evidence in this area, but the
evidence appears to me firm enough to be taken quite seriously. In
addition to these two sets of reasons for optimism, imaginal techniques can probably facilitate cognitive reorganization (Meichenbaum, 1978) with the resulting changes in decision-making, and can
help people gain a greater measure of both acceptance of their
spontaneous inner life and control over their mental resources.

CONCLUSION

The 11 general principles or sets of issues presented above
represent one way of structuring both what we know and what we don't
about the flow of thought as it pertains to therapy. In reflecting
on them, they seem a bit plain. They are not as rich as the fine-
grained lore of the experienced clinician. They are high-order
generalizations based on our common experimental or clinical experience, and many readers could clearly supplement them with numerous
astute further statements. Nevertheless, they help one to think
about the field. They serve as guideposts, or as an inventory of
certain kinds of knowledge. They also serve as the rudiments of a
broad program of future investigation into the fundamentals of
phenomena central to human functioning.

REFERENCES

Ahsen, A. Eidetics: an overview. Journal of Mental Imagery, 1977,
     1, 5-38.
Anderson, M. P. Imaginal processes: therapeutic applications and
       theoretical models. In M. J. Mahoney (Ed.), Psychotherapy
       process. New York: Plenum, 1980.
Beck, A. T. Role of fantasies in psychotherapy and psychopathology.
       Journal of Nervous and Mental Disease, 1970, 150, 3-17.
Cautela, J. R., and McCullough, L. Covert conditioning: a learning-
       theory perspective on imagery. In J. L. Singer and K. S. Pope
       (Eds.), The power of human imagination: new methods in psycho-
       therapy. New York: Plenum, 1978.

Festinger, L., Ono, H., Burnham, C. A., and Bamber, D. Efference
    and the conscious experience of perception. *Journal of
    Experimental Psychology Monograph*, 1967, 74 (4; Whole No. 637).
Fiske, D. W. *Strategies for personality research*. San Francisco:
    Jossey-Bass, 1978.
Foulkes, D., and Fleisher, S. Mental activity in relaxed wakeful-
    ness. *Journal of Abnormal Psychology*, 1975, 84, 66-75.
Freud, S. *The interpretation of dreams*. New York: Wiley, 1961.
    (Originally published, 1900.)
Freud, S. A project for a scientific psychology. In *The standard
    edition of the complete psychological works of Sigmund Freud*
    (Vol. 1). London: Hogarth, 1966. (Originally published,
    1895.)
Kazdin, A. E. Covert modeling: the therapeutic application of
    imagined rehearsal. In J. L. Singer and K. S. Pope (Eds.),
    The power of human imagination: new methods in psychotherapy.
    New York: Plenum, 1978.
Klinger, E. *Structure and functions of fantasy*. New York: Wiley,
    1971.
Klinger, E. Utterances to evaluate steps and control attention
    distinguish operant from respondent thought while thinking out
    loud. *Bulletin of the Psychonomic Society*, 1974, 4, 44-45.
Klinger, E. *Meaning and void: inner experience and the incentives
    in people's lives*. Minneapolis: University of Minnesota
    Press, 1977. (a)
Klinger, E. The nature of fantasy and its clinical uses. *Psycho-
    therapy: Theory, Research and Practice*, 1977, 14, 223-231. (b)
Klinger, E. Modes of normal conscious flow. In K. S. Pope and
    J. L. Singer (Eds.), *The stream of consciousness: scientific
    investigations into the flow of human experience*. New York:
    Plenum, 1978. (a)
Klinger, E. Dimensions of thought and imagery in normal waking
    states. *Journal of Altered States of Consciousness*, 1978, 4,
    97-113. (b)
Klinger, E., Barta, S. G., and Maxeiner, M. E. Current concerns:
    assessing therapeutically relevant motivation. In P. C.
    Kendall and S. D. Hollon (Eds.), *Cognitive-behavioral inter-
    ventions: assessment*. New York: Academic Press, in prepara-
    tion. (a)
Klinger, E., Barta, S. G., and Maxeiner, M. E. *Motivational corre-
    lates of thought content frequency*. In preparation. (b)
Lang, P. J. Imagery in therapy: an information processing analy-
    sis of fear. *Behavior Therapy*, 1977, 8, 862-886.
Leuner, H. Guided affective imagery: an account of its develop-
    ment. *Journal of Mental Imagery*, 1977, 1, 73-92.
Marks, I. Behavioral psychotherapy of adult neurosis. In S. L.
    Garfield and A. E. Bergin (Eds.), *Handbook of psychotherapy
    and behavior change: an empirical analysis*. New York:
    Wiley, 1978.

Meichenbaum, D. Why does using imagery in psychotherapy lead to change? In J. L. Singer and K. S. Pope (Eds.), The power of human imagination: new methods in psychotherapy. New York: Plenum, 1978.

Neisser, U. Cognitive psychology. New York: Appleton-Century-Crofts, 1967.

Perky, C. W. An experimental study of imagination. American Journal of Psychology, 1910, 21, 422-452.

Pope, K. S. How gender, solitude, and posture influence the stream of consciousness. In K. S. Pope and J. L. Singer (Eds.), The stream of consciousness: scientific investigations into the flow of human experience. New York: Plenum, 1978.

Rossi, E. L. Dreams and the growth of personality: expanding awareness in psychotherapy. New York: Pergamon, 1972.

Singer, J. L. Daydreaming: an introduction to the experimental study of inner experience. New York: Random House, 1966.

Singer, J. L., and Pope, K. S. (Eds.). The power of human imagination: new methods in psychotherapy. New York: Plenum, 1978.

Sokolov, E. N. The modeling properties of the nervous system. In M. Cole and I. Maltzman (Eds.), A handbook of contemporary Soviet psychology. New York: Basic Books, 1969.

Starker, S. An application of the hypnotic serial fantasy technique. International Journal of Clinical and Experimental Hypnosis, 1971, 19, 66-70.

Tomkins, S. S. Affect, imagery, consciousness (Vol. 1). New York: Springer, 1962.

Weimer, W. B. Structural analysis and the future of psychology. Forthcoming.

ACKNOWLEDGEMENTS

Original research described in this paper was supported by Grant No. MH 24804 from the National Institute of Mental Health and by grants from the University of Minnesota Graduate School.

THE IMAGINATION AS A MEANS OF GROWTH

Edward Joseph Shoben, Jr., Ph.D.

California School of Professional Psychology

Los Angeles, California

It may be well at the outset to remind ourselves that, like most human attributes, imagination is a two-edged sword. If it represents a means of fruitful adaptation, of joy through enlarged creation, it also defines a major facilitator of anxiety. In a very real sense, imagination--that aspect of the cognitive process that produces and communicates products that differ markedly from their perceptual origins--is a distinctively human means for shaping the future. As such, it has both advantages and disadvantages. Although our concern here is primarily with the former, at least a sidelong glance at the latter seems necessary.

On critical occasions, when a perceived threat dominates the environment, what Cannon (1932) called the emergency reactions of flight or fight tend to take over. Among other animals, anticipatory responses tend to be of short duration and to serve basically if not exclusively for preparing for an assault or for literally running away. With us humans, we have the option of attempting to modify the dangerous circumstances. We can erect defenses, or we can institute preventive or corrective measures. The catalogue here ranges from damming flooding streams to using fireproof safes for important documents. More crucially, it includes such activities as pleasing a parent or boss, pacifying an enemy, ingratiating ourselves with a group in which we seek membership, lying, cajoling, seducing, and so on. This power to grapple with what Clark Hull

(1951) once called "the not here and the not now" permits us to
alter in some degree the character of reality itself, to function
as the collaborator with nature and with chance in the making of
our future instead being only the passive object of the future's
revelations.

Even at times of full security, then, we can anticipate trouble.
We needn't wait for the first cold snap or snowfall to store a food
crop; we don't have to break bones to avoid high ledges, and we
needn't have repeated accidents to take reasonable precautions on
Los Angeles freeways. But this adaptive power, no less remarkable
for its obviousness, leaves us susceptible to all kinds of false
alarms; we respond at times to dangers that exist only in our
imagination. An illustrative and classic example of imagination-
bred anxiety is furnished by Robert Frost:

> I always have felt strange when we come home
> To the dark house after so long an absence
> And the key, rattled loudly into place,
> Seemed to warn someone to be getting out
> One door as we entered at another.

This vague feeling of discomfiting fear, undeniable though unpro-
voked, is all too familiar.

Its strangeness, however, may be somewhat alleviated--or at
least set in a different perspective--when we recognize that imagining and dreaming lie on the continuum of human cognition. That continuum runs from logical reasoning and systematic theorizing,
through creative imagination and through dreams and dreamlike
experiences, to the hallucinations of the psychotic.

In dreams, of course, all things are possible. As dreamers,
we accept essentially without question the violation of those
natural laws on which we securely rely when we are awake. We
readily fly through the air; we encounter monsters; we hold discourse with infants or with animals, and we talk with the dead or
the nonexistent. As long ago as 1911, Schroetter (Rapaport, 1951)
experimentally induced a dream in a subject who crawled through the
eye of a needle and then walked dryly across the Danube. Such wonders, whether they provide us with delight or inspire terror, surprise us not at all _if_ they happen when we are asleep; and we are
interested but not at all startled when we hear of such experiences
from others, so long as they occurred in dreams.

But similar events mark the _waking_ life of some people. William
Blake, for instance, held a number of essentially casual conversations with the prophets Isaiah and Ezekiel, and the accounts suggest
that he accepted these visitations quite calmly despite their high
improbability from points of view other than his own. Before he

painted his memorable <u>Ancient of Days</u>, Blake saw an apparition
above the stairs of his house for nearly a week before he recorded
it in oils. As Bronowski (1944) puts it, Blake's brother, Robert,
"went about the house after 1787 as he had done before, although
it happened he died that year." Dreams resemble these odd occurrences that, in their transgression of the principles that ordinarily rule the natural world, psychology tends to label hallucinations
or, possibly, eidetic imagery. In consequence, our dreams--one
manifestation of our imaginations--may help us to understand Blake's
rich poems and pictures. They may also help those who have been
spared the horror of psychotic episodes to understand and to achieve
a measure of sympathy for the mentally ill. Indeed, Immanuel Kant
once observed that "the madman is a waking dreamer," and Schopen-
hauer, a hundred years later, wrote of dreams as a brief madness
and of psychosis as a prolonged dream. More recently, Jung characterized the schizophrenic as "a sleeping person in a waking world."

     In a comparable fashion, the qualities of our dreams permit
our comprehending the recurrently curious elements of experience
reported in folklore. In the 17th century, Thomas Hobbes (1651)
was almost prescient in his perception of the relationship of dreaming to the content of folk tales: "From the ignorance of how to
distinguish dreams and other strong fancies from vision," he wrote,
"did arise the greatest part of the religion of the Gentiles in
time past, that worshipped satyrs, fawnes, nymphs, and the like."
Following this lead, Hobbes went a long way toward the explanation
of the belief in fairies, in ghosts and goblins, and in the power
of witches. Three centuries afterwards, contemporary anthropolo-
gists tend to derive myth, folklore, and much of primitive religion
from the process of dreaming, that universal exercise of the human
imagination; and when the nightmare is included in the dream,
psychoanalysts like Ernest Jones (1949) also find in this source
the origins of vampires, incubi, and other products of the imagination's darker, and more disturbing, work.

     For Freud (1900), as everyone knows, dreams are forms of wish-
fulfillment. That is, the dream is motivated by some kind of
desire; its content represents a way of fulfilling that desire.
In general, children's dreams tend to be relatively straightforward
and simple wish-fulfillments; whereas in the dreams of adults, both
the motivating wish and the means of gratifying it tend to undergo
disguises of various types. Affecting the apparent or manifest
content of the dream is a latent content, the issue of distorting
dream mechanisms that mask the character of the motivating wish
from both the dreamer and others. We need not maintain that all
dreams take the form of wish-fulfillments to find utility in
Freud's emphasis on the two factors of <u>motive</u> and <u>content</u>. And if
his stress in dream analysis fell on identifying the more covert
motivations bound up with specific dreams, he was far from dis-
interested in finding the sources of content-elements in dreams

among the dreamer's fund of historic experiences. While Freud noted
that a dream "may select its material from any period of life," he
followed others in observing that recent perceptions, especially
those of the preceding day, contribute principally to the dream's
content. Dominant motives may thus be conceived as the principles
determining the choice of content from a hoarded pool of previously
registered sense impressions. Ella Sharpe (1937) puts it this way:
The motives that energize a dream are like a magnet that, drawn
across a table on which there are a hundred objects, will select
the iron ones. Thus, she says, the wish "will gather together out
of the whole reservoir of past and present experiences just those
particular ones that are responsive to the 'magnet.'" It seems
probable that a similar relationship between motive and past experience holds in virtually all imaginative acts. What must be under-
scored is that what Sharpe calls "the whole reservoir of past and
present experiences" includes the perception of the thoughts and
imaginings of other people. If dreams explain in some significant
degree the phenomena of folklore, so does our familiarity with folk
tales account for some of the content of our dreams. Imagination
cumulates. As E. H. Gombrich has observed in the case of visual
art, "all pictures owe more to other pictures than they do to
nature." Imaginative quality arises less from direct imitation or
recording than from the connection, rearrangement, and fusion of
percepts, only some of which may be "remembered" or "conscious."

    In the light of this formulation, the similarities between
dreams and poetry are well worth exploring. W. H. R. Rivers (1923)
once suggested that it is quite possible "to take the images of
the manifest content of a poem and discover more or less exactly
how each has been suggested by the experience, new or old, of the
poet." There are dangers here. Not only are the hazards technical, but they risk diverting attention from the poet's imaginative
product and its pleasures and insights to his biography. But
Rivers' hypothesis holds particular interest for us here for two
reasons: it squares entirely with Freud's conception of dreaming
and with the contention that imagination works universally like
dreams, through the interplay of motive and past experience, and
it has been remarkably confirmed by John Livingston Lowes' The Road
to Xanadu (1927), a painstaking search for the origins in experience of Coleridge's poems, "The Ancient Mariner" and "Kubla Khan."
A literary scholar, Lowes spoke like a psychologist when he proposed that "The imagination never operates in a vacuum. Its stuff
is always fact of some order, somehow experienced; its product is
the fact transmuted." His method was to familiarize himself systematically and thoroughly with everything that Coleridge appeared
to have read just prior to composing the poems.

    In relation to "The Ancient Mariner," Lowes read through vol-
umes on early voyages of discovery, including those by Cook and by
Dampier, and worked his way through an extensive notebook that

Coleridge kept at the appropriate time. While no reaching back into history can, of course, uncover all of the reading, perceptions, and experience of a person long dead, Lowes was nevertheless able to build a highly persuasive case as to why "The Ancient Mariner" took the form and embodied the images that it did rather than others. He did not, obviously, argue that Coleridge worked by means of a deliberate synthesis of his readings; rather, he held that the poet unconsciously combined and rearranged and melded bits of information into the unique elements of the poem--that he ran the magnet of his wish to create a literary work through the filings of his experience, and under the influence of acquired craftsmanship and aesthetic purpose, he produced a work of art that is continuous in its structure, spontaneous in its content, completely original and completely derived from experience.

Rivers' hypothesis is also supported by Robert Gittings' study (1954) of the background of Keats' "The Eve of St. Agnes." Whatever its musical qualities, this poem has been repeatedly faulted for its anachronisms. The medieval room that defines its setting would simply not contain fringed carpets, and medieval beds were simply not sheeted with linen. But more than 125 years after the composition of the work, Gittings took seriously an account by Keats of a visit in 1820 to Stansted House near Chichester. At Stansted House there were precisely such carpets; there were also tapestries, including a well known one from Arras. Anachronistic or not, the House was furnished with all kinds of rich curtains, bed-hangings, and luxuriant fabrics. During the lengthy ceremony of dedication that had led him to visit the place, Keats examined intently a great, three-arched window, filled with diamond panes and carrying stained glass panels of armorial inscriptions.

Returning to London, the poet resumed his work. Originally, he had suffused "The Eve of St. Agnes" with a starkly medieval atmosphere. After the Stansted visit, he had new perceptions to add to the store he had collected from observing old structures from the Lake Country to the southern coast. Out of them, he created the gold-fringed carpets and linen sheets for Madeline's room, and the three-arched window resulted in:

> A casement high and triple-arch'd there was
> All garlanded with carven imageries
> Of fruits, and flowers and bunches of knot-grass,
> And diamonded with panes of quaint device,
> Innumerable of stains and splended dyes,
> As are the tiger-moth's deep-damask'd wings;
> And in the midst, 'mong thousand heraldries,
> And twilight saints, and dim emblazonings,
> A shielded scutcheon blush'd with blood of queens and
>   kings.

As Gittings notes, "The wonder is not that Keats' unconscious eye
should be so influenced, but that his conscious art should work so
magnificently upon the picture that his experience presented to
him."

Therein lies the mystery that emerges even as demystification
takes place. The imagination seems to work fundamentally and possibly entirely through the interaction of motives, including professional aspirations and even crassly commercial yearnings, with
observations, perceptions, accumulated experience. Great artists,
great scientists, and great businessmen seem understandable to a
significant degree on the basis of their strong motivation, especially for achievement, and their attentiveness as observers, their
absorption of information from virtually any quarter. And yet there
is the residue that we name genius or talent, typically enlarged by
a rigorously learned craft or discipline, and--most puzzling of all
--marked by a felicitousness in their "dream work," in the way that
they recombine and fuse elements of their experience, that is not
yet understood and may not prove entirely understandable. J. B. S.
Haldane (1970), the cosmologist, once remarked that, as astrophysi-
cal knowledge becomes greater, "The universe not only seems queerer
than we imagine, but queerer than we can imagine." Conceivably,
Haldane's comment may apply to the processes of imagination itself.

But for the rest of us, interested more in imagination as a
means of personal growth than of public accomplishment, this analysis of our human capacity to deal in various ways with "the not
here and the not now" may suggest some useful leads. Not the least
of these leads is the strong implication that the imagination works
more productively if it is fed with information and experience.
Knowledge and a large stock of deeply reflected-upon perceptions
may not yield imaginative products, but the imagination does not
seem to function effectively without relatively extensive experience or in persons who have not schooled themselves in the discipline of close observation.

Close observation seems to share characteristics with other
habits; it can become stronger with practice and with reinforcements, including self-administered reinforcements. One vehicle for
developing closer observation is Crawford's (1954) method of attribute listing, a more or less systematic attempt to describe an
object concretely, thinking of specifications, limitations, needs,
etc. For example, the attributes of an ordinary screwdriver might
include these:

        It has a round steel shank.
        It has a wooden handle riveted to the shank.
        It has a wedge-shaped end to enter a screw head.
        It is manually operated.

Torque is applied to achieve a twisting movement.
Pressure is exerted to keep the end in the screw head.

The list is obviously not exhaustive. Illustratively, however, it
permits one to consider how to improve a screwdriver by altering
its attributes, by _imagining_ what it would be like and how it would
work as modifications were introduced. One could change the handle,
for instance, from wood to plastic because plastic is a better insu-
lator and tends to outlast wood. The shank could be shifted from a
round to a hexagonal shape to permit readier manipulation by a
wrench or by pliers; this change would also allow the application
of more force than manual operation typically supplies. The handle
and shank could be joined by a gear ratchet that would facilitate
the interaction of torque and pressure instead of entailing a degree
of conflict between them. These changes have, of course, already
been made; but they occurred only after a surprisingly long period
in which the screwdriver remained almost as unevolved as the shark!

Another aspect of the imagination seems to be the identification of similarities in ostensibly dissimilar situations or objects.
In E. M. Forster's phrase, "Everything connects." It is here that
metaphor serves the imagination in significant ways. In few places
are those ways better exemplified--is the principle that "everything
connects" better shown--than in a sonnet of Edwin Arlington Robinson,
entitled "The Sheaves." The opening octave sets a scene at once
ambiguous and clear:

Where long the shadows of the wind had rolled,
Green wheat was yielding to the change assigned,
And as by some vast magic undivined,
The world was turning slowly into gold.
Like nothing that was ever bought or sold
It waited there, the body and the mind;
And with a mighty meaning of a kind
That tells the more the more it is not told.

Obviously, we are observing a field of ripening wheat, and Robinson
has invited us to attend to some "vast magic," the nature of which
is far from specified. Neither does he tell us anything about the
"It" that "waited there" except in negative terms: it is not a
commodity to be traded in the markets, and its essence is not to
be formulated in words; it somehow "tells us the more" by withhold-
ing verbal communication about itself. But there is a promise in
those last two lines, and a mood is struck to which we almost
inevitably respond with heightened alertness: "a mighty meaning
of a kind/that tells the more the more it is not told" seems in
some important way worth attending to.

The closing sextet fulfills the promise:

So in a land where all days are not fair,
Fair days went on till on another day
A thousand golden sheaves were lying there,
Shining and still, but not for long to stay--
As if a thousand girls with golden hair
Might rise from where they slept and go away.

Here is the condensation of dream-work, linking elements of experience in a fashion that seems compelling despite the complete unpre-
dictability of those last two lines. No one could have guessed
that the thousand sheaves of newly matured wheat could symbolize a
thousand girls with golden hair, and yet no one can deny the aptness of the improbable association or the touching evocation of the
evanescence of beauty. The sheaves, shining and still, are "not
for long to stay," and the golden-haired girls "go away." In these
14 lines, our imagination feeds on Robinson's in at least three
ways. We have a deeper appreciation than before about the similarities that can be found in disparate things (ripening sheaves of
wheat and sleeping girls with golden hair); we have learned that
ambiguities can be profitably ransacked for rich meanings that may
be more effectively communicated by an unexpected image than by a
formalized concept (the wheat told us nothing about the momentary
but heartbreaking beauty of its ripeness, but that picture of sleeping girls rising and going away evokes an understanding outside
words); and we have discovered, if we have followed the sonnet
openly, something about ourselves--our capacity to respond to a
field of wheat as a symbol rather than as an agricultural or economic unit, the catch in our throats when we recognize the implications of "in a land where all days are not fair/Fair days went on"
until that moment of beauty occurred, and our sense of the value
inherent in beautiful moments despite their fragility and their
essential impermanence.

How will this kind of experience become translated into behavior? Perhaps it won't. It depends on the extent and on the ways
in which it is assimilated, reflected upon, put--imaginatively--to
use. Henry Cowell (1926), the composer, has described the techniques he used to gain control over his auditory imagery through
practice, a procedure that Agnew (1922) reports is common among
those who write music. In Cowell's account, he repeatedly practiced hearing over and over "in his head" musical selections that
he had heard. In the course of this self-training, he began to
"hear," first in bits and snippets and then in longer passages,
new compositions. But they flashed through his awareness, leaving
no traces that he could capture on a score. "With superhuman
effort," he says, he finally gained control of this spontaneous
imagery, was able to hold it in memory as he had learned to hold
the music that he had actually heard, and could write it down. If
imaginative products often appear to have been turned out effort-
lessly, imaginative powers seem not to grow without cultivation or

without the investment of often painfully mustered energies.

Most of all, however, growth through the imagination entails
some sense of the diverse ways with which we deal with the world in
which we live. If we put ourselves in the position of a Robinson
Crusoe, the only inhabitant of a small and isolated island (or if we
try the impossible but instructive task of trying to recreate, with
adult equipment, the big, buzzing, booming confusion that is the
baby's universe), we are likely to find ourselves deeply concerned
with two virtually simultaneous experiences. First, we are preoccupied with the dimensions and character of our new world. Will
it furnish shelter and enough to eat? Does it endanger us because
of wild animals, poisonous plants, or stinging insects? Does its
weather define a troublesome problem for us, or is it mostly benign
and balmy? Whatever the answers to these kinds of questions, we
perceive our island as objective, external to us, and profoundly
not-us. While it may have a form and contours that are distinctively
its own, the island as landscape and as terrain remains unresponsive
to us; it engages us in no conversation, raises no moral issues, has
no intelligence that matters to us, and impresses us as entirely
indifferent to our situation, whether we call that situation a
plight or an opportunity. To survive, we will have to understand
that environment, to learn to describe it, and to develop the skills
to continue our existence within its context; but we feel unrelated
to it and very much like the alien in that milieu of sea and sky,
earth and stars, and plants, animals, and diurnal variations, all
quite independent of our presence.

A. E. Housman catches that latter part of our experience: "A
stranger and afraid/In a world I never made." On the one hand, our
reaction to our island is intellectual. We certainly need to know
a great deal about our new world, to analyze its components in
relation to our requirements for food, protection against the elements, and safety from predatory beasts, and to generate a sense
of its geography and biology. We may even have a curiosity, a
positive interest, in so strange a place. But we also react with
feelings: we perceive it as beautiful or repellant, as comfortable
or terrifying, as supportive or harsh. Most of all, there is that
anxious sense of being a lonely stranger in an uncaring cosmos.

The point, of course, is both elementary and important. Our
response to our lonely island comprises intellectual and emotional
components that, so long as we simply examine our objective, external environment and cadge a bare and simple living from it, leave
us divided. We are chivvied by cycles of outwardly oriented work
and inwardly determined affects that seldom achieve harmony and
congruence with each other. On rare occasions they may--in those
infrequent moments when we feel that the island is ours, that we
are identified with it, and that we somehow belong to its trees
and beaches and birds. But our habitual sense of things is one of

separation, the separation that comes with an ordinary consciousness of self and not-self, of I and the world.

Two issues here seem critical. The language of ordinary consciousness is a descriptive one, consisting mostly of nouns and adjectives, that permits us to label and to manipulate more effectively both the external environment and, at least in some measure, our internal states of emotion. Words like "water," "edible," "sharp," and "hard" are likely to prove high in survival value. In terms like this, conforming to the attributes of the environment and accepting the evidence of the outside world without attempting to alter it, the rudiments of science lie. Improved by more sophisticated methods of observation, enriched by concepts of measurement, and obedient to the rules of logical reasoning, such terms eventually become more or less mathematicized and develop into the idioms of physics or biology. But words like "lonely," "hungry," "anxious," "ugly," and "harsh" seem to have a rather different destiny. They move into propositions like "I don't like this," "This is not what I wish," and "I wish for something better." The intrusion of wish puts us back in the context of the dream, that cognitive process through which longings are, however complicatedly, expressed and fulfilled.

From that dreaming, based in discontent and the power to wish for something different and presumably "better," a new model of island existence is born. A hut goes up beside the pond; a garden is planted from seeds dropped by local plants that have proved edible, and we erect a fence around both hut and garden to keep out bothersome animals. We hew and trample paths to places where we can fish, pick fruit, or enjoy the scenery. In short, we begin to construct, guided by our dreams, the foundations of a crude civilization, to give a distinctively human shape to our natural surroundings that is the basis for our feeling in a more intimate and symbiotic relationship to them. The labor involved demands a special language, the language of practical endeavor, so that we can reflect upon our efforts and increase their efficiency and their effectiveness. Such a language comprises basically verbs and words of movement and action. "Lifting," "cutting," "joining," "carrying," and "arranging," for example, are likely to bulk large in its vocabulary. Here is the tongue of engineering and medicine, popular publishing and plumbing, architecture and agriculture--the practical arts and the applied sciences that are so aptly named because the mixture in them of "art" and "science" is so complete. But the language of the dream out of which the constructive labor grew--the language of imagination--has two characteristics that seldom appear in the languages of either ordinary consciousness or practical endeavor. One is its focus on referents in "the not here and the not now," its function of fulfilling wishes--often in complex ways, sometimes seriously, sometimes quite playfully-- rather that of describing nature or of clarifying and guiding

practical labor. The other is its necessary reliance, as we have
seen, on previous experience for its content. No matter how the
elements of experience may be recombined, melded, or connected in
a novel fashion, the basic content of imagination derives from
earlier registered observations and perceptions. Its essence,
therefore, is metaphor, that <u>fabrication</u> that we have noted of
similarities among disparate things. The language of imagination
is a device for modeling the world we would like to create, not for
reporting the world that we discover and not for facilitating the
work of reshaping that alien and external environment that presents
itself to our senses.

A pair of parentheses seem worth interjecting at this point.
First, this conception of three different languages that correspond
to three different organismic conditions--the language of ordinary
consciousness, the language of practical endeavor, and the language
of imagination--suggests the groundwork for a rough discrimination
between science and art as human activities. Science begins with
the world as it is, external to us and independent of us, and
develops intellectually confirmed representations of that world.
Art, on the other hand, begins with wishes, with the discontent
that is bound up with feelings and emotions, and develops evocative
visions of the world that exists within us, that we dream about,
that we experience precisely when we are <u>not</u> in a state of ordinary
consciousness or thinking about the work that we must do. Whatever
the overlap and the commonality among the sciences and the arts
(and they are many), this quite different point of origin marks a
central difference between them. Second, the role of metaphor is
not to reveal truth but to enlarge our awareness of human possibilities relative to inherent human longings; most of all, it provides
a sense of linkage between us and our surroundings, a sense that
person and habitat, humanity and the universe, are at least congruent with each other and intimately related to each other. Biblical
Eden and the heavens of the great religions take just this form:
the cities and rural communities of human civilizations are quite
freed from the frustrations, the boredom, and the active unhappi-
ness that account for so much of earthly life. We needn't be concerned with these dream-created conceptions theologically or meta-
physically to recognize their reach as imaginative products. And
if the metaphors of imaginative thought fall short of inducing that
sense of unity between human beings and their environment, then
they still become a means of approximating that impossible but
yearned-for process by which one person shares his experience with
another and thereby breaks through that barrier of separateness
that is a component of ordinary consciousness.

Wallace Stevens offers us a helpful and moving clarification:

You like it under the trees in autumn,
Because everything is half dead.

The wind moves like a cripple among the leaves
And repeats words without meaning.

In the same way, you were happy in spring,
With the half colors of quarter-things,
The slightly brighter sky, the melting clouds,
The single bird, the obscure moon--

The obscure moon lighting an obscure world
Of things that would never be quite expressed,
Where you yourself were never quite yourself
And did not want nor have to be,

Desiring the exhilaration of changes:
The motive for metaphor, shrinking from
The weight of primary noon,
The A B C of being,

The ruddy temper, the hammer
of red and blue, the hard sound--
Steel against intimation--the sharp flash,
The vital, arrogant, fatal, dominant X.

The weight of primary noon, the A B C of being, the dominant
X are all features and symbols of the objective environment, the
not-us and the not-me, in which we exist as strangers and afraid in
a world we never made. Outside the imagination, the main business
of communication, the process to which we as human beings are con-
demned and which is so inherent and distinctive a part of us, is
to describe this external context in ever more precise and comprehending ways. But "the motive for metaphor" is at once to escape
it, to enlarge it, and to transmute it from an environment into a
home. The function of the imagination, with its metaphorical
language, is to associate the experience of being human with the
alien world that provides the context of that experience and to
unify, at least at times, human minds with the multiform tumble of
events that occur outside it.

Once again we must remind ourselves of dangers. The motive
for metaphor can lead to distorted images of both ourselves and
our world, and the imagination, qua imagination, includes no self-
corrective mechanism. As we observed at the outset, the creation
of worlds in the not-here and the not-now can leave us vulnerable
to false alarms and subject us to intense anxieties. Like other
cognitive processes, our imaginative potentials can go awry: when
a schizophrenic patient was asked to interpret the proverb, "When
the cat's away, the mice will play," he responded, "When there's
nobody here, the voices come; they take advantage of me." Not
only psychotics find that their imaginations "take advantage" of
them.

And yet a central dimension of human and personal growth concerns itself with this sense of being intimately associated and identified with our venue. Although the moments may be rare, we are likely to develop as people most quietly but most positively and substantially on those infrequent occasions when we feel that although we can know only, as St. Paul says, in part, we are also a part of what we know; and activated by those imaginative experiences, we are a bit more likely to perform what Wordsworth called: "That best portion of a good man's life/His little, nameless, unremembered acts/Of kindness and of love."

REFERENCES

Agnew, M. The auditory imagery of great composers. _Psychological Monographs_, 1922, _31_, 279–287.

Bronowski, J. _William Blake_. London: Secker and Warburg, 1944.

Cannon, W. B. _The wisdom of the body_. New York: Norton, 1932.

Cowell, H. The process of musical creation. _American Journal of Psychology_, 1926, _37_, 233–236.

Crawford, R. P. _Techniques of creative thinking_. Englewood Cliffs, New Jersey: Hawthorn, 1954.

Freud, S. The interpretation of dreams. In _The basic writings of Sigmund Freud_. New York: Modern Library, 1938. (Originally published, 1900.)

Gittings, R. _John Keats: the living year_. London: Heineman, 1954.

Gombrich, E. H. _Art as illusion_. New York: Ballinger Foundation, 1961.

Haldane, J. B. S. _Science and everyday life_. London: Lawrence and Wishart, 1970.

Hobbes, T. _Leviathan_. London: Bohn, 1839. (Originally published, 1651.)

Hull, C. L. _Essentials of behavior_. New York: Appleton-Century, 1951.

Jones, E. _On the nightmare_. London: Hogarth, 1949.

Lowes, J. L. _The road to Xanadu_. London: Constable, 1927.

Rivers, W. H. R. _Conflict and dream_. London: Kegan Paul, 1923.

Schroetter, K. Experimental dreams. In D. Rapaport (Ed.), _Organization and pathology of thought_. New York: Columbia University Press, 1951.

Sharpe, E. F. _Dream analysis_. London: Hogarth, 1937.

IMAGERY, RAW AND COOKED: A HEMISPHERIC RECIPE

Paul Bakan, Ph.D.

Simon Fraser University

Burnaby, B.C. Canada

I would like today to consider the matter of imagery in the light of functional hemispheric asymmetry of the brain. It is becoming very clear that the notion of cerebral hemispheric asymmetry is becoming a part of the basic belief system of modern psychological thought. In 1864, Broca showed that the faculty of articulate language is localized in the left hemisphere of the brain. With the left hemisphere controlling speech, and the use of the right hand, two of man's most distinguishing features, it is no surprise that the left hemisphere became known as the dominant hemisphere, and the right one, the minor hemisphere. But only a year after Broca's discovery, the English neurologist, J. Hughlings Jackson, began to develop what I have called the dual dominance model (Bakan, 1971). This model allows that just as the left hemisphere is dominant for speech, so may the right hemisphere be dominant for other functions. Jackson suggested, in fact, that perception may be localized in the right hemisphere. His program was formulated specifically in 1874 when he wrote:

> That the nervous system is double physically is evident enough. . . . I wish to show that it is double in function also, and further in what way it is double in function . . . the posterior lobe on the right side . . . is the chief seat of the revival of images. . . . The patient (with a right posterior lesion) would have difficulty in recognizing things; he would have difficulty in relating what had occurred, not from a lack of words, but from a prior inability to revive images of persons, objects, and places of which the words are the symbols. (Jackson, 1958)

35

Jackson's interest in right hemisphere dominance for perceptual and imagery functioning had little effect on the thinking of neurologists and psychologists. The notion of a dominant and a nondominant, or minor, hemisphere held sway, at least until the Second World War. With a sharp increase in war-related head injuries, it became obvious that injuries to the same areas of the right and left sides of the brain produced different psychological deficits. A syndrome of visuo-spatial deficit following right hemisphere injury made it clear that indeed Jackson was right when he suggested that perception might reside in the right hemisphere. As a result of further observations of split-brain patients and normal subjects in recent years, it is now clear that the dual dominance model is a reasonable one. The right and left hemispheres do different things, and do things in different ways. Furthermore, it appears likely that there are individual differences in people's relative reliance on their right or left hemispheres, or what Bogen (1969) has called their hemisphericity.

The upshot of research on hemispheric functioning suggests that the left and right brains respectively mediate two basically different modes of cognition. This is the latest chapter in the long history of man's belief in the duality of his mind. This belief has led to dichotomies such as buddhi-manas, emotion-reason, nonverbal-verbal, synthetic-analytic, intuition-intellect, respondent-operant, imagination-intellect, unconscious-conscious, primary process-secondary process, stoned and straight thinking, and so on. The general tendency in the literature is to localize imagery or the imaginative faculty in the right hemisphere, where it can find its place with things like emotion, intuition, primary process, the unconscious, and the non-verbal side of our psychological existence. Zangwill (1972) says, "We may see in the evocation of images, activity, governed primarily by the right hemisphere, in precisely the same way as linguistic analysis is governed by the left." Fischer (1975b) exemplifies this view when he writes, "The right hemisphere is concerned with nonverbal information processing, visuospatial gestalts and fields, multivalued metaphors, music, imagery: it is our analogical, intuitive mind." And in a psychoanalytic context, Stone (1977) says that the task of "making the unconscious conscious" may involve the kind of dominant hemisphere processing of visual, unverbalized constructs fed into it from the minor hemisphere."

I would like now to consider the evidence for the proposition that imagery is largely a right hemisphere function. Then after making a strong case for the proposition, I will raise some doubts about it. And finally I will try to reformulate the question of the relationship between imagery and the hemispheres. This will entail a distinction between raw and cooked imagery, a metaphor I borrow from Levi-Strauss (1969).

LATERALIZED BRAIN INJURY AND IMAGERY

    Consider first the evidence from cases of brain injury.
Humphrey and Zangwill (1951) reported on three patients with posterior parietal lesions of the right hemisphere, in which a loss of
dreaming was spontaneously reported following the injury. In
cases where there was a loss of dreaming, the patient also reported
deterioration of imagery in the waking state. It appears that the
brain mechanisms underlying the imagery of dreaming and the imagery
while awake are closely related. The first patient with a right-
sided war wound reports "almost no dreams nowadays," and also
reports his waking imagery as "very dim" after the imagery, despite
his having been a good visualizer before the injury. The authors
conclude that in this case, "all thought processes of a predomi-
nantly visual character (including dreaming) were markedly depressed."
In a second patient with damage to the parieto-occupital areas of
both the right and left hemispheres, the patient says:

        . . . if someone says: can you visualize what your
    house is like? Well, I can do that, but I can't visu-
    alize a lot of things, such as faces sometimes or places
    I've been to and tried to recall . . . and I never dream.
    . . . Lying awake at night trying to go to sleep I think
    only in words, never in pictures.

The third patient was left handed, with a right posterior parietal
injury. He showed "marked impairment on all tests commonly held to
demand visualization" when tested one month after injury. This
patient did not dream and had difficulty in evoking imagery for
about five years after the injury. After five years he noted a
return of dreaming and at the same time great improvement in waking
imagery. Very little has been reported about restitution of imagery
after brain damage, but this report of restitution in a left handed
patient seems to parallel reports of greater restitution from language disorders in left-handed patients who sustain left hemisphere
damage (Hecaen and de Ajuriaguerra, 1964). There appears to be a
relationship between handedness and the effect of lateralized hemispheric damage.

    Humphrey and Zangwill report still another case, which they
did not personally observe, where a patient with right occipito-
parietal abscess was operated on in 1938 and had entirely ceased
dreaming up to the time of the writing of their paper in 1951. In
still another case reported by Nielsen (1955), a drainage tube
passing through the right occipital lobe resulted in diminished
ability to produce visual images and a simultaneous cessation of
dreaming.

    What happens to imagery after left hemisphere damage? Henry
Head (1926) analyzed a large series of patients with language

disorders due to left hemisphere pathology. He had a clear impression that there was little impairment of spontaneous visual imagery in these patients. He says:

> But it is remarkable how rarely it (visual imagery) is
> affected. . . . Thus, none of the specific forms of
> aphasia interfere directly with the spontaneous recall
> of visual images. But both nominal and semantic defects
> limit the power to employ these mental processes for the
> purposes of consecutive and logical thinking. . . .
> There is sometimes a difficulty in the evocation of visual
> images in response to words. . . . Mental pictures remain,
> but the means of converting them into the materials for
> logical thought have been disturbed or grossly diminished.
> (pp. 370, 373, 392)

What do we learn from the split-brain patient about imagery and the hemispheres? Bogen (1969), one of the surgeons who performed the split-brain surgery, noted changes in dreaming after commissurotomy, the operation where the commissures connecting the right brain to the left brain are split. He reports that the operation is typically followed by alteration in dreaming, and that several patients deny any dreams after the operation, even though they experienced frequent visual dreams before. Hoppe (1977) has studied the dreaming and fantasy behavior of these split-brain patients and finds that they "reveal a paucity of dreams, fantasies, and symbols." "Their dreams," he says, "lack the characteristics of dream work; their fantasies are unimaginative, utilitarian, and tied to reality; their symbolization is concretistic, discursive, and rigid." Hoppe also found this to be true in a patient with a right hemispherectomy. What has happened to the characteristics of the dream work, the bizarre, the surrealistic aspect of the dream in these patients? Perhaps it is no longer there after the brain is split. Alternatively, the dreams and dream work are still happening in the right hemisphere, but the split-brain patient is unable to report on the dreams because the lack of communication between the right and left hemispheres makes it impossible for the speaking left hemisphere to verbalize the dream experience of the right hemisphere. It just may be that the left hemisphere does not know and cannot tell what the right hemisphere is dreaming.

Further study of the brain-injury literature offers further evidence of a close relationship between imagery and the right hemisphere. Let me just cite a miscellany of findings before going on to some telling evidence from the literature on epilepsy. Jones (1976) asked patients with right hemisphere damage to learn pairs of words by linking them with an image that would mediate recall. The recall of these patients was impaired with respect to a normal group. When asked to learn pairs of words linked by sentences, the recall of right hemisphere damaged patients was about equal to that

of a normal group. This result suggests impaired use of imagery
mediation after right hemisphere damage.

The relationship between imagery and the right hemisphere has
been used explicitly in the rehabilitation of patients suffering
language disorders after left hemisphere damage. Patten (1972)
successfully treated patients with verbal memory defects due to
left hemisphere lesions, by teaching them to encode memory items
visually through use of a peg list of images.

IMAGERY AND EPILEPSY

Somewhat related to brain injury and brain splitting is epilepsy, a disease associated with some form of brain malfunction.
Epileptics experience at times an epileptic aura just before the
seizure begins. These auras assume a variety of forms including
tics, twitches, vocalizations, pains, smells, and imagery experiences. Jackson (1880) described a particular kind of aura characterized by imagery. Images preceding seizures were described by
patients as "dreamy feelings," "dreams mixing up with present
thoughts," "a feeling of being somewhere else," and feeling "as if
I went back to all that occurred in my childhood." Jackson called
such experiences of imagery "dreamy state" auras, and noted a close
association between these auras and motor activity involving the
left side of the body, such as spasms on the left side, or head
turning to the left side. Such left-sided movements are known to
be associated with epileptic discharge in the right hemisphere.
Jackson therefore concluded that "dreamy state" auras occur at the
beginning of right hemisphere epileptic discharge, i.e., the dreamy
state aura is a localized symptom for right hemisphere epileptic
discharge. More recently, Arseni and Petrovici (1971) reported an
association between auras involving imagery and epileptic discharges
originating in the right hemisphere, particularly the right temporal
lobe. They also found that auras involving changes of the body
image are associated with right hemisphere seizure activity. A
close relationship between the right hemisphere and the body image
has also been found by Luria (1973).

Wilder Penfield, the Montreal surgeon known for his surgical
treatment of epilepsy, developed a form of brain mapping by elec-
trically stimulating different brain areas in conscious human
patients undergoing brain surgery for epilepsy. In the course of
these studies he was able to produce "dreamy state" auras like
those described by Jackson. These states, including hallucinatory
experiences, visual illusions, and deja vu experiences, were almost
always produced by stimulation of the right temporal lobe. Quoting
Penfield and Perot (1963):

It is . . . most significant that stimulation within the
. . . speech area of the temporal lobe on the dominant
side never produced visual experiential responses,
although such responses are most numerous in that area on
the non-dominant side. . . . Stimulation in that area
. . . is apt to produce recall of visual experiences.
. . . Illusions of familiarity and strangeness are almost
always produced by discharge or stimulation on the non-
dominant side. . . . Since stimulation produces . . .
detailed recall of past experiences in these areas and
nowhere else . . . it seems likely that these areas play
in adult life some role in the subconscious recall of
past experience.

SENSORI-MOTOR FACTORS AND IMAGERY

It is evident to people who work with imagery that relaxation
is conducive to the experience of imagery. There appears to be an
inverse relationship between activity of the motor system and imagery. Consider the period of REM sleep where imagery in the form of
dreaming is most likely to occur. An important characteristic of
the REM state is the profound relaxation resulting from the reduction of muscle tone, especially in the anti-gravity muscles. All
mammals lie down in a relaxed, flaccid state during REM sleep.
Brain-injured patients suffering from muscular rigidity show a
severe reduction of muscle tonus during REM sleep; and in epileptics there is a sharp reduction of seizure discharges during REM
sleep (Bakan, 1978a). When motor activity occurs during sleep, it
usually occurs outside of REM sleep. Sleep talking, sleep walking,
and sucking movements of the newborn usually occur in non-REM sleep.
Sigmund Freud, a knowledgeable student of the dream, observed "this
very motor paralysis during sleep is one of the fundamental conditions of the psychic process which functions during dreaming"
(Freud, 1938).

The left hemisphere appears to have a closer relationship to
motor activity than does the right hemisphere. Perhaps imagery
activity, associated with the right hemisphere, is incompatible
with a high degree of motor activity. When Baldwin (1970) uni-
laterally stimulated the cortex, he found that left hemisphere
stimulation evoked more motor responses than right hemisphere stimulation. Studies of the effect of lateralized brain injury on motor
function suggest a relative dominance of the left hemisphere in
motor control. Left hemisphere lesions in the motor cortex produce
motor symptoms on both the right and left side of the body, but
right hemisphere lesions usually produce motor symptoms on one
side, namely the left side (Semmes, 1968). It has been shown that
only left hemisphere lesions can produce impairment in learning
and performance in tasks requiring bimanual coordination (Wyke,

1971). Sperry, in describing the performance of split-brain
patients, reports that "the dominant hemisphere, in particular has
good motor control over both hands" (Sperry, 1966).

I have discussed elsewhere (Bakan, 1978a) the possible relationship between the functional paralysis of REM sleep, the right
hemisphere, and the workings of the sympathetic and parasympathetic
systems. The left hemisphere may have closer relations with the
sympathetic system and the right hemisphere with the parasympathetic
system. The sympathetic system associated by Cannon with "fight or
flight" capability is intimately related to the activation of the
muscular motor mechanisms, whereas the parasympathetic system is
involved in the mechanisms of relaxation. In fact, it has been
shown (Baust, 1973) that during REM sleep there is a "striking
decrease in sympathetic tone."

Martin (1972) has distinguished between two modes of ego functioning associated respectively with effort and relaxation. His
description of these states closely parallels those used to describe
left and right hemisphere function. The effort mode, he says, is
used for rational, deductive, linear, analytic, logical, and focused
thinking; the relaxation mode for non-rational, mosaic, inductive,
synthesizing, and analogical thinking. The relaxed mind, he says,
involves a return to an earlier, more fundamental, poetic, ideo-
graphic, and figurative level. In passing from effort to relaxation, there is a shift of perception from higher to low power, a
widening of the field of consciousness to include what had previously been peripheral and subconscious. Roland Fischer (1975a) has
also suggested an inverse relationship between imagery and willed
motor activity. He says that an "increase in interoceptive visuo-
spatial and audio-spatial imagery is paralleled by a decrease in
willed motor activity, reflecting a high sensory/motor (S/M) ratio
or a high non-dominant/dominant hemisphere ratio."

Some years ago I did a study in which the state of body relaxation was manipulated, to study its effect on the imagery experience
in a sensory deprivation situation (Morgan and Bakan, 1965). We
found that sensory deprivation imagery was facilitated when Ss
were lying down as compared to the sitting up position. Perhaps
relaxation facilitates the production of images and other forms of
primary process material as well. This may be the real reason for
the success of the psychoanalytic couch. Relaxation has been shown
to enhance free association (Kroth, 1970), recall of early childhood memories (Berdach and Bakan, 1967), and a tendency to confuse
images with external reality in the Perky effect (Segal and Glickman, 1967). Kenneth Pope (1978) has recently demonstrated again
the important influence of physical posture on the quality of
consciousness.

INDIVIDUAL DIFFERENCES IN IMAGERY

I would like next to consider the matter of individual differences in the experience of imagery, in the light of functional
hemispheric asymmetry. For many years, investigators in the field
of imagery have been intrigued with the wide variation among people
in the ability to form images. Typologies based on imagery have
been suggested by Galton, Charcot, Bartlett, and Jaensch among
others. To a large extent, these typologies tend to be dichotomous,
classifying people as preferring either a verbal or an imagery mode
of thinking (Richardson, 1977).

The verbalizer-visualizer dichotomy seems to parallel the left-
right hemisphere dichotomy. This certainly follows the trend of
brain hemisphere literature, which attributes language functions
largely to the left hemisphere, and non-verbal and imagery functions
to the right hemisphere. This trend of thought suggests an interesting possibility. Could it be that verbalizers show a relative
dominance or preference for the use of the left hemisphere, and
that visualizers or imagers show a relative dominance or preference for the use of the right hemisphere? Can the cognitive style,
determining the degree to which imagery is preferred in thought and
consciousness, be a function of the nature of the lateral (i.e.,
right-left) organization of the brain? I suggest that we make a
jump from hemispheres to people. If right hemispheres are better
at imagery, is there a sense in which right hemisphere people are
better at imagery than left hemisphere people? A right hemisphere
person is a person with a bias or preference for use of the right
hemisphere in his or her psychological functioning. Such a person
is said to have right hemisphericity. Similarly, the left hemisphere person with bias or preference for use of the left hemisphere
is said to have left hemisphericity. This leads to the problem of
determining the hemisphericity of an individual. To deal with this
question, I would like now to consider the phenomenon of conjugate
lateral eye movements, or CLEMS for short.

CLEMS OR CONJUGATE LATERAL EYE
   MOVEMENTS

About 10 years ago, I proposed a hemispheric typology based on
right or left hemisphericity. The direction of the hemispheric
bias or preference is inferred from the lateral direction of certain conjugate lateral eye movements, CLEMS, and leads to a classification of individuals as right or left hemisphere people. A
conjugate lateral eye movement, associated with thought or reflection, has been described by Teitlebaum (1954) and independently by
Day (1964). If an experimenter facing a subject asks the subject
a question requiring thought or reflection, the subject usually
turns his eyes to the right or left (often his head as well) upon

beginning to reflect on an answer. Day observed that the direction
of the eye movement, right or left, was reasonably consistent for
most people, that about half the people move their eyes to the
right, and about half to the left, and perhaps, most important,
that there were differences between right movers and left movers in
various aspects of their cognitive, personality, and physiological
functioning.

In 1969 I suggested a hemispheric basis for the right-, left-
mover classification, by equating the tendency to move eyes left,
with right hemisphericity, and the tendency for eyes to move right,
with left hemisphericity. This is because the relationship between
the lateral direction of the eye movements and the cerebral hemispheres is essentially contralateral. This has been known since
Fritsch and Hitzig showed in 1870 that stimulation of the frontal
eye field of one hemisphere in the monkey leads to a turning of the
eyes to the opposite side. This contralateral relationship has
been shown to be essentially the same for humans.

This leads to the following model: CLEMS are symptomatic of
easier excitation in the hemisphere contralateral to CLEM direction.
Individuals who tend to move their eyes to the right, as they begin
to reflect on a question, have a central nervous system, organized
in such a way as to facilitate left hemisphere activity. The
reverse is the case for left movers. In hemisphericity terms, it
follows that subjects who make right CLEMS are "left brained,"
and those who make left CLEMS are "right brained." Since each
hemisphere appears to serve a primary mediating function for certain
cognitive and emotional "styles," it follows that subjects making
left CLEMS will have a type of psychological functioning reflecting
a bias toward the style of the right hemisphere. Likewise, the
right CLEM subject will have reflected in his psychological functioning a bias toward the style of the left hemisphere.

The literature comparing right and left CLEM subjects is a
rapidly growing one and I shall not take the time to review it here
since it has been reviewed elsewhere (Bakan, 1978b; Gur and Gur,
1976; Ehrlichmann and Weinberger, 1-78). But I would like now to
review the CLEM research as it bears specifically on the imagery
problem. This typological approach to imagery will hopefully
increase our understanding of the relationship between imagery and
the hemispheres.

I first raised the question of the relationship between CLEM
direction and imagery in 1969 (Bakan, 1969). In a list of questions used to elicit lateral eye movements, I included the following question: "With your eyes open, try to have an image of a man
(or woman for female subject) crying." Subjects were then asked
to rate the clarity of the obtained image on a five-point scale,
1 for "no image" to 5 for "very clear image, just like real." On

average, the left movers reported more vivid images than the right
movers, but the difference was not significant at the .05 level;
it was significant at the .10 level.

Harnad (1972) studied some CLEM correlates among mathematicians.
He found that left movers reported more frequent use of visual imagery in their work. This was confirmed in a university sample by
Croghan (1974), who found that left movers report a significantly
greater use of visualization in responding to mathematical questions.

Meskin and Singer (1974) found support for the hypothesis that
persons given to producing more visually oriented or imagery-related
material, as their habitual response pattern, shift their eyes more
to the left, while persons more prone to thinking in logical-verbal
sequential terms are more likely to shift their eyes to the right.

In a study of eye movements and imagery in the obese, Rodin
and Singer (1976) found that obese subjects were less likely to
make left CLEMS and reported having significantly less visual imagery in their daydreams than did normals. This is consistent with
other studies which have shown overweight people more externally
and less internally responsive.

Richardson (1977) administered to right and left movers a
self-report questionnaire of individual differences on a verbalizer-
visualizer dimension of cognitive style (VVQ). In two independent
studies with high school subjects, he found significant relationships, indicating that left movers tended to respond more visually
and less verbally. For example, left movers were more likely than
right movers to agree to the following items:

My daydreams are sometimes so vivid I feel as though I
actually experience the scene.

My powers of imagination are higher than average.

My dreams are extremely vivid.

My thinking often consists of mental pictures or images.

But here is where things get somewhat troublesome. A third experiment with a university rather than a high school sample turned up
a reversal of these results. Richardson says that what is so odd
about these results is their systematic reversal of the previous
results. For 11 out of 15 items, the right movers were more likely
to respond as left movers, and vice versa.

The relationship between CLEMS and imagery may have an important bearing on the results of psychotherapy. In a recent study
(Tucker et al., 1978) subjects being treated for "speaking anxiety,"

i.e., fear of making a speech, were classified as right or left movers. Subjects were treated by one of two therapeutic techniques, either a "coping imagery" cognitive therapy, or a verbal self-instruction technique. Contrary to the expectations of the experimenters, the left movers (right hemisphere people) were most effectively helped by the verbal therapy, and the right movers by the imagery therapy. The extension of this research design to other forms of imagery therapy would be of great interest. The old adage, different strokes for different folks, may possibly be reworded to right strokes for left folks and left strokes for right folks.

Van Nuys (1979) has found a relationship between CLEM direction and dream recall. When he asked male subjects the question, "How many dreams a week do you remember on the average?", he found that right movers and bidirectional movers reported 2.8 and 3.2 dreams respectively, whereas left movers reported an average of 5.8 dreams per week. The author attributes this difference to a greater ability of left movers to access the right hemisphere.

The evidence thus far presented on the relationship between CLEM direction and imagery, though not conclusive, is at least consistent with the hypothesis of a close relationship between right hemisphericity (as indicated by left CLEMS) and a more active imagery life. Now to confuse things a bit, let me tell you about some recent research done at Simon Fraser University with my student, Bill Glackman (Glackman, 1976). This was a comparison of male right and left movers on a number of imagery related tasks.

First, a memory study, where subjects were asked to learn groups of three nouns projected as slides. There were three groups, each given a different form of mediation instructions. A free instruction control group was told to use any method they felt was suitable to learn the words; an imagery group was told to form an interactive imaginal scene in which images designated by the nouns were in contact with each other; and a verbal group was told to connect the nouns with verbal links to form a verbal unit. Half the words were concrete nouns and half were abstract nouns.

Overall recall was best for the imagery instructions and worst for the free instructions. Concrete words were recalled better than abstract words as has been shown before. The right movers had slightly higher recall scores than the left movers. But the most interesting finding was a significant CLEM by instruction interaction (p of .01). Though there was hardly any difference between right movers and left movers in the free instruction group or the verbal mediator group, there was a difference between right and left movers under the imagery mediator condition. The right movers recalled words significantly better than the left movers, when instructed to learn by forming an imaginal scene. The right movers show better recall of the words under instructions to use imagery--

on the surface, a somewhat paradoxical finding.

In the next study, a battery of tests consisting of visuo-spatial tasks, a form of the Betts Imagery Vividness Scale, and a measure of CLEM direction, was administered to a group of 69 male university students. A brief description of the tests follows:

Shepherd-Metzler Block Rotation Task

Each item consists of five two-dimensional pictures of a configuration of 10 blocks connected together in a three-dimensional space. The subject looks at the first figure and is to identify which two of the remaining four pictures shows a configuration of blocks which is the same as that in the first figure except for a three-dimensional rotation.

Card Rotation Task

Presents a row of nine irregular shapes. The subject looks at the first one and marks each other with a plus if it is a two-dimensional rotation of the first, and with a minus if it is a rotation of its mirror image.

Hidden Patterns Test

The subject identifies figures which have embedded in them a specified target pattern.

Paper Formboard

The subject marks lines on a complete geometric shape to show where it should be cut in order to produce an array of pieces like those shown alongside the complete figure.

The above four tests were selected to represent the spatial-visualization factor identified by Wilson et al. (1973) in a factor analytic study of cognitive measures. These tests involve visualization and manipulation of visualized objects in the imagination.

Betts Questionnaire

The next seven measures were taken from the Sheehan (1967) revision of the Betts Questionnaire on Mental Imagery. This task requires seven-point ratings of the subjective vividness of each of five directed images in each of seven modalities--vision, audition, cutaneous, kinaesthetic, gustatory, olfactory, and organic.

Gordon Test of Visual Imagery Control

This scale (Gordon, 1949) requires that the subject indicate whether he can, cannot, or is unsure of attaining 12 specified interrelated visual imaginal scenes.

CLEMS

This measure is based on the number of right and left CLEMS in response to 20 questions.

Let us consider first the correlates of the CLEM measure taken from the correlation matrix of these measures before factor analysis of the matrix. The correlations between the number of right CLEMS and the other measures is shown in Table 1.

An interesting pattern emerges from these correlations. First, it appears that people who tend to make right CLEMS (left hemisphere people in our scheme of things) do better on the spatial-visualization tests. Correlations with three of the four spatial-

Table 1

Correlations Between Number of Right
CLEMS and Test Scores*

Shepherd-Metzler Block Rotation	.494
Card Rotation	.467
Hidden Patterns	.207
Paper Formboard	.329
Betts Questionnaire--Visual	.147
Auditory	.119
Cutaneous	.321
Kinaesthetic	.150
Gustatory	.253
Olfaction	.240
Organic	.279
Gordon Test	-.123

*Correlation of .230 required for significance at .05 level

visualization tests are significantly (.05) and positively related
to the proportion of right CLEMS, and the correlation with the fourth
approaches significance.

Looking at the correlations with the Betts Questionnaire which
involves self-reports of imagery vividness, the results are less
dramatic, but nevertheless all seven correlations are positive, with
those for cutaneous, gustatory, olfactory, and organic imagery
being significant at the .05 level. This means the right movers,
who do better on the spatial-visualization tests, also tend to
report that their directed images are more vivid.

The only negative correlation with right CLEMS was with the
Gordon Test of Visual Imagery Control. This correlation was low
and not statistically significant. The Gordon Test also shows negative correlations with most of the spatial-visualization measures
and the imagery vividness measures which tend to be positively
related to right CLEMS.

The correlation matrix of variables being considered was factor analyzed and rotated to four factors in a varimax rotation.
These factors in order of percentage variance accounted for are:

1. _Vividness of non-visual imagery_. It has high loadings
(.51-.83) on all of the Betts scales except that for visual imagery.

2. _Spatial visualization_. This has high loadings (.67-.83)
on the four paper and pencil tests of spatial visualization.

3. _Vividness of visual imagery_. The only variable loading
high (.90) on this factor is the visual vividness part of the Betts
Questionnaire.

4. _Visual imagery control_. The Gordon Test of visual imagery
control is the only variable with a high loading (.90) on this
factor.

The CLEM variable loads relatively high (.65) and positively
on the spatial visualization Factor 2. In fact, it loads almost as
high as the tests defining the factor. The next highest loading
for CLEMS is positive (.23) on the first factor, non-visual imagery
vividness, followed by Factor 3 (.21) visual vividness, with very
little weight (.07) on the fourth factor, visual imagery control.

If right CLEMS are indicative of easier activation or preferred
usage of the left hemisphere, then we are faced with the prospect,
based on the experiments described here, that important aspects of
imagery such as use of imagery mediators in learning, spatial visualization, and vividness of imagery are dependent on left hemisphere function. But this is paradoxical in light of the commonly

held "wisdom" that puts imagery in the <u>right</u> hemisphere.

Have we then come full circle? Are we asking meaningless questions? I think not. There <u>are</u> relationships between imagery, the
hemispheric functioning of the brain, and the hemisphericity of
individuals. When you do not get a clear answer to a question, it
is often the question that is at fault. I think part of the problem is that imagery is not a unitary function. Asking questions
about imagery is like asking questions about disease. Just as it
is often easier to answer a question about a particular disease
rather than disease in general, so it may be more rewarding if we
talk about particular kinds of imagery. It may be time to talk
about different kinds of imagery as mediated by different kinds of
hemispheric organization.

Steven Starker (1974) has distinguished between two modes of
imagery, an active thought imagery, and a passive spontaneous mode
of mental imagery. Perhaps this is a good place to start. There
seems to be a continuum of imagery between two poles. At one pole
imagery can be said to be vivid, directed, active, voluntary and
reality-oriented. Going along to the other pole, imagery becomes
fuzzy, spontaneous, passive, involuntary and fantasy-oriented. How
different is the imagery experienced in doing the Card Rotation
Task and the imagery experienced in a dream. In the first case, an
irregular shape has to be rotated as it is and as its mirror image
in order to compare it with other irregular shapes. This seems to
exemplify the first pole of imagery--clear, directed, active, voluntary, and oriented to reality and the solution of a specific problem. In the dream, on the other hand, imagery may have a wide
range of clarity; it occurs spontaneously and involuntarily in a
passive experiencer and generally in a context not fully congruent
with reality. In a sense, this dichotomy suggests to me a psychoanalytic metaphor--namely, a dimension from primary to secondary
process <u>imagery</u>.

With this framework, it is tempting to suggest that there are
two kinds of imagery mediated by the two cerebral hemispheres, primary process imagery mediated by the right hemisphere, and secondary process imagery mediated by the left hemisphere. I think this
is a gross oversimplification of the matter. So let me continue
with metaphors and consider a raw-cooked model of the relation
between imagery and the hemispheres.

IMAGERY RAW AND COOKED: SPECULATIONS
  ON A HEMISPHERIC RECIPE

The following statements constitute a body of speculation
designed to take account of the evidence that the right hemisphere
is very important for imagery, and the somewhat paradoxical results

of our experiments which indicate a possible left hemisphere
advantage in certain tasks which involve imagery.

1.   The right hemisphere has a primary role in imagery. It
mediates the making of pictures in the head or images in other
modalities. It is crucial for the production of raw imagery. This
basic ability to produce images is what gets lost after certain
right hemisphere brain injury. This loss may also be the basis for
a variety of visuo-spatial difficulties noted after right hemisphere injury.

2.   This raw imagery may appear spontaneously under certain
conditions as sleep, muscular relaxation, free association, mind-
wandering, and under the influence of certain drugs. Under these
conditions it may have primary process qualities and may be
described as regressive, primal, affective, illogical, etc. There
is some evidence suggesting that reduced interhemispheric communication is conducive to dream imagery, and this may also be the case
for raw imagery in general (Bakan, 1978a).

3.   At times when the hemispheres are in good communication,
there may be processing or cooking of the raw right hemisphere
imagery by the left hemisphere. The left hemisphere may request
that images be constructed for help in the solution of problems as
posed in visuo-spatial tests. Or the left hemisphere may request
conversions of words to vivid images as "form a clear image of an
apple." Or the left hemisphere may take hold of raw imagery from
dream recall or daydreaming, and bring to bear upon it some form
of logical, analytic, or reality-oriented processing. This kind of
processing or cooking of raw imagery may constitute the contribution of the left hemisphere and it may be because of this that the
right mover or left hemisphere person does well at "imagery" tests
of the spatial and vividness type, as we have shown. Most so-called
tests of imagery put a premium on some such kind of processing.
Head's (1926) observations of left hemisphere damaged patients are
telling in this respect. He said that in these patients, "mental
pictures remain, but the means of converting them into materials
for logical thought have been disturbed or grossly diminished."
He already perceived the role of the left hemisphere for the processing of right hemisphere mental pictures.

It is not as easy to measure the prevalence of, or preference
for, raw imagery in the thinking of an individual. I think that a
need for such measures grows out of the model suggested here. But
if such tests were available, I expect that left movers, or right
hemisphere people, would do better at them.

In sum, imagery is neither localizable in the right or left
hemisphere. Components of imagery exist in both. There is raw
imagery and cooked or processed imagery, mediated respectively by

the right and left hemisphere.

CODA

Whenever I get myself out on a dualistic limb, as I may have
done here with respect to imagery, I meditate on the beautiful
statement of Dr. Jekyll when he faced similar problems: "I saw that
of the two natures that contended in the field of my consciousness,
even though I could rightly be said to be either, it was only
because I was radically both" (Stevenson, 1964).

REFERENCES

Arseni, C., and Petrovici, I. N. Epilepsy in temporal lobe tumours.
    European Neurology, 1971, 5, 201-214.
Bakan, P. Hypnotizability, laterality of eye movement and func-
    tional brain asymmetry. Perceptual and Motor Skills, 1969, 28,
    927-932.
Bakan, P. The eyes have it. Psychology Today, 1971, 4, 64-67, 96.
Bakan, P. Dreaming, REM sleep, and the right hemisphere: a theo-
    retical integration. Journal of Altered States of Conscious-
    ness, 1978(a), 3, 285-308.
Bakan, P. Two streams of consciousness: a typological approach.
    In K. S. Pope and J. L. Singer (Eds.), The stream of conscious-
    ness. New York: Plenum, 1978(b).
Baldwin, M. Neurological syndromes and hallucinations. In W. Kemp
    (Ed.), Origin and mechanisms of hallucinations. New York:
    Plenum, 1970.
Baust, W. The problem of sympathetic tone and automatic functions
    during sleep. In V. J. Jovanovic (Ed.), The nature of sleep.
    Stuttgart: G. Fisher, 1973.
Bender, M. The oculomotor system. New York: Hoeber, 1964.
Berdach, E., and Bakan, P. Body position and free recall of early
    memories. Psychotherapy: Theory, Research, and Practice,
    1967, 4, 101-102.
Bogen, J. E. The other side of the brain, II: an appositional
    mind. Bulletin of the Los Angeles Neurological Societies,
    1969, 34, 135-162.
Croghan, L. M. The relationship between conjugate lateral eye move-
    ment and verbal and spatial abilities. Dissertation Abstracts
    International, 1975, 35(9-B), 4644-4645.
Day, M. E. An eye-movement phenomenon related to attention, thought
    and anxiety. Perceptual and Motor Skills, 1964, 19, 443-446.
Ehrlichman, H., and Weinberger, A. Lateral eye movements and
    hemispheric asymmetry: a critical review. Psychological
    Bulletin, 1978, 85, 1080-1101.

Fischer, R. Transformations of consciousness: a cartography, I.
    The perception-hallucination dichotomy. Confinia Psychiatrica,
    1975a, 18, 221-244.
Fischer, R. Cartography of inner space. In R. K. Seigel and L. J.
    West (Eds.), Hallucinations. New York: John Wiley, 1975b.
Freud, S. The basic writings of Sigmund Freud. New York: Modern
    Library, 1938.
Glackman, W. G. Imagery and conjugate lateral eye-movement.
    Unpublished master's thesis, Simon Fraser University, Burnaby,
    B.C., Canada, 1976.
Gordon, R. An investigation into some of the factors that favour
    the formation of stereotyped images. British Journal of Psy-
    chology, 1949, 39, 156-167.
Gur, R. E., and Gur, R. C. Correlates of conjugate lateral eye
    movements in man. In S. Harnad, et al. (Eds.), Lateralization
    in the nervous system. New York: Academic Press, 1976.
Harnad, S. R. Creativity, lateral saccades and the nondominant
    hemisphere. Perceptual and Motor Skills, 1972, 34, 653-654.
Head, H. Aphasia and kindred disorders of speech, Vol. 1.
    Cambridge: Cambridge University Press, 1926.
Hecaen, H., and de Ajuriaguerra, J. Left-handedness. New York:
    Grune and Stratton, 1964.
Hoppe, K. Split brains and psychoanalysis. The Psychoanalytic
    Quarterly, 1977, 46, 220-244.
Humphrey, M. E., and Zangwill, O. L. Cessation of dreaming after
    brain injury. Journal of Neurology, Neurosurgery, and
    Psychiatry, 1951, 14, 322--25.
Jackson, J. H. On right- or left-sided spasm at the onset of epi-
    leptic paroxysms, and on crude sensation warnings and elabor-
    ate mental states. Brain, 1880, 3, 192-206.
Jackson, J. H. Selected writings of John Hughlings Jackson,
    J. Taylor (Ed.). New York: Basic, 1958.
Jones, M. K. Reduced visual inventiveness after focal right hemis-
    phere lesions in man. Dissertation Abstracts International,
    1976, 36, 416-B.
Kroth, J. A. The analytic couch and response to free association.
    Psychotherapy: Theory, Research and Practice, 1970, 7,
    206-208.
Levi-Strauss, C. The raw and the cooked. New York: Harper and
    Row, 1969.
Luria, A. R. The working brain: an introduction to neuropsychol-
    ogy. New York: Basic, 1973.
Martin, A. R. Cultural impairment of our inner resources: an
    empirical inquiry. American Journal of Psychoanalysis, 1972,
    32, 127-146.
Meskin, B., and Singer, J. Daydreaming, reflective thought and
    lateral eye movements. Journal of Personality and Social
    Psychology, 1974, 30, 64-71.

Morgan, R., and Bakan, P.   Sensory deprivation hallucinations and
    other sleep behavior as a function of position, method of
    report, and anxiety. . Perceptual and Motor Skills, 1965, 20,
    19-25.
Nielsen, J. M.   Occipital lobes, dreams and psychosis.   Journal of
    Nervous and Mental Disease, 1955, 121, 50-52.
Patten, B. M.   The ancient art of memory.   Archives of Neurology,
    1972, 26, 25-31.
Penfield, W., and Perot, P.   The brain's record of auditory and
    visual experience.   Brain, 1963, 86, 595-696.
Pope, K. S.   How gender, solitude and posture influence the stream
    of consciousness.   In K. S. Pope and J. L. Singer (Eds.), The
    stream of consciousness.   New York: Plenum, 1978.
Richardson, A.   Verbalizer-visualizer: a cognitive style dimension.
    Journal of Mental Imagery, 1977, 1, 109-126.
Rodin, J., and Singer, J. L.   Eye-shift, thought and obesity.
    Journal of Personality, 1976, 44, 594-610.
Segal, S. J., and Glickman, M.   Relaxation and the Perky effect:
    the influence of body position and judgments of imagery.
    American Journal of Psychology, 1967, 60, 257-262.
Semmes, J.   Hemispheric specialization: a possible clue to mecha-
    nism.   Neuropsychologia, 1968, 6, 11-26.
Sheehan, P. W.   A shortened form of the Betts Questionnaire on men-
    tal imagery.   Journal of Clinical Psychology, 1967, 23, 386-
    389.
Sperry, R. W.   Brain bisection and consciousness.   In J. C. Eccles
    (Ed.), Brain and conscious experience.   New York: Springer,
    1966.
Starker, S.   Two modes of visual imagery.   Perceptual and Motor
    Skills, 1974, 38, 649-650.
Stevenson, R. L.   The strange case of Dr. Jekyll and Mr. Hyde.   New
    York: Airmont, 1964.
Stone, M. H.   Dreams, free association, and the non-dominant hemis-
    phere: an integration of psychoanalytical, neurophysiological,
    and historical data.   Journal of the American Academy of Psy-
    choanalysis, 1977, 5, 255-284.
Teitlebaum, H. A.   Spontaneous rhythmic ocular movements: their
    possible relationship to mental activity.   Neurology, 1954,
    4, 350-354.
Tucker, D., Shearer, S., and Murray, D.   Article in Cognitive
    Therapy and Research, 1978, 1, 263-273, cited in Brain Mind
    Bulletin, April 17, 1978, 3, No. 11, 1.
Van Nuys, D. W.   Lateral eye movement and dream recall.   Unpublished
    manuscript.   Personal communication, 1979.
Wilson, J. R.   Sex and age differences in cognitive abilities.
    Unpublished manuscript, University of Hawaii, 1973.
Wyke, M.   The effects of brain lesions on the learning performance
    of a bimanual coordination task.   Cortex, 1971, 7, 59-72.
Zangwill, O. L.   Remembering revisited.   Quarterly Journal of
    Experimental Psychology, 1972, 24, 123-138.

DISCOVERIES ABOUT THE MIND'S ABILITY

TO ORGANIZE AND FIND MEANING IN IMAGERY

Joseph E. Shorr, Ph.D.

Director, Institute for Psycho-Imagination Therapy

Los Angeles, CA. 90048

> We are dealing, after all, with the private process of
> theory construction or innovation, the phase not open
> to inspection by others and indeed perhaps little under-
> stood by the originator himself. (Albert Einstein)

Why the mind organizes images that a person may "see" upon
being asked to imagine certain directed imaginary situations, is
currently a mystery. If we observe the well-known "phantom limb"
phenomenon it seems that such accidents of nature reveal a property
that is contrary to common sense--meaning, from a psychobiological
point of view, a phenomenon contrary to the way in which the brain
is normally designed to understand its role in its own consciousness. Hallucinations provide a similar example of this property
of the mind.

Gary Schwartz (1978) says that the mechanism by which these
"biocognitive constructions take place is currently a mystery."
Schwartz (1978) also says:

> The fact that this problem has received so little
> attention up to now is consistent with the basic
> phenomenon itself! Since the brain has no direct
> experience that it is responsible for, the creation
> of three-dimensional experience requires accidents
> of experience (e.g., phantom limbs, hallucinations)
> or the development of new technology (e.g., brain
> stimulation) to "see" beyond its own constraints.

To this I add an additional dimension, that of observable

psychological phenomenon of the manner and style of a person's
imagery productions and the ability to find meaning in them from
the context of their life experiences. In this way, perhaps
insight can be offered about this mystery.

Additionally, it may tell us more about the subjective, intro-
spective flow of images that is known as the stream of consciousness.

When a person is asked to imagine an imaginary situation and
then asked to describe the flow of his imagery, what he reports
very often bypasses his censorship. Afterwards, when he examines
his imagery, the person may begin to get subjective meaning from
his production. As such, it has projective qualities.

In this paper I will try to show some of the "discoveries"
that have been found in the use of directed imagery offered to
patients, and about the mind's ability to organize and find meaning
in them. The imagery use is within the context of Psycho-
Imagination Therapy as previously reported by Shorr (1972, 1974).

Jerome L. Singer (1974), in referring to Psycho-Imagination
Therapy, said, "It seems much closer in orientation to observable
psychological phenomena than many of the imagery techniques." I
find the phrase "observable psychological phenomena" to my liking.
The direct observation of a person's reported imagery avoids theorizing that is doctrinaire and the sterility of premature experimental work for the appearance of a scientific standard. It is
my own trial and error thinking of the patients' reported imagery,
combined with thoroughly studied lifestyles and conflicts of
patients, that has led to assumptions that a particular imaginary
situation will reveal certain personality information.

In doing clinical work involving imagery, some sort of trial
and error creativity takes place. It is beyond my own capacities
to set up an experimental design in advance of clinically using an
imaginary situation to determine what specific kinds of imageries
purport to reveal about a person. Of course, once several hundred
persons are asked to do the same imaginary situation, their
reported images can be examined for commonalities of themes or
conflicts with an idea towards possible empirical validation.

In determining subjective meaning, consensual validation
between myself, as therapist, and the patient was the general procedure used. When total agreement was reached by the patient and
myself, as therapist, we could then assume that the imagery production was, indeed, indicating particular meanings. This procedure was then repeated with hundreds of persons on each imaginary
situation offered. In time, after hundreds of records of one image

production were reviewed, certain unmistakable patterns emerged
that appeared with extremely high consistency and reliability.

In all attempts at subjective meaning in the use of imagery,
it is the patient who leads the discussion and makes the connections that are necessary to effect such conclusions. The therapist
takes an essentially non-directive position, allowing the patient
to explore possible meanings until he or she is satisfied with the
possible meaning. With thoroughly studied patients, agreement from
the therapist as to subjective meaning occurs at an extremely high
proportion of times.

In teaching a class in Imagery and Human Growth at UCLA in
1972, it occurred to me that the Russian type dolls with succeedingly smaller sizes inside the other, sometimes having four or five
dolls inside the larger doll, might reveal succeeding layers of
personality. It was at best a construct with a possible logical
basis.

Experience with the Russian dolls did not seem to reveal very
much. No general consistency of responses emerged. In fact, my
idea seemed to bog down and the students became bored. I persisted,
and modified my approach into using boxes. This time I attempted
to use three separate boxes in succeedingly smaller sizes. Eventually I chose a large box, a medium-sized box, and a small box.
Each person was asked what he or she imagined was in each box.
What would they reveal?

I collected "three boxes" responses from hundreds of people.
As I examined the responses I began trial and error thinking and
observation. After months of study and observation of patients'
responses, it seemed that the large box was showing how the person
appeared in his or her interaction with the social environment.
The middle box took longer to make sense to me. After months of
study and observation of patients' responses, the small box appeared
to represent the inner core of the person, or so it seemed.

Still it was trial and error creativity. A few weeks went by.
It occurred to me, why not ask the imager to imagine that he or
she was whatever he or she imagined was in the boxes, and then finish certain sentences. Out of this came: I feel ____, The adjective that best describes me is ____, I wish ____, I must ____, I
need ____, I secretly ____, I will ____, Never refer to me as ____.
Then clearer than ever came the meaning of the three boxes. Now
the middle box emerged in concept as the coping and defense mechanism between the large box and the small box. What I had anticipated about the large and small boxes were confirmed.

Several thousand persons have now done the three boxes!

Remarkably, it seems this special imagery has had an exceptionally high consistency to reveal what by trial and error I, in consensual validation with patients, discovered it might reveal.

Not all of my trial and error thinking can be remembered, so at its best I can look back upon it and call it trial and error creativity.

What still baffles and amazes me is why the human mind organizes the three boxes in this particular manner. Of equal mystery is the fact that not one single person has ever guessed or surmised the interpretation we have come to believe as true in advance of or while doing the imagery.

Shortly after the three boxes seemed to be firmly established as an enormously revealing imaginary situation, it subsequently became an important test item in the Shorr Imagery Test (1974). Soon my mind wandered to other possibilities. Would three balls, three windows, three doors, or three anything give us the same kind of delineations of meaning and personality information?

I attempted some of these other imaginary situations upon myself. Certain confusions seemed to occur. Perhaps I was trying too hard or knew what I was looking for. Clear categories of interpretation did not seem to emerge. I then decided to try it on others in my training classes and with patients.

It was the three doors that seemed to yield the most information in my trial and error activity. For, in asking a person to imagine three doors (left, right and center) and then to imagine opening each and to report what he or she saw, did and felt, one concept clearly emerged. In about 98% of the persons asked, the center door could subsequently be interpreted through consensual validation to concepts and dynamics about sexual matters or about relationships with the opposite sex.

Not unlike dream work, it may not be the manifest content of the center door imagery that is explicitly sexual. Subjective meaning can become clearer from the dialogue and subsequent imagery associations to the center door imagery. However, one will be surprised by a fairly large number of specific sexual references and references to actual persons that the imager is intimately involved with.

The right and left doors could yield much material. Here indeed was observable psychological phenomena. But, subjective meaning and interpretation of these doors was not easy to discover. In fact, no clear-cut patterns of meaning emerged. I tried collecting hundreds of three-door responses, but my intuitive judgment yielded confusion. I thought many times, "There is certainly a great deal of material here, but what does it mean?"

For the next year I would periodically return to this "three door" image, but it was only the center door that could reveal meaningful material. The meaning of the right and left doors eluded me--or perhaps there was no special meaning to it at all.

One day I tried the image with one patient and something sparked in my mind. The material I was getting in the left door in combination with the center door was the essence or the nucleus of that person's <u>central</u> conflict. The right door was presenting some form of <u>resolution</u> to the conflict or some aspect of a hoped-of future.

I felt elated. And I collected further records of the three doors. Soon my elation was jolted, for I had come across two persons who reversed the proceedings. The right door revealed what I had found in others as occurring in only the left door. It seemed amazing to me. Right or left handedness made no difference, and neither were there any sex differences.

I found that five persons in approximately 15 reversed the left/right doors and their meaning. Once I became alerted to this possible reversal, I could proceed to gather vital personality information that had previously escaped me.

It is my opinion that what will be revealed in the left door, in combination with the center and right doors, will contain many of the central aspects of that person's conflicts, styles and defenses. But for clarity, it must be stated that sometimes the left door will reveal the core conflict of the person. This may be reversed in some people so that the right door reveals the core conflict. The resolution of the conflict may also appear in the left or right door. Once the pattern can be seen, valuable material results.

Another imaginary situation that contains the "three" is titled "The Three Gates." In this image the subject is asked to imagine three gates in a row, one behind the other, and to open each in turn and then report what he sees, does and feels.

Again, I collected hundreds of responses to this imaginary situation from patients. Again consensual validation between myself and the patients ensued. After several months certain patterns became clear. In about 90% of the persons responding to "The Three Gates" imaginary situation, the first and second gate response led into the deeper levels of the unconscious of the person, that then seemed to be revealed from what they saw, did and felt as they entered the third gate.

With hundreds of respondents, it now seems clear that a highly reliable view of the person's unconscious can be observed from the patient's responses to the opening of the third gate. This seems to be true in 90% of the respondents. About 5% of the persons reverse this and give the first gate the same prominence that ordinarily appears in the third gate. Ordinary observation of the responses can quickly orient the interpreter to the point (first or third gate) that reveals the deeper levels of the unconscious.

There is a very small group of persons that go past the third gate to a fourth gate before revealing heavily unconscious material. Only actual experience with one's own imagery and that of others will yield the clarity I believe exists in the "Three Gates" imagery.

I have found using the same procedure that nearly all respondents--when asked to imagine putting their hand into a cave three times, each time a little deeper--will usually get to some deeper aspect of unconscious material the deeper they imagine going into the cave. Reversals have not occurred in this particular imaginary situation. When the material from all three responses, each going a little deeper, is examined, much usable personality dynamics can be elicited. Subjective meaning that the patient elicits from such material invariably bypasses censorship and informs both of us about unconscious phenomena.

Speculation as to why the third gate and the third, or deepest, hand insertion into the cave gives certain subjective meanings, is still speculation at this point.

Another unconscious imagery that I found extremely useful in uncovering "deeper" aspects of the personality is the imaginary situation in which the subject is asked to look into a pool of water and then to imagine three consecutive images one following the other. Again this seems to follow a pattern that reveals the third image as revealing unconscious material. Naturally, the first and second may reveal significant material as well. Invariably it is the third, or on occasion a fourth, image that in the greatest majority of times seems to reveal "deeper" levels of the personality.

One can ask the subject to imagine he or she is what he or she sees, for example in the third image, and finish the sentences, such as I feel _____, The adjective that best describes me is _____, I wish _____, I must _____, I need _____, I secretly _____, I will _____, I fear _____, and Never refer to me as _____. This adds fuller dimensions leading to meaningful dialogue and greater subjective meaning.

In yet another category of imagery productions (1978) called "Body Imagery" (1973), the mind's way of organizing and finding meaning in such imagery offers additional points and comments.

For example, when a person is asked to imagine "the body part core of his identity," respondents appear to have little difficulty in coming up with a body part such as hands, heart, guts, head, etc., etc. Yet in actuality there is no evidence that there is a body part core. But, the relative ease by which persons can arrive at such a body part clearly shows that human beings can assign such meanings. In consensual validation with patients, persons who say "hands," for example, invariably say they "saw" hands because they are what they do. Others say they are so much in their heads that their body part core is their head, etc., etc.

The mind organizes body imagery in yet another manner when a person is asked to imagine, for example, "In what part of your body does your mother or father reside?" In actuality, we know that a parent does not reside within a person. Yet, with relative ease most persons respond to this imaginary situation such as "my heart," "my guts," "my head," "my vagina," etc., etc. With consensual validation one can ascertain why a person sees and feels his or her parent resides in one particular body part or another. "My mother is in my heart," or "My father is in my head" are common responses that have real meaning to the respondent. The respondent can differentiate a bad introjected parent from a good parental introject.

It is possible for respondents to imagine eliminating the bad introjected parent. The therapist can ask the patient to imagine getting the bad introject out of his or her body in such a fashion as to not hurt himself or herself in the process. An amazing fact is that persons who are able to remove the bad introjected parent may "feel better" or remove the negative influence of that bad introjected parent.

Observation of persons eliminating the bad introjected parent and the feelings, struggles and style the person experiences in the process reveals observable data that is unmistakably real to that person. Since imagery and imagination is the method the person uses in this exorcism, it is remarkable to observe, but does not tell us why the mind does and can perform in this manner.[1]

---

[1]Body imagery offers at least a dozen other methods in which the person can organize imagery and find meaning in it. See Shorr's chapter, Clinical Use of Categories of Therapeutic Imagery, in Singer and Pope, "The Power of Human Imagination," 1978, Plenum Press, New York.

One of the most interesting ways in which the mind organizes imagery is the concept of "Dual Imagery" (1976). In dual imagery the subject is instructed to imagine two <u>different</u> objects, forces, persons, animals, or feelings. Take, for example, two <u>different</u> animals. Invariably the person, after imaging two different animals, can then be asked to describe each animal with an adjective. Following this the subject is asked to imagine one animal speaking to the other. Another way in which this might be clarified is to have them walk down a road together. From this the attempt is made to look for the outstanding differences between the animals. Dual imagery thus provides complementary opposites within the experience.

Clinical experience indicates that the subject, in referring to the outstanding differences between the two animals, is referring to some aspect of conflict within himself. The more polarized the differences the more polarized is the possibility of conflict within himself.

Dialogue about the two different images can bring forth projective qualities often unaware in the subject.

To divert for a moment, I would like to remind the reader that a great deal of work has been done about similarities of things. Similarity plays a fundamental role in theories of knowledge and behavior.

Tversky (1977) says of similarity that, "It serves as an organizing principle by which individuals classify objects from concepts and make generalizations. Indeed, the concept of similarity is ubiquitous in psychological theory."

If we say "A is like B," then it is directional, it has a subject and a referant. We say the portrait resembles the person rather than the person resembles the portrait; or the son resembles the father rather than the father resembles the son. Similarities are central to connative meaning.

Rosch (1973, 1975) supports the view that perceptual and semantic categories are naturally formed and·defined in terms of focal points or prototypes. For example, Rosch asks:

(A)   103 (variant) is virtually 100 (prototype), or

(B)   100 is virtually 103

Most subjects preferred (A): to place the prototype in the second position and the variant in the first position. (103 is virtually 100.)

In dual imagery the person, in imagining two different

feelings, objects, persons, etc., is using an organizing principle
that is ubiquitous in psychological theory. The person is able to
form concepts and make generalizations assigning meanings and values
that lead to a view of opposites, even to polarization. The degree
of opposition between the two images invariably leads to assumptions
of conflict within the person. Sometimes the conflict is between
two parts of the person, and sometimes it is between some aspect of
self and others.

In this paper the attempt has been made to show certain discoveries about how people get meaning and organize their responses
when asked to report certain directed imagery.

Finally, I would like to say that our images are so fleeting,
no device for trapping them should be overlooked.

REFERENCES

Rosch, E. On the internal structure of perceptual and semantic
      categories. In T. E. Moore (Ed.), Cognitive Development and
      the Acquisition of Language. New York: Academic Press, 1973.
Rosch, E. Cognitive reference points. Cognitive Psychology, 1975,
      7, 532-547.
Schwartz, G. E. Psychobiological foundations of psychotherapy and
      behavior change. In A. Bergin and S. L. Garfield (Eds.),
      Handbook of Psychotherapy and Behavior Change, 2nd ed. New
      York: Wiley and Sons, 1978.
Shorr, J. E. Psycho-imagination therapy: the integration of
      phenomenology and imagination. New York: Intercontinental
      Medical Book Corporation, 1972.
Shorr, J. E. In what part of your body does your mother reside?
      Psychotherapy: Theory, Research and Practice, 1973, 10, 31-34.
Shorr, J. E. Psychotherapy through imagery. New York: Inter-
      continental Medical Book Corporation, 1974.
Shorr, J. E. Shorr Imagery Test. Los Angeles: Institute for
      Psycho-Imagination Therapy, 1974.
Shorr, J. E. Task imagery as therapy. Psychotherapy: Theory,
      Research and Practice, Summer, 1975, 12.
Shorr, J. E. Dual imagery. Psychotherapy: Theory, Research and
      Practice, Fall, 1976, 13, No. 2.
Shorr, J. E. Clinical use of categories of therapeutic imagery.
      In J. L. Singer and K. Pope (Eds.), The Power of Human Imagi-
      nation. New York: Plenum, 1978.
Shorr, J. E. Imagery as a projective device. Imagery Bulletin of
      the American Association for the Study of Mental Imagery, Los
      Angeles, July, 1978. I, No. 2.
Shorr, J. E. Imagery as a method of self-observation in therapy.
      Imagery Bulletin of the American Association for the Study of
      Mental Imagery, Los Angeles, May, 1979, II, No. 2.

Singer, J. L. Imagery and daydream methods in psychotherapy and
    behavior modification. New York: Academic Press, 1974.
Tversky, A. Features of similarity. Psychological Review, July,
    1977, 84(4), 327-352.

IMAGERY IS MORE POWERFUL WITH FOCUSING: THEORY AND PRACTICE

Eugene T. Gendlin, Ph.D.

University of Chicago

Chicago, Illinois

THEORETICAL INTRODUCTION

Let me begin with an extremely brief and summarized theoretical statement. How might we think about "the unconscious," that rich source of imagery and of course, of other processes? I would like to say simply: the unconscious is the body. Of course, we need to devise entirely new kinds of concepts about the body, for this and many other reasons. The body is no mere physiological machine. The body is inherently interactional. Let me say more clearly what this means:

We guide our behavior most of the time by a bodily sense of each situation. We do not speak to ourselves about each facet of a situation--if we did, we could not handle any situation at all. To do any simple thing, we must "know" what led up to the situation, what we are trying to bring about or avoid, who the people present are, how to walk, sit, speak, and countless other facets. We can think only very few of these explicitly. All the rest are "known" in a rich, holistic feeling of the whole context, which we can have only in a bodily concrete way.

What we mean by "body" must therefore be reformulated. We do not mean only what physiology formulates. The living body is a complex interactional system. We live with our bodies, and we feel in our bodies what goes on around us, as well as what we are about to say and do (Gendlin, 1962).

There is a way of feeling and having this whole complexity. This way is called "focusing," and I will say more about it later.

65

First, we must rethink our concepts of the body. From the
very start it must be interactional--a body-environment unit. I
have had to build concepts anew from this beginning (Gendlin, 1979).
Every living event is a body-environment unit. "Environment"
includes many kinds of objectifications: food and air, other people, symbolic behaviors, imagery.

The body implies, and can produce, whole complex sequences of
interaction in situations between people. A single system encom-
passes body, feeling, situation, and action. What another person
does affects our feeling of the total situation. Certain behaviors
of our own, or by others, change situations in certain ways, and
also engender certain feelings. At the simplest level certain
"emotions" arise in us at certain junctures in such situational
interaction. The body can produce whole sequences of moves, each
move is a body-emotion-situation-action unity. Such sequences, when
they aren't actually happening, are called "stories." A story consists of a sequence of interactions between people, each interaction
is body, it is also felt, it involves a situation and other people.
The body produces many stories of this kind every 24 hours. Every
person makes up such stories every night. I am referring to dreams,
of course.

Just as we don't want to think of the living body as mere
physiological events, so also we don't want to think of images as
merely entities, pictures like a painting hanging on a wall. Any
event of life includes body and also environment, and a kind of
forward-moving action of the living body into some environment. An
image can be thought of as a living body's move, a living into a
special kind of "environment." The imagery level must be a kind of
environment, a kind of objectification. One can live further in
feeding or breathing, which are the life of the body spread out
into space. One can also live further by acting toward others in a
situation--again such action is life spread out. Analogously, one
can live forward into an imagery space. Again, an image is spread
out, it is a kind of environment, although a symbolic kind.

Although I stated these kinds of environment in the order I
did, just now, I do not believe that images are copies of ordinary
interaction between people. Just the opposite. It requires symbolic imagery first to form human culture and its interactions
between humans. Imagery and culture must have formed together.
Human interaction, however actual and concrete, is always symbolic.

From this absurdly rapid summary I wish to take the main conclusions: We can understand that imagery is a special kind of
bodily living in an environment with other humans. We can think
of the body as inherently an interactional process so that body,
emotion, situation, action, and other people are always inherently
a single system.

This changes how we think about an image. Instead of asking
only about the image itself, what is pictured, what bodily change
was involved in the bodily living which made this image? And we
can also ask: What further bodily living is now implied, now that
the image-event has occurred? It will not be the same as before.

I am altering the basic assumptions: rather than an image
being viewed as a representation, I view it as itself living.
Rather than statically being what it seems to be, like a picture
hanging unchangingly on a wall, I ask both what it stems from, and
what change its very formation made.

For example, take food. One can say that hunger represents
food, hunger is, of course, about food. But we also know that if
the food occurs and is eaten, then the hunger is changed by that
very food. I want to think of symbols, and especially images, in
this way. A symbol, say an image, is like the act of eating, it
stems from the living body's implying of a certain next process.
And, if it occurs, it also changes the body so that now it implies
something different as its next process.

Therefore, we will consider imagery, now, in relation to the
bodily way it forms, and also, we will ask about the changed body
as a result of its formation. This leads to a different way of
practice with imagery, a constant return to the body between each
image and the next.

But the kind of attention which must be paid to the body is
rather special, and different from the ways known until now. That
brings us to focusing.

FOCUSING INVOLVES A VERY SPECIFIC
  KIND OF BODILY AWARENESS

In focusing, one attends inwardly to the sense of the body,
but quite differently from how that is done, for example, in Gestalt
Therapy. One does not simply scan the body, finding tension, say,
in the shoulders, or some odd sensation in the chest. We are not
now speaking of sensations that seem merely bodily (even though
they will turn out to have relations to how one lives or lived).
Say you just walked into this room and sat down. Now you can pay
attention to your sense of this whole situation. This, too, will
be a bodily sensing, but it will not be a scanning of all the parts
of your body, rather you will find directly this specific bodily
sense--your sense of this situation. It will be somewhere in the
middle of your body, the area from your throat to your belly. It
will not be a mere body sensation like a too tight belt or indigestion. It might be quite similar to indigestion, but it will be a
sensing of meaning, a sense of . . . . At first it won't be clear

what it is a sense of, beyond the fact that it is of this situation.
As you keep your attention near it, you may find it coming into focus.
Suddenly, it is no longer just a diffuse discomfort with the situation (or a diffuse comfort, or however it feels), but something quite
specific. "Oh . . . ." you may say, not yet having found words to
say it yet. Suddenly you "know"--again in this bodily sensed way of
knowing, in which we "know" the thousands of facets of any situation.
Quite quickly, usually, you can then think "what it is," and this
is usually something focal, important, central, for example: "Oh,
that's what worries me. . ." or "Oh, that's what's funny about what's
going on. . . ." You can now tell yourself in words what that is,
or at least, you can name it briefly. There is a bodily change,
which comes along with this coming into focus. There is a release,
a relief, a flow of energy that was stuck before.

In a new book called Focusing (Gendlin, 1978), I have presented
very specific instructions for how to bring about what I just
described too simply. There are quite specific steps, first for
enabling this holistic "felt sense" to form (it must form, it isn't
just there--and that requires some 30 seconds or a minute of quiet
time), and then there are other specific steps for enabling that
felt sense to come into focus, to "shift." By "felt shift" we mean
this bodily release. Although it feels like merely release, new
energy, the body is subsequently found to be very different. The
problem may not be solved in one such round of focusing, but what
one can now think and do is already very different. The way the
whole situation exists in the body is changed.

This focusing process is the essence of psychotherapeutic
change--it is a specific series of steps, newly defined, for what
happens at those moments when a person actually changes in a concrete way. Unless change occurs unmistakably in the body, it does
not, in my opinion, occur at all (Gendlin, 1968). But now can
there be change in people anyway? What they deliberately try to do
to themselves usually is only another example of their personality,
and doesn't change what needs changing. What others tell the person does not usually, through the intellect, make real change. How
then is change possible at all? It is only when more is worked
with than just the person's conscious ego. But where is this "more,"
and how does one contact it? The focusing steps are an exact answer
to this question.

I might now return for a moment to the difference I explained,
between Gestalt and focusing ways of attending to the body. Even
if one works with tense shoulders, there is still a need to sense
the overall feel of these shoulders--the meaningfulness of the tension. And this meaningfulness is not sensed in the shoulders, but
in the center of the body, as in focusing. Gestalt (and every
other method I know) is aided by the specificity of focusing.
Focusing helps each method to do that, which happens when the method

works.

Let me now return to imagery. It happens that, during focusing,
one sometimes cannot get words, or even that recognition of, "Oh. . .
that's what it is" directly. One can sometimes let an image come
from the as yet unopened "felt sense." That, of course, is not just
any old image. It is an image living forward from the felt sense of
the whole (the whole problem, the whole situation). Such images are
powerful.

The first difference in practice, that I propose, is to let a
felt sense form first, and then to let an image form from it.

The second difference in practice is what happens just after
an image forms in this way. Now one must not let the image flow
into another image, and another, and so on, at least one must not
continue to do that and nothing else. One major powerful image,
probably the first one that came and felt powerful, needs to be
held for a little time, and in that time one needs to sense the
bodily impact--the felt sense in the body--which this image makes.
The occurrence of the image will have made for a new and changed
felt sense. This new and changed felt sense must be allowed to
form in the body. The question is: What is the holistic bodily
feel, which this image gives you?

In my opinion real change in people does not come to any great
extent from the mere having of images as such. It comes if one
works directly with the bodily change that image-formation makes.
If this is ignored, the most important effect of imagery is ignored.

But, someone will ask, didn't you just say that the formation
of images is bodily change? How then can there be anything better
than a long chain of images; won't that be a long chain of bodily
change? Now you have contradicted yourself and told us that a
chain of image-image-image (without direct attention to the bodily
felt sense) makes little change!

Something like the same problem also exists with thinking,
action, and every other kind of symbolic interaction. It can occur
so that, at each point, there is a new bodily shift. Or, it can
occur as a largely separated sequence of only thinking, or only
action, only images. Now, of course, this "only" is really impossible. Even the most abstracted and separated thought is still an
event in a living body, and therefore some kind of change. What
exactly is the difference?

The difference is this: If one lets a holistic bodily "felt
sense" form, that is a holistic process. The whole body's living
is involved in forming the whole sense of a problem, or a situation. It is a rearrangement of everything in so far as it is

relevant. And the difference I am concerned about is whether we engender such a whole living reorganization every little while, or only once (or not at all).

If one simply has an image from this moment, without first letting a felt sense form, that will not be a powerful change. If one then lets the images play on and on, again it won't be a powerful change. However, if one stops any image and, seeking what its impact is, lets a felt sense form in the body, this will be a powerful change. Also, if one lets the image form from a felt sense, then there is a powerful change first in the formation of that felt sense, and then again in living that felt sense further via the image. The question is whether there is a holistic bodily change at every step, or not.

In this conception of the body there are two basic assumptions: first, that the body lives its whole complexity forward, and always implies a forward movement. If the whole, as it is just now patterned, cannot be lived forward, there is a blockage. The body lives forward as best it can, but not wholly. Our problems are like that, and require a change, or a series of changes, in concrete bodily story-implying (if you like that way of putting it).

Secondly, I assume that there are different kinds of environment in which living forward can happen, and that felt-sense formation is one of them, and imagery another.

I cannot here say much in detail about the new and odd kind of "space"--and the new kind of "environment" involved in the formation of a felt sense in focusing. It is not in the usual image space, nor in the body as usually attended to. There is a new level, a new kind of awareness. One senses a new kind of "it," that felt sense there. Along with sensing such as "it," one also senses in a fresh direct way that "Oh . . . I am not it." There is a discovery that one is none of these contents. But this is no mere disembodied watcher. Rather, a new flow of energy and a new sense of self-in-touch, makes this new self very concrete and alive, no mere observer. And yet one finds this newly formed "felt sense" over here, and oneself over here next to it, with a new kind of space in between.

But, although this new level, this new plane, this new space, is not the space of imagery, nevertheless imagery is very powerful. Once a felt sense of the whole issue has formed, one can live on from it in words, imagery, action, and in other ways. Living on in imagery is one of the most powerful ways. (Living on in creative body movement as in dance may be even more so, and is akin to imagery.) Therefore, it is often best if one first lets an image form from the felt sense, and only then one finds words for what the image's impact is.

Words, in focusing, come of their own accord once there is the "shift," but before that happens one must often try out various words. Most useful at that stage are very descriptive words like "heavy," "tight," "burdened," "queasy," rather than content-words that have to do with the problem. (The latter kind may come, however.) Whatever words one uses, the key is whether they receive a bodily signal, in response to the words. When words come, one must not try to decide if they are right, rather, one needs to check them against the bodily sense, directly--just as if one were asking another person. One repeats the word and asks, "Is that right?" "Does that do anything?" Then one quietly attends, one must first regain the felt sense, else one cannot "ask" it. Only when it is there again can one ask and await a signal, some loosening, some relief, some small or large stirring, which lets one know that the word or words are, indeed, a bit of further living from the felt sense, and not just words.

Something quite similar is done with images that come. One can just ask, "What is the bodily impact of this image" but, then one must, of course, attend directly inwardly to sense it directly. Or, one can once again regain the felt sense of the whole problem ("Is this problem all solved?"--little waiting, trying to say it's solved, "Ah. . . there it is again, that discomfort. . .") When the sense of the whole problem has returned, one can then set the image, as it were, before this sense, asking: "Is this image right for it?" There may now be a distinctly sensed change in the body, a release, a stirring, a moving inside, in response to the image. One can feel oneself changing right there and then, concretely.

The very coming of a felt sense is a holistic body change. Living further from such a felt sense is further change. It isn't possible to say exactly whether the way a word or image fits is again a holistic "shift," or only a small signal, a little bit of such change. What matters is whether or not we work with the bodily formed felt sense of the whole problem or not. If we work with this bodily forming and shifting, it might be to let the image come from it, it might be on the return from an image to then form the whole sense it engenders in the body, or it might be to see if the image makes a further change in the felt sense already formed and regained.

It must also be noted that imagery comes very well and very richly during highly relaxed states, while this is not the case with focusing, the felt sense and its shifts. One cannot focus when one is too relaxed. Focusing is at the entry point to altered states, at the door, so to speak, but not far into relaxation. It is certainly more relaxed than our usual living, and most people must relax a bit in order to focus. However, as soon as one passes beyond the entry line and becomes very relaxed, focusing becomes impossible. Focusing requires that this "door" to altered states be open, or, I could say, it opens this door. But focusing occurs

in the doorway, so to speak. Focusing requires <u>letting</u> a felt
sense form, and this letting needs relaxation. But it also requires
a very deliberate attention, a kind of frame-holding over the murky
sense of the problem, which cannot be done with very much relaxation.
Focusing also requires a distinct questioning, as I said above, an
active putting the word before the felt sense, an active being next
to it, attending to it, finding it again, and so on. None of this
works even in an otherwise rather moderate state of alteration due
to relaxation.

In meditation, for example, when something feels off, one needs
to come out of meditation and to an ordinary awareness (open one's
eyes, wait till the sparkles subside, move one's shoulders a little),
then focusing becomes possible. Focusing can let one free the body
of the cramp, the stoppage, the physical effects of the problems
one carries in the body; then meditation is much easier and better.

Thus, I am far from asserting that focusing is the deepest
level, or the only kind of important process, or the only method
of working with oneself, or anything like that. It is a very specific process, located at a crucial juncture in relation to altered
states, and in relation to personality change. It can powerfully
aid other useful methods, and should not be thought of as excluding
them. We have been teaching focusing for some years to many different kinds of people and in relation to many topics, spirituality,
psychotherapy, stress-reduction, education, creativity, to mention
a few. (See Focusing, the references in the back.) Focusing,
when there is a "felt shift," has EEG correlates (Don, 1977), and
further research especially in conjunction with imagery would be
very desirable. A beginning of such research already exists
(Olsen, 1975).

In summary, I believe that whatever your way of working with
imagery may be, you will find your method enhanced quite powerfully,
if you employ focusing. It is quite likely that this kind of
holistic formation of a directly felt bodily sense of the whole
issue is already what you wish for, in your method, and occasionally
get. It is likely, too, that this return from the image, at each
point, to a direct sensing and having of its bodily impact, is also
something you already want, and occasionally get. If so, focusing
is the specific way of teaching and engendering that. Imagery and
body-sense are inherently related, but on different planes. It is
much more powerful if one not only works with the body and imagery,
but devotes specific attention to the formation of the body's
holistic sense of the issue. That is the formation of something
directly sensed in the body, yet implicitly meaningful. Such a felt
sense is not just there, waiting to be noticed. It must first form,
and does so in an oddly new space. Its formation is a major change,
and enables the further major change of a "felt shift." When imagery stems from such a felt sense, and when the impact of an image

is used to engender a felt shift, that is when working with imagery is most powerful.

REFERENCES

Don, N. S. Transformation of conscious experience and its EEG correlates. Journal of Altered States of Consciousness, 1977, 3(2), 147-148.

Gendlin, E. T. Experiencing and the creation of meaning. New York: Free Press, 1962.

Gendlin, E. T. Focusing. New York: Everest House, 1978.

Gendlin, E. T. A process model. Unpublished draft.

Gendlin, E. T., Beebe, J., Cassens, J., Klein, M., and Oberlander, M. Focusing ability in psychotherapy, personality and creativity. Research in Psychotherapy, Vol. 3. Washington: APA, 1968.

Olsen, L. E. The use of visual imagery and experiential focusing in psychotherapy. Unpublished doctoral dissertation, University of Chicago, 1975.

TREATMENT OUTCOME IN RELATION TO VISUAL IMAGERY,

SUGGESTIBILITY, TRANSFERENCE, AND CREATIVITY

Joseph Reyher, Ph.D.

Michigan State University

East Lansing, Michigan

The rapidly proliferating development of treatment procedures utilizing visual imagery is an index of the excitement being generated by its return from ostracism. This excitement is a welcome quickening of the pulse in the growing malaise of psychotherapy research. To wit, it does not make any difference what you do, just do it convincingly (Frank, 1979), and be enthusiastic (Shapiro and Morris, 1978). Simpler yet, just put everyone on a waiting list (Bergin and Lambert, 1978). Unfortunately, visual imagery methods are sufficiently varied as to obscure what it is about them that warrants the excitement and interest. To aid my own thinking, I have ordered these by classifying them into four disparate categories: guided imagery, behavior modification, active imagination and spontaneous visual imagery, which I call emergent uncovering psychotherapy. In guided imagery, the client is given standard scenes as stimuli with the purpose of symbolically addressing ignored parts of the self, archetypes and recurrent problems in living. By artful manipulation of the client's imagery, these sources of emotional difficulty can be ameliorated or resolved symbolically. It is an absorbing, creative interaction between both participants. In behavior modification (systematic desensitization, implosive and flooding methods, modeling, rehearsal, covert conditioning), visual imagery is used as a means to interfere with undesirable stimulus-response or antecedent-consequent relationships. Visual imagery is used to stimulate anxiety, promote relaxation or to activate drives and affects. In active imagination, visual imagery and dream continuation is used to overcome personal and interpersonal problems by creative problem solving and conflict resolution (Greenleaf, 1978). In emergent uncovering (Reyher, 1978), free association with eyes closed in a viz a viz relationship is used to generate anxiety, symptoms, resistance and security operations (face-saving devices) to pave the way for the depiction of underlying repressed strivings by visual imagery.

These categories of clinical application are not exhaustive; they only represent nodal points on a spectrum of methods laid out by Singer (1974) in his excellent review. Each of us has gone his own way believing, as we must, that visual imagery plays an essential role in whatever success, which we dearly prize, we claim for our methods. When research shows that all methods are equally effective, those of us with strong personal investments in a particular modality are apt to belittle research on psychotherapy as being irrelevant rather than discount the efficacy of our own methods. The ideal of parsimony moves aside for personal investment. This personal investment, a nonspecific effect, is a powerful factor in achieving a favorable treatment outcome (Shapiro and Morris, 1978).

The current status of systematic desensitization, the most intensively researched method of psychotherapy, epitomizes the inevitable progression of complexity and uncertainty whenever a particular modality of treatment is scrutinized. Initially, the method appeared to be a model of simplicity and logic involving the combination of relaxation and a hierarchy of scenes. However, neither the scenes nor the hierarchy have proved to be influencing variables. The scenes can be scrambled or the hierarchy reversed or the subject made tense instead of relaxed, the results are the same. In the face of these findings, Wilkins (1972) looked elsewhere for explanations: the expectations of the client and other unknown aspects of the patient-therapist relationship. Kazdin and Wilcoxson (1978) recently reviewed the same body of literature and they concluded that expectancy had not been controlled. The procedures of the control groups characteristically lacked credibility. Unfortunately, this does not elucidate matters any more than such concepts as the placebo effect, suggestion or transference. Until the mechanisms mediating these effects are identified, they merely give the illusion of scientific understanding. Most of us resort to such nonspecific explanations because we are without recourse and we know empirically that they can have a powerful effect on some dependent variables some of the time. On the optimistic side, however, two reviewers (Wilkins, 1972; Mathews, 1978) have suggested that visual imagery may play some role in favorable treatment outcomes. Unfortunately, instructed imagination methods of treatment, particularly guided imagery, are especially susceptible to interpretation in terms of non-specific effects. However, as we shall see, this may be their strength rather than their weakness.

NONSPECIFIC TREATMENT EFFECTS

What are these nonspecific effects? Although defined differently by various investigators, they are the processes which mediate the so-called placebo effect; hence, like the word "normal," "placebo" is an omnibus term. Frank (1961) has identified four nonspecific effects as being common to successful psychotherapy: 1) confidence in the therapist's competence, caring and acceptance; 2) the setting has connotations of healing; 3) a rationale or myth, which explains illness, health, deviancy, normality, to provide meaning and an optimistic perspective; and 4) a procedure prescribed by the rationale. These necessary conditions interrelate in five ways to produce positive treatment outcome. These are: 1) new cognitive and experiential learning; 2) creation of favorable expectations; 3) enhanced feelings of mastery and capability; 4) overcoming a sense of alienation; and 5) emotional arousal.

Hypnosis and Suggestibility

Hypnosis consistently has enabled us to gain clearer glimpses of significant phenomena than any other treatment modality, viz, hysteria, multiple personality, amnesia, transference, and suggestibility. True to form, nonspecific effects are particularly visible in hypnosis. In fact, the real-simulator design was developed by Orne (1959) to guard against the strivings of highly suggestible subjects to please the experimenter. On the basis of clinical lore and scattered research, I (Reyher, 1977c) formulated the putative psychodynamics of high and low suggestible subjects. The verification of these group differences not only would invalidate the real-simulator design because of the confounding of these group differences with the manipulated variables (Reyher, 1973), but it also would cloud the findings of outcome research unless the distribution of high and low suggestible clients were taken into account. I have little doubt that research will show that these subsets of individuals do not distribute themselves evenly across treatment modalities (Crowne and Marlowe, 1964).

Among those persons who score high on scales of suggestibility are those who seek approval from others, particularly authoritative persons, and who anticipate rejection because of self-conceptions of personal insufficiency. Accordingly, they react with intense anxiety and anger which they must suppress or repress when they objectively are made to feel insufficient through failure or when they perceive signs of disapproval, real or imagined. I call this complex of aversive cognitions and affects dystonia (Reyher, 1978). They tend to be submissive, conforming and generally pleasing. This is a coherent set of strivings and security operations[1] (Reyher, 1978). Sheehan (1971) has reported that about fifty

---

[1] Security operation is Sullivan's (1953) term to denote those interpersonal behaviors by which we attempt to prevent or offset a decrease in self-esteem.

percent of high suggestible subjects are oriented to behave in
accordance to the expectations of the hypnotist-experimenter rather
than to the overt demand characteristics of the research design.
They also score high on submissiveness. Smyth (1977) reported
cogent evidence that high suggestibility is associated with diffuse
attention, and a recent analysis of his data, taking into account
dystonia, showed that high suggestible subjects react with more dystonia to failure on a signal detection task and the items of a suggestibility scale. On the other hand, among those individuals who
score low on hypnotic susceptibility scales are those individuals
who are more concerned with strivings of mastery and autonomy
rather than generalized approval seeking. Accordingly, they are
more disposed to confer approval upon themselves for behaving and
performing in accordance with their own standards rather than those
of others. Approval from others is meaningful only when it is
deserved. Since they are less dependent on the approval of others,
they are more apt to be competitive, defiant and moved to anger;
consequently, they are likely to respond with poorer performance
to task motivating instructions than to hypnotic suggestions
(Dhanens and Lundy, 1975). They also have been characterized as
possessing a generalized unwillingness to cooperate (Spanos and
Bodorik, 1977). Unlike those high susceptible individuals who seek
approval indiscriminantly to reduce anxiety about personal unaccep-
tance, they tend to have received less severe punishment in childhood (J. Hilgard, 1970) and to have had mothers who were more
approving and less anxious (London, 1976). They are characterized
by a different coherent set of strivings and security operations.

The pursuit of security most aptly characterizes that subset
of high suggestible subjects identified by Sheehan and discovered
in Smyth's data, whereas autonomy and self-actualization most aptly
characterizes a sizable proportion of low suggestible subjects.
This conclusion, however, is discrepant from current stereotypes of
high and low suggestible subjects. Nevertheless, Table 1 shows
opposed configurations of correlations[2] representing safety needs
and antagonistic esteem (Assor, 1979) which also are opposed and
congruent with my psychodynamic formulations of low and high suggestible persons. An added insight is that these two configurations
of correlations reflect risk- and nonrisk-taking orientations in
interpersonal relationships. Both orientations are distinctively

---

[2]The impressively high correlations in Table 1 reflect
the virtues of Aronoff's sentence completion test (Aronoff and Messe,
1971). Its ipsative construction allows for the organization of
an individual's strivings to find expression in the way they are
actually organized. The projective or response free nature of the
instrument also minimizes response bias because of the wide variety
of discrepant values, and perspectives available to the testee for
legitimizing his response.

Table 1

Comparison of Correlations (SCT)[a] Taken From
Assor With Respect to Safety and
Antagonistic Esteem[b] in Males[c]

Variable	Striving	
	Safety	Antagonistic Esteem
Dependency[a]	.22*	-.30**
Personal incompetence[a]	.61***	-.35**
Self-esteem[a]	-.75***	.69***
Gratification esteem[a]	-.61***	-.11
Mistrust-withdrawal[a]	.80***	-.41***
Affiliation[a]	-.52***	.03
Academic achievement[a]	-.35**	.47***
Power (TAT)	-.10	.25*
Antagonistic esteem[a]	-.56***	

[a]Aronoff's sentence completion test.

[b]Individuals characterized by competition and dominance.

[c]n = 59

*p < .05

**p < .05

***p < .001

different ways of maintaining self-esteem when the individual is faced with the possibility of failure.

Until proven otherwise, it would be a good research strategy to assume that risk- and nonrisk-taking persons are not evenly distributed across treatment groups and levels of suggestibility as measured by individual hypnotic susceptibility scales. I also would

assume that their response biases on objective tests differ because
they reflect their distinctive strivings and self-conceptions.

Suggestibility

Even if individual and group differences are taken into account,
outcome studies must also control for alterations in suggestibility
associated with different treatment procedures. An investigation
by Reyher, Wilson and Hughes (1979) into the circumstances associated with elevated and lowered suggestibility found, as predicted,
that suggestibility increased whenever an individual adopts a
passive-receptive attitude with respect to oral instructions in good
faith. I call this hypersuggestibility, level 1. One of the three
passive-receptive groups silently observed their imagery while their
suggestibility was assessed by ten test suggestions masquerading as
statements of fact. Another group received the same instructions
with the exception that they described their imagery. Yet another
group was recruited for research on hypnosis, not perception as
were the others, and the same suggestions were given except they
were acknowledged as such. Since speech is a left cerebral hemisphere function, and since suggestibility appears to be a right
cerebral hemisphere function, we expected the group that described
their spontaneous visual imagery to show the least suggestibility.
Indeed, this was the case. The three passive-receptive groups and
the one receiving a formal induction were equivalent; hence, the
formal induction did not provide an advantage. In fact, the highest mean was associated with the passive-receptive group that was
instructed simply to sit quietly with eyes closed while waiting
for further instructions.

In the clinical situation, it should be kept in mind that the
goal (symptom amelioration) is shared by both participants and functions as an indirect suggestion under conditions of hypersuggestibility induced by the instructions. The instructions may be for
guided imagery, acupuncture, systematic desensitization, progressive relaxation, biofeedback, osteopathic manipulation, faith healing, exorcism, a placebo, a formal induction of hypnosis, LeMaze
training, autogenic training, a chiropractor doing his thing or
even a physician going through a physical examination. These procedures all serve as vehicles for the adoption of a passive-
receptive attitude, providing that a given procedure is not anxiety-
producing for a particular person. Anxiety activates adaptive,
analytical (interpretive) responses, including defenses. Reyher
and Wilson (1973) showed that the prospect of a formal hypnotic
induction is anxiety-producing for some persons and interferes with
their adoption of a passive-receptive attitude. When the procedure
was designated as hypnosis, a significantly greater rate of GSRs
was produced than when the procedure was designated as relaxation.
The advantage of a formal induction for those persons who are not
made anxious is the opportunity for the initiation of a regressive

transference which allegedly is associated with a higher degree of
suggestibility (Reyher, 1977a).

Suggestibility and Regressive
  Transference

The use of hypnosis in a medical setting has impressed me with
respect to the apparently greater effectiveness of suggestion than
what is customarily observed in the laboratory. Equally apparent
is the patient's adulation of the practitioner. This is particularly strong in those areas of medicine, such as obstetrics, which
represent the vital concerns of an individual. There is the same
adulation of rock stars, faith healers, cult leaders, popes, royalty,
military heroes, and some politicians. This adulation is best
understood, I believe, as regressive transference. By this I mean
a state dependent reactivation of parental images (an image) in the
client. Freud also conceptualized hypnosis as a regressive transference. The uncritical overestimation of the hypnotist is akin
to falling in love.

A regressive transference is readily initiated in many of us
during crisis, particularly physical threats of life (Reyher, 1977a)
and when an individual despairs of self-actualization, or loses his
capacity to cope with everyday survival, or is unable to maintain
self-esteem and rid himself of dystonia. Whether a physician, a
cult leader, demagogue, or captors, the effects are the same.
The individual incorporates the values and beliefs of his saviors
because they have become parental surrogates. Freud recognized the
powerful effect of a regressive transference in furthering the painful process of self-discovery, and an investigation (Beutler and
Pollack, 1978) showed that there is a relationship between improvement in psychotherapy and the acquisition of the therapist's values.
The Stockholm effect, the growth of mutuality between both captors
and hostages, appears to be a function of a regressive transference
in them both. As time runs out in a hostile environment they lean
more on each other for approval to offset a lowering of self-esteem.
Feeling helpless and anxious about one's personal, social, physical,
or spiritual well-being constitute stimuli for the reactivation of
percepts of parents or caretakers in early childhood who, at the
time, appeared to be all-powerful. This state of affairs may
reflect a distinctive brain state context and an amnesic barrier
(Weingartner, 1977) that allows access to vital regulatory neurophysiological centers (Reyher, 1977a). One indicator of this
alleged brain state context (altered awareness) is an additional
elevation of suggestibility which I call hypersuggestibility,
level 2. Another indicator is the overestimation of the provider,
protector or captor. In operational terms, Anna Freud's concept
of identification with the aggressor and regressive transference
are the same.

Many of us unwittingly, and wittingly, foster hypersuggestibility, level 2, by assuming a demeanor of unquestionable self-
assurance and competence and by relating to our patients/clients in
a paternalistic manner. The laying on of hands further approxi-
mates the conditions associated with infant caretaking, particularly
feeding, and, therefore, the initiation of a regressive transference. A paternalistic manner is the essence of a good bedside manner by the physician and mediates his magic. Ralph August's film
on Caesarian birth with hypnosis as the sole anaesthetic is a good
illustration of the effectiveness of a paternalistic manner, even
to the point of a register that approaches baby talk. This mode of
speaking also characterizes the speech of someone conducting hypnosis, and it should be noted that both the hypnotist and the physician use this same register as is the case in most situations
wherein one person tends to the needs of another (Ferguson, 1978).
The communications of both the physician and the hypnotist to their
patients/clients almost exclusively involve instructions as well as
prescriptions and proscriptions reminiscent of childhood caretaking.
LaBaron (1979) found that women facing abortion exhibited higher
suggestibility, greater transference and less anxiety when they
were treated in a paternalistic manner rather than in an equalitar-
ian manner. However, Maria Della Corte and I found that type of
induction was irrelevant for college student volunteers for research
on hypnosis. The necessary conditions for a regressive transference
did not obtain.

Perhaps the most visible aspects of a regressive transference
are placating security operations, e.g., submissiveness, diffidence,
flattery, that are symptomatic of approval seeking. Sheehan and
his associates have demonstrated that student subjects who are
highly susceptible to an hypnotic induction are more responsive to
the subtle cues pertinent to the expectations of the experimenter-
hypnotist than are student subjects who are insusceptible. Moreover, Sheehan and Dolby (1979) have likened this special involvement of highly suggestible subjects with the experimenter-hypnotist
to Freud's concept of transference. As we shall see in another
context, their dreams--in this case their nocturnal dreams--are
populated by parental surrogates.

The available evidence indicates that the probability of initiating a regressive transference is increased to the extent that the
conditions of early childhood or infancy can be reconstituted to
cue the reactivation (state dependent recall) of omniscient parents
whose approval and good will is the infant's major striving. This
reconstitution is most complete when an individual feels helpless
in relation to threats to life and a physician adopts a paternalistic manner wherein he speaks in the baby talk register, gives
instructions--which includes prescriptions and proscriptions--and
he ministers to the individual's most pressing needs. The stimulus
complex of infancy is more closely approximated to the treatment

and includes touch, manual manipulation of limbs, holding, or simply the laying on of hands. The probability of offsetting a regressive transference is minimized when the individual engages in self-help--plans to escape if a hostage--and engages in self-initiated speech. In evaluating treatment outcome, the closeness of the treatment situation to either extreme (regressive versus autonomy) must be assessed in conjunction with the shared expectancies of the participants, and how these are moderated by personality variables.

Our investigations into creativity, particularly when the aspiring individual is at impasse, further elucidate the foregoing psychodynamic processes. I also believe that I have learned how noncognitive processes (repressed strivings) can aid and abet problem solving via the good offices of spontaneous visual imagery.

CREATIVE PROBLEM SOLVING

Anecdotal Reports of Problem
  Solving Dreams

The autobiographical accounts of eminent persons in science, mathematics, literature, and the arts amply document that spontaneous and bizarre visual imagery can be a vehicle of inspirational insight and problem solving (Lindauer, 1977). Psychoanalysts, particularly Freud and Kris, also have implicated infantile or pregenital sexual strivings as the underlying motive in creativity. If this is true, spontaneous visual imagery should be especially revealing of this connection because of its intrinsic concreteness and its aptness as a modality of substitute drive gratification. Using emergent uncovering methods (Morishige and Reyher, 1975, Reyher, 1977a, 1978), it can be objectively demonstrated that spontaneous visual imagery, no matter how innocent the initial imagery, may indeed be an indirect depiction of anxiety-producing strivings. Kekule's insight into the molecular structure of benzene is an example of imagoically mediated insight that would appear to have sexual origins. Although he might be unwilling to submit to emergent uncovering techniques if he were alive, such a presumption has instructional and heuristic value and, thereby, serves a communicative function. As the story goes, after having laid aside his work, Kekule dozed in front of a fire and watched lines of dancing, hand-holding molecules turning about like serpents. They became snakes, and at that moment when one seized its own tail and whirled mockingly in front of him, he knew that the molecular structure of benzene was a closed ring. Based on informal inquiries, I have reason to believe that such dreams are not uncommon and certainly not peculiar to eminent people. In fact, some of my informants have been very reluctant (a security operation) to describe them in full because of their obvious sexual features or implications. One of these is particularly apt because it not only illustrates

the major components of the model, but it took 56 years for my
informant, a relative, to divulge its obvious sexual allusions.

It was an inauspicious moment when our informant, now an elderly
man, had to choose between consummating his marriage or traveling
alone to a distant hunting and fishing lodge to troubleshoot the
engine failure of a diesel-electric generator. It was the only
source of power of the lodge where he was to be employed as handyman.
He was unfamiliar with diesel engines and never had seen one dis-
assembled. Such was the plight of this 21-year old bridegroom in
1926. Torn between spending the night with his bride or pleasing
his new employer, he chose the latter. Despite his hopes of success, his labors proved fruitless and he lay down tired and discouraged. While falling asleep he had a vision of a large trans-
parent cylinder, which clearly showed the inside of a diesel engine
that he knew about but had never seen. His attention was drawn to
the nozzle which squirted kerosene into a hole, a hot spot heated
externally by a blow torch. As he watched, he noticed that spurts
of kerosene were not going into the hole. Suddenly he knew the
cause of the engine failure, and without further ado, he roused himself and dismantled the housing for the fuel injection nozzle and
hot spot. He properly aligned the nozzle, and the engine started
on his next attempt.

The analogy between the nozzle squirting kerosene into a hole
and penile ejaculation in a vagina is striking and strongly implies,
as our informant recognized, that imagery generated by sexual strivings served as a vehicle for problem solving. Because of the obvious sexual significance of his dream, it was not until our informant
reached the age of 78 that he could relate these "embarrassing"
details. Freud (1948a, 1948b, 1958) and Kris (1952) have speculated
as to mechanisms mediating the expression of sexual strivings and
creativity. For Freud, creativity involves a temporary regression
to childhood primary process thinking and a sublimation of repressed
sexual strivings consciously experienced as curiosity about how
things work. The plastic materials of the artist and imager are
easily shaped into vehicles of representation by primary process
which might prove to have artistic merit. Kris, however, adopted
Hartmann's (1939) constructs of neutralization (of sexual and
aggressive energy) and adaptive regression instead of Freud's drive
organized creativity taking the form of derivatives (substitutes
for the true objects of drives). He coined the term "regression in
the service of the ego," and postulated the existence of preconscious, cognitive processes. These perform the creative work, and
they are ultimately based on an unconscious fantasy of impregnation
by the paternal penis. These cognitive processes are potentiated
by neutralized sexual and aggressive energy released incidental to
a partial lifting of repression in the service of the ego. A
finished creative product, bereft of drives, may be presented
unannounced to awareness as in Poincare's discovery of the Fuchsian

functions or the ego might be bypassed and inspiration is presented
in the form of images of visions, as in Kekule's mocking, whirling
snake. It is this latter possibility that provides the connection
between problem solving and spontaneous visual imagery. Like Freud,
Kris considered the ultimate motive for creativity to be pregenital
sexual strivings, but he specifically inferred the dynamic of
impregnation by the paternal penis.

Laboratory Studies on Primary Process
Mediated Problem Solving on
Impersonal Tasks

Ruben Gur and myself (1976) explored the contribution of disguised drive representation (primary process thinking[3]) and visual
imagery in creative problem solving in the laboratory. Student subjects were asked to visualize the tasks that were given to them
and to describe whatever visual images spontaneously came into their
mind's eye. We found that only hypnotized subjects benefitted, and
that this gain was restricted to figural tasks. The nonhypnotized
subjects not only failed to benefit on the figural tasks, but they
did very poorly in the verbal tasks. Consistent with the instrumental role of sex, the hypnotized subjects also showed higher disguised drive (sex and aggression) representation which is an index
of primary process thinking. We considered our findings to be consistent with the construct of regression in the service of the ego.

Wiseman and myself (1973) also reported findings favorable to
Kris's position. In a brilliantly conceived investigation, Wiseman
(1962) used the Rorschach inkblots as stimuli for dreams under hypnosis with the expectation that the inkblots and the dreams they
gave rise to would subsequently show the earmarks of the dreamwork,
specifically primary process thinking. Indeed, a standard

---

[3]In previous communications (Reyher, 1977a, 1977b, 1978), I
have reinterpreted displacement and condensation, the principal components of primary process thinking, in terms of principles of
organization intrinsic to the nervous system. Analogic functions
(displacement) selectively reactivate percepts while synthetic functions (Gestalt principles) thematically and temporally organize
these percepts into drive gratifying fantasies. The reactivation
of percepts in accord with the aims and objects of drive-related
strivings, even when they are subject to repression, accounts for
reveries, daydreams and dreams. Syntax is the meaning provded by
agent-action--effect via some instrumental object. It is temporally
organized and constitutes a cause and effect commerce with the environment in the gratification of drives, including approval, which
grammarians refer to as subject, verb, object. Both spontaneous
visual imagery and language follow this same Indo-European format
(Reyher, 1969).

administration of the Rorschach one week later was associated with
an increase in primary process thinking (high drive representation
and logical deviations in percept formation). Germane to our
present concerns were a variety of changes on Rorschach dimensions
that are considered to be associated with creativity.[4] This significant investigation survived replication and incorporated both
waking and simulating subjects.

Hypnosis clearly added something in both the foregoing investigations. They suggest that hypnosis involves an attenuation of
self-critical functions and a corresponding increase in tolerance
for drive-related mentation. The attenuation of self-critical cognitive functions, however, does not include a reduction in an
appreciation for the logical relationships in which the problem is
embedded; otherwise, problem solving would not take place. Irre-
spective of the role of hypnosis, both creative problem solving and
visual imagery have taken on new interest in the light of recent
claims that the right cerebral hemisphere is the origin of each.
However, contrary to prevailing opinion, recent research shows that
analytical problem solving use of visual imagery appears to be a
left, not a right, cerebral hemisphere function. Bakan (1979) has
resolved this apparent anomaly by invoking a raw (drive-laden) and
cooked distinction between right and left hemisphere visual imagery.

Laboratory Studies on Primary Process
Mediated Career and Personal Problems

While pondering the results that Ruben Gur and I reported, I
realized that Wiseman's ingenious method for testing Freud's theory
of dreams might well increase the involvement of the dream work in
problem solving. If primary process thinking plays a key role in
mediating insights and inspiration, then the dream work potentially
could be harnessed to problem solving. Why not use the elements
of an unresolved problem-at-hand in one's career (type of work) to
serve as the day residue, instead of inkblots, to form a reservoir

---

[4]A variety of significant changes in Rorschach categories supported Kris's construct of regression in the service of the ego.
An increase in creativity, as indexed by an increase in human movement (M), an increase in drive, as indexed by animal movement (Fm),
at the price of increased anxiety, as indexed by inanimate movement
(m), but not at the expense of adaptation or, in more operational
terms, there was no decrease in reality contact, as indexed by form
(F) and good form quality (F+). As expected in terms of the dream
work paradigm, there was an increase in fresh perspectives, as
indexed by the reversal of figure and ground (S), and an increase
in synthetic functions, as indexed by use of the total inkblot (W),
to form percepts. Pine and Holt (1960) also have presented support-
ing evidence for Kris's position.

of material for the fabrication of manifest content. Hopefully,
novel transformations of the elements of the problem-at-hand wrought
by the dream work would cast the problem in new and productive perspectives. Robert Dave and I worked out the experimental design
which included a dream induction group, a rational-cognitive problem solving group and a group of individuals on a waiting list.
The subjects responded to advertisements for individuals who were
at an impasse on some problem and who wished to participate in
research on creative problem solving via hypnosis. Hypnosis only
was used in the dream induction group. A means of induction was
used that provided no challenges and otherwise minimized the possibility of the subject failing or inferring failure. In my clinical
practice I have found that an induction patter synchronized with an
interesting piece of music often was successful when other means of
induction were not. Side 1 of Tubular Bells suited this purpose
well because of its unusual sounds and rhythms. The underlying
logic is that both music, particularly rhythm, and hypnosis are
right cerebral hemisphere functions.

The kinds of problems-at-hand brought to us by the respondents
were widely distributed and included personal as well as career
problems. Prior to the suggestion for them to dream, or to have
dreamlike thoughts about the problem-at-hand, they were asked to
visualize the elements of the problem and to report whatever imagery
came into their mind's eye. This was repeated three times (trials).
One week after the administration of either treatment, there was
an interview for the control subjects; the experimenter who conducted a particular treatment telephoned the subjects to assess whether
they had become unstuck. Davé, a graduate student in the clinical
program, ran the dream condition and an undergraduate ran the
rational-cognitive treatment. Davé also conducted the interviews
for control subjects. The results (Davé, 1979) strongly favored
the dream induction group which included both personal and task-
related problems.

The hypothesis under investigation specified that novel transformations of the elements of the problem-at-hand mediated by primary process would be instrumental in problem solving. However,
obvious imagery mediated solutions did not occur. None of the
subjects could relate specific imagery to the problem-at-hand in
the laboratory. One subject attested to such mediation at call
back, but the others who claimed success could not specify how
their imagery led to problem resolution. This led me to consider
the possibility that the favorable treatment outcome merely was due
to nonspecific effects (shared expectancies or suggestion or the
combination of them both). In this case, the power of shared expectancies is magnified by their status as suggestions to be carried
out and by the special relationship (transference) that obtains
between hypnotist and subject. Such individuals have strong needs
for approval and are more apt to be placating, submissive, and

anxious about the possibility of rejection. Moreover, our subjects
were not the typical student subjects, but people (both students
and community persons) who.were distraught by failure to resolve a
vital career or personal problem. They were coming to us for help.
Even their dreams were more like those of clients in the beginning
phase of emergent uncovering psychotherapy than they were like
student subjects (Reyher, 1977b, 1978). Consequently, our subjects
are better conceptualized as clients rather than run of the mill
student subjects, and the experimenters are better conceptualized
as experimenter-therapists rather than as just experimenters.
These observations prompted Maria Della Corte and myself to compare
the imagery and dream phases of the research with respect to both
degree of drive activation and deviations of logic, and as expected,
the dreams were higher on each of them (U=34, df=2; p < .002).
Drive activation was assessed using a modified version of our Drive
Activation Scale (Burns and Reyher, 1976) and deviations in logic
was assessed by the Analogic-Synthetic Scale. Interrater reliability on the two scales was .85 and .75, respectively.

Creative Strivings at Impasse

These subjects were indeed exceptional. To objectify my
impressions further, Maria Della Corte compared these dream protocols with those collected by Wiseman (1962) and she found that they
were significantly higher in implausibility, bizarreness and drive
activation. They also were distinguished by more references to
powerful or fantastic adult figures, babies, and references to the
sun and sunlight and an abundance of phallic symbols. She also
found a very significant under-representation of aggression and a
disproportionate number of symptomatic reactions. There is no
doubt that these subjects were very different from the typical
sample of student subjects. One subject in particular illustrates
the clarity in which displacement and condensation are seen to
create a fantasy out of the underlying repressed aims and objects
of an apparent Oedipus complex.

Subject 1, Trial 2. This female undergraduate had been unable
to develop an image to embody the essence of a poem she was writing.
The treatment was "successful."

Imagery: I, it recalled to mind a painting I had done of this
silver structure that I've been sort of like stringing together
with my hands. And beside it there's the virgin and she has . . .
I don't want to get into the painting, she . . . she has constructed
this structure, the virgin has. And it's piled one on top of the
other, but it's very very haphazard and it's no good image, no good
image (S's eyes pop open and El asks her to close them. S does so
with a short laugh).

Dream: There, there is a girl which is myself with braceleted

arms laying on a marble floor. It's very cold and white. And she's
in draperies. Silk, Persian. And these gentlemen enter. She knows
not who they are. She knows not who they are (almost sung).
(Laugh) They're neither armed nor decorated in any recognizable
sense. And these men conduct her to a boat which is wooden and has
a very plain prow and no figurehead. No sails, but a mast. And
she's taken, or she rises and then finds herself in a throne room
facing the father god of resurrection who pushes the sun down
through her shoulders. And it expands within her and is released,
if you'll excuse me, in urine. Now I realize the disparity of an
image like that. That's all.

In the imagery phase, there was resistance (opening of eyes),
anxiety (laughter) and the rejection of the concept virgin (interference in integration of percept and concept) and what might be
phallic images. In the dream phase the anxiety-producing aims and
objects of the sexual drive are sufficiently blatant to suggest
that father is the object and that impregnation by rape is the aim.
The sailboat is a percept that includes multiple features (mast,
prow and figurehead) suitable for the indirect depiction of a penis
as is the sun (it rises, is hot and is the source of all power and
energy). Even without having had the opportunity to apply emergent
uncovering techniques long enough to achieve objectification, the
dynamic is precisely that which Kris specified. Several other
protocols also suggested the same dynamic. I was stunned by this
turn of events because I had considered this to be too restrictive.

The following protocols further illustrate the implausibility
and bizarreness of the reported imagery as well as the ubiquitous
presence of features lending themselves to the indirect depiction
(phallic symbols) of the repressed aims and objects of drives.
Most importantly, these are more. blatant in the dream phase than
the imagery phase and document the greater uncovering properties
of the former, a key technique in emergent uncovering psychotherapy.

Subject 34, Trial 3. The female freelance poet with three
prior publications was experiencing a creative block. The treatment
was unsuccessful.

Imagery: I see a very straight middle-class lady's face. And
I smelled dust, stuffiness. Like a meeting. It has to do with
people. It's not, it's an unpleasant smell but it isn't meant to
be. It's a very ordinary smell. Like this middle-class lady, she's
very comfortable with that smell.

Dream: I was looking at this, at earth and I could see underneath. And there was this clump of carrots growing. And they were
growing one at a time. And they were kind of, they were synchro-
nizing. And they were making room for each other as they were
growing. And they were nudging and pushing against each other and

they were brilliant orange. And they had a big bright green top,
green tops. And as they pushed into the ground they would move and
they sort of clasped like . . . like hands. And then all of a sudden there was a large tree. Well, it was a drawing of a tree. But
all the leaves were in the shape of a huge ball and the very oak
tree with very thick branches and very big. And all of a sudden
there was this big oak tree there. The sky is very black and again
it's a very flat horizon. Very flat terrain. That's it.

Subject 17, Trial 2. This undergraduate had been unsuccessful
in developing a symbol for the concept of self. She claimed that
the treatment was a "success."

Imagery: It was the shield again. This time there were no
swords, and the shield was more like a pear-point. The top of it
tapered up, so like at the top there were three points. (According
to Freud, the concept "three" represents male genitals.) One high
point in the center and two lower points. And there was a circle
inside with the lightning. And then the image of the shield seemed
to reverberate out like there was one image inside of another image
inside of another image. And they got progressively longer and
smaller until the one with the earth in it . . . and the earth was
with the lightning. Two parallel pieces of lightning. And the
earth was divided. It was split in two.

Dream: There was a reverberation of the earth. One inside of
another so that it looks like waves of the earth. Images. And
that turns into a picture of Stonehedge (sic) in England. And
you're seeing it from the side. And then Stonehedge seems to turn
on its side so it's a circle on something like a square piece of
ground. Then there's the one who's all dressed up in royal robes
and I thought for a moment that he was the pope. But I wasn't sure.
He was just some royal person. And he knighted someone. And then
there was a symbol of the peace symbol except for the prongs were
made out of a, like a three-pronged pitchfork. There was a circle
around it. Part of the pitchfork end was out of the circle. And
then it disappeared.

There were other dreams that were apparently nonsexual but
regressive. The one below documents the severity of some of the
problems encountered centering around self-esteem and the desir-
ability of having a psychotherapist involved in data collection or
on call.

Subject 9, Trial 1. This female was experiencing a "mental
block" on a problem in environmental design. The treatment was
"successful."

Imagery: The little girl who wanted and needed those things
and always wanted something to do was always told to go play by

yourself and you really don't need those things. Is that valid?
She feels angry but she won't complete anything she starts 'cause
she wants to punish them by not giving her what she wanted.

Dream: It first starts out, um, with a series of different
shapes, very large shapes composed of different kinds of materials.
And a little infant is crawling through the semi-circles and triangles and very strange types of shapes and is happily playing
through them except there seems to be that it's leading nowhere.
There's no end, there's no beginning, there's just the constant
crawling through shapes. Ten shapes then leave the ground and
they're floating up in the clouds. And most of them seem to be circles now. There's no beginning, there's no end. They just go round
and round. And there is not only an infant but a form that is
crawling through the shapes in a very consistent kind of way, like
forming a chain. And it becomes more and more involved and more
tangled up in the circles and at a point. It's like it's trapped
because it's all wound up in these circles that it's been entwining
through. And it's up above the clouds and it's very peaceful up
there, very quiet. And there's sunshine and white clouds below and
it's a very light feeling. But it's trapped in the circles and
it's struggling to get out.

Subject 9, Trial 2

Imagery: It's a question of simplicity versus complexity.
Simplicity holds no value, it gains no recognition. Simplicity is
a waste of my time. The more elements that are involved the better.
Take on the impossible. There's always those words of "you can do
it." And then sometimes I don't want to. I feel that I must. And
I feel very heavy. Very very heavy.

Dream: I am a musical note. I'm an eighth note. Nothing
special, just an eighth note. The eighth note is trying to sit
high, love. It's sitting on a page of music. But it cannot sit
long enough. It continues to move around. The player tries to
play the eighth note but it's very impossible. The eighth note is
so heavy it falls off the page. The eighth note then stumbles on
the stage and is feeling safe. It is dancing and enjoying itself.
It becomes animated. It spreads legs and arms. And it's pretty
spontaneous and it's dancing. It tried to fly through the air but
all of a sudden it becomes much too heavy. And it falls. It
crushes into the wall. The eighth note then tries other things.
They're not well defined. But it's no longer in its own environment. Seems to be very diminutive now, but very heavy. And, uh,
it seems to have a lack of spontaneity. Rather that of mechanical
precision because it was trained to be a note. That's all.

Trial 3

Imagery: It's far more fun to conceive the problem than it is
to execute it. There's a fear of execution. But one must not be
as capable of perfecting it as the concept. It's a fear of the
actual doing. Not being capable of doing it. Also things move far
too slowly. It's painful, it's very painful to sit with a project.
There's so little gained by completing it. It moves far too slowly.
One becomes involved with the microcosm of one square inch and painstaking hours are spent with the one square inch that really has no
long range humanitarian benefit. It's so irrelevant, insignificant,
and difficult.

Dream: There are many duplicate images of me, but one of which
is hanging from a noose from a very tall ceiling. And I'm just
about ready to die from hanging myself. But all these duplicate
images of me are standing on top of one another on their shoulders
all the way to reach me at the top to try to hold me up so that I
don't choke. And there must be eight or ten of them standing on
top of one another. And the load is very heavy and it's very pre-
carious and the whole load of bodies is swinging back and forth
slightly almost ready to fall over. But they have to hold up the
top of me which is just about to hang and I am ready to die.

Regressive Transference Revisited

Fortunately, such disquieting dreams in response to uncovering
techniques are rare when the relationship is not defined as psychotherapy (Maria Della Corte, 1979). However, our subjects were at
an impasse concerning a vital problem for which they were coming
for help. For them it was tantamount to initiating psychotherapy.
In fact, the circumstances delimiting the dream group are congruent
with the necessary conditions (Reyher, 1977a) for the development
of a regressive transference, namely, an individual made anxious by
a medical, spiritual, or personal condition that he cannot treat
himself turns to others who claim to possess the requisite skills.
The pressure to become dependent was intensified by the administration of a hypnotic induction, which apparently reactivated childhood recollections of omniscient parents, i.e., images depicting
parents, powerful figures, and/or children and helpless animals.
In addition, a sense of trust was evidenced in the atypical direct-
ness in the depiction of repressed strivings. Their protocols were
more like those of clients undergoing emergent uncovering psychotherapy than run-of-the-mill volunteer undergraduates. Accordingly,
they might have been so highly motivated to earn the approval of
the experimenter-hypnotist that they lowered their criteria for
accepting a resolution of their impasse. It seemed likely that
their proffered explanations for impasse resolution were less
stringent when compared to their usual criteria for assessing the
adequacy of their own work. Crowne and Marlowe (1964) also have

concluded on the basis of laboratory findings that persons strongly
motivated to seek approval tend to be compliant, conforming, and
anxious about rejection and threats to self-esteem. This potential
source of artifact in the alleged resolution of impasse is compounded further by the possibility of uncontrolled experimenter
bias and personality differences between experimenters.

These considerations led to another investigation which replicated the procedures of the dream induction group and which enabled
me to assess the foregoing potential confounding nonspecific effects.
Two undergraduate experimenters (Trudy Simon and Mike Marin), who
were blind to the purpose of the investigation, were trained by
myself in the procedures. These included the suggestibility scale
used by Reyher et al. (1979) and a five point Lickert type scale
for rating their anxiety at different points in the procedure. The
experimenters also rated the subjects on their strivings to please
them (transference) by noting appeasing, flattering remarks (security operations). The specific threats to self-esteem in this situation was failure to form images and/or dreams and to experience
the suggestions.

Fifty-three respondents were run through the procedure of
which 50 percent reported some degree of improvement at call back.
A particular effort was made to have them describe the imagery
which mediated their improvement. Our efforts met with absolutely
no success. This, of course, is in line with a wide variety of
investigations wherein subjects could not specify the antecedents
to their behavior (Nisbett and Wilson, 1977), but who doubtlessly
engaged in security operations to avoid looking foolish (dystonia),
most notably, rationalization, guessing and not trying. The
choice of security operation is a function of the individual's prevailing level of dystonia, the self-conceptions he is trying to
ratify (e.g., "I'm smart"), and those he is trying to controvert
(e.g., "I'm dumb"), and whether his modus operandi is risk-taking
or nonrisk-taking (Gavrilides, 1980).

After the debriefing of the subjects, I debriefed the two
experimenters on their understanding of the objectives of the study.
They both were absolutely convinced that I had expected the treatment to be effective. About six weeks later, another experimenter,
who was indifferent to the outcome of the investigation, called
back those subjects who earlier had claimed some degree of improvement to learn more about the intervening cognitive processing of
their laboratory experience. Her most salient impression was that
many of them strove to give the impression that the research was
effective (a security operation) even though they might also have
clearly indicated that they really had not improved. Yet another
ad hoc experimenter tried to predict their rating of improvement
on the basis of these telephone transcripts with little success
(r=.46).

The crucial comparisons were between those subjects who claimed some degree of improvement and those who did not. The dependent variables were suggestibility, transference, and anxiety. All three were significant (two-tailed t-tests) with suggestibility showing a whopping mean difference. The improved group passed an average of 7.38 items whereas the non-improved group passed an average of only 4.69. There were ten items. The total group mean was 6.04, which is significantly higher than the mean (4.19) following a formal hypnotic induction procedure (Reyher et al., 1979). Thus, not only was the group as a whole more suggestible than typical student volunteers, but the mean suggestibility score for the improved group was particularly high. Since they also had high scores on the transference and anxiety scales, I concluded that both their suggestibility scores and their improvement scores were inflated by compliant behaviors (security operations) to carry our approval.

Anne Stern (1975) also reported unusually high suggestibility for females who responded to advertisements asking for volunteers in research involving the enhancement of female sexual responsiveness via hypnosis. Aside from the success of her treatment, of paramount concern to me in the present context is the implication that we possessed a method that could cure or ameliorate a vital personal problem. Under these conditions, they were apt to experience a regressive transference and, therefore, an intensification of their strivings for approval. Individuals so characterized are anxious to please the experimenter-hypnotist by meeting his expectations. By carrying out suggestions and by responding favorably to the treatment, they avoid dystonia and gain approval.

Thus, our favorable treatment outcome can be best explained in terms of nonspecific effects, namely, personality variables of the subjects disposing them to adopt a passive-receptive attitude under circumstances wherein both participants shared expectations of success. The enthusiastic participation of the experimenter-hypnotist in the treatment procedures also has been identified as a nonspecific effect (Morris and Shapiro, 1978). It took me a long time to arrive at this conclusion because of my investment in demonstrating the validity of my paradigm for enlisting the dream work in the service of problem solving in the laboratory.

Creativity in Relation to Insufficiency of Repression

I think it unlikely that primary process thinking can be used to resolve the very conflicts that generate it. Moreover, there is evidence that the dream procedure may be counterproductive for persons at impasse. This is consistent with Freud's conception of the unsuccessful artist as one who is unable to sublimate infantile sexual strivings. Unlike highly successful individuals, their interests are relatively direct outlets for repressed strivings.

In terms of Kris, their interests do not exist in a conflict-free
ego sphere. Theoretically, it is possible that an aversive or
phobic reaction might develop in an attempt to resolve an impasse.
Subject 9 is an example of this possibility. Fortunately, an aversive reaction did not permeate her creative endeavors, perhaps
because the elements or her subject matter, environmental design,
did not provide apt vehicles for her dreams. Subject 23 (below),
however, showed a progressive eruption of blatant derivatives in
his dreams, which extensively utilized the elements of the problem-
at-hand as vehicles (manifest content). The treatment was unsuccessful.

Subject 23, Trial 2. This male graduate student in physiology
was trying to devise a means of measuring the quantity of blood
flow in a cerebral artery.

Imagery: It's a, not really the anatomy that I described
earlier but evidently a symbolic resemblance and, well at least a
resemblance. And it is a vision of the western hemisphere of the
earth. Evidently the a, North American continent symbolizing the
hypothalamus which they both somewhat resemble the shapes somewhat, part of the area of Central America being the capillary system I just described leading down to the pituitary which I guess
is, which resembles what I see as South America which again is a
very shocking resemblance. I don't see at all the biological
picture.

Dream: It began as I pictured the northern portion of South
America. And again elements which were not distinct, but certainly
not the dashed, fast lines of the prior dream. Elements were moving in a northerly direction or, more correctly around the Gulf up
into the Central America area presumably, then dispersing into the
United States, the United States area at least. It was a slow
motion and I guess the idea or the impression was that these moving
objects are persons. Then I perceived a very nondescriptive,
somewhat of a, possibly a black X or a flare of some sort approximately in the Louisiana-Mississippi southern area. Just a, just a
kind of a rash over this area that I suppose somewhat distorted
the picture.

Trial 3

Imagery: It's a, not a silhouette, but just a three dimensional or superficial image of this hypothalamic-pituitary axis
that I described with a structure between them containing capillaries. I, once in a while I note the redness of the capillaries.
They appear as much thicker vessels than I know they must be.
Every once in a while, just a flash of cutaways of those tissues,
as if a slice has been taken out of it, as in a pie so like I'm
seeing the whole structure for the most part. There's a triangular

slice taken out where I can look in and see the cytology of the hypothalamus and the pituitary.

Dream: Well, obviously my choice of words seem to suggest to me in describing the slice-outs as pieces of pie, I envisioned black-birds coming to peck at the, these tissues . . . whatever blackbirds have to do with pie. Anyway, they were unable to diminish it all it seems, until I realized in fact that they hadn't diminished it. And then it seemed as though it somewhat disintegrated from the pituitary upward, leaving a shambled hypothalamus remnant. But then just this picture remained for a while until I then saw a sunset, a quite beautiful sunset which blocked out the picture of the tissue. And after the sun had set I then saw a view from above some clouds, looking down upon these clouds as if in an airplane climbing over the clouds. A quite attractive sight. Then things got dark as the night. I pictured briefly the other visions that I previously described from other dreams. And that was it.

The first hint of the emergence into awareness of an aggressive striving occurred in the imagery phase of trial 3 when he described the cutaways, pie-like, of the tissues. Once again in the dream he sees the "slice-outs" and is taken aback by the blackbirds that came to peck at them. Note the neutralization or sublimation of the aggressive strivings by the superimposition of the beautiful and tranquil sunset.

Clinical Documentation of an
Artist as Impasse

The foregoing protocols only can leave unanswered questions because they were not generated by clients. Accordingly, I will synopsize the sessions of emergent uncovering psychotherapy of an aspiring young artist leading up to a disruption of her work on a project.

The client, a 22-year old female art major, was foundering in her course work; however, this did not constitute the basis of her desire for psychotherapy. Neither was her lesbianism and her rejection of middle-class mores, including the shaving of her legs and the use of cosmetics. She complained of being anxious about sexual encounters and her inability to orgasm. Only later, because of intense feelings of shame, did she reveal her greatest concern: putting her fingers down her throat to induce vomiting following the ingestion of fattening foods. Although a beautiful young woman with a stunning figure, she disliked her body and was discontent with the major facets of her life, including her failure to complete college, her inability to find the most congenial mode of artistic expression, and the fragility of her interpersonal relationships. She tended to gush, laugh anxiously, use hyperbole, and demean herself. She claimed being very close with her father, distant from her beautiful mother, and envious of her younger brother's "great looks, terrific body and athletic ability." A Freudian would classify her as a hysteric.

The introduction of emergent uncovering produced the usual, objective resistances and self-effacing security operations (Reyher, 1978). After about seven months into psychotherapy, she announced that she had begun a weaving that was absorbing her interest and producing waves of excitement. She described a wall hanging made from lengths of thin ropes enclosed by black material to form long, flexible cylinders. She intertwined these to form a wreath with an opening about a foot in diameter. She intended to insert into this opening a bunch of ropes, wrapped in flesh toned gimp, of varying lengths. She twisted outwards the end of the cylinder with the largest opening so that it faced the observer. She thought her creation was ugly and did not want anyone to see it, but she kept one of the smaller cylinders on her person because she liked to hold it and play with it. Highlights from succeeding sessions in emergent uncovering psychotherapy document the origins of her creation in insufficiently repressed strivings.

She described a dream, while exhibiting great resistance and manifesting symptoms, wherein her mother sat on her bed and made a sexual advance. She found the dream repugnant. During the course of subsequent free imagery, using the dream as a stimulus, she saw the profile view of a horse's head with prominent ears and pointed snout. Then the ears and snout became more pointed. Its head turned towards her and opened its mouth, frightening her. Then she saw a female warrior carrying a pointed spear and wearing a crown with multiple points. Next, she saw a bat with wings spread and wearing a tasseled stocking hat, standing erect. She interjected that the bat's spread wings made her feel anxious and vulnerable. She opened her eyes. Upon closing her eyes she saw a crooked finger (her mother has a crooked finger) placed over the tip of an arrow. Then the arrow turned into a baby bottle. Following this there was a series of images showing, from the waist up, ample breasted, beautiful women. She saw herself sucking a nipple of one of them. Then she saw her mother dressed in a nun's habit choking a young boy who was lying nude on the bed. She felt herself being choked and became very disturbed. The boy was making thrusting pelvic movements, which she felt. With great distaste she recognized her identification with the boy.

At the beginning of the next session a rabbit hopped by the sliding glass door to my office and we both watched it for a short time. I asked her to revisualize the horse's head from the last session. Instead, she saw the rabbit with a scissors about to cut off its ears. Then the scissors changed into her mother's fingers which then changed into a mouth. Later there were women in shiny dresses (wrappings) and one snake swallowing another, which bore a

resemblance to the gimp-wrapped cylinders. She also had the feeling of her head going down between her legs and biting something.
At the end of this session I asked about the weaving, and she said,
"I love it, and I hate it, but I must do it." In the next session
she said that she had experienced a connection between her mouth
and her vagina. When she forced herself to vomit, she observed
that she used her fingers in the same way as when she masturbated.
With some reluctance, she mentioned that she found the induced
vomiting to be pleasureful. She saw two fingers move into the back
of a throat and, scissors-like, pull down on the uvula. Then she
saw two fingers move to the side of her neck and massage it. Her
neck elongated and turned into a penis. Later she reported having
had the sensation of biting on a penis and having blood in her
mouth. She then saw her father's penis bitten off.

In the next session she described a feeling of growing larger
and smaller, which she has known all her life, particularly after
having gone to bed. She saw a cherub blowing a trumpet and it
turned towards her and the bell (flaring mouth) of the trumpet was
prominent. (Note the analogy between the bell, the horse's open
mouth, and the open end of the outward-facing cylinder.) Later,
she felt as though she were reaching under her bed, in her parent's
house, where she had always thought a crocodile lurked. Now, however, the thought of it was not frightening. It felt coarse and
bumpy. Then it turned over and she stroked its belly. "He" liked
it and she, with some embarrassment, said that she was turning him
on. When she moved her hand towards its genitals, it violently
righted itself and moved away. As it moved away her hand traveled
down its tail and grabbed the tip and held it. It felt like a
penis. Then it turned into a snake (a cobra) and it opened its
mouth wide. It had her father's teeth and there was a pointed thing
coming half-way out of its mouth. Images of the cherub, the
trumpet and the crocodile returned. Then she saw herself as a baby
boy which she later saw "immersed" in the belly of the crocodile.
When asked to revisualize a previous scene of her father nude, she
saw him wearing only shorts; the fly was open and it was dark and
forbidding. She then saw her hand reach into the fly and unscrew
his penis. Her hand then screwed it onto her vagina, but it shrank
until it became very small, tiny. When her father grew a new penis,
she became depressed and, with great difficulty, she said that her
clitoris was like a tiny penis.

In our most recent session, she would not lie back on the
couch because she felt too vulnerable. It turned out that she was
wearing a tight revealing top and thought that I would look at her
breasts. She finally leaned back and, feeling deeply ashamed, told
me that she frequently had been inducing vomiting with her fingers,
following eating bouts. Again, with great resistance, she revealed
that the sensations of vomiting were like orgasms; in fact, at times
they were so intense that she almost fainted. Amidst great distress

and requests for reassurance, she described a dream in which she was at a psychotherapy meeting wherein I was demonstrating a technique by massaging her neck and shoulders. This reminded her of a dream that she had when she was 16, but she could only tell me a few fragments because of insuperable conscious resistance stemming from embarrassment. Her father was in it, as well as others, and it involved her rape on a large bed.

Sometime in the course of these sessions she had stopped work on her project. She said that if she hung it on the wall it would scare her. In fact, it acquired such phobic quality that she put it out of sight, in a drawer. I am now asking myself some pointed questions. Would she have finished her project if emergent uncovering psychotherapy had been suspended during the course of her creative work? Will she ever resume it? At the end of psychotherapy will nonpathological strivings serve equally well as a source of inspiration? Is creativity optimized by a particular range in the blatancy of derivatives?

Optimizing Imagery Mediated
Problem Solving

In terms of the dream work paradigm, what are the optimal conditions for spontaneous imagery to mediate inspiration or insight?

1. A period of intense, fruitless mental effort must be followed by a cessation of analytical thinking to permit elements of the problem-at-hand to be used as derivatives of anxiety-producing, drive-related strivings.

2. The cessation of analytical thinking must not be accompanied by a disregard for logical relations. The imager must recognize the relevance of the imagery, even if bizarre, to the problem-at-hand, i.e., reverie, doze, light sleep.

3. The aims and objects of an active striving should be sufficiently repugnant and anxiety-producing to cause a shift in direct to indirect (derivatives) reactivation of percepts and their synthesis into a fantasy or dream having implausible or bizarre aspects (condensation).

4. The imager's self-protective system must not permit too direct representation of repressed, drive-related strivings otherwise, the impasse might become permanent or, in the case of artists, poets, musicians, and writers, they may develop aversive reactions to their own products though these are valued by others.

5. The better suited the elements of the problem-at-hand to serve as vehicles (indirect depictions) of repugnant drive-related strivings, the more likely the resulting fantasies or dreams will

be relevant to a solution of the problem-at-hand.

6. The imager must possess the requisite knowledge and skills (left cerebral hemisphere functions) in order for his imagery to become the instigator of inspiration and insight.

7. Once the imager fully appreciates the significance of his inspiration or insight, his approval-seeking from mentors and colleagues must not override what he must do to bring his nascent insights to fruition. If it should be inconsistent with the fashions and conventions of the time, he must be able to take the inevitable interpersonal risks in order to allow himself to become absorbed in the task of transforming it into a contribution. This means some degree of alienation from family and friends may have to be suffered by everyone.

In our investigations of people at impasse, conditions 1, and perhaps 6, were satisfied, but conditions 2, 3, 4, 5 and 7 were not assessed. In fact, our solicitations for persons at an impasse in problem solving might just possibly have violated condition 4 because many of their hypnotically induced dreams resembled the spontaneous imagery and nocturnal dreams of clients undergoing emergent uncovering psychotherapy. This certainly was the case for my client at impasse. Our solicitations screened out those persons who generally are successful in their craft. More than likely they have sufficient confidence in their methods to work through or wait out an impasse without being thrown into dystonia. For them, naturally occurring periods of spontaneous imagery may provide hints and fresh perspectives which eventually lead to solutions. When they do achieve sudden inspiration or insight via imagery, it is noteworthy, and some of them ought to find their way into the anecdotal literature because of their intrinsic interest.

Imagery consistent with the dynamic of impregnation by the paternal penis in the hypnotically induced dreams of several subjects and in the nocturnal dream of the illustrative client, caught me by surprise, as I had always rejected this possibility out of hand. Although I am not ready to consider its presence as a precondition for creativity, I certainly am sensitized to its presence in the imagery of aspiring artists at impasse.

A recent investigation by Domino (1976) also shows that creativity is associated with primary process thinking. The nocturnal dreams of students who were assessed as high in creativity were characterized by more primary process than were the dreams of their less creative peers. This finding suggests that they also have more primary process available to them while awake and when they suspend analytical, problem-solving activity, or even during it. In any event, his data are consistent with the formulations of both Freud and Kris, as well as other contemporary investigators of creativity (P. Bowers, 1979), who discuss creative persons in the same or similar terms, e.g., divergent thinking and unconventional behavior. Bowers explored the effect of effortless thinking on creativity and she found that measures of creativity and effortless thinking were correlated for students but not for creative writers. Although her instructions did not encourage imagery specifically, they ought to have been ample. Consonant with the impairment of our subjects on verbal tasks (Gur and Reyher, 1976), in contrast to figurative tasks, the creative quality of Bower's writer-subjects suffered somewhat. The concreteness of visual imagery precludes abstract thinking which is mediated by conceptual-verbal vehicles of representation (Reyher, 1977a, 1978).

EPILOGUE

It is clear that powerful nonspecific effects can overwhelm whatever specific treatment effects may exist. The shared expectations of both participants operating through elevated suggestibility, induced by the treatment procedures, may account for more improvement than other factors. If all the treatment procedures in outcome research are equally credible, then all should show the same improvement. This seems to be the case. The initiation of a regressive transference should even be more powerful, but it is contingent on a more restricted set of circumstances wherein the client feels helpless and the practitioner takes charge. A variety of investigations, particularly those of Sheehan and his associates in combination with my clinical observations, strongly suggest that high and low suggestibility is moderated by disparate constellations of personality variables. Of those persons who score high on a suggestibility scale, there is a large subset of persons most aptly characterized as approval-seeking, submissive and non risk-taking, whereas a large subset of low suggestible persons can be most aptly characterized as autonomous, competitive and risk-taking. If these two subsets of people are as populous as I suspect, comprising at least 50 percent of the population, then both clinical and laboratory research designs may be seriously confounded because they most probably are not evenly distributed across groups or conditions.[5] An investigation by Gavrilides (1980) reinforces this possibility.

---

[5]An example of such confounding is an investigation by Nash, Johnson and Tipton (1979) concerning transitional objects in relation to age regression. Since the real and simulating subjects differed on the dependent variables, was this the result of the age regression in the real subjects or was it a function of group differences in capacity for regressive transference and/or a reflection of the disparity in strivings to please the experimenter?

He assigned adult males in the working community to high and low
risk categories. Risk was defined as the opportunity to be observed
as being insufficient or unsuccessful in one's vocation and avoca-
tion. When these persons were subjected to a stressful interview,
the risk-takers, as predicted, were significantly higher in personal power functions (viz, attractiveness, attire, carriage, savoir
faire, etc.), and showed greater happiness. They also manifested
less anxiety and fewer placating security operations. Personal
power was positively related to happiness (r=.51, df=38, p < .001)
and negatively related to anxiety (r=.46, df=38, p < .003).

Since the term creativity has little consensual validation, I
believe that there may be some merit in differentiating between
innovation and creativity with the former referring to new applications and extensions of current fashions or conventions of thought
and the latter referring to the employment of new conceptions that
prompts others in the same endeavor to relinquish their established
way of conceptualizing their subject manner. Einstein and Freud
were creative; Edison was innovative. It also is important to
recognize that the whole brain is involved in problem solving, not
just one hemisphere, and that the unconventionality often noted in
the behavior of creative persons illustrates that approval seeking
is minimal and autonomy is high.

Visual imagery continues to show great promise as a treatment
modality because it maximizes nonspecific effects generated by both
participants. It already has shown its versatility by serving a
vital role in a variety of treatment paradigms. These virtues arise
from the "fact" that images are reactivated percepts that are
related to the aims and objects of whatever strivings are active
at the moment, especially those of childhood which often are subject to repression. Although emergent uncovering psychotherapy is
able to generate distressing drive-laden imagery of progressively
increasing blatancy for many clients, therapists untrained in
psychoanalytic concepts and methods are likely to be intimidated by
the severity of symptoms, the blatancy of drive expression, the
intensity of transference and their own emotional reactions. A
less stressful procedure might be to utilize emergent uncovering
methods only until the origin of strivings in repressed conflicts
can be identified. Implosive methods might then be used. It
might also prove useful to apply guided imagery methods in an
attempt to resolve these conflicts on a symbolic level. The efficacy of these interventions can be assessed objectively by monitoring client security operations and risk-taking behavior and by
applying emergent uncovering methods to assess if the same strivings are still pathogenic; that is, do they still produce resistance,
symptoms, and anxiety along with their indirect depiction
(derivatives)?

REFERENCES

Aronoff, J., and Messe, L. Motivational determinants of small
    group structure. Journal of Personality and Social Psychology,
    1971, 17, 319-324.
Assor, A. The relationship between motivation of perceivers and
    their evaluations of high and low status persons. Unpublished
    master's thesis, Michigan State University, 1979.
Bakan, P. Imagery, raw and cooked: a hemispheric recipe. Paper
    presented at First Annual Conference on Imagery of the American
    Association for the Study of Mental Imagery, June 22-24, 1979,
    Los Angeles, California.
Bergin, A., and Lambert, M. J. The evaluation of therapeutic out-
    comes. In S. L. Garfield and A. E. Bergin (Eds.), Handbook of
    psychotherapy and behavior change (2nd ed.). New York: Wiley,
    1978.
Beutler, L. E., Pollack, S., and Jobe, A. "Acceptance," values,
    therapeutic change. Journal of Consulting and Counseling
    Psychology, 1978, 46, 198-199.
Bowers, P. Hypnosis and creativity: the search for the missing
    link. Journal of Abnormal Psychology, 1979, 88, 564-572.
Burns, B., and Reyher, J. Activating posthypnotic conflict:
    emergent uncovering psychotherapy, repression and psycho-
    pathology. Journal of Personality Assessment, 1976, 40,
    492-501.
Crowne, D. P., and Marlow, D. The approval-motive: studies in
    evaluative dependence. New York: Wiley, 1964.
Dave, R. Effects of hypnotically induced dreams on creative prob-
    lem solving. Journal of Abnormal Psychology, 1979, 88,
    293-302.
Della Corte, M. The effect of preceding stimulus conditions on
    spontaneous visual imagery. Unpublished master's thesis,
    Michigan State University, 1979.
Dhanens, T. P., and Lundy, R. M. Hypnotic and waking suggestions
    and recall. Journal of Clinical and Experimental Hypnosis,
    1975, 23, 68-79.
Domino, G. Primary process thinking in dream reports as related
    to creative achievement. Journal of Consulting and Counseling
    Psychology, 1976, 44, 929-932.
Ferguson, C. Talking to children. In J. Greeberg (ed.), Universals
    of human language: Volume I: Method and theory. Stanford
    University Press, 1978.
Frank, J. D. Persuasion and Healing. Baltimore: Johns Hopkins
    University Press, 1961.
Freud, S. "Civilized" sexual morality and modern nervousness.
    Collected papers, Vol. 2, J. Riviere (trans.). London:
    Hogarth Press, 1948a.
Freud, S. Leonardo da Vinci, A. A. Brill (trans.). London:
    Routledge and Kegan Paul, 1948b.

Freud, S. On creativity and the unconscious. Papers on the
     psychology of art, literature, love, religion. New York:
     Plenum, 1958.
Gavrilides, G. Personal power functions in relation to general
     happiness, interpersonal risk, and interpersonally induced
     anxiety and security operations. Unpublished doctoral disser-
     tation, Michigan State University, 1980.
Greenleaf, E. Active imagining. In J. L. Singer and K. S. Pope
     (Eds.), The power of human imagination. New York: Plenum,
     1978.
Hartmann, H. Ego psychology and the problem of adaptation,
     D. Rapaport (trans.). New York: International Universities
     Press, 1939.
Hilgard, J. R. Personality and hypnosis: a study of imaginative
     involvement. Chicago: University of Chicago Press, 1970.
Kazdin, A. E., and Wilcoxon, L. A. Systematic desensitization and
     nonspecific treatment effects: a methodological evaluation.
     Psychological Bulletin, 1976, 83, 729-758.
Klopfer, B., and Kelly, D. M. The Rorschach technique. New York:
     World Book Co., 1942.
Kris, E. Psychoanalytic explorations in art. New York: Inter-
     national University Press, 1952.
LeBaron, S. Suggestibility and type of physician-patient relation-
     ship. Unpublished doctoral dissertation, Michigan State
     University, 1979.
Lindauer, M. S. Imagery from the point of view of psychological
     aesthetics, the arts, and creativity. Journal of Mental
     Imagery, 1977, 1, 343-362.
London, P. Kidding around with hypnosis. International Journal of
     Clinical and Experimental Hypnosis, 1976, 24, 105-121.
Mathews, A. Fear reduction research and clinical phobias. Psycho-
     logical Bulletin, 1978, 85, 390-414.
Morishige, H. H. A., and Reyher, J. Alpha rhythm during three
     conditions of visual imagery and emergent uncovering psycho-
     therapy: the critical role of anxiety. Journal of Abnormal
     Psychology, 1975, 84, 531-538.
Nash, M. R., Johnson, L. S., and Tipton, R. D. Hypnotic age regres-
     sion and the occurrence of transitional object relationships.
     Journal of Abnormal Psychology, 1979, 88, 547-555.
Nisbett, R. E., and Wilson, T. D. Telling more than we can know:
     verbal reports on mental processes. Psychological Review,
     1977, 84, 231-259.
Pine, F., and Holt, R. R. Creativity and primary process: a study
     of adaptive regression. Journal of Abnormal Psychology, 1960,
     61, 370-379.
Reyher, J. Emergent uncovering: a method for producing and objec-
     tifying psychopathology, repression and other psychodynamic
     processes. Paper presented at the meetings of the American
     Psychological Association, Washington, D.C., 1969.

Reyher, J. Can hypnotized subjects simulate waking behavior. The American Clinical Hypnosis, 1973, 16, 31-36.

Reyher, J. Clinical and experimental hypnosis: implications for theory and methodology. In W. E. Edmonston (Ed.), Conceptual and Investigative Approaches to Hypnosis and Hypnotic Phenomena. Annals of the New York Academy of Sciences. New York: New York Academy of Sciences, 1977a.

Reyher, J. Spontaneous visual imagery: implications for psychoanalysis, psychopathology and psychotherapy. Journal of Mental Imagery, 1977b, 2, 253-274.

Reyher, J. Suggestibility, motivational psychodynamics, and task variables. Paper presented in a symposium, Personality and development in response to hypnosis, at the meetings of the American Psychological Association, San Francisco, 1977c.

Reyher, J. Emergent uncovering psychotherapy: the use of imagoic and linguistic vehicles in objectifying psychodynamic processes. In J. L. Singer and K. S. Pope (Eds.), The power of human imagination. New York: Plenum, 1978.

Reyher, J., and Wilson, J. G. The induction of hypnosis: indirect vs. direct methods and the role of anxiety. American Journal of Clinical Hypnosis, 1973, 4, 229-233.

Reyher, J., Wilson, J. G., and Hughes, R. Suggestibility and type of interpersonal relationship: special implications for the patient-practitioner relationship. Journal of Research in Personality, 1979, 13, 175-186.

Shapiro, A. K., and Morris, L. A. Placebo effects in medical and psychological therapies. In S. L. Garfield and A. E. Bergin (Eds.), Handbook of psychotherapy and behavior change (2nd ed.). New York: Wiley, 1978.

Sheehan, P. Countering preconceptions about hypnosis: An objective index of involvement with the hypnotist. Journal of Abnormal Psychology Monograph, 1971, 78, 299-322.

Sheehan, P. W., and Dolby, R. Motivated involvement in hypnosis: the illustration of clinical rapport through hypnotic dreams. Journal of Abnormal Psychology, 1979, 88, 573-583.

Singer, J. L., and Pope, K. S. The use of imagery and fantasy techniques in psychotherapy. In J. L. Singer and K. S. Pope (Eds.), The power of human imagination. New York: Plenum, 1978.

Smyth, L. S. The influence of attention, anxiety, and brain asymmetry on hypnotic suggestibility. Unpublished doctoral dissertation, Michigan State University, 1977.

Spanos, N. P., and Bodorik, H. L. Suggested amnesia and disorganized recall in hypnotic and ask-motivated subjects. Journal of Abnormal Psychology, 1977, 86, 295-305.

Stern, A. Enhancement of female sexual arousal through hypnosis. Unpublished doctoral dissertation, Michigan State University, 1975.

Sullivan, H. S. The interpersonal theory of psychiatry. New York: Norton, 1953.

Weingartner, H., Miller, H., and Murphy, D. L.   Mood-state-dependent
     retrieval of verbal associations.   Journal of Abnormal Psychol-
     ogy, 1977, 86, 276-284.
Wilkins, W.   Desensitization and getting it together with Dawson
     and Wilson.   Psychological Bulletin, 1972, 78, 32-36.
Wiseman, R. J.   The Rorschach as a stimulus for hypnotic dreams:
     a study of unconscious processes.   Unpublished doctoral disser-
     tation, Michigan State University, 1962.
Wiseman, R. J., and Reyher, J.   Hypnotically induced dreams using
     the Rorschach inkblots as stimuli: a test of Freud's theory
     of dreams.   Journal of Personality and Social Psychology, 1975,
     27, 329-336.

VISUAL IMAGERY: THE LANGUAGE OF THE
RIGHT BRAIN

Evelyn Virshup, M.A., A.T.R.
Bernard Virshup, M.D.*
*USC School of Medicine

Los Angeles, California

Neurological research has rediscovered the concept that we have two separate brains, capable of two separate ways of perceiving the world. As early as 1844, Wigan, in his book, The Duality of the Mind, wrote "that a separate and distinct process of thinking or ratiocination may be carried on in each cerebrum simultaneously." Since then, with the splitting of the brain in severe epileptics, Sperry, Bogen and others have been able to elucidate the cognitive characteristics and styles of the two hemispheres. The left or major hemisphere, controlling the right side of the body, appears to predominate in verbal, sequential, and analytic problem solving, while the right or minor hemisphere predominates in perceptual, holistic, manipulo-spatial and parallel processing, and in gestalt formations. The right brain also serves as a perceptual feedback system, while the left selectively focuses on aspects of the input, utilizing analytic sequential processing aimed at problem solving (Eaton, 1977).

Developmentally, the imagery processing system precedes the language system. Therefore, early memories prior to the development of the language system are accessible in the visual or imagery system but are inaccessible through the verbal system. In addition, Gazzaniga (1978) has pointed out the parallels between the split brain patient and the young child in terms of two separate independent streams of consciousness co-existing 1) in the absence of the corpus callosum (the fibers connecting the two hemispheres), and 2) due to the late myelination (the myelin sheath which covers nerve fibers has protective, nutritive and insulating qualities) of the corpus callosum increases from birth through approximately age 10-11, due to physical maturation. This factor may underlie the qualitative changes in cognitive functioning that occur

developmentally, beginning with the sensorimotor, concretistic pre-
occupational, and formal operational stages of cognitive development (Piaget, 1929).

Based on many concepts of cognitive development, including
those of Jung, Piaget, Dewey and Kolb, a tentative hypothesis for
understanding cognition is suggested. A person experiences events
and situations; or senses, intuits, and feels, as a response
to events and situations; and then makes tentative reflections and
observations (right brain processes). Then analytical, evaluative
and logical conceptualizations occur; and active, practical actions
occur (left brain processes).

The creative experience has been hypothesized to involve shifting between right and left hemisphere modes of cognition (Assagioli,
1965). That is, intuitive ideas emanating from the right hemisphere
must then be analyzed by the left hemisphere in order to deduce the
parts contributing to the whole.

The right brain processes of tentative reflection include
fantasy, daydreaming, free thinking (allowing one's mind to wander
in any direction without restraints or organization), and meditation. Arieti (1976) lists these attitudes as among those necessary
for fostering creativity, in his book, Creativity, the Magic Synthesis. Unfortunately, our educational system has traditionally
emphasized the left brain processes, without validating, and in
fact often deprecating the importance of, the right brain processes
which are essential ingredients of cognition.

Among right brain skills also neglected by the educational
system are manipulo-spatial skills of actively exploring and altering the spatial environment, by using the hands, as in activities
involved in drawing, arranging, and constructing. The right brain
is vastly, if not absolutely, superior to the left in constructing
perceived relations by manipulating (Nebes, 1972). In addition,
since the right brain has stored images in childhood inaccessible
through verbal recall, manipulo-spatial activities evoke imagery
linked to these early learning experiences.

Perhaps as a result of unbalanced educational emphasis, a
dichotomy is often observed, of people who function in mostly one,
or the other mode, rather than in an integrated manner, sequentially and synergistically. This has led to several paradoxes and
difficulties.

Many people live rich and fulfilling lives without having
fully developed their left brain functions. They may have marvel-
ously free, imaginative, creative abilities, expressed through the
arts, and in their relationships with others.

However, we find many people who approach life using their right brain processes, allowing others whose left brain processes dominate, to define them as inadequate, incompetent and worthless. Even worse, these people may deny their right brain functions, and, being without adequately developed left brain functions, find themselves leading lives of depression, despair and frequently addiction.

It is necessary to help such people to recognize the value, richness, and worth of their right brain processes, and by doing so, to restore their self-esteem and self-confidence.

We also find people whose lives are largely dominated by left brain processes, also as a result of the unbalanced educational emphasis. By overemphasizing the analytic, evaluative, logical and practical aspects of life, they deny themselves the freedom of fantasy and the richness of imagination.

Thus, it is important to be aware of and to respect the nature of different people's strengths and shortcomings, and perhaps, if possible, to add to the shorter dimensions without deprecating the others. Visual imagery alone is valuable, but visual imagery synthesized and integrated with conceptualization, by, for example, sharing our inner experiences with others verbally, gives us greater contact with our experiential process and more tools to make effective impact on our world.

It is understandable, after a lifetime in a culture that views art as an elitist activity and a frill, and daydreaming as impractical, that we should feel a resistance to "dreaming" on paper. Others may view us as "silly"; our work will look inadequate, and will confirm our lack of "talent." We will appear exposed and vulnerable. Furthermore, we probably won't have pastels and paper for drawing available; and it may be messy, if we do. Most people in our culture have these reactions. Art is not integrated into our society, or into most people's lives.

And so, the inarticulate right brain's complexities, passions and conflicts often remain unexpressed, frustrated and a source of pain and confusions. To ease the pain and obliterate the confusion, many have turned to drink, drugs and food, and have never "understood" why. When verbal therapy alone doesn't help, perhaps drawing out the right brain will.

The importance of the arts therapies such as art, music, movement and psychodrama has been twofold:

First, the arts therapies have clearly been useful in expressing and understanding the right brain concepts and processes, which, being mostly nonverbal, have previously been considered to be unconscious. Since many behavior patterns were established in

preverbal days, and before myelination of the corpus callosum, it
has been quite difficult to elicit deep personality concepts and
motivations through verbal therapies. With the focus on these
relatively new therapies, such processes have been made more easily
available, and clarified, so that such terms as unconscious and
resistance have lost some of their prior significance.

Through the process of art therapy, "every individual, whether
trained or untrained in art has a latent capacity to project his
inner conflicts into visual forms" (Naumberg, 1966). Betensky
(1973) elaborates this viewpoint:

> Every work of art . . . expresses and means something
> . . . since the spontaneous, simple unsophisticated
> process of working with art materials involves visual
> patterns within an interaction between the person and
> the materials used, there is reason to assume that
> there is a similarity between the two patterns, one
> inside the user of the material and the other outside
> him, in the product made by him with the material.

Janie Rhyne (1973) utilizes "art media as a bridge between inner
and outer reality, encouraging people to create their own visual
artforms and to use these as messages they send to themselves.
Made visible, these messages can be perceived by their maker."

Since drawing was the first form of expression and communication before the written word, and since the imagery processing system precedes the language system, the use of art techniques as
developed in art therapy taps the right brain memories and early
learning experiences within each of us.

Second, spontaneous art, when not dominated by left brain
concepts of representational drawing and the emphasis on technical
skills, is, like dreams, a "Royal Road" to the rich world of fantasy and creativity, available to everyone, "talented" or not. It
is not just a method of therapy or of visual representation. It
is an important language, which has almost been lost to many of us,
because of the technological and rational bias of our times.

As an example of one effective art therapy technique, for
therapy or for self-expression, I often present kite string which
my clients soak in ink and drag across the paper, making abstract
designs. They turn the paper around sideways and upside down until
they find some image they can develop with pastels or felt tipped
pens. If no images are forthcoming, they intuitively put color
down, again turning the paper around to find new inspiration. When
they have done this right brain process, I ask them to write stories
or poems about their drawings to identify with their images in the
Gestalt manner. The process of organizing and ordering a sequential

story about the drawing taps into left brain functions. The process produces for the clients a series of pictures dealing with their right brain concepts and beliefs. Many examples of these drawings can be seen in my book, <u>Right Brain People in a Left Brain World</u>.

An important element of the process is the spontaneity of the artwork. There is an illusion of lack of control over the product; the "string did the drawing." The images perceived are intuitive. They occur without preconception and planning, and often occasion surprise and laughter.

Another important element is the bypassing of "resistance." When words are not used, concentration is on selecting and using colors, and developing the image. Thus, the critical evaluative left brain functions are suspended, and images of clear and simple power are produced.

Later, when the artwork is viewed and when people deal with their individual drawings in attempts to integrate the symbolism into their conscious rational framework, defense mechanisms are used as necessary for their own individual comfort; but the evidence lies in front of them, plainly to be seen.

It should be clear by now that art as a language of the right brain cannot be fully comprehended by thinking or talking or reading about it. It is an experiential right brain language that, in general, speaks only to the right brain. I can only indicate that its symbolism, metaphor and power exist; I cannot describe it further.

This naturally leads to some degree of resistance and frustration. "I don't understand what you are talking about!" "It doesn't make sense!" are frequent signs that the individual has not allowed him/herself to experience the process. These comments are never heard after even one excursion into the realm of art as an experiential trip into the wonders of the right brain.

REFERENCES

Alperson, E. D. Nonverbal and verbal integration. In W. A. Anderson (Ed.), <u>Therapy and the arts</u>. New York: Harper Colophon, 1977.

Arieti, S. <u>Creativity, the magic synthesis</u>. New York: Basic Books, 1976.

Assagioli, R. <u>Psychosynthesis</u>. New York: Hobbs, Dorman, 1965.

Betensky, M. <u>Self-discovery through self-expression</u>. Illinois: Chas. C. Thomas, 1973.

Bogen, J. E. <u>The other side of the brain</u>, I and II. Bulletin, Los Angeles Neurological Society, 1969.

Eaton, E. Intra and inter hemispheric processing of visual infor-
    mation in process and reactive schizophrenia. Doctoral disser-
    tation, University of Southern California, 1977.
Galin, D. Hemispheric specialization: implications for psychiatry.
    In R. G. Grenell and S. Gabay (Eds.), Biological foundations
    of Psychiatry. New York: Raven Press, 1976.
Gazzaniga, M. S., and Le Doux, J. The integrated mind. New York:
    Plenum Press, 1978.
Kolb, D. Organization psychology: a book of readings. New York:
    Prentice-Hall, 1974.
Kolb, D. Learning style inventory technical manual. Boston:
    McBer and Co., 1976.
Naumberg, M. Dynamically oriented art therapy: its principles and
    practice. New York: Grune and Stratton, 1966.
Nebes, R. Dominance of the minor hemisphere in commissurotomized
    man on a test of figural unification. Brain, 1972.
Piaget, J. The child's concept of the world. London: Routledge-
    Kegan-Paul, 1929.
Rhyne, J. The Gestalt art experience. California: Brooks/Cole,
    1974.
Sperry, R. W., Gazzaniga, M. S., and Bogen, J. E. Interhemispheric
    relationships; the neocortical commissures; syndromes of hemis-
    phere disconnection. In P. J. Viken and G. W. Bruyen, Handbook
    of clinical neurology, Vol. 4. North Holland, Amsterdam, 1969.
Sperry, R. W. Lateral specialization of cerebral function in the
    surgically separated hemispheres. In F. J. McGuigan and R. A.
    Schoonover (Eds.), The psychophysiology of thinking. New York:
    Academic Press, 1973.
Virshup, B. The wounded physician: a handbook for coping in medi-
    cal school. In publication.
Virshup, E. Art and the right hemisphere. Art Education. Vir-
    ginia: NAEA, 1976.
Virshup, E. Right brain people in a left brain world. Los Angeles:
    Guild of Tutors Press, 1978.

IMAGES OF INDIVIDUATION: A JUNGIAN APPROACH TO

THE PSYCHOLOGY OF IMAGERY

John R. Battista, M.D.

Department of Psychiatry

University of California, Davis

Jung is not generally appreciated as a pioneer in the study of imagery. Yet Jung dedicated his life to understanding the relationship between imagery and psychological development, a process he called individuation (Jung, 1916a, 1916b, 1933, 1939, 1945, 1967, 1968a, 1968b, 1970). In the course of these studies he made three important discoveries. First, that images serve to compensate for the limited perspective of our conscious awareness. Second, that there is a patterned series of images which parallel the individuation process. Third, that cultivating and attending to these images can facilitate the process of individuation.

Jung's understanding of the role of imagery in the functioning of the psyche is an integral part of his perception of the psyche as a self-regulating system that attempts to balance and synthesize the various functions of psychological life (Jung, 1927, 1946). Particularly important is the balance between the complex of consciousness, called the ego, and the unconscious complexes, including the shadow, anima, animus and self (Jung, 1939). Jung viewed these unconscious complexes as seeking to inform and correct the one-sided adaptation of our conscious lives. In this sense the psyche strives to achieve a state of integration and wholeness, what Jung called self-realization.

Jung viewed images as the central means by which the unconscious complexes can be balanced and integrated with conscious life. At a minimum images serve to compensate for the narrowed perception of consciousness and act as a kind of safety valve within the psyche. However, when images are used to establish a positive relationship between conscious and unconscious complexes, they serve to make individuals aware of those aspects of themselves with which they are

unaware and thus facilitate the individuation process toward a state
of self-realization.

It is not surprising therefore that Jungian analysis makes
extensive use of imagery, not only in the form of dreams, but active
imagination, sand play, drawing and other creative endeavors. Images
are not treated as signs to be analyzed into bits of information to
be used by the ego in order to better control the individual's adaptation to external reality; but rather, as symbols that point beyond
the realm of cognitive consciousness, whose function is to transform
the limited nature of our awareness.

Jung's study of images went beyond just understanding their
role in the dynamics of the psyche. Over the course of many years,
Jung began to realize that there is a pattern of imagery which is
related to the individuation process. He found the same pattern of
images not only in dreams, active imagination, fantasy, sand play,
drawing and hallucinations, but also in the myths, rituals and initiation rites of preceding ages. Jung thus began to view images as
objective instruments with which to understand the individuation
process in a particular individual.

Much of the controversy concerning Jungian psychology has cen-
tered around Jung's hypothesis that the repetitive archetypal images
he discovered implied some kind of collective historical unconscious
from which these images are inherited. This hypothesis is not sup-
portable in any concrete, physical form and blinded many people to
Jung's more basic empirical discovery--that the human psyche is
structured in such a way that it is predisposed to mature in a particular manner and to experience the world in a particular way. In
this form, Jung's ideas about imagery in relation to the individuation process becomes quite compatible with the structuralist and
information-system's approaches of contemporary psychology (Muchielli, 1972; Piaget, 1971; Peterfreund, 1971). That is, what is
inherited is not the images themselves, but a structure which pre-
disposes human beings to experiencing particular images. Much of
the interest among Jungian analysts today is not trying to verify
Jung's hypotheses about the racial inheritance of ideas, but rather
to develop an understanding of how the structure of the psyche Jung
discovered evolved historically. Neumann's work (Neumann, 1970),
attempting to show that individual psychological development reca-
pitulates the evolution of consciousness of the species as a whole,
may well provide a valuable key in understanding this mystery.

However, the value of Jung's work on the relationship of imagery to the individuation process for those of us interested in personal development does not rest in a theoretical explanation of the
etiology of an objective psyche, but rather, in our capacity to
utilize Jung's understanding of the relationship between imagery
and individuation to facilitate that process. In order to

accomplish this we must first have an appreciation for the process
itself.

Jung saw the process of individuation as divided into two main
movements. In the first movement a conscious ego perspective is
separated from the individual's originally unified, but unconscious,
experience of life. In the second movement, the individual ego is
consciously reintegrated with this unified state, called the self.
In order for this integration to occur, those aspects of the self
which were denied, repressed, projected or left unexperienced must
be confronted and experienced. The images of individuation which
facilitate this process can thus be more fully appreciated if we
have some understanding of the first, or differentiation stage of
this endeavor.

Initially the infant lives in a state of undifferentiated
unity. There is no separation of inner and outer, subject and
object. The infant is complete, yet unconscious of its self. In
order for self-realization to occur, the infant must differentiate
itself from the mother with which it is united and a part.

As the infant develops in utero, its increasingly independent
biological system separates itself from the mother. The infant's
needs continue to be met by the mother but the unity between them
becomes less perfect, and more of a dynamic interplay. This interplay is deepened and made more complex by the advent of birth and
the physical separation of mother and child.

The infant's needs inevitably become frustrated as the mother
becomes more independent of the child and the child more separate
from the mother. These experiences of frustration serve to accen-
tuate the infant's nascent sense of separateness and individuality.
However, the infant's ego is nearly helpless and unable to cope in
the world around it. Left to itself the infant would die. The
infant is thus gratified to have its needs met and return it towards
its original state of non-separateness.

This dynamic interaction between child and caretakers around
separation and re-integration becomes an axis upon which further
differentiation can take place (Edinger, 1973). It marks the
original separation of ego and self. It is important to understand
in this regard that the mother is the child's first conscious
experience of the self. The nature of the mother-child interaction
thus gives form to the ego's relationship to the self.

The ideal mother provides both gratification and encourages
individuation. She is balanced in her frustrating and nurturing
qualities. However, all human mothers overgratify or overfrustrate
and generally do both. This is a result not only of the mother's
personality, but of the child, and what their interaction evokes

in the two of them. Depending on how this interaction takes place,
the child's ego and image of mother becomes structured in a particular form. A permissive mother who loves having a child close
to her will evoke a strong, positive image of mothers in a child.
To compensate for this, unconscious images of a devouring, engulfing
mother are constellated because such a mother inhibits a child from
fully differentiating its ego. Alternately, a critical mother crip-
ples the child's sense of well being and gives a negative cast to
the ego's images of mother. To compensate for this, images of the
great mother, the nurturing madonna, may be constellated. Jungian
analysts (Edinger, 1973; Harding, 1965; Jacobi, 1965, Neumann,
1970; Whitmont, 1969) have stressed that the unconscious fear of
being devoured by the terrible mother and longing for reintegration
with the divine mother leads to another stage in the individuation
process, the heroic quest. However, for our purposes, the point
is more that this heroic quest takes place consciously in the second half of the individuation process when these two unconscious
aspects of the mother interaction are confronted and dealt with.

     As the child moves out into society as a family member, the
child is taught how to act in particular ways. Those aspects of
its potential sexual expression which are left unactualized in this
process, as well as compensatory images to balance the one-sided
nature of the child's sex role adaptation, constitute an unconscious
contrasexual complex known as the anima in the male and animus in
the female. Similarly, those characteristics of the self which are
not acceptable to the socialized child constitute a same sexed
unconscious complex known as the shadow.

     During adolescence the child is transformed into an adult
through its separation from the family as an independent person.
This process generally involves accepting some social role or collective identity which both expresses and defends the person in
his new independent position. This defensive, yet adaptive, role
of the individuals is called their persona.

     With the establishment of the persona the first movement of
the individuation process is completed. The individual ego has
become consciously separated from its self by identifying with a
collective, social role. The scene is now set for this process to
be reversed. It is as if the individual's assertion of itself as
a fully conscious, independent person motivated solely by its own
wishes, wants and desires activates the compensating images of the
second movement of the individuation process. Those aspects of
the self which were sacrificed in establishing a social identity are
to be confronted and integrated. The unconscious complexes established during this process are to play an active role in bringing
this reintegration about. Jung observed that this reintegration
process generally takes place in the second half of life, after
what we would call the mid-life crisis. However, today we see many

people interested and involved in this process at a much earlier
age. Sometimes this represents a failure of the individuals to
fully separate themselves and establish an identity, but not uncommonly such a quest is a legitimate and viable concern.

The first level in this process is to confront one's persona,
or social adaptation to life. Many people come to therapy with
complaints about their adaptation. In our psychologically sophisticated society people commonly get extensive feedback about how
they are seen by others. In addition, discomfort in social situations can make individuals acutely aware of their need to relate
to other people through socially stereotyped roles. These confrontations with one's persona can greatly facilitate this aspect of
the individuation process for those individuals who are ready to
give up their protective role and relate more as themselves. However, it is important to distinguish those individuals with persona
related complaints who have never established a viable persona from
those who have outgrown theirs. Individuals who have never established a viable persona have not completed the first movement of
the individuation process and need assistance in establishing an
ego perspective separated from the unconscious forces, i.e., ego
oriented psychotherapy. On the other hand, individuals who have
established such a persona separation need assistance in reintegrat-
ing their ego and unconscious forces, i.e., psychotherapy oriented
towards self-integration.

The nature of the person's persona images can be helpful in
making this distinction. Persona images generally take the form
of the persons themselves. Individuals who have never established
a viable persona may appear naked or find themselves overwhelmed
by primitive, non-human forces. Individuals who have established
a persona adaptation may appear overly dressed or dressed in uniform. For example, individuals who are unaware of their falseness
in relationships may find themselves appearing in their dreams as a
model or actor. Persons too attached to their role, as when a doctor needs to relate to everyone as a physician, may find themselves
dressed in uniform or unable to take off their clothes.

Such self representations can facilitate the persons' confrontation with their persona. In addition, the place or circumstances
in which the individuals find themselves in their imagery can help
clarify the nature of their adaptation to life. For example, the
overly abstract, initiative individuals may find themselves alone
on a mountain top unable to see the path down because of the clouds
all around them. When this confrontation is successful, these persons will feel more natural in their social functioning and appear
more natural in their imagery. Rather than finding themselves
strange or uncomfortable in their images, they will be accepting of
themselves.

Such a resolution of persona problems commonly ushers in the next level of the individuation process. This generally involves confronting one's shadow, or rejected aspects of the self. The confrontation with one's shadow generally follows the confrontation with one's persona because it involves a somewhat deeper and more unconscious aspect of the psyche. The persona involves confronting one's conscious adaptation to life, while the shadow involves confronting unconscious aspects of the person which have been split off and rejected from consciousness.

Shadow imagery generally takes the form of same sexed persons. They have a distinctly evil or negative cast to them. Sometimes they appear in primitive, stereotyped forms such as witches or men in black capes, but not uncommonly they appear as brothers, sisters, or other persons close to the individual. The persons must confront these qualities in themselves, a process often facilitated by realizing the projection of one's shadow onto people or institutions around one. In order to integrate these bad or negative aspects of one's self, individuals must learn to see their positive side, how they are perversions of a potential strength that the person is in need of, or come to understand that they are rooted in some fear of proceeding further in their self-confrontation. Not uncommonly this confrontation and transformation will appear in imagery—they will finally turn and meet the frightening figure they have been running from, establish some relationship to them, and find them transformed into some helpful figure or guide.

When this confrontation and integration takes place, a third level of the second movement of the individuation process may begin. This involves confronting the contrasexual elements of one's potential self—the anima of the man or animus of the woman. These complexes are more unconscious than the shadow because they represent latent or unrealized aspects of the person which have never been conscious rather than elements which were rejected or repressed from consciousness. The confrontation with anima or animus figures thus generally constitutes the person's first experience with the transpersonal dimensions of the psyche.

This confrontation normally occurs in a concrete, outer form well before the person confronts these elements in the symbolic, inner form of imagery. Most people's first experience of the anima or animus occurs through falling in love. In romantic love persons become possessed by their anima or animus which is projected onto their lover. Thus, they are in love with projected aspects of themselves rather than with the person as s/he is. Following this, the person is left with the challenge of loving another human being who does not match the archetypal expectations found in his love, of anima-animus projections. For this to occur, the person must begin to confront the anima or animus within himself. The use of imagery can greatly facilitate this process.

The nature of the person's relationship to contrasexual figures in imagery can help to clarify the individual's relationship
to latent aspects of himself. For the woman who has been put
down and rejected by men, her animus may take the form of an allur-
ing young man impelling her to look at his penis--to become related
to the seeking of masculine power. To the man who is frightened by
women and repressive of his emotional side, his anima may be constellated in the form of a beautiful woman who tries to give him a
magic potion. Thus, anima and animus figures not only confront
individuals with how they relate to members of the opposite sex,
but impel them to confront those aspects of contrasexuality of which
they are unaware. As this occurs, the person may begin to have
imagery in which s/he is united or allied with members of the
opposite sex.

When this occurs, the person achieves a realization of the
various aspects of personality. What remains is for the individual
to confront the self, that aspect of psychological life which tran-
scends any individual differentiation or limitation.

This confrontation of ego with the self marks the final, deepest and most intriguing aspect of the individuation process. The
ego must consciously realize the wholeness of the self, yet in order
to do so, it must give up its sense of importance and control.
Neumann (1970) calls this process the sublimation of the ego to the
self.

Imagery of the self is always characterized by a numinous,
transcendent quality. Dreams and fantasies of this phase of the
individuation process generally are highly organized and present a
theme or story. The person is commonly cast in some mythic garb or
engaged upon some mythic task. In the course of this adventure
the person may well confront other mythic characters--the king,
queen, knight, fair maidens, dragons and other beasts. The self,
the goal of the quest or journey, is commonly represented by Christ,
a ring of power or some mandala figure.

The tale of the ego's confrontation with the self is well known
and can be found in many myths (Campbell, 1956), as well as the life
of Christ (Edinger, 1973; Jung, 1968). Jungian analysts have often
stressed the Quest of the Holy Grail (Johnson, 1977a, Jung and Von
Franz, 1970), as a myth of masculine initiation, while Amor and
Psyche (Neumann, 1971; Johnson, 1977b) have served as a myth for
feminine initiation into the self. Jung (Jung, 1968, 1970) was
particularly interested in alchemy as a symbol for the entire individuation process.

Initially, the hero or heroine may be tested by a number of
trials. Although individuals may first be called upon to prove
their courage by slaying various beasts and performing difficult

tasks, eventually they are called to submit themselves to that which
is greater than they are, the self. The most frequent difficulties
involve the ego's attempt to possess the self and thus maintain its
control. This result is an inflation or aggrandizement of the ego
(Edinger, 1973). Instead, the individual must submit to the self,
to be contained by it, and thus transformed (Henderson, 1967).
This requires an attitude of humility and service.

We are now in a position to review a series of images in order
to see how this process takes place in a particular individual. I
have selected a series of three dreams that span an eight-year
period in my own life for this purpose.

The night before I entered Jungian analysis I had the following
dream. I was part of the American Western Spirit Company in retreat
from an overwhelming Asian force. The barren, rolling plain was
filled with fighting. My job was to set a charge and blow it up on
command as the enemy streamed over the charged area. I was terrified of death.

We retreated and retreated until I finally fell backwards over
a shallow embankment down to a sandy beach along the ocean. I
played dead as our forces were overrun and prayed to God for help
and assistance.

Suddenly I found myself on a train in the middle of an Oriental
city. A Chinese woman rode up on a bicycle and took my picture.
This gave me a sense of being watched and I became nervously attuned
to everything around me.

A young boy started running to catch the train as it began to
pull out. He frightened me and I aimed my gun at his heart through
my telescopic sight. He ran harder and harder, his chest heaving,
arms pumping forcefully to catch the train. Finally only his chest
was visible through the sight as I slowly began to squeeze on the
trigger. However, his complete determination to catch the train
calmed my fear and I put down the gun and helped him aboard. He
was myself as a boy.

The train became a yellow school bus bouncing along a wide
broad river at the edge of a European city. A swarm of Boy Scouts
carrying a large banner swarmed around behind the bus, cutting it
off from those behind. We followed the river past the New Jersey
First Brigade and continued out into the country. We went by a
large blue lake and smoothly ascended a long, gentle hill. As we
began to descend the other side I became entranced by a gigantic
castle-fortress off in the distance. The castle was surrounded by
a barren field and barbed wire fence. I felt I had to go into the
castle, although I was frightened by the prospect of walking across
that barren field, sure to be seen.

I set out on foot accompanied by my analytically-oriented
friend, Joel. We saw no one and finally came to the old covered
portico of the house. We knocked at the massive door and it swung
open. The sounds of a ping pong game greeted us from down a stairwell leading into a urine-smelling darkness.

Joel began to feel sick and didn't want to continue on, so I
travelled down the curved stairwell alone. Soon the light and sound
ceased. I am surrounded by a frightening, yet exiting silence. I
come to series after series of passageways leading off in every
direction but continue down through the maze following my intuition.

I think I hear footsteps behind me--I stop to make sure, but
there is nothing. However, when I walk I hear someone walking
behind me. When I stop they stop. I am frightened.

On and on, down and down I go until I sense that I am coming
to the end. I finally enter a small room with one remaining door.
Suddenly I hear the follow reverberation of steps and voices from
above and flee through the last door into a room with no other
exits.

I take up the lotus position and enter samadhi. Within that
state, with my eyes shut, I see my friend, Joel, enter the room with
another friend of mine, Mills, who is wearing a German army uniform.
They see me rocking and drooling like an acute psychotic, totally
beyond help and understanding. They feel sorry for me and leave.

Some time later, Steve, a quiet, self-contented, physically
fit friend, returns and leads me up the stairs again. I ask him
if everything will be all right. He says yes, as long as I stay
away from the S.H.O. types (S.H.O is a radical medical students'
organization). The door opens to the outside and I am flooded with
light from the beautiful spring courtyard of the dormitory where I
lived my last year at Princeton.

Although I didn't comprehend it at the time, this dream outlines the course I needed to follow in order to come to terms with
myself. The phophetic and prognostic significance of initial
dreams has been emphasized by many Jungian analysts.

First, the dream revealed my current situation--the nature of
my psychological adaptation to life. There is a great battle raging between Eastern and Western spiritual forces. I was aware of
being attracted to Eastern spirituality, but unaware of my association with the Western Spirit Company. Consciously I was identified with the East and the struggle of the Vietnamese people. I
was quite surprised, and even ashamed, at finding myself identified
with the West in my dreams. This thus revealed the nature of my
persona problem. I was consciously identified with the East, but

unconsciously very frightened by the power of these forces.

It is only through prayer for salvation that I am saved from destruction by this battle. This showed my need for help and assistance from beyond the realm of my conscious intellect. The necessary solution is then told loud and clear. I must confront my fear of women. For a strange woman appears who makes me very nervous which almost results in my destroying myself as a child. The necessity is made clear. I must overcome my femininely-related fear which threatens to kill myself as a child. I must become reunited with my natural, fully committed youthful self. This reunion would take me beyond the collective social role of the Boy Scouts or New Jersey First Brigade into a confrontation with myself, that fascinating, yet frightening castle, which no human can approach without being seen or put at the mercy of the power there.

Initially I am accompanied on this journey by my analytically oriented friend, my intellect. However, my intellect becomes sickened by all the filth it must encounter and turns back. I must find my way to the inner-most aspect of the castle of my self following my intuition as a guide.

However, I find that something is shadowing me. I feel it is evil and am frightened of it. It is only when I settle in the final room and enter a state of samadhi (enter a state of self-realization) that I come to find that my shadow is my critical intellect. Its problem is that it is attached to German authoritarian intellectualism which causes me to mistake my own self-realization as psychosis and thus to take pity on my self.

I needed to be led out of this confrontation with my shadow by Steve, characterized by humility, fitness and self-containment. He advised me to stay away from the radical politics of the S.H.O. Through that I come to re-enter the springtime of my senior year at Princeton, a time, not surprisingly, when I had my first conscious experience of spirituality, my self, but became frightened that I had gone crazy.

A second dream, a couple of years later, helped to further elucidate the problem I was having. I was driving along a highway with many cars on it, but turned to the right at the first light onto a beautiful, peaceful, tree-lined road. On my left a ways down I turned to enter a large stone mansion owned by a French composer, Jacques Baptiste. As I turned into the driveway the dream took on a strange numinous quality and I felt the events were of great significance for me.

I entered the house and my wife, Sandy, was there. She explained the significance of the 13 steps leading from the living room up to the second story. Each step represented a whole

different facet of the composer. The lower steps were concerned
with the composer's personal life, while the final steps concerned
the composer's music as a manifestation of the powers of the universe. The process was so profound and enrapturing that I fell
into a trance on the floor, only to be awakened by Sandy saying,
"You see, women can be significant and understand these things too!"

I then walked down a series of circular stone steps into the
basement. The basement was candle lit and filled by a choir singing
an early Christian chant. A monk was translating an ancient holy
text into English.

I walk out of the basement and get in a car with Herbie, a
childhood friend of mine. We go through all kinds of freeways and
tunnels. He asks me if I know the way home--I answer yes, but turn
away from the road leading back to our home town, Mountain Lakes.

We come to a large brownstone building with a large courtyard
and porticos on two sides. I walk through the porticos and enter a
rapturously beautiful garden. In the distance on a hillside is an
old, tudor-style monastery. All is lush, green, fragrantly in bloom
and perfectly cared for.

As I wander through the garden I begin to hear entrancing
baroque polyphonic music. The further I go the more intense and
encompassing the music is until I hear it all around me and am carried away with it. As I go farther and farther I come to a choir
that is singing a call to Daniel.

I continue to walk. The music is everywhere. Incredibly
beautiful, complex and yet totally integrated--counterpoint melody
upon counterpoint melody, changing and evolving through all of the
instruments and voices--creating an overwhelming melodic structure
that leaped from the music and sent my heart soaring. I knew that
this was my path, that this music was my own, that this was meant
for me. I began to realize that I am about to meet God-Christ.
Just as the music is about to climax it stops and there is total
silence. I see an angel up in the sky, a cardboard angel, slowly
floating down until it falls over at my feet. Behind me I hear a
single voice laughing, "Hah! Hah! Hah! Hah!" I turn around, furious,
It is my brother and I cry out to him, "Don't laugh, that could have
been me."

I awoke in an altered state--the numinous quality of the music
still with me but also the fear of the fallen cardboard angel and
my brother laughing. "Don't laugh, that could have been me"--what
did that mean?

The situation of my ego consciousness had shifted. I had
turned off the great highway of life and had begun to confront my

hidden personality, my soul or inner self (Jacques Baptiste).
Through my interaction with my wife (Anima) I come to understand
the full depths and diversities of my ego as it is illuminated by
the spirit of the self. Here is the mysterium conjunctionis, the
mystic union of male and female. She points out how I desperately
need to respect my feminine side.

I then descend from this second story of inflated higher knowledge back down into the unconscious basement of my self which is
now somewhat illuminated by candlelight. There I find early Christian spirituality, but leave it to travel with a childhood friend
of mine. I have hooked up with my youth and become less frightened
of my self. Thus, when he asks me if I know the way back home, I
say yes, but rather than return to our childhood home, seek out
another, more complete home.

I pass through the porticos into a magic garden made just for
me. I become entranced again, although not totally captured by my
anima emotions. In this state I hear a call to Daniel and then go
on believing I am to meet God or Christ. At the last moment an
angel falls from the sky and my brother laughs at me sinisterly.
I say, "Don't laugh, that could have been me!"

Don't laugh, that could have been me to become so inflated that
they think to find God outside themselves. Such a complex needs our
compassion, not our ridicule and judgment. So I needed to correct
the judgment of my discriminating intellectual side, my shadow.

Daniel was called for in the dream itself. Of what significance could that be? Daniel was called by King Nebuchadnezzar to
interpret his dream.

> For as all the wise men of my kingdom are not able
> to make known unto me the interpretation: but thou art
> able; for the spirit of the holy gods is in thee.
> Then Daniel, whose name was Belteshazzar, was
> astonished for one hour, and his thoughts troubled him.
> The king spake, and said, Belteshazzar, let not the
> dream or the interpretation thereof, trouble thee.
> Belteshazzar answered and said, My Lord, the dream be
> to them that hate thee, and the interpretation thereof
> to thine enemies.
> The tree that thou sawest, which grew, and was
> strong, whose height reached unto the heaven, and the
> sight thereof to all the earth;
> Whose leaves were fair, and the flowers and the
> fruit thereof much, and in it was meat for all; under
> which the beasts of the field dwelt, and upon whose
> branches the fowls of the heaven had their habitation:
> It is thou, O king, that art grown and become

strong: for thy greatness is grown, and reacheth unto
heaven, and thy dominion to the end of the earth.

And whereas the king saw a watcher and a holy one
coming down from heaven, and saying, Hew the tree down,
and destroy it; yet leave the stump of the roots thereof
in the earth, even with a band of iron and brass, in the
tender grass of the fields; and let it be wet with the
dew of heaven, and let his portion be with the beasts of
the field, till seven times pass over him;

This is the interpretation, O king, and this is the
decree of the Most High, which is come upon my lord the
king:

That they shall drive thee from men, and thy dwell-
ing shall be with the beasts of the field, and they
shall make thee to eat grass as oxen and they shall wet
thee with the dew of heaven, and seven times shall pass
over thee, til thou know that the Most High ruleth in the
kingdom of men, and giveth it to whomsoever he will.

And whereas they command to leave the stump of the
tree roots; thy kingdom shall be sure unto thee, after
that thou shalt have known that the heavens do rule.

Wherefore, O king, let my counsel be acceptable
unto thee, and break off thy sins by righteousness, and
thine inequities by showing mercy to the poor; if it may
be a lengthening of thy tranquility.

All this came upon the king Nebuchadnezzar.

At the end of twelve months he walked in the palace
of the kingdom of Babylon.

The king spake, and said, Is not this great Babylon,
that I have built for the house of the kingdom by the
might of my power, and for the honour of my majesty?

While the word was in the king's mouth, there fell
a voice from heaven, saying, O king Nebuchadnezzar, to
thee it is spoken; the kingdom is departed from thee.

And they shall drive thee from men, and thy dwell-
ing shall be with the beasts of the field; they shall
make thee to eat grass as oxen, and seven times shall
pass over thee, until thou know that the Most High
ruleth in the kingdom of men, and giveth it to whomsoever he will.

The same hour was the thing fulfilled upon Nebuchadnezzar; and he was driven from men, and did eat grass as
oxen, and his body was wet with the dew of heaven, till
his hairs were grown like eagles' feathers, and his nails
like bird's claws.

And at the end of the days I Nebuchadnezzar lifted
up mine eyes unto heaven, and mine understanding returned
unto me, and I blessed the Most High, and I praised and
honoured him that liveth for ever, whose dominion is an
everlasting dominion, and his kingdom is from generation

to generation.

And all the inhabitants of the earth are reputed as
nothing; and he doeth according to his will in the army
of heaven, and among the inhabitants of the earth: and
none can stay his hand, or say unto him What doest thou?

At the same time my reason returned unto me; and
for the glory of my kingdom, mine honour and brightness
returned unto me; and my counsellors and my lords sought
unto me; and I was established in my kingdom, and excellent majesty was added unto me.

Now I Nebuchadnezzar praise and extol and honour the
King of heaven, all whose works are truth, and his ways
judgment: and those that walk in pride he is able to
abase.

The interpretation of King Nebucchadnezzar's dream is for his
enemies--which in his case are pride and righteousness. Only by
suffering for his pride did he come to understand his limited role
in the order of the universe. That there is a greater power who
ruleth over him, to whom he should pay reverence and respect.

The parallels to my own dream are many--most interestingly the
king saw a watcher and holy one come down from heaven while I saw
an angel. Lucifer, the fallen angel of pride is the problem,
revealed in my dream. It is my pride that causes the inflation of
my ego. It is pride that inhibits my ego from accepting the help
and assistance of my feminine side required to submit my ego to
the self, the true source of power.

A third dream some eight years after the original dream brought
some resolution to my struggle with the feminine and allowed me to
come closer to my self.

I dreamt I was back in the house I was raised in. A war had
been going on with the forces of the East but just ended. My
mother was there and I asked her what had brought the war to an end.
She shrugged her shoulders saying she didn't know, it just ended.
I looked out the window and felt compassion for the people, a woman
and two children, behind a smashed window in the living room of the
home with which he had been fighting.

Just then an earthquake began. I was between our dining room
and living room. I fell into the living room and the quake became
more and more intense until the entire room felt like it was accel-
erating very rapidly--as if we were taking off in a space ship.

I saw Jesus' head surrounded by a deep blue halo at the window. The room became like a car on a train. Everything calmly moving along and people coming and going from the car as they pleased.
Finally everyone settled down into a car and there was no more

movement. Then Jesus came inside and was with us--everyone stood
up and rejoiced.

It was Christmas day and a white-haired, paunchy Southern
minister was conducting the service. I opened a present from my
mother-in-law. It was a loaf of fresh hot cheese bread. It was
warm and perfect so I offered it to everyone as our communion bread.
When the minister came to collect the bread to distribute it, he
broke off a small piece and gave me communion first. I felt Christ
enter me and felt Jesus holding me in his loving arms. I tried to
recite the Lord's prayer but ended up reciting holy scripture in
unison with the minister, now transformed into Jesus.

After we had returned to our normal states the minister called
me up to the pulpit saying something very special had happened and
wanting me to tell everyone else about it. I was frightened to talk
and at first a couple of people left. Then I just simply told my
experience the best I could and everything went well. When I got
to what I had said in the minister's arms I became confused and had
to ask the minister what we had recited. He said that it was First
Corinthians, Two.

At that point I arrive back at my childhood home all alone.
The house is dark and scary and I can feel something evil in it.
Then my Christian friend Clem says, "It'll be OK--Jesus has been
inside--it's safe to enter."

In this dream the war between the Eastern forces and myself
had finally ended for reasons unknown to my mother. The reason is
because my fear of the Eastern spiritual wisdom was part of my war
with my mother. I was fighting to free myself from my mother complex, from the undifferentiated unified state of my birth. My fear
that it would devour me, my sense of myself, my sense of I.

In healing this wound with my mother I am able to find communion
between my ego and myself as a result of a gift given to me by my
mother-in-law, my adopted, spiritual mother. This mother, through
offering the bread of communion, allows me to experience the Christ
consciousness within me while in the compassionate arms of Jesus,
the outer and original Christ. The inner Christ is thus differenti-
ated from the outer Christ as I accept one and am accepted by the
other. The self is thus separated from the symbol of the self. In
doing so I speak out something said in First Corinthians, Two that
protects me in confronting the evil that still remains in me as a
result of my childhood.

First Corinthians, Two says:

As for me, brothers, when I came to you, I declared
the attested truth of God without display of fine words

or wisdom. I resolved that while I was with you I would
think of nothing but Jesus Christ--Christ nailed to the
cross. I came before you weak, nervous, and shaking with
fear. The word I spoke, the gosple I proclaimed, did not
sway you with subtle arguments: it carried conviction by
spiritual power, so that your faith might be built not
upon human wisdom but upon the power of God.

And yet I do speak words of wisdom to those who are
ripe for it, not a wisdom belonging to this passing age,
nor of any of its governing powers, which are declining
to their end; I speak God's hidden wisdom, his secret
purpose framed from the very beginning to bring us to our
full glory. The powers that rule the world have never
known it; if they had, they would not have crucified the
Lord of glory. But, in the words of Scripture, "Things
beyond our seeing, things beyond our hearing, things
beyond our imagining, all prepared by God for those who
love Him," these it is that God has revealed to us through
the Spirit.

For the Spirit explores everything, even the depths
of God's own nature. Among men, who knows what a man is
but the man's own spirit within him? In the same way,
only the Spirit of God knows what God is. This is the
Spirit that we have received from God, and not the spirit
of the world, so that we may know all that God of his own
grace has given us; and, because we are interpreting
spiritual truths to those who have the Spirit, we speak
of these gifts of God in words found for us not by our
human wisdom but by the Spirit. A man who is unspiritual
refuses what belongs to the Spirit of God; it is folly
to him; he cannot grasp it, because it needs to be judged
in the light of the Spirit. A man gifted with the Spirit
can judge the worth of everything, but is not himself
subject to judgment by his fellow-men. For (in the words
of Scripture), "who knows the mind of the Lord? Who can
advise Him? We, however, possess the mind of Christ.

So the point was made that it is only by submitting the ego to
the self and the powers of the spirit that we can hope to understand the true nature of reality and root out the evil and ignorance that still resides within each of us. However, for me and
those I have worked with, the individuation process does not end in
some state of perfect bliss, wisdom and contentment.

The struggle to confront the repressed and latent aspects of
ourselves, to submit our conscious ego perspective to the greater
transforming power of the self, continues. The purely self-
realized being whose ego serves merely as a channel for the expression of the self remains a myth--a state we enter for a time that
transforms us, but which is balanced by a return to the everyday

reality of our conscious ego perspective. So the process continues, more of a spiral with the issues repeated time and time again at more subtle and complete levels. Not so much the orderly linear progression laid out in this paper for the sake of clarity and brevity. No matter what, I am impressed with the great power of spontaneously occuring images to make us aware of our current situation in life and what it is we must do. The essential point of this paper, and of Jung's work as I understand it, is that by establishing a positive relationship with our unconscious through images, we can be transformed and led into a fuller, and more whole reality that lies beyond our wildest thoughts and fantasies--a world of meaning and fullness, seemingly created just for us.

REFERENCES

Campbell, J. The hero with a thousand faces. New York: Median
    Books, 1956.
Edinger, E. Ego and archetype. Baltimore: Penguin Books, 1973.
Harding, M. E. The I and not I. Princeton: Princeton University
    Press, 1965.
Henderson, J. Thresholds of initiation. Middleton, Connecticut:
    Wesleyan Universities Press, 1967.
Jacobi, J. The way of individuation. New York: Harcourt, Brace,
    World, 1965.
Johnson, R. A. He. New York: Harper and Row, 1977a.
Johnson, R. A. She. New York: Harper and Row, 1977b.
Jung, C. G. (Symbols of transformation) (R. Hull, trans. and
    H. Read, M. Fordham, G. Adler and W. McGuire, Eds.). Prince-
    ton: Princeton University Press, 1967. (Originally published,
    1912.)
Jung, C. G. (The structure of the psyche) In R. Hull (trans.)
    and H. Read, M. Fordham, G. Adler and W. McGuire (Eds.), The
    collected works of C. G. Jung, Vol. 8. Princeton: Princeton
    University Press, 1968. (Originally published, 1931.)
Jung, C. G. (The concept of collective unconsciousness) In
    R. Hull (trans.) and H. Read, M. Fordham, G. Adler and
    W. McGuire (Eds.), The collected works of C. G. Jung, Vol. 8,I.
    Princeton: Princeton University Press, 1968. (Originally
    published, 1936.)
Jung, C. G. (The phenomenology of the spirit in fairytales) In
    R. Hull (trans.) and H. Read, M. Fordham, G. Adler and
    W. McGuire (Eds.), The collected works of C. G. Jung, Vol. 9,I.
    Princeton: Princeton University Press, 1968. (Originally
    published, 1948.)
Jung, C. G. (General aspects of dream psychology) In R. Hull
    (trans.) and H. Read, M. Fordham, G. Adler, and W. McGuire
    (Eds.), The collected works of C. G. Jung, Vol. 8. Princeton:
    Princeton University Press, 1968. (Originally published, 1948.)

Jung, C. G. (On the nature of dreams) In R. Hull (trans.) and
     H. Read, M. Fordham, G. Adler and W. McGuire (Eds.), The
     collected works of C. G. Jung, Vol. 8. Princeton: Princeton
     University Press, 1968. (Originally published, 1948.)
Jung, C. G. (Psychology and alchemy) In The collected works of
     C. G. Jung, Vol. 12. Princeton: Princeton University Press,
     1968. (Originally published, 1953.)
Jung, C. G. (On the nature of the psyche) In R. Hull (trans.)
     and H. Read, M. Fordham, G. Adler, and W. McGuire (Eds.), The
     collected works of C. G. Jung, Vol. 8. Princeton: University
     of Princeton Press, 1968. (Originally published,1954.)
Jung, C. G. (A study in the process of individuation) In R. Hull
     (trans.) and H. Read, M. Fordham, G. Adler and W. McGuire
     (Eds.), The collected works of C. G. Jung, Vol. 9, I.
     Princeton: Princeton University Press, 1968. (Originally
     published, 1950.)
Jung, C. G. (Aion) In The collected works of C. G. Jung, Vol.
     9, II. Princeton: Princeton University Press, 1968.
     (Originally published, 1951.)
Jung, C. G. (Mysterium conjunctionis) In The collected works of
     C. G. Jung, Vol. 14. Princeton: Princeton University Press,
     1970. (Originally published, 1955/56.)
Jung, C. G. (The transcendent function) In R. Hull (trans.) and
     H. Read, M. Fordham, G. Adler, and W. McGuire (Eds.), The
     collected works of C. G. Jung, Vol. 8. Princeton: Princeton
     University Press, 1968. (Originally published, 1958.)
Jung, C. G. (The structure and dynamics of psyche) In The
     collected works of C. G. Jung, Vol. 8. Princeton: Princeton
     University Press, 1968. (Originally published, 19 .)
Jung, E., and Von Franz, M. The grail legend. New York: Putnam,
     1970.
Muchielli, R. Introduction to structural psychology. New York:
     Avon, 1972.
Neumann, F. The origins and history of consciousness. Princeton:
     Princeton University Press, 1970.
Neumann, E. Amor and psyche. Princeton: Princeton University
     Press, 1971.
Piaget, J. Structuralism. New York: Harper, 1971.
Peterfreund, E. Information, systems and psychoanalysis. New
     York: International Universities Press, 1971.
Whitmont, E. The symbolic quest. New York: Harper, 1969.

SYMBOLIC ASPECTS OF HYPNAGOGIC IMAGERY

ASSOCIATED WITH THETA EEG FEEDBACK

George W. Oliver, Ph.D,* Louis Breger, Ph.D.** and
Robert Zanger, M.A.*

*Newton Center for Clinical Hypnosis, Los Angeles,
California, **Department of Humanities, California
Institute of Technology, Pasadena, California

In recent years, dream research has focused on the physiological correlates of sleeping and dreaming, and, in particular,
on REM sleep. Also, comparisons have been made between the dream
content of REM and non-REM states including sleep-onset stages
(Foulkes and Vogel, 1974; Foulkes and Fleisher, 1975). However,
very little work has been done with these kinds of techniques to
learn more about the meaning and function of the dream contents to
the individual dreamer.

Foulkes (1973), among others, has stressed the importance of
paying attention to the idiosyncratic meaning of dream symbols,
and Vogel (1973) has suggested that an unconscious resistance may
be operating within researchers in this field against delving into
the depths of the unconscious through the symbolic meaning in
dreams. In this spirit, I have begun an exploration of the experimental territory at the meeting point of the physiological and symbolic approaches to the study of hallucinated imagery and altered
states of consciousness. This has been done by looking in depth
at the hypnagogic or "sleep-onset" imagery reported by a small
number of subjects from the altered states of consciousness associated with theta EEG feedback.

To begin the historical perspective of this presentation and
also to give the audience some feeling for the experience of hypnagogic imagery, I would like to quote some remarkable excerpts from
an article written by Edgar Allan Poe in 1846. (The phrase,
"illusion hypnagogique", was coined in 1848 by Maurz.)

> There is a class of fancies, of exquisite delicacy,
> which are not thoughts; they seem to be rather (psychal)

131

than intellectual. They arise in the soul (alas, how
rarely!) only at its epochs of most intense tranquility--
and at those mere points in time where the confines of
the waking world blend with those of the world of dreams.
I am aware of these "fancies" only when I am on the
brink of sleep, with the consciousness that I am so.

I so regard them, through a conviction that this
ecstasy, in itself, is of a character supernal to the
Human Nature--is a glimpse of the spirit's outer world;
and I arrive at this conclusion by a perception that the
delight experienced has, as its element, but the absolute-
ness of novelty.

At times I have believed it impossible to embody
(in words) even the evanescence of fancies as I have
attempted to describe.

I can startle myself from the point (of blending
between wakefulness and sleep) into wakefulness and thus
transfer the point itself into the realm of Memory--con-
vey its impressions, or more properly their recollections,
to a situation where (although still for a brief period)
I can survey them with the eye of analysis.

My work is based on an experimental approach using both a
physiological parameter and subjective reports of the experience
of the altered states of consciousness associated with the biofeedback use of that parameter. In 1970, Stoyva discussed the
logic and the value of this combined approach in what he called
"the public study of private events." In the same year, Green,
Green and Walters presented preliminary results of a similar study
which they called "a subliminal dredging operation" which they were
using in an investigation of creativity. Following the pioneering
work of Kamiya in 1969, Brown (1970) first reported hallucinated
imagery associated with theta EEG feedback. Budzynski and Stoyva
had shown in 1969 an association between EMG feedback and hallucinated imagery, which Green et al. also showed correlated with the
use of hand temperature feedback. The work of these investigators
and others turned around the earlier experimental paradigm of using
physiological measures to monitor subjects as they drifted into
dream-like states of reverie and into sleep. In 1964, Bertini,
Lewis and Witkin, using a system of partial sensory deprivation and
physiological monitoring, published accounts of hallucinated imagery which show many of the phenomena which will be presented in
this work. Foulkes and Vogel (1965) found that bizarre and symbolic imagery was reported most from non-REM descending stage one
sleep (as defined by the EEG activity between 4-7 HZ and electro-
oculogram data). The various stages of drowsiness and sleep had
previously been explored and defined in 1957 by Kleitman and Dement.
Earlier in 1943, Kubie reported hypnogogic imagery associated with
the use of a feedback technique based on amplified breathing
sounds. Davis, Davis, Loomis, Harvey and Hobart (1938), in their

early EEG studies, observed that subjects reported visual and bodily fantasies and dream-like feelings immediately after brief moments of loss of EEG alpha rhythm during drowsiness.

A summary model of the brain/mind conditions necessary for the experience of sleep-onset hallucinations can be assembled from the writings of West (1968), Deikman (1971), and Stoyva (1973). These conditions are as follows:

1. A reduced input to the brain from both outside and inside the body which then releases the organizing and inhibiting effects that these inputs have on the brain.

2. The combination of a residual awareness and a degree of internal arousal.

3. A shift from active to "passive volition"; that is, a shift from "making it happen" to "letting it happen."

4. A shift of the autonomic nervous system from a sympathetic to a parasympathetic predominance.

The other half of the historical background of this work is the rich literature of the study of symbolic process mainly as seen in dreams. In his first formulation in 1900, Freud saw dreams as a form of disguised wish fulfillment and he described the basic mechanisms which relate the elements of the dream to their possible symbolic origins. He also introduced the important technique of free association. Silberer, a student of Freud's, published in 1914 descriptions of his own hypnagogic imagery in which he identified a kind of symbolic imagery which he called "autosymbolic phenomena" and which appeared to relate symbolically to thoughts and other aspects of inner experience which occurred shortly before the hypnagogic image was experienced. As we will see later, autosymbolic imagery is a significant part of the imagery reported by the subjects in this study. While Freud placed emphasis on symbolic references to experiences in the dreamer's past, Silberer was the first investigator to view dreams as symbolic anticipations of the future. In 1920, Freud reported an observation of the repetitive play of a child, and this observation was an important development in the understanding of such issues as strivings for mastery as a part of symbolic process. This approach was supported by Griffith's study (1936) of the symbolic play and dreams of children in which she found such processes as problem solving and rehearsal expressed in symbolic form. Piaget (1951), also observing the play of children, discussed the neglected work of Silberer and pointed out that there is a constant and continuous "coming and going" from the unconscious to the conscious in symbolic process. Piaget also emphasized an important aspect of Freud's concept of condensation which is the fact that in this "coming and going" from the unconscious, images

can refer symbolically to the present and past simultaneously. This
becomes clear from a study of hypnagogic imagery.

The role of such processes as problem solving and conflict
resolution were demonstrated by Erickson (1954), and French and
Fromm (1964). Jung (1964) stressed that symbolic imagery in dreams
was unique and idiosyncratic, not only to each individual dreamer,
but also to each therapist-patient relationship. Breger (1969,
1973) and his co-workers have further investigated how dreams can
be a part of an adaptive response to stress in adults and how symbolic structures in children can reorganize in a developmental
response to internal change and as a part of changing perceptions
of, and responses to the world.

The most important development in this field has been the growing understanding of dreams as a problem solving activity that
expresses strivings for mastery while relating the conflicts of the
present to the experience of the past in the advancement of current
developmental issues.

In general, the procedure I used was an adaptation of those
described by Green et al. and by Bertini et al. Bipolar, theta EEG
with an auditory feedback was used as a kind of depth gauge to
guide the subject into a twilight state of consciousness where he
is not aware of his surroundings and where he can experience brief
and sometimes startingly vivid hallucinated images, the memory of
which is extremely fleeting and over which he has no control whatever. In fact, any attempt to control the appearance of the imagery prevents its appearance. In this state one usually cannot use
language or speak, but one can learn to rouse enough after experiencing an image to describe it verbally and then drift back into
the state where another image may appear, and so forth. Images
were reported in a series of seven to ten weekly sessions with each
subject. On the average, between 20 and 45 images were reported
per session. A total of 500 images was collected from two subjects.

Each session took place in the subject's own home and lasted
between 90 minutes and four hours. Rather than use any of the
various automatic procedures of Tart (1969) or Green et al., I
used instead the method of Bertini et al. of continuous reporting
which usually kept the subjects from falling asleep. This also
facilitated the reporting of imagery, the memory of which is very
brief. I was present in a close and immediate sense throughout
each session and roused the subjects on the few occasions when they
did slip into sleep. At the end of reporting images for each session, I would then review all of the images one by one, recording
the subject's associations and other comments. Throughout the sessions, it was clear that my close support was an important factor
in the subject's being able to report so many images in such a sustained and potentially revealing project.

Because this has been a venture of hypothesis discovery rather than testing, I have sacrificed the objectivity one might gain by using a content analysis by independent raters of the images reported by a large number of subjects. Instead I collected a long series of images from a small number of subjects whom I already knew well as friends. This has enabled me to translate the unique and idiosyncratic picture language used by each subject by immersing myself in an abundance of information about each subject, including my interactions with them and my previous knowledge of their lives.

The process of interpretation followed two basic strategies: first, gathering lists of repeated themes or repeating kinds of images together with associations and the sequential context of each image; second, working with long sequences of images considering the many interweaving and multileveled meanings and implications often borrowing clues and connections from other images and sequences in other sessions. As I worked with these 500 images, several categories of apparent symbolic reference emerged. These categories can be divided into two groups: the first group contains symbolic referants to various "here and now," present-time aspects of the experiment itself, such as symbolic statements about the nature of the images themselves, about the altered states of consciousness, the nature of one's thoughts, the biofeedback, one's bodily feelings, and the subject's relationship with the researcher. The second group of images appears to refer to current issues in the subject's life, as well as life-long themes.

In the next section of this presentation I would like to give examples of images that seem to refer to these various aspects of the subjects' experience in the experimental situation. It will become apparent that it is in the nature of symbolic images to refer to more than one issue or theme at a time, and therefore most images fit into more than one category.

IMAGES THAT REFER TO THE NATURE
   OF THE IMAGES THEMSELVES

In the first category are the images that relate to the images themselves, especially to the fleeting and utterly involuntary way they appear. In the second session, after a series of images that seem to relate to control, keeping control, and losing control, Jeff reported, "Herd of elk, reindeer ran through a clearing in a dense forest . . . interspersed with meadows at the same time. Thinking about fleeting qualities of things." Earlier in the session he had reported, "There's a lot of flash imagery . . . like still shots on a movie screen that go by too fast to catch." Just as Silberer reported the translation of thoughts into images, here the fleeting nature of the images become elk and reindeer appearing

for a moment in a forest clearing and running too fast to catch;
that is, to hold long enough to put into words.

Frank expressed similar issues in the following image: "Being
in a control room with a lot of TV monitors, sitting at the controls,
clearly black and white." Some of his later comments about this
image: "I didn't feel I was in control of it. I just felt I was
watching it, I didn't know what to do with any of those things; I
was just there, passive participation." In addition, this image is
also referring to other aspects of the hallucinated imagery. Most
of Frank's images were vividly colored and in their vividness they
many times convinced him, as he "saw" them that he was looking at
something "real." Likewise the black and white TV monitors are a
kind of representation that closely resembles the real world in
front of the TV cameras. A third level of meaning is important
here, namely that black and white images also refer to the experience of being deceived, and this symbolic device appears in many
of Frank's images. This meeting of a related group of themes in
one image is an example of Freud's concept of condensation.

IMAGES REFERRING TO ALTERED STATES
OF CONSCIOUSNESS

The process of repeatedly submerging into an altered state of
consciousness is graphically described in this image reported by
Jeff: "A guy in a swimming pool, pushed around on a float, and
being dunked time after time." The metaphor of going or being
"down" as a reference to an altered state of consciousness is very
common and is mixed with other themes from the experimental situation in the next example: "A scene looking up at a table in a
gallery with extraterrestrial people looking down . . . reminded me
of a surgical theater of some sort." In the altered state of consciousness one seems to be in another world. The gallery here
clearly refers to the array of images, and in addition the image
conveys a sense of surgical exposure that these images are revealing to me, the experimental observer. Needless to say, the issues
of alienation and of exposure to vulnerability in an intimate
relationship are recurrent themes in Jeff's imagery and in his life.

Sinking down into the heavy, thick space associated with "being
in theta" is combined in the next example with other aspects of
this experience: "Sank down through a series of granite images,
sometimes raw granite, like rock, and sometimes sculptured granite,
from the inside." Putting unpredictable imagery into the form of
language is a repeated transition between the illogical, uncontrolled, non-verbal raw granite and the logical, structured, verbal,
sculptured granite. Themes concerning relations between order and
chaos appeared several times throughout Jeff's imagery.

IMAGES REFERRING TO OTHER ASPECTS
   OF THE EXPERIENCE

The next example from Jeff's imagery is a pictorial representation of his thoughts in this state of consciousness: "Thinking
about thought fragments that occur in this state . . . a cluttered
room associated with that . . . and a conversation, small fragments,
having to do with pieces of thoughts." In this case, there was an
auditory hallucination associated with the visual image of the
cluttered room.

The following image seems to be a symbolic representation of
Jeff's experience with the biofeedback instrument: "Bunch of people in a room chanting "OM," swaying back and forth, and a water
bed over in a corner with me lying on it, chanting also, I'm leading the chanting." During the session, he was in fact lying on a
water bed. In the image, the warbling tone of the biofeedback
became a chant and a swaying back and forth; he "led" the "chant"
with his own brain waves.

The last image Jeff reported is a symbolic reference to his
relationship to me and, more specifically, a reference to his feelings about our ending the rather special intimacy we had while he
was a subject in my research:

> Having a rifle, and looking through the scope . . . at
> someone at a great distance who was doing the same thing
> simultaneously, and firing and then wondering if you
> could get out of the road of what you knew was coming;
> it was a fun trip.

The image also seems to be saying that he sees separation as a kind
of mutual annihilation.

Thus far in this presentation I have been discussing individual images. Now I would like to discuss a group of 18 images
reported by Frank, all of which appear to have meanings closely
related to those discussed already for the image of being in a TV
control room with rows of black and white TV monitors. The central
theme in this group is that of deception and the interpretive process has begun with this "autosymbolic" image which comments on the
immediate experience in the same way as the "autosymbolic phenomena"
reported by Silberer. Other themes closely related to deception in
this group include imitation, disillusionment, disappointment, and
failed nurturance. This group of images will also give us an
interpretive base from which to then understand six repeating
sequences of images which will be presented next.

You will notice that while nearly all of the 300 images that
Frank reported were in some way colored, often vividly, most of the

images in this group are either white or black and white. This
supports the hypothesis that the colors white and black themselves
are symbolic here for deception and failed nurturance.

I will now go through the images one at a time and give the
basis for their interpretation. Frank related the large white
letter "Y" to the letter he had just received from the YMCA dis-
continuing his student status and he was quite annoyed about this.
It was clear that the "Y" had failed him at a time when he could not
afford the regular fee. White appears again in the image of his
mother's china dishes out of reach in a china cabinet. His comment
about them was, "I never ate off them." The white pearls on black
velvet were worn at his mother's funeral. Her death in his arms
five years earlier had been a turning point in his life, and he had
also been disillusioned by the hypocrisy of several members of her
family at the funeral. His helplessness to prevent her death may
relate symbolically to the image from childhood of the disappear-
ance of the picture from a black and white TV set which someone had
just turned off. In two different sessions Frank reported images
of white milk bottles at the hospital where he worked. The first
time his comment later was, "Almost like watching black and white
TV." This image confirms the symbolic association between nurturance and both the color white and black and white TV. His comment
the second time was, "You can see through them." This comment
gives a clue to the possible meaning of a number of images involving transparency. The one included here was of a group of trans-
parent faces to which his association was, "I can see through people." In Frank's lifelong struggle not to be deceived and disappointed by people, he frequently took pride in his ability to
"see through and not be fooled by" their facades and their hypocrisy. Thus, it becomes more understandable why in this group of
images there is the repeating theme of eyes, watching, looking at,
and seeing through. This leads us back to where we began with
Frank's repeated concern while experiencing these extremely vivid
images of what is real and what is not real. In this regard, his
comments about the image of the parrot with a ruby for an eye are
very important for the emphasis I have put here on deception. His
associations included the following:

> I just know where that's from. I thought it was real.
> It might have been; I might have seen that in some kind
> of art show, or something . . . I don't think it was
> real, though . . . the thing that stood out was the eye.

From time to time, after having experienced a particularly vivid
image (which, while he was "seeing" it, he believed was "real"),
Frank wondered whether his mind had not actually gone; for example,
to the art gallery where the parrot with a ruby eye was on display
as a piece of sculpture. From these comments it became evident
that the images of beautiful stuffed animals with glass eyes

represent the beautiful images he "sees," but later realizes were
not real objects, not real living animals as they appeared to be,
but only hallucinations which he was fooled into believing were
real. The beautiful fake eyes clearly represent the fact that his
"eyes" are deceived by images which are not the reality they appear
to be. Thus, the image of the parrot with the ruby eye seems to
be a picture symbol for hallucinated imagery. It is tempting to
ask why of all animals did he choose a parrot? One then realizes
that the parrot is one of the very few animals that can talk, and
then it is very hard not to assume that the image of the parrot
with a ruby eye is a symbol for the whole process of hallucinating
images and then reporting them out loud to an observer.

The importance of the theme of deception is further supported
by the story associated with the image of the mounted head of a
black Catalina goat which he had seen in the home of a friend. It
turns out that the friend did not actually hunt and kill the goat,
but came upon it already dead. Thus, the mounted head with its
glass eye was not only an imitation of a live goat, but also as a
hunting trophy it misrepresented its owner as a real hunter.

As another example of the nature of the symbolic process
involved in hypnagogic imagery, I want to discuss one more image
from this group, namely the black and white image of a pin-up girl
from Playboy. This image he saw upside-down. The original photo-
graph was printed in color, so Frank's seeing it in black and white
is consistent with a pin-up being not a real woman, but only a tantalizing picture of one. In addition, this suggests that he views
women in general as somehow deceptive and disappointing.

This image is the basis for understanding another symbolic
device in this picture language, namely, that when the image is
upside-down, there is an element of deception or disappointment in
its meaning. Also the phenomenon of several symbols representing
the same theme is an example of the aspect of condensation which
Piaget calls "polysymbolization."

It is tempting to suggest that Frank's hypnagogic imagery
represents a process that continues to be working through the death
of his mother at the same time as it struggles to find solutions to
his ongoing concerns about being deceived and disappointed. Remarkably enough, as we go on now to look at sequences of the images
that Frank reported, we will not only see how he symbolically con-
siders and reconsiders these and other related issues, but we will
also see symbolic representations of a variety of solutions to
these difficult issues as he repeatedly strives to master them.

THE INTERPRETATION OF SEQUENCES OF IMAGES

The group of images which I have just discussed alerted me to

the possibility that in Frank's picture language color itself
might be used in symbolic ways. Whereas the color white seemed to
be associated with his mother, the image of his father's green
Chevy suggested that perhaps the color green was similarly associated with his father. A list of images with green in them was
assembled and to my amazement another group of closely related
themes appeared which included the following:

A middle-aged man in a green work uniform.
This man in a uniform could be some kind of authority figure.
A Victorian lady in a greenish dress.
His roommate's green dress shift which he was
envious of.
A man with a steel hard hat and green pants standing in front of a gate. The man and the gate may be
blocking his way. This image reminds me of the "hard-
headed" members of Frank's doctoral committee who were
making it very difficult for him to complete his
dissertation.
The green Chevy his father had when he was a little
boy.
The green religious hat that the priest wore on
certain occasions when Frank was an altar boy. At that
time he was very much in awe of the priest.
A green neon Sears sign which reminded Frank of how
much he disliked Sears because he was fired from a job
there once.

It then occurred to me to see if I could find sequences of
images where both white, or black and white, and green appeared.
In the last three sessions I found the six sequences of images
which are shown in the next chart. When these sequences are lined
up in this way, many images which previously could not be interpreted now became meaningful. The sequences suggested a possible
meaning for the color red, and the sequences themselves, taken as
a group, all seemed to be saying something similar. I will now
trace through the symbolic structure that these sequences of images
appear to have.

The initial green image of each sequence seems to relate to
figures who either block his way, reject him, or whom he is envious of or in awe of. In each case the next image refers straight-
forwardly to some source of good nurturance, a sandwich, chairs
and tables in a cafeteria, cookies, research subjects who are
supplying him with the data he needs, and Gerber's baby cereal.
Interestingly enough, none of these images of apparently satisfactory nurturance is white. But then something goes wrong. The
sandwich is followed by a riot on a black and white TV monitor in
another TV control room. The cafeteria is followed by a black and

white movie; white pearls on black velvet seen at a funeral replace the Christmas cookies. The white "Y" of the disappointing YMCA follows the helpful research subjects, and the Gerber's baby cereal is replaced by a can of an imitation fruit juice which Frank does not like. The doubly deceptive mounted goat's head and the doll's house furniture that imitates real furniture support the apparent meaning of this step in the sequence. Now the question arises as to what comes next. What comes next is the color red and a group of images that seem to be symbolic of the adult roles he has in his life. The red pistachio nuts he bought for himself the day of that session. The red-haired girl was a girl friend when he was working as a jazz musician. 225 was the room number of the laboratory where he worked as a graduate student. The red street sign pointed the way to the hospital where he worked. The nuts and bolts were at his father's hardware store where he worked one day a week without pay to help out his father. The red Christmas card refers to his relationship with his current girl friend, and the kitchen knives that he took care of seem to be symbolic of the help he gave his mother in the kitchen.

At the time when he was reporting these images, Frank's situation in graduate school paralleled to a remarkable degree the repeating progression of these sequences of symbolic themes. Frank was struggling with a very critical doctoral committee that he felt was making it much more difficult than necessary to complete his dissertation. Also he felt very strongly that his committee chairman, with whom he previously had a close relationship, and who had previously supported him in many ways, now had let him down when he needed him most by leaving the university and dropping out of academic life. He was now forced to complete his graduate work largely on his own.

Therefore, the sequences of symbolic images seem to be saying that when authority figures block his way and reject him, he has sources of support that he can fall back on. However, he can never trust those who have helped him before, no matter how loyal and dependable they might have appeared, and in the end he can trust only himself, and in the end he will have to survive and succeed on his own.

In more developmental terms, the imagery suggests that Frank's strivings for mastery have been carrying him out of a life style where he was dependent on others and to that extent not in control. It further suggests that his goal is to instead take care of himself and others, and thereby attain an autonomy for himself and a control over others in a way that will protect him from being vulnerable to rejection and disappointment.

DISCUSSION

In this work it has been shown that subjects can learn to use
theta EEG feedback to remain for extended periods of time in altered
states of consciousness where they can experience and report brief,
involuntary hallucinated imagery. This confirms the earlier work
of such writers as Green et al. and Bertini et al.

This work has also confirmed my initial expectation that both
the appearance and the content of the imagery is exquisitely sensitive to the subject's relationship to many aspects of the experimental situation and especially to the subject's relationship to
the researcher conducting the study. The symbolic meanings are
very difficult to interpret in depth without an extensive collection of them gathered over time and without the subject's associations to them. Interpretation of the imagery can yield penetrat-
ing insights into the subject's core conflicts, perceptual styles,
and coping strategies.

The images appear to be structured according to the well-known
mechanisms proposed by Freud and are also consistent with the theories of the more recent writers I reviewed at the beginning of this
presentation. It has been especially significant to me to confirm
the early reports of "autosymbolic phenomena" in hypnagogic imagery
by Silberer.

From this in depth study of the hypnagogic imagery of two subjects, it seems reasonable to propose that hypnagogic imagery may
be a unique window on that point in human information processing
where the ongoing experience of the moment is converted into symbolic form, or at least where it is commented on in a symbolic
language that is remarkably unique to each person. This symbolic
picture language appears to use images from the past as well as the
present, and indeed it seems to the point of continuous interchange
between the past and the present using mechanisms of symbolic
processes.

In more metaphorical language, the flow of imagery seems like
the movement of a multidimensional fabric as it is woven on a loom
of information processing. This moving fabric seems to have a
structure and a continuity determined by the interweaving of a
variety of recurrent themes and issues from the recent and distant
past as they interact with the flow of immediate experience.

This loom seems to be kept moving both by the passage in time
of experience and by the endlessly repetitive creation and release
of tension which is created by apparently built-in mechanisms striving for conflict resolution, the solving of problems both new and
old, symbolic rehearsal of new behaviors, and striving towards
goals such as survival, mastery, and perhaps creativity, curiosity,

and play--and doing all these things seemingly simultaneously.

REFERENCES

Bertini, J., Lewis, H. B., and Witkin, H. A. Some preliminary
    observations with an experimental procedure for the study of
    hypnagogic and related phenomena. In C. T. Tart (Ed.), Altered
    states of consciousness. New York: Wiley, 1969. (Originally
    published, 1964.)

Breger, L. The meaning of dreams, Research Symposium #3, California
    Department of Mental Hygiene, 1969.

Breger, L. From instinct to identity. Englewood Cliffs, New Jersey:
    Prentice-Hall, 1974.

Brown, B. B. Recognition of aspects of consciousness through asso-
    ciation with EEG alpha activity represented by a light signal.
    Psychophysiology, 1970, 6, 442-452.

Budzynski, T., and Stoyva, J. M. An instrument for producing deep
    muscle relaxation by means of analog information feedback.
    Journal of Applied Behavior Analysis, 1969, 2, 231-237.

Davis, H., Davis, P. A., Loomis, A. L., Harvey, E. N., and Hobart, G.
    Human brain potentials during the onset of sleep. Journal of
    Neurophysiology, 1938, 1, 24-38.

Deikman, A. J. Bimodal consciousness. Archives of General Psychi-
    atry, 1971, 25, 481-489.

Dement, W. C., and Kleitman, N. The relation of eye movements dur-
    ing sleep to dream activity: an objective method for the study
    of dreaming. Journal of Experimental Physiology, 1957, 53,
    339-346.

Dement, W. C., and Kleitman, N. Cyclic variations in EEG during
    sleep and their relation to eye movements, body motility, and
    dreaming. Electroencephalography and Clinical Neurophysiology,
    1957, 9, 673-690.

Erickson, E. H. The dream specimen of psychoanalysis. Journal of
    the American Psychoanalytic Association, 1954, 2, 5-56.

Foulkes, D. Position paper presented to the Association for
    Psychophysiological Study of Sleep, San Diego, California,
    May, 1973.

Foulkes, D., and Fleisher, S. Mental activity in relaxed wakeful-
    ness. Journal of Abnormal Psychology, 1975, 84, 66-75.

Foulkes, D., and Vogel, G. Mental activity at sleep onset. Journal
    of Abnormal Psychology, 1965, 70, 231-243.

Foulkes, D., and Vogel, G. The current status of laboratory dream
    research. Psychiatric Annals, 1974, 4, 7-27.

French, T. N., and Fromm, E. Dream interpretation. New York:
    Basic Books, 1964.

Freud, S. The interpretation of dreams. New York: Basic Books,
    1953. (Originally published, 1900.)

Freud, S. Beyond the pleasure principle. In J. Strachey (Ed.),
    Standard edition of the complete psychological works of
    Sigmund Freud. London: Hogarth Press, Vol. 18, 1955.
    (Originally published, 1920.)
Green, E. E., Green, A. M., and Walters, E. D. Voluntary control
    of internal states: psychological and physiological. Journal
    of Transpersonal Psychology, 1970, 2, 1-26.
Griffiths, R. A study of imagination in early childhood. Psychol-
    ogy, 1970, 2, 1. (Originally published, 1935.)
Jung, C. G. Man and his symbols. London: Aldus Books, 1964.
Kamiya, J. Operant control of the EEG alpha rhythm and some of its
    reported effects on consciousness. In C. T. Tart (Ed.),
    Altered states of consciousness. Garden City, New York:
    Wiley, 1969.
Kubie, L. The use of induced hypnagogic reveries in the recovery
    of repressed amnesic data. Bulletin of the Menninger Clinic
    1943, 7, 172-182.
Maury, L.-F. Alfred. Le Sommeil et les Reves. Paris: Didier &
    Cie, 1878. (Originally published, 1848.)
Piaget, J. Play, dreams, and imitation in childhood. New York:
    Norton, 1962. (Originally published, 1951.)
Poe, E. A. Marginalia. Graham's American Monthly Magazine, 1846,
    28, 436.
Silberer, H. Report on a method of eliciting and observing certain
    symbolic hallucination phenomena. In D. Rapaport (Ed.),
    Organization and pathology of thought. New York: Columbia
    University Press, 1951, 195-207. (Originally published, 1909.)
Silberer, H. On symbol-formation. In D. Rapaport (Ed.), Organiza-
    tion and pathology of thought. New York: Columbia University
    Press, 1951, 208-233. (Originally published, 1909.)
Silberer, H. Hidden symbolism of alchemy and the occult arts. New
    York: Dover Publications, 1971. (Originally published, 1914.)
Stoyva, J. M. The public (scientific) study of private events.
    In E. Hartman (Ed.), Sleep and dreaming. Boston: Little
    Brown and Co., 1970, 353-368.
Stoyva, J. M. Biofeedback techniques and the conditions for hallu-
    cinatory activity. In F. J. McGuigan and R. A. Schoonover
    (Eds.), The psychophysiology of thinking. New York: Academic
    Press, 1973, 387-405.
Tart, C. T. Toward the experimental control of dreaming. In C. T.
    Tart (Ed.), Altered states of consciousness. Garden City,
    New York: John Wiley & Sons, 1969, 74-88.
Vogel, G. W. Invited comments on Foulkes' position paper, presented
    at the Association for Psychophysiological Study of Sleep, San
    Diego, California, May, 1973.
West, L. J. Hallucinations. In J. G. Howells (Ed.), Modern Per-
    spectives in World Psychiatry. Edinburgh: Oliver and Boyd,
    1968, 265-287.

FUNCTIONAL ATTRIBUTES OF MEDIATIONAL IMAGERY:

A DEVELOPMENTAL VIEW TOWARD HABILITATION OF RETARDED ADULTS

Dan Tomasulo, Ph.D.

Young Adult Institute and Yeshiva University

New York, New York

Abstract: Mental imagery can play a significant role when
teaching activities of daily living to retarded adults.
The technique of combining imagery instructions with pictures is discussed with an emphasis on those features which
facilitate memory and acquisition of the skill being
taught. The theoretical underpinning which accounts for
the effectiveness of the technique draws from the work of
A. Paivio, Z. Pylyshyn, G. Bower, K. Nelson and J. Piaget.
Experiments carried out by the authors show the developmental and facilitative nature of the technique. Proposed topics for research are discussed.

The study of mental imagery is a process which involves a
marriage between the poet and the scientist. The discussion of
mental imagery for the purpose of theoretical exploration becomes
merely an esoteric exercise if it does not have an observable
counterpart in reality. On the other hand, an experimental investigation of the imaginal process, for reasons which are important to
the mechanics of scientific thinking, necessarily reduce many of
the intriguing elements of mental imagery to understandable and
identifiable dependent variables.

The purpose of this paper is twofold. The first is to look
at the mental image with respect to the question of whether or not
it can be used as an irreducible psychological construct. Although
the various theoretical perspectives reviewed will not answer that
question definitively, they will initially broaden, then hopefully
focus our perspectives on the functional psychological values of
imagery. The second and obviously most important topic this paper

145

will cover is the practical uses of mental imagery with respect to
the particular population of retarded adults.

The conceptual models of mental imagery (Pylyshyn, 1973; Bower,
1972; Anderson and Bower, 1973), would suggest that the concept of
a particular object or idea is represented through the image. One
way we can experience feeling for this conceptual model is through
an imaginal representation of a zebra. We can quite readily repro-
duce a conceptually appropriate image which satisfies the request.
What is significant to note, however, is that we fail to incorporate
specific (propositional) information to this image. In our imaginal
representation of the zebra, we are aware that the image is
equipped with stripes. However, the question of how many stripes
the zebra has is not initially available. This is not because we
are unable to provide such information, but rather because the
imaginal representation of the concept need only provide general
cues in order for the concept to be retrieved. As a mnemonic
representation the mental image can be understood as a dependent
variable reflecting ·a static representation indicative of a known
concept. Brainard (1971) puts forth the image as a "dependent
variable" notion asserting that the picture-like qualities of the
image are conscious forms which signify the activation of the
representation.

The study of mental imagery is influenced by the type of yard-
stick we use to measure it. As cognitive psychology is interested
in learning what we know, it must intimately explore the problems
and virtues of relying on recall for verification. If we follow
the view that the image is not an irreducible psychological construct, then our use of memory to retrieve the image confounds what
we learn about the imaginal process. Did we recall an image of an
object as the result of previously associated attributes connected
to the object, or does the mental image in some way reflect a gross
indicator of mental operations used to define criteria for classification of an object?

Having raised the question of the origin of imagery in a mediational context, it would seem important to examine the possible
explanations for the facilitative effects of imagery instructions.
One explanation offered by Bower (1972) suggests that imagery
enhances associative connections between terms through a relational
organization. This interpretation is important in that it sets the
foundation for entertaining the functional attributes of imagery
terms which force the consideration of a perceptual-developmental
link. The framework within which such a proposal can be made is
begun by Bower's experiment where two imagery groups were compared.
One group was instructed to have the two imagined objects interact
while the other group received separation instructions. The
results indicated that, "The important component is the interactive
relation between the imagined objects" (Bower, 1972, p. 80). This

parallels the finding by Epstein, Rock and Zuckerman (1960) in
which it was found that two pictured objects are more easily associated when they are in a spatial interaction than when placed in
non-interacting positions. Rohwer (1966) found that nouns in a
paired associate learning task were recalled better when connected
by prepositions and verbs as opposed to connectives. Bower points
out that "this recall pattern with pictures, images and words is
probably being produced by the same relational generating system"
(p. 81).

The argument then is for relational organization as the facilitating property behind mental imagery. The interesting feature of
this argument is that it has used terminology and rationale which
is not unfamiliar. Katherine Nelson (1974) has proposed a conceptual model which accounts for a child's initial translation of
meanings into words. The basis of this model rests on the assumption that dynamic functional relations among objects are translated
into conceptual cores. The identificational features of these
cores are then labeled as the particular concept. The theory is
based in part on what is, coincidentally enough, known as the
Relational Concept theory. There seems to be a connection between
what Bower is proposing happens during imagery, and what Nelson is
proposing occurs during conceptual development prior to acquisition
of meaning.

Nelson suggests that when an infant develops a concept (and
the corresponding identificational image), the child's direct
experience with the object in the world accounts for an initial
appreciation of a dynamic functional attribute of the object (the
rolling quality of a ball, for instance), and subsequent appreciation of other dynamic functional attributes (bouncing and throwing).
Over time a synthesis of the various functional relations create
the core of the child's concept. This is important because it
identifies which elements are essential to the construction of a
meaningful image for the child, and consequently what attributes
are recalled during the retrieval of the object's image.

If we abstract what is being said by the conceptual-propositional theorist with respect to the origin of the mental image,
and incorporate what Nelson proposes as the process by which concepts develop, then we are left with an approach to understanding
the dynamics of how best to employ the mediational aspects of
mental imagery. To this end we may hypothesize that a highlighting
of the functional properties by displaying the object actively
using its functional attributes would be most effective in the
retrieval of the concept. This is essentially what occurs during
the sensori-motor period of cognitive development as outlined by
Piaget (1928). The young child's active engagement with the
environment fosters the understanding that the things which are
similar can be acted upon with similar sensori-motor schemes. Basic

categories are thereby established and a functional relationship
between the sensori-motor schemes and later preoperational and operational stages are developed. The important feature to note here
is that although the young child's use of mental imagery may serve
as a useful auxiliary to advance the knowledge of particular operational states, the extent to which a mental image may be employed
is limited to the stage of mental operations at which the individual
is functioning (Piaget and Inhelder, 1971).

We have discussed so far the parameters by which a mental image
of a concept may be more effectively retrieved and to what factors
the use of a mediational image may be limited (such as level of
cognitive functioning).

Having dealt with the dynamics of the origin of the mental
image, we now need to explore those theories which deal with the
psychological significance of the phenomena. In particular, those
theories which outline the functional aspects of mediational imagery
will be discussed.

Paivio's "Conceptual Peg Hypothesis" (1971) proposes that the
more concrete the stimulus term in a paired association, the better
(stronger) the associated response will be. The concreteness of
the stimulus member is rated as having an imagery value. This
value relates to the degree to which mental imagery acts as a mediator in the association. As such, the more concrete the stimulus
member, the higher its imagery value and consequently, the stronger
the response is associated to the stimulus. In the paired associate arrangement, the stimulus term functions as a "peg" to which
its associated response is paired in learning trials. The main
characteristic of the Conceptual Peg Hypothesis is that it predicts
that the more concrete the stimulus term, the higher its imagery
arousing value and consequently, the better the recall of the
response item. On a continuum from the most to the least concrete
(having the least image arousing value) are objects, pictures of
objects, concrete nouns and abstract nouns. An example of the
continuum would be: an apple, a picture of an apple, the word
"apple," and the abstract classification of "fruit." It is reasonable to assume that cognitive processes involved would differ
depending on the nature (concreteness of the stimulus). Using a
picture (e.g., line drawing) of an object as an example, it would
have to attain a certain degree of meaningfulness before it could
be used to hook an association on. As Ausubel (1968) has proposed,
the conditions which surround meaning are concerned with symbolically expressed ideas being related in a non-arbitrary, substantive
fashion to what the learner knows. This view has as its corner-
stone the assumption that what is meaningful is in some way related
to what is known. The line-drawn picture is a representational
learning, the line-drawn stimulus member is the new material to be
learned, and the conceptual representation of the object which is

being imagined would reflect existing knowledge. Within this theoretical structure, the meaningfulness of the line-drawn stimulus
is a function of the individual's previous experience of the object.
It would then seem that the closer or better the representation of
the line drawing to the real object, the more readily the image of
the object will be aroused. The concreteness value of the image
(and consequently its mediational strength) is related to a lack
of ability of the stimuli (because of its abstractness or ambiguity)
to effectively arouse a representational image. As the image in
Paivio's theory is an irreducible psychological construct, the
emphasis is focused on finding the minimal perceptual (visual)
qualities (i.e., color, size, orientation, etc.), as well as the
minimal cognitive abilities (i.e., attention, memory, etc.) which
will evoke the image. Again, if we integrate the information we
have gathered from reviewing the other theories, we are able to fit
with Paivio's theory possible features which will evoke the image
in a more efficient and effective manner. Specifically, we are
now able to know that line drawings (pictures) have a high imagery
arousing value because (according to Paivio) they are considered to
be more concrete than word labels. If we add the work of Pylyshyn,
Bower and Nelson to this information, we would hypothesize that
depicting an object in an inter-active functioning position by
using line drawings would evoke a stronger mediational image than
if objects were depicted in a static, non-interactive state.

When the mental retardation literature relevant to the question of mediational strength of the image was reviewed, an article
by Ashford and Baumeister (1977) was found to have explored some
of the above issues. Their article suggests that less intelligent
individuals may use less efficient stimulus selection strategies
than their more intelligent counterparts. They hypothesized that
an elaboration linking the stimulus and response terms in PA learning would facilitate integration of the entire stimulus compound
and as such, provide a functional cue for forming associations.
In terms of the two attentional orientations, it appears that
Ashford and Baumeister find that "elaboration of the entire stimulus compound" rather than "fractionation" is most appropriate.

The predictions which follow from this reasoning are that:

1. Faster learning will occur with interactive stimulus
components as opposed to non-interactive components.

2. A greater probability that all components of the interactive conditions will elicit the correct response.

3. Higher functioning regarded subjects will integrate components within an interactively depicted stimulus compound.

Less intellectually able subjects can be expected to cue-select on the basis of fractionation of the compound rather than elaboration. The major finding in the study is that the higher functioning retarded individuals (unfortunately the authors do not mention the chronological age of their subjects) generates functional cues for learning. This elaboration effect is developmentally related in that the less intelligent individuals do not appear to use the thematic nature of the interactive pictures as a functional cue in PA learning. The authors were led to the conclusion "that inter-active stimulus component depiction produces increased utilization of the stimulus compounds as meaningful units by retarded persons, the degree of increase being directly related to developmental level." As such, it would seem that the functional depiction of the stimulus term would be an important feature in highlighting the stimulus member in the picture to paired associate method.

This assumption was examined in a pilot study (Tomasulo, 1978) where two groups of retarded adults were matched for IQ and sex, and were presented with line drawn pictures of objects in a paired associate learning design. In one group imagery instructions were given which highlighted the functional attributes of the stimulus member in an interactive manner with the response member. (As an example, the stimulus picture of a boat would be associated to the response picture of an apple by asking the subject to imagine the apple in the boat floating on the water.) In the other group, imagery instructions, which did not highlight the functional properties of either member, were given and an association linking the members together was asked for. As an example, the uses of a boat and the properties of an apple would be discussed but no specific reference was made for the subject to imagine the functional properties in particular being amplified in the association.

The results were obtained by computing the correct number of anticipations made by each subject in each group after being presented with the stimulus picture. A highly significant main effect ($F = 11$, $p < .01$) was found between the two groups. This clearly indicated the effectiveness of imagery as a mediator with retarded adults when the functional attributes of represented objects are highlighted. Thus, it seemed that the elements outlined by Nelson which account for the development of a conceptual representation of an object when presented in line with Paivio's Conceptual Peg Hypothesis significantly improve the memory of retarded adults. This suggests that if we view an image in the same manner as the conceptual-propositional theorists (Bower, 1972; Anderson and Bower, 1973; Pylyshyn, 1973), a potentially systematic approach toward strengthening the psychological significance of the image may be introduced.

But how does this help retarded adults?

Independent functioning skills are the most important of all

adaptive behaviors. The goal of independence in teaching such
skills is not easily achieved. Skills which are taught on one day
are not readily recalled by retarded students the next. Training
on such self-help skills usually requires repetitive demonstrations
by the trainers over long periods of time.

Common sense would indicate that those retarded individuals
whose memory is functionally superior should achieve the goal of
independence more readily than their less retentive peers. It follows that those who can learn to improve their memory will also
improve their potential to become functionally autonomous. In the
same vein, those retarded individuals who would best profit from
vocational skills training programs would be taught more efficiently
and more rapidly if they were better able to employ their memory.

A pictorial method of teaching porter skills to mentally
retarded adults was developed in an effort to achieve the goal of
vocational competence in this area (Tomasulo, 1976). Essentially,
particular cleaning tasks were analyzed into their component parts,
clustered into meaningful "chunks" of behavior, and associated to
line draw pictures which represented the particular portion of the
task being taught. After learning the components of the particular
portion of the task, and making the association to the picture, a
series of learned tasks could be recalled and ultimately a wide
variety of porter skills could be followed throughout.

The initial success with such teaching methods prompted the
development of more elaborate and comprehensive picture training
systems. To accomplish this, a wide variety of functional skills
(e.g., grooming and hygiene, ironing, dishwashing, etc.) were
analyzed and clustered for picture presentation. Although this
represented the extension of an effective method, it was obvious
that an examination of the essential elements of the system would
be needed in order to identify and elaborate the mechanics of its
success.

Tomasulo, Sullivan and Biango (1978), and Robinson-Wilson
(1977) introduced explicit instructions for employing particular
picture association models (hair washing and individual recipes,
respectively). The significant feature highlighted by these
articles is the fact that those who were being taught the skill
would be able to follow through independently once they have
learned to associate the tasks to the pictures. Many of the suggestions which have been outlined above were employed when the functional skills training program by Tomasulo et al. (1978) was introduced. We found that once a particular skill had been taught using
the pictures, it was able to be maintained simply by having the
student use the pictures as cues.

The emphasis now has been to abstract information from the

existing programs and research with the hopes of generating an even
more effective training method. The most notable feature to date
which seems worthy of investigation is a phenomenon found during
the pilot study (Tomasulo, 1978). The researchers found that when
particularly absurd and comical imagery instructions were given to
the subjects, there almost always seemed to be a stronger association and higher recall for the response card. We hypothesized that
if an absurd image could be recalled better than a non-absurd image,
the factors which account for the effect should somehow be linked
to the dynamics of the interaction of the images. If we follow the
information we have used to date, then it would seem best to look
at how the absurd images address the functional properties of the
objects. When we reviewed the imagery instructions we had given
the subjects, we found that in the case of the absurd image we
asked for an interaction between two objects which defies the
natural function of the objects. As an example, the two objects
mentioned before (an apple and a boat), were instructed to interact
together in an absurd manner. The apple sitting in the boat as the
boat floats on the water creates what I have called a "thematic
dissonance." The common function of the boat is not to carry an
apple, just as the apple was not meant to be a passenger in the
boat. The creation of the image where the two interact in the
present manner does not allow for a known thematic label to be
given to the image. The uniqueness of the interaction of the
objects is a matter of their not having complementary thematic
functions.

We also noticed that it seemed the higher functioning subjects
(according to such measures as IQ and Adaptive Behaviors) were the
ones who were able to appreciate the thematic dissonance by laughing
at the absurdity of the image. As such, the testing of the strength
of absurd images will be done using a comparison between mildly and
severely retarded adults on a variety of paired associate learning
tasks where interactive line drawings will depict objects employing
their natural function (i.e., a foot going into the shoe); the
object interacting in a mildly absurd manner (a hand going into the
shoe); and finally, the object interacting in a highly absurd manner (a hammer going into the shoe). We would expect that the higher
functioning subject would profit most from the high absurd imagery
while the lower functioning subject would do best with the object
depicted in its natural functional role. If this is true, a developmental trend towards an increased appreciation of thematic dissonance can be established. This would allow for a training program
where self-generated mnemonics could be gradually introduced to
recall a sequential learning of new skills. The teaching of
retarded adults to self-generate an implicit mnemonic cue seems a
most worthy pursuit toward the goal of totally independent
functioning.

While the above-stated research is the current interest for

this author, there are a variety of research questions related to the present topic which need to be investigated. The following are proposed suggestions:

1. Experimenter-imposed awareness of functional attributes vs. subject-generated awareness of functional attributes. A study by Borys (1978) found that free recall in experimenter-imposed conditions of verbal and imaginal elaborations was superior to subject-generated condition. A further investigation of this effect could be extended to include an elaboration on functional attributes of pictured objects which can be imposed by the experimenter for one mixed group of high and low-functioning subjects, and self-generated for another mixed group (that is, that elaborations on what functions the object serves would be drawn into the subject's state of awareness through a series of questions asked by the experimenter). I would hypothesize that lower-functioning subjects will have significant difficulty with self-generated awareness imagery elaborations; and consequently, they will do poorly in a test of free recall. While they will probably score better with the experimenter-imposed elaborations, they will not score nearly as well as the high-functioning group. If the stated results are found, a training program which would help low-functioning clients improve their memory could be designed. One way of achieving this would be through directed interaction with the actual object in question; elaboration on the functional attributes of the object by the trainer; and a stating of these functional attributes by the client after interaction with the object and hearing the elaborations by the trainer. This would hopefully foster an awareness of the object's function which would serve to improve memory.

2. The use of imagery to promote operational relations through anticipation of object function.

Piaget and Inhelder's imagery experiments with children (1971) were seen as indicative of a particular level of functioning (preoperational, concrete operational, etc.). These experiments could then be used to screen high (concrete operational) from low (preoperational) retarded adult subjects. This should correlate to high and low IQ and adaptive behavior scores.

Objects, but not their anticipated function (wheel rolling, pitcher pouring, match burning, etc.) would be presented to the two groups. It is hypothesized that higher-level subjects will have significantly better anticipation of function scores than their low-functioning counterparts. This would be predicted from Piaget's discussion which suggests that anticipatory images are limited by cognitive structures.

Once again, if the stated results are obtained, a training program (similar to the one previously mentioned) would be designed

for use with low-functioning clients. The goal would be for the
clients to be able to match a static representation of an object
with a correct depiction of the object employing its primary function. A retest of the trained group when compared to a control
group on Piaget and Inhelder's experiments would be hypothesized to
show that a greater number of imagery tasks could be completed correctly than was previously possible. This would be indicative of
a change in operations (most likely from pre-operational to concrete
operations). Such a finding would be important because it supports
the intuitive notion that training directly on the adaptive behaviors will somehow improve the overall functioning ability of the
individual.

REFERENCES

Anderson, R., and Bower, G. Human associative memory. Washington,
    D.C.: V. H. Winston and Son, 1973.
Ashford, A., and Baumeister, A. Processing of interactive and non-
    interactive pictures in PA learning by retarded persons.
    American Journal of Mental Deficiency, 1977, 82(2), 187-193.
Ausubel, D. Educational psychology--a cognitive view. New York:
    Holt, Rinehart and Wilson, 1968.
Bower, G. H. Mental imagery and associative learning. In . Gregg
    (Ed.), Cognition in learning and memory. New York: Wiley,
    1972.
Borys, S. Effect of imposed vs. self-generated imagery and sentence
    mediation on the free recall of retarded adolescents. American
    Journal of Mental Deficiency, 1978, 83(3), 307-310.
Brainard, C. J. Imagery as a dependent variable. American
    Psychologist, 1971, 26, 599-600.
Epstein, W., Rock, I., and Zuckerman, C. B. Meaning and familiarity
    in associative learning. Psychological Monographs, 1960, 74,
    (4, Whole No. 491).
Nelson, K. Concept, word and sentence: inter-relations in acqui-
    sition and development. Psychological Review, July, 1974, 81
    (4).
Paivio, A. Imagery and verbal processes. New York: Holt, Rine-
    hart and Winston, 1971.
Piaget, J. Judgment and reasoning in the child. New York:
    Harcourt, Brace and World, 1928.
Piaget, J., and Inhelder, . Verbal imagery in the child. London:
    Routledge and Kegal Paul, 1971.
Pylyshyn, Z. What the mind's eye tells the mind's brain: a
    critique of mental imagery. Psychological Bulletin, July,
    1973, 80(1).
Robison-Wilson, M. Picture recipe cards as an approach to teaching
    severely and profoundly retarded adults to cook. Education
    and Training of the Mentally Retarded, February, 1977, 12(1).

Tomasulo, D. Imagery as a mediation in PAL with retarded adults,
    unpublished manuscript.
Tomasulo, D., Sullivan, A., and Biango, N. Pictures as cues for
    functional skills training, unpublished manuscript.

II: PSYCHO-IMAGINATION THERAPY

A GROUP STUDY USING THE GROUP SHORR IMAGERY

TEST AS THE TOOL OF OUTCOME THERAPY

Gail E. Sobel, M.A.

Institute for Psycho-Imagination Therapy

Los Angeles, California

For the past 10 years the Department of Psychology at Los Angeles City College has offered a course entitled Group Dynamics I as part of the Human Services curriculum. The testees in this two-group study were first or second year students at the college during the fall semester of 1977, and participants in the Human Services program.

The purpose of this study was to examine the effectiveness of the group dynamics process in one classroom setting, by assessing any notable changes in the level of conflict expressed by the subjects over a 20-week semester.

The experiment group (E) was devised of students enrolled in the group dynamics experience, while the control group (C) subjects were not. A test-retest design was applied to the groups which were comprised as follows:

Experiment Group I (enrolled in Group Dynamics Class)

Number of Subjects: 24

Mean Age: 28 years, 3 months

Male: 3

Female: 21

Ethnic Constitution: White, 12; Black, 10; Latin, 2

Control Group II   (enrolled in Human Services Curriculum but
   not presently in a Group Dynamics Class)

Number of Subjects: 16

Mean Age: 30 years, 4 months

Male: 4

Female: 12

Ethnic Constitution: White, 5; Black, 4; Latin, 7

The E groups consisted of 12 members each that met twice weekly
for 50 minutes each session for 15 weeks. Additionally, each group
participated in two eight-hour marathons during a 20-week semester.
Students were encouraged to openly share their feelings and concerns
with and about each other. Preliminary exercises were practiced in
the first three weeks, and the final weeks were reserved for reviewing of the class experience.

The tool of measurement used was a projective test in the tradition of the Rorschach, entitled Group Shorr Imagery Test (GSIT)
(Shorr, 1976).

The GSIT is a group administered projective test of adult personality developed in 1974-75 by Dr. Joseph E. Shorr and his associates at the Institute for Psycho-Imagination Therapy in Los
Angeles. Dr. Shorr is a noted author, lecturer and clinical psychologist who has spent 15 years in the development of psychotherapy through imagery. His previous work in developing the concepts of Dual Imagery, Task Imagery, Self Imagery, Body Imagery,
etc., have shown the importance of visual imagery as an indicator
of personality conflicts.

The GSIT is called an Imagery Test, not because the quality
or quantity of a subject's imagery is measured, but because visual
imagery is the projective device used to elucidate and score various areas of personality with major emphasis on conflicting issues
(Shorr, 1976). The authors believe that unconscious conflicts are
a major source of psychological disturbances within individuals and
that the presence of such conflicts is graphically illuminated and
brought to awareness by the test items.

The test consists of 15 items in which the testee is asked to
imagine a particular situation and then to expand upon the image
evoked. The items were selected based on clinical experience, as
being those that accurately reflect areas of emotional conflict.

Because the test seeks out the phenomenological world of each subject, their particular level of intelligence, within reasonable boundaries, does not limit its use. It is not culture-bound, and therefore is not restricted .to any particular social, economic or cultural level.

The test was administered to the subjects by the use of a pre-recorded tape that is part of the test kit. The subjects responded in writing to each imaginary situation on the corresponding record blank. The testees were encouraged to close their eyes, since closed eyes seem to allow for a better flow of imagery, although this was not an absolute requirement.

It was emphasized that the GSIT is not a test of knowledge and that there are no right or wrong answers. Subjects were also encouraged to report the first image that came to mind, although some editing does not effect the test results since all images are the unique production of the individual.

The following examples of some test items and a brief explanation of the areas of conflict they are thought to illuminate are included to clarify for the reader.

Item 3, Forces: "Imagine that above you and behind you is a force. What is the force? How are you in relationship to the force? Can you humanize the force?"

The forces above and behind usually relate to authoritative forces with which the person is in conflict. Humanizing the forces concretely identifies them, allowing for possible confrontation.

Item 6, Gold Throne: "Imagine being seated on a gold throne and tell me what you see, what you do, and what you feel."

This items refers to the person's ability or lack of ability to accept power or authority for himself, to deal with that power, and to deal with conflicts about being or not being powerful.

Item 8, Mirror: "Imagine looking into a mirror and seeing some-one other than yourself. Whom do you see? Say something to that person and have that person make a statement back to you. Now have each person (mirror image and self) finish the following sentences:

I feel _____
Best adjective to describe me _____
I wish _____
I must _____
I secretly _____
I need _____   I will _____

This item is thought to be getting at the individual's conflict with a significant other or with a significant part of the self.

The test was first administered to Group I (E) and Group II (C) during the week beginning September 26, 1977, and each group was retested the week of January 23, 1978. The same classroom was used and every effort was made to duplicate the environment to reduce the possible introduction of disruptive variables. The testing time for both groups was approximately 55 minutes.

All subjects were told that their participation was voluntary, that they might stop at any time, and that their records forms required only an identification number for test-retest comparison. Additionally, it was explained that the purpose of the study was to examine the effectiveness of the group dynamics experience and that they would be viewed as a group rather than as individuals.

It was suggested the subjects close their eyes before each test item was presented, to then experience their particular imagery in response, and, only upon completion of that process, to open their eyes and fill in the corresponding blank on the record form.

Ninety-five volunteers took part in the initial September testing, and 52 subject's participated in the January retest. Several factors may have contributed to the large reduction in the number of retest subjects. Perhaps too much time elapsed between the tests, resulting in a lack of interest on the part of the subjects, anxiety during or following the first test experience, absenteeism or the 35% attrition rate typical at Los Angeles City College. Of the total number tested and retested, 80 protocols were usable for the purposes of this study.

The scoring of any projective test is, to a certain extent, subjective. However, a 1977 test-retest study involving 104 psychology undergraduates at San Diego University showed the following results:

The GSIT was administered to 104 introductory psychology students at San Diego State University. The test was administered again five weeks later. Each session lasted approximately one hour and consisted of a tape-recorded administration of the GSIT, which was filled out individually by the subjects. The resulting protocols were divided among the four investigators and scored according to the criteria presented in the GSIT Manual (Shorr, 1976). Five of the six inter-rater reliabilities of the investigators were significant, r (8) = .65, .65, .71, .76, and .88, p < .05 or better.

To establish interscore reliability of my own scoring results, I employed the expertise of an associate, experienced in the administration and scoring of the GSIT. Using a random sample of 12 protocols scored for comparison, the results yielded a correlation between two scorers of R = .99 (Chart 1).

CHART 1

Group I (E)

Subject	Test Score 9/27/77	Retest Score 1/26/78
4	72 (70)	61 (61)
9	76 (77)	59 (60)
14	77 (77)	70 (68)
17	60 (63)	63 (64)
20	52 (53)	52 (50)
22	63 (64)	59 (59)

*My findings in parentheses.

Group II (C)

Subject	Test Score 9/27/77	Retest Score 1/26/78
2	73 (74)	71 (73)
5	71 (71)	68 (68)
7	60 (62)	60 (60)
10	48 (49)	49 (51)
12	51 (51)	55 (55)
15	58 (59)	58 (57)

*My findings in parentheses.

Each conversation and each list of sentence completions on all the protocols was scored for degree of conflict. (Each image must be scored separately based on its own merits, avoiding any effect from previous images.) The five scoring levels are:

		Score
P1	A positive response	1
C1	A conflict response	2
C2	An increased conflict response	3
C3	A severe conflict response	4
C3*	An extreme conflict response	5

C1 is scored when there is evidence of some conflict in the response. C2 is scored when there is overt conflict in the response. C3 is scored when there is severe conflict in the response. C3* is scored when images of blood, mutilation, suicide or murder occur, or when the subject refuses to answer in a dangerous situation (GSIT Manual, 1976). The scoring sheet is laid out so that conflict scores can easily be converted to number scores and the number scores added to produce a quantitative conflict score. The higher the total score, the conflicted the individual is considered to be. The minimum possible score on the GSIT is 21 and the maximum is 105.

Examples of scoring criteria for each item, and all possible levels of response are included in the test manual.

As previously stated, my intent, when selecting this project for investigation, was to examine and evaluate by testing, any measurable conflictual level reduction effect by the class process called "Group Dynamics" at Los Angeles City College. I chose the Group Shorr Imagery Test as the tool of measurement because it is a test with which I have had a great deal of experience, it is easily administered to groups, and because I felt a measure of degree of conflict to be an appropriate reflection of possible change in individuals as a result of group process.

The selection of student subjects, enrolled in the same program but not in the same class, seemed, at the onset of the study, to allow for little variance between the E and C groups. When compiled, however, the data resulting from the first test reflected a significant difference between the groups prior to the experiment, T = 2.09 < .05, invalidating the original E and C test model.

The E group was then compared to itself before and after the group dynamics experience (test-retest results) and found to be

significantly changed, $T = 2.75 < .05$, $R = .78$. The C groups
results, on the other hand, when compared over time, showed no significant difference, $T = 1.89 > .05$, $R = .96$.

In other words, the data reflects that even though the E and C
groups were not well matched for experimental purposes, the subjects
enrolled in the group process class (E) did show marked reduction
in their measurable level of conflict, while those not participating
in the class (C) did not. When the quantitative scores of the E
group were viewed individually, 19 out of 24 subjects scored lower
levels of conflict.

This examiner is led to conclude that the group dynamics class
did have a positive impact on the majority of subjects, and that the
effect was measurable by the assessment device.

Felton (1976), in his article about the class entitled, "The
Vital Classroom," states:

> I have found that through the use of such a course, stu-
> dents discover they have power, strength and responsibil-
> ity for what they do and what happens to them. For most
> community college students such feelings are new and often
> scary, although exciting. Particularly because of the
> high minority-ethnic population at Los Angeles City Col-
> lege, most students are accustomed to believing and feel-
> ing themselves to be powerless and victimization-prone.
> Thus, when they discover their own power and control over
> their personal lives, they see and then expand great new
> horizons for themselves in their intra-psychic and inter-
> personal relating behaviors.

As with any test, the usefulness of the GSIT can be assessed
in terms of scoring consistency. My findings, coupled with the
results of the San Diego State University study, show the test
capable of an unusually high degree of inter-score reliability and
that the procedures for administration and scoring are standardized. As such, the test is an invaluable projective tool for the
measurement of outcome therapy.

References

Felton, G. The vital classroom. Education, Summer, 1976, 96(4).
Los Angeles City College Catalogue, 1976.
Shorr, J. E. Psycho therapy through imagery. New York: Inter-
    continental Medical Book Corporation, 1974.
Shorr, J. E. Manual for the Shorr Imagery Test, Los Angeles, Ca.,
    1976.

USE OF THE SHORR IMAGERY TEST WITH A

POPULATION OF VIOLENT OFFENDERS

David Tansey, Ph.D.

Private Practice
San Diego Group
San Diego, CA.

ABSTRACT

The Shorr Imagery Test (SIT) was administered to 17
violent offenders incarcerated at the California
Institute for Men in Chino, California. The results
were used in three ways: first, to confirm or deny from
quantitative data what Yochelson says makes up "criminal
thinking"; second, to describe the population in terms
of structural difference found in the results; and
third, to quantitatively describe four of the modal
members of the population on items where their conflict
scores differ from the general population norms·.

INTRODUCTION

The Shorr Imagery Test (1) is a projective measure of individual personality. It can be quantitatively scored for degree of
conflict and for several other kinds of structural data. It can
be used qualitatively for personality description. In this paper
we use each of these three facets of the test to examine the personalities of men incarcerated for a variety of violent criminal
offenses.

METHOD

Subjects: the subjects were 17 men incarcerated in the
California Institute for Men, a medium security prison at Chino.
All had been convicted of violent crimes such as murder, rape or

Table 1

Response Frequencies for Sentence Completions

	Standard	Criminal	z
"Never refer to me as . . . "			
Bad or Controlling Character	39	29	0.80
Stupid, Inadequate or Insane	29	47	1.50
No Identity	18	12	0.61
Racially or Sexually Negative	7	6	0.15
Physical or Sexual	4	0	0.84
Non-characterological	3	6	0.64
"Worse than loneliness is. . ."			
Negative Reaction to or in Self	31	24	0.59
Lack of Others	27	59	2.67**
Non-characterological	18	18	–
Too many Others or Others in a Negative Situation	12	0	1.51
Negative Reaction from Others	8	0	1.21
"No one can repair the damage caused by. . ."			
Feeling Helpless or Hopeless	40	12	2.24**
Significant Others	25	12	1.18
Self or Self-Blame	16	35	1.89**
Significant Situation	12	35	2.49**
Unspecified Others	5	6	0.17
No Response or Reject	3	0	0.72
"My Whole Life is Based on Proving. . ."			
Something Specific About Myself (Others not mentioned)	50	71	1.62
Myself or My Identity	23	24	0.09
Abstract Generalization	18	6	1.25
Nothing	5	0	0.94
Something Specific About Myself to Others (Others Mentioned)	4	0	0.84

$*p < .05$
$**p < .01$

aggravated assault. They were volunteers who had been told that
participation would not reflect on their records and that individual
results would not be shared with them or with the prison administration. They did not differ significantly in age from the standard
population.

Procedure: the SIT was administered individually to the subjects. The resultant data were used in three ways.

1. "Criminal thinking". Ten "thinking errors characteristic
of criminals," as described by Yochelson and Samenow (1976), seemed
amenable to verification with the SIT. The conflict and frequency
tabulation data that might support Yochelson and Samenow's ideas
were compared against the results from the standardized population.

2. Structural data. The SIT data from the subject population
was compared with the standardization population. Differences were
examined and analyzed.

3. Modal subjects. Protocols of four subjects were selected
where their conflict scores on items found to differ from the
standardization population matched those of the subject population.
Qualitative personality descriptions were developed based on these
items.

RESULTS

"Criminal thinking": Volume 1 of the Yochelson series contains
a list of 47 "thinking errors characteristic of the criminal." Ten
of these seemed amenable to verification with the SIT.

We shall take up each of the thinking errors that seemed vari-
fiable in order.

1. Yochelson says a criminal's worst fears are of apprehen-
sion, bodily injury or put down. If we accept that the sentence
completion, "Worse than loneliness is _____," reveals the subject's
worst fear, we would expect "non-characterological" or "negative
reaction from others" would be more frequent in our criminal population. As Table 1 shows, there was no statistical difference in
these proportions observed. Actually, in 59 percent of the subjects
our incarcerated criminal population could think of nothing worse
than loneliness. This response was significantly more frequently
given (.27, .59, p < .01) by the criminal subjects. We may speculate that the isolation from freedom and significant others of a
prison rather than Yochelson and Samenow's paroled or not guilty by
reason of insanity hospital population leads to the difference.
Yochelson suggests that criminal loneliness really means boredom
and action-wanting, rather than missing the warmth and enjoyment of

companionship for its own sake.

2. Yochelson says the criminal oscillates between a "zero state" in which he believes he is, is known to be by all others, and will always be a nothing; and being "tops." In the zero state he feels worthless, helpless, futile and blazingly angry but with no despair or psychomotor retardation. When "tops" he knows all, owns all and can accomplish anything. If we accept that the small box reveals how a person feels about his inner self or core, the inner aspects of himself, we would expect more conflict for the criminal sample than in our standard population. As Table 2 shows, this is not observed (2.91, 3.12, n.s.). If we accept that the image outside relates to two parts of self-image in this instance, we would expect more conflict for the criminal sample than in our standard population. As Table 2 implies, a trend in this direction

Table 2

Item Mean Conflict Scores

Item	Standard Population M	s.d.	Criminal Population M	s.d.	t
1 S	2.59	0.81	2.94	0.83	-1.66
1 C	3.14	0.82	3.47	0.62	-1.59
2 L	2.73	0.78	3.24	0.44	-2.63**
2 M	2.75	0.81	2.71	0.85	0.19
2 S	2.91	0.84	3.12	0.70	-0.98
3	2.79	0.99	3.29	0.59	-2.03*
4	3.04	0.96	3.12	0.78	-0.33
5 S	2.62	0.98	3.00	0.94	-1.50
5 I	2.69	0.88	3.12	0.49	-1.96a
5 0	2.85	0.83	3.24	0.66	-1.85a
6	2.25	1.04	1.76	0.75	1.87a
7	1.93	0.99	1.65	0.70	1.12
8 S	2.31	1.05	2.41	1.00	-0.37
8 S	2.86	0.88	3.18	0.53	-1.46
8 0	2.81	0.94	3.12	0.60	-1.32
9	2.63	1.36	3.35	1.27	-2.06*
10	2.67	1.12	2.88	1.11	-0.72
11	2.17	1.20	1.71	0.99	1.51
13	2.51	0.84	2.53	0.80	-0.09
14	2.92	0.93	3.00	0.79	-0.34

*p < .05
**p < .01
a_p < -1

is observed.   (Inner, 2.69, 3.12, p < .0515; Outer, 2.85, 3.24, p < .0655.)

3.   Yochelson says that "criminal pride" corresponds to an extremely and inflexibly high evaluation of oneself. It is the idea that one is better than others, even when this is clearly not the case; that one is a powerful, totally self-determining person. Maintaining and reinforcing this pride is a matter of psychic survival to him--were he to bend, he would break. If we accept that the large box reveals how we want to be seen in the world, the image we want unconsciously to cast, we would expect more conflict for the criminal sample than for our standard population. As Table 2 shows, this is observed (2.73, 3.24, p < .01). If we accept that the bridge size and gorge depth reveal something about the subject's achievement drives, we would expect that there would be trends toward longer bridges and deeper gorges. This is partially observed. There are no significant changes in the proportions of bridge sizes reported in the frequency tabulations of Table 3. More do put the depth of the gorge at infinity (.01, .12, p < .01) or give an unclassifiable answer (.03, .12, p < .05), and less give answers between 15 feet and less than 31 feet (.14, .00, p < .05).

4.   Yochelson says that "power thrusting"; an excitement seeking effort to move from the zero state to the state of being a powerful somebody is a characteristic of criminals. The observed increased conflict for our criminal sample in the large box also can support this notion. If we accept that the gold throne relates to the person's ability to accept and deal with power and with conflicts about being or not being powerful, we would expect more conflict for our criminal sample than the standard population. As Table 2 shows, this is not observed; if anything, the trend is in the other direction (2.25, 1.76, n.s.). We may speculate that the manipulative negative competition ascribed to criminals shows up about as often as the integrative, positive competition ascribed to noncriminals by Yochelson and Samenow.

5.   Yochelson says that criminals are perfectionistic, but only in areas of their choice. If we accept that the bridge image reveals the person's style of approaching difficult areas, we would expect more conflict in our criminal population than in the standard sample. As Table 2 shows, this is not observed (1.15, 1.93, n.s.). We may speculate that the image did not sufficiently tap into areas where the criminals chose to be perfectionistic with conflict.

6.   Yochelson says that criminals are loners because they consider themselves one of a kind. They are thrusting for power and trying to control others, secretive and exploitive. If we accept that the person who opens the closet door will be a significant other in the subject's life, we would expect that the criminal would open his own door more frequently than in our standard

Table 3

Frequency Tabulations

	Standard	Criminal	z
Item 4, How Big?			
Tiny, under 1/2"	1	0	0.41
1/2" - under 4"	17	12	0.52
4" - under 18"	24	29	0.45
18" - under 37"	33	29	0.33
37" - under 10'	8	6	0.29
10' and above	0	6	2.67**
Small	1	6	1.52
Medium	0	0	-
Large	5	0	0.94
Infinite	3	0	0.72
Unclassifiable	8	12	0.55
Item 4, How Far?			
Immediate, under 1'	4	6	1.38
1' - under 5'	14	18	0.44
5' - under 11', One floor	20	18	0.99
11' - under 20'	3	12	1.74*
20' - under 51'	11	0	1.44
51' and above	5	6	0.17
Small	0	6	2.67**
Medium	0	0	-
Large, very far	12	6	0.73
Infinite, can't see	25	24	0.09
Unclassifiable	6	6	-
Item 7, How Large?			
Under 15'	11	12	0.12
15' - under 31'	14	24	1.07
31' - under 100'	13	6	0.83
100' - under 600'	14	24	1.07
600' - under 1 mile	9	6	0.41
1 mile and above	12	6	0.73
Small	7	0	1.13
Medium	2	0	0.59
Large	9	18	1.15
Infinite	2	0	0.59
Unclassifiable	8	6	0.29

Table 3   (cont)

	Standard	Criminal	z
Item 7, How Deep?			
Under 15'	14	12	0.22
15' – under 31'	14	0	1.65*
31' – under 100'	8	18	1.33
100' – under 600'	20	29	0.85
600' – under 1 mile	11	6	0.63
1 mile and above	11	6	0.63
Small	3	0	0.72
Medium	0	0	–
Large	14	6	0.92
Infinite	1	12	2.78**
Unclassifiable	3	12	1.74*
Item 13, Who?			
Me, myself	24	24	–
Parent	21	0	2.09**
Spouse	14	12	0.22
Sibling	6	18	1.76*
Friend	19	6	1.32
Stranger, someone	8	12	0.55
Other relative	3	6	0.64
Personality	3	0	0.72
No one	2	6	0.99
Not closed	1	0	0.41

*$p < .05$
**$p < .01$

population. As Table 3 shows, this is not observed (.24, .24, n.s.). Rather, parents are significantly less likely (.21, .00, $p < .01$) and siblings are significantly more likely (.06, .18, $p < .05$) to open the door. However, there is no significant difference if we compare the proportion who believe any relative will open the door. We may speculate that the criminal feels he can control others still, so no differences show up.

7,8,9. Yochelson says the criminal says "I can't" when he does not want to do something or act responsibly; thus, he really means "I won't." Any they say the criminal portrays himself as a victim when he is held accountable for his deliberately irresponsible behavior, but that this is not a firm conviction. The overriding criminal characteristic is a lack of interest in responsible performance. If we accept that the sentence completion, "No one can repair the damage caused by _____" reveals the subject's feelings of hopelessness or helplessness about his problem or of his problems as internally or externally caused, we would expect our criminal population to take proportionately less responsibility and to feel more helpless. The opposite is observed in two of three proportionate changes. Our criminal population certainly feels less helpless or hopeless (.40, .12, $p < .01$) than our standard population. More feel personally to blame for their situations (.16, .35, $p < .01$). At the same time, they are more likely to blame a significant situation (.12, .35, $p < .01$) including three subjects who blame jail itself as their unrepairable cause. Evidently, our prisoner sample rejects helplessness and hopelessness and either accepts responsibility or avoids responsibility by blaming the situation. Since the zero state is not depressed, we should not be surprised that the criminals don't feel helpless or hopeless. If the men were being truthful or scoring points, accepting responsibility is an appropriate response in this situation. If they were playing the victim, they would blame the situation.

10. Yochelson says criminal thinking, with its fantasies, schemes and fears, is pervasive in the criminal's mind, invading every thought and coloring every action. If we accept that the SIT conflict score is a measure of the intensity of internal conflict, we would expect conflict would be higher for the criminals than for the standard population. As Table 4 shows, this is observed (56.24, 59.94, $p < .05$).

In summary, one of Yochelson and Samenow's suggestions concerning criminal personality is supported, six get partial or mixed support, and three are not supported.

Structural Data: what can we say about the criminal based on the SIT structural results. According to the Sentence Completion Response Frequency of Table 1, their worst fear is of being lonely, isolated from the company of significant others, as they are. They

Table 4

Total Conflict Score

	Standard Population	Criminal Population	t
N	118	17	
M	56.24	59.94	2.51*

*$p < .05$

reject helplessness and hopelessness and either accept responsibility with rather more conflict or avoid responsibility by blaming
situations. Let us consider the Tables 2 and 4 conflict data.
First, there is more conflict overall. From the large box it
appears that criminals have more conflict in the way they relate to
the world, their social manifestations of behavior or interaction.
According to the image of the force above and behind, they evidently experience more conflict with the press that surrounds them.
According to the image inside and outside which relates to self-
image, self-other concepts or inner versus outer conflicts, they
tend to have more conflict there. The image of the animal from
head and animal from guts indicates that our criminal population
has significantly more conflict in the interaction between intellect
and affect.

The differences in Frequency Responses are in Table 3. According to their size responses to the image of the hole in the floor,
our criminal population seems slightly more open to sexuality and
slightly closer to it, but also more concrete with a tendency to be
less human. The deeper gorge suggests that they see the dangers
involved in a task as greater without a significant increase in
rewards. They appear to have a significant relationship more likely
with a sibling than with a parent.

The differences in content responses reported in Table 5 are
several. The increased frequency of nonresponse suggests to me more
resistance or defiance. Three changes, increased non-response,
increased (H) response and decreased O response, are all on the
inner and outer image, suggesting this was a difficult image for
them to deal with. They were so busy denying or depersonalizing
this image they could not simply let the more abstract or diffuse
images into consciousness. This tendency to avoid the abstract for
the concrete might also explain the higher frequency of trees,
grass, flowers and hence overall greater B. Yochelson suggests that
criminal thinking is more concrete and this result would support
that idea.

Looking at the yes/no tabulation of Table 6, they are somewhat
more likely to qualify failure. They are more likely to accept a
situation rather than fight it, if their response to the ability to
get out of prison can be taken as an indicator.

Modal Subjects: four cases were selected where the conflict
scores on the large box, the force above and behind, the image
inside and outside and the animal from head and guts matched those
of the average for the criminal population. A quantitative statement about each of the four was prepared and they follow.

One experienced himself as a superior being who felt trapped,
captured by the police, and pressed by authority. His inner image

Table 5

Content Responses for Standard and Criminal Population, with Z Scores

Item	H			(H)			A			(A)		
1	1	0	0.41	1	0	0.41	67	65	0.16	1	0	0.41
2L	8	12	0.55	2	0	0.59	22	6	1.54	1	6	1.52
2M	8	12	0.55	3	0	0.72	20	6	1.40	0	0	–
2S	6	12	0.92	1	0	0.41	19	12	0.70	0	0	–
3A	11	12	0.12	7	6	0.15	1	0	0.41	1	0	0.41
3B	14	24	1.07	4	6	0.38	3	6	0.64	0	0	–
4	21	6	1.47	3	0	0.72	13	6	0.83	0	0	–
5I	38	35	0.24	8	24	2.05**	4	6	0.38	0	0	–
5O	39	47	0.63	5	24	2.80**	3	0	0.72	0	0	0.41
8	78	88	0.95	14	6	0.92	1	0	0.41	0	0	–
15V	33	53	1.61	4	6	0.38	4	0	0.84	0	0	–
15O	33	53	1.61	4	0	0.84	2	0	0.59	0	0	–
Total	24	29	1.22	5	6	0.60	13	9	1.62	–	–	–

Item	B			I			O			-			(A)		
1	6	6	–	19	12	0.70	6	0	1.04	–	–	–	0	18	4.66*
2L	2	6	0.99	59	59	–	7	0	1.13	–	–	–	0	12	3.79**
2M	3	6	0.64	55	65	0.78	11	0	1.44	–	–	–	0	12	3.79**
2S	3	12	1.74*	64	47	1.35	8	6	0.29	–	–	–	0	12	3.79**
3A	0	12	3.79**	25	18	0.63	54	47	0.54	–	–	–	3	6	0.64
3B	0	6	2.67**	16	18	0.21	25	12	1.18	–	–	–	37	29	0.64
4	2	6	0.99	36	47	0.88	25	35	0.88	–	–	–	0	0	–
5I	1	0	0.41	11	6	0.63	36	12	1.97**	–	–	–	2	18	3.14**

Item	B			I			O			-		
50	4	0	0.84	13	6	0.83	33	6	2.28**	3	18	2.68**
8	6	0	-	?	0	0.52	3	0	0.72	2	6	0.99
15V	2	0	0.59	39	18	1.68*	18	12	0.61	0	12	3.79**
150	2	0	0.59	36	24	0.97	23	12	1.03	0	12	3.79**
Total	2	4	1.80*	31	26	1.45	21	12	3.01**	4	13	5.45**

*p < .05
**p < .01

Table 6

Yes-No Tabulations for Standard and Criminal Populations, with Z Scores

Item	Yes			Qualified Yes			Yes and Qualified Yes			No			Qualified No		
7 Cross	85	88	0.33	9	0	1.29	94	88	0.92	6	6	-	0	6	2.67**
10 Out	78	82	0.38	3	0	0.72	81	82	0.10	18	18	-	1	0	0.41
14 Out	56	41	1.16	17	12	0.52	73	53	1.69*	25	41	1.39	2	6	0.99

*p < .05
**p < .01

revealed a troubled inadequate component that depended on an impulsive outer self for direction. Intellect and affect were an owl and a rodent who avoided one another. But one notes that owls and rodents are mortal enemies.

The second of our four modal subjects presented himself as a caged dog who could contend with some forces in his environment but sex was a terrifying enemy. He did not visualize component areas of self or self and other and unable to relate to affect and intellect.

The third presented himself as secretive and self-protective, but a pretty neat fellow overall. There was conflict for him between the power of religion and the power of the authorities without much capacity to take over. He experienced himself as not worth very much and dependent on others for recognition, but perfect at the same time. He appeared to be in a struggle with his own racial identity. He experiences the relationship between intellect and affect as a dog chasing a rabbit; his intellect tries to keep up with feeling and perhaps destroys it.

The fourth modal subject presents himself as deluxe but undervalued and cold. He is under pressure from his father; there is conflict between good and bad parts of himself in which the impulses win. There seems to be no contact between affect and intellect, but both are painful for him.

DISCUSSION

We set out on this project to learn something about the responses of convicted violent male offenders to the SIT. We imagined we might be able to say something about recidivism, but it was immediately apparent we would do no better than others have. But interest developed in examination of these personalities as a study in themselves. Yochelson's ideas that there is a criminal personality, deliberately irresponsible, action seeking, prideful and contradictory do gain a measure of support. There do seem to be be clear differences in the ways these men responded to the SIT, and personality descriptions that carry the flavor of these men can be written from their responses to the SIT imagery and sentence completions.

In conclusion, I feel the Shorr Imagery Test can be used effectively with this population to reveal the kind of personality with which we are dealing. Clearly, more work is needed but I think it is interesting that in seven of the 10 cases, at least some support was given for the ideas of Yochelson and Samenow about characteristics of the criminal personality.

REFERENCES

Shorr, J. E., and Tansey, D. <u>Manual for the Shorr Imagery Test</u>.
    Institute for Psycho-Imagination Therapy, Los Angeles, 1976.

Yochelson, S., and Samenow, S. E. The criminal personality, vol. I,
    a profile for change. New York: Jason Aronson, 1976.

IMAGERY EXPERIENCE OF DISABLED PERSONS

Clifford O. Morgan, Ph.D.

University of New Mexico

Albuquerque, New Mexico

DISABILITY THROUGH IMAGERY EXPERIENCE

A positive attitude regarding the potential of physically disabled persons is an important value for professional helpers. The helper who has not resolved his/her own conflicts regarding physical trauma and subsequent disability may transfer these negative feelings to the patient. For example, if the helper has an underlying belief that s/he would be completely helpless and that s/he would not be accepted by others if s/he were suddenly spinal cord-injured, then this attitude could be indirectly communicated to other severely disabled people. It is unlikely that the patient would see positive aspects in his/her situation if the helping staff s/he contacts really believe that the situation is negative and hopeless.

Conversely, a helper with realistic, positive attitudes regarding the potential of the disabled person in spite of the handicap, would be therapeutic for the person. Specifically, these positive feelings from the helper could be transferred to the patient who then may introject these positive values into the patient's own frame of reference.

The patient's psychological response to his or her disability and the way others respond to the patient have significant implications for the patient's return to normality (Marinelli and Orto, 1977). A positive response would include: (1) value changes in which the patient would see as valuable those aspects of life not closed to the person, (2) value changes where physique becomes less important, (3) containment of the disability effects so that the evaluation of the total person is not affected by a single

181

characteristic, and (4) acceptance of the disability as a characteristic of the person (Wright, 1960). Professional staff with positive values regarding the potential of the disabled patient are in
a much better position to facilitate these necessary patient
responses than are helpers with negative attitudes.

Attempts to reduce and/or change negative attitudes toward
disabled persons have been grouped into three broad categories:
(1) contact with disabled individuals, (2) information about the
disabled individual, and (3) a combination of contact and information (Anthony, 1972).

Research findings indicate that either contact or information
alone do not significantly change attitudes towards persons with a
disability (Anthony, 1972). Contact in combination with information does seem to have a favorable impact on the non-disabled person's attitudes (Anthony and Carkhuff, 1970). However, it is not
always possible to arrange positive contact and information for
professionals. The procurement of rehabilitated disabled individuals to participate in attitude change programs is not always possible. Time limitations, as well as economic constraints, are also
barriers to changing attitudes through contact and information
programs.

This study presents an experimental method to assess and change
prejudicial attitudes of professionals who either work or will work
with disabled people. This new technique utilizes visual imagery
which allows a person to experience underlying feelings and attitudes regarding physical disability.

METHOD

Instrument

A structured procedure was adapted from the Shorr Imagery Test
(Shorr, 1974). It is called the Disability Through Imagery Experience (DTIE). Subjects are given six imaginary situations to visualize. Each of the situations has instructions for the visualizer
such as statements to make and sentences to complete. These items
help the person identify specific feelings, conflicts, and to
interpret the individual meaning of the image for the person.
Upon completion of the six situations, the subject summarizes his/
her new awareness regarding their conflicts surrounding personal
disability. These situations and instructions are given in Table 1.

The purpose of the first administration of the DTIE is the
identification of negative feelings and attitudes. However, the
awareness of conflicts does not necessarily resolve the conflicts.
Therefore, a procedure is used to allow a person to experience the

Table 1

Disability Through Imagery Experience

Image Number	Instructions
	Imagine yourself with a disability.
	Now imagine the most opposite image.
	Imagine the you with the disability saying something to the opposite image.
	Now have the opposite image say something to the image of yourself with a disability.
1	Speaking as if you are the image with a disability, finish the sentences.

    I feel

    The adjective which best describes me is

    I wish

    I must

    I secretly

    I need

    I will

What references have these images to you?

Imagine meeting a disabled person who is helpless on the ground.

Make a statement to him/her.

2   Have him/her make one back to you.

I want every disabled person to think of me as (finish the sentence).

The only good disabled person is (finish the sentence).

Table 1 (cont'd)

Image Number	Instructions
	Imagine a flower.
	Imagine the flower becoming traumatized.
3	Now humanize the flower.
	Imagine going down the road with this person.
4	Imagine that you are to escort a group of disabled people of the opposite sex to you from one place to another.
	The interpretation I make of this experience to my sexual feelings are
	Imagine entering the body of a disabled person.
	Finish these sentences.
	I feel
	The adjective which best describes me is
5	I wish
	I must
	I secretly
	I need
	I will
	Never refer to me as
	What does this mean to you?
	Imagine lying on a hospital bed in a crowd of people.
	Have the people make a statement to you.
	Make a statement back to them.

Table 1 (cont'd)

Image Number	Instructions
	Finish these sentences.
	I feel
6	The adjective which best describes me is
	I wish
	I must
	I secretly
	I need
	I will
	Can you get out of the bed?
	How do you go about getting out?
7	What have you become aware of regarding yourself and your conflicts regarding disability through these images?

Note: Adapted from Shorr Imagery Test.

same situation, but in a more positive context. This procedure is called transforming and focusing for change (Shorr, 1977).

The subject is instructed to go over his or her previous images and identify aspects which are unsatisfactory to the person. Then the DTIE is redone. If the subject's initial response to any of the situations in the DTIE indicates a generally acceptable and positive image, that particular situation is not redone. The subject him/herself is the judge of whether the image was acceptable or not. Following the second administration of the DTIE, the subject again summarizes his/her new awareness regarding his or her attitude toward disability.

This procedure is designed for group administration, and subjects write their responses on prepared answer sheets. The procedure is meant to be used in the context of a class or workshop setting where information regarding disabled people is given. It

is helpful to have a group discussion regarding the experience
following the completion of the exercise. Ethical considerations
suggest that if a subject has unresolved conflicts regarding the
experience, then an appropriate person should be available for con-
sultation.

Scoring

Each of the six imagery situations is given an overall rating
on a scale from 1 to 4, 1 being an essentially completely negative
image, and 4 a completely positive image. A rating of 2 is given
if the image is more negative than positive, and a rating of 3 is
given if the image was mostly positive, but with some negative
aspects. As a help in deciding on the final rating for each of the
six situations, raters look at each statement and sentence completion, and if, in their judgment, the item is a devalued statement
(negative), the item is assigned a minus (-); if the item is judged
as positive, it is assigned a positive (+); and if the item appears
neutral or the rater cannot decide, it is assigned a neutral (0).
These positive and negative assignments are then added up, and if
there are mostly minuses (-), the image is rated a 1. An image
with mostly positives (+) is rated a 4 and ratings of 2 and 3 are
given depending on the ratio of minuses to plusses. Neutrals are
not counted.

A subject's overall rating can be found by adding each of the
six ratings and dividing by six. Raters are trained by written
explanations of the scoring system, sample scored items and group
discussions of rating procedures.

Subjects

Thirty-five undergraduate (15) and graduate (20) students
enrolled in an introductory rehabilitation counseling class over
two semesters were given the DTIE procedure. There were 26 females
and nine males with an average age of 28. Twenty-six of the students were Anglos, seven were Hispanic, one Black, and one Asian-
American. Twelve of the students were disabled themselves. No
control subjects were used.

Raters

Three counseling and guidance graduate students who were not
participants in the classes were selected to rate the responses on
the DTIE. A two-hour group training session was held, and the raters then scored the DTIE response sheets. Interjudge reliability
for the 70 response sheets was $\underline{r}$ = .83 (Pearson product moment
coefficient).

RESULTS

Pre- and Post-Transformation
   and Focusing

Overall scores for subjects on the first administration averaged 1.8, or more of a negative than positive attitude. After
transforming and focusing on the second administration of the DTIE,
subjects averaged 3.1, or more of a positive than a negative attitude. There was a significant difference in the subjects' scores
on the DTIE after transforming and focusing ($\underline{T}(68) = 7.95$, $p < .001$).
These results are given in Table 2.

Case Study

Excerpts from one subject's written responses are included to
demonstrate an example of an actual subjective experience of the
procedure. Here is what she wrote about the first image:

> In image #1, I visualized myself as a quad., but I
> was also unable to speak. I felt trapped, helpless,
> frustration, and felt like others would not accept me, as
> me. In other words, I would constantly have to be prov-
> ing my "worth" as a human being. I also felt the tremen-
> dous need to be independent.
> In focusing, I found that I can't change how others
> will react to me all the time (i.e., they might stare, or
> think I'm a vegetable), but I know for myself my own value

Table 2

Means, Standard Deviations and $\underline{t}$ Test of
Differences Between Means Pre- and Post-Focusing
on the Disability Through Imagery Experience

Disability Through Imagery Experience	Pre-		Post-		
	M	S	M	S	$\underline{t}$
	1.82	.62	3.14	.73	7.95[*]

Note: N = 35

*$\underline{p} < .001$

as a person, and I don't feel like I have to constantly
"prove" myself. I see that I can still be independent,
but a different kind of independent. I will have to
rely on others for menial tasks (i.e., dressing, cooking),
but I can still be independent in my mind. I still kind
of worry about what type of job I would be able to get,
especially one that wouldn't be menial (i.e., sorting
scraps, etc.), but given time I'm sure I'll find something.

DISCUSSION

Using imagery, a person can identify negative or positive attitudes s/he possesses regarding physical disability. By transforming
and focusing for change, a person can also experience previously
negatively held images in a more positive manner. Whether these
positive attitudes would generalize to other situations is speculation at this point. However, there is evidence that imaginary
rehearsal does generalize to "real life" situations.*

The DTIE is an experimental procedure which needs reliability
and validity development. This study needs to be replicated using
an independent measure of attitude such as the Attitude Toward Disabled Persons (Yuker, Block and Younng, 1970) scale, as well as a
control group.

This procedure was not designed to be used with the disabled
person, but rather with the helper of the disabled. The study does
suggest, however, that the basic procedure of visualization, transformation and focusing for change is applicable with the physically
disabled. The use of imagery as a method for helping the disabled
cope with their handicap is a new exciting area begging for exploration.

REFERENCES

Anthony, W. A., and Carkhuff, R. R. The effects of rehabilitation
    counselor training upon trainee functioning. Rehabilitation
    Counseling Bulletin, 1970, 13, 333-342.
Anthony, W. A. Changing society's attitudes toward the physically
    and mentally disabled. Rehabilitation Psychology, 1972, 19
    (3), 117-126.

---

*E. Klinger, Therapy and the flow of thought. Paper presented
at the meeting of the American Association for the Study of Mental
Imagery, Los Angeles, California, June 22, 1979.

Marinelli, R. P., and Orto, A. E. The psychological and social
     impact of physical disability. New York: Springer, 1977.
Shorr, J. E. Shorr imagery test. Los Angeles: Institute for
     Psycho-Imagination Therapy, 1974.
Shorr, J. E. Go see the movie in your head. New York: Popular
     Library, 1977.
Yuker, H. E., Block, J. R., and Younng, J. H. The measurement of
     attitudes toward disabled persons. Alberton, New York:
     Human Resources Center, 1970.

THEORY AND APPLICATION OF PSYCHO-IMAGINATION THERAPY

Pennee Robin, MFCC

Institute for Psycho-Imagination Therapy

Los Angeles, California 90048

There is a constant flow of images through the human mind. This fertile outpouring can be an important dimension of the therapeutic process. Psycho-Imagination Therapy, as developed by Joseph E. Shorr, uses as one of its major modalities the Imaginary Situation (IS). Other modalities, including the Self-and-Other Question, Finish-the-Sentence, the Most or Least Question, are discussed in Shorr's books, Psycho-Imagination Therapy (1972), and Psychotherapy Through Imagery (1974).

This workshop is designed to present an introduction to the Imaginary Situation. I find this approach to be exceptionally effective in revealing, both to the therapist and to the patient, the latter's conflicts, coping strategies, and avenues of healthy conflict resolution.

Psycho-Imagination Therapy, based on the interpersonal personality development theories of Harry Stack Sullivan and R. D. Laing, involves both therapist and patient in an existential phenomenological duet. The Imaginary Situation provides both with a window into the innermost aspects of the patient.

Shorr's creativity is evidenced by his skillful weaving of theory and technique.

Psycho-Imagination Therapy puts great emphasis on how the patient has been defined falsely by others and how he must learn to define himself in line with his true identity. It is also an open system which allows the therapist to create newer approaches as they become

necessary--within the framework of a self-and-other
theory (Shorr, 1972).

Shorr has devised Imaginary Situations to help reveal whatever
specific psychological dynamic may seem relevant to the therapeutic
process at a particular time. They also expose forgotten, repressed,
and distorted attitudes, feelings, emotions, and behavior patterns
more rapidly and efficiently than many more conventional approaches.
As used in Psycho-Imagination Therapy, the constant flow of images
bypasses the conscious censor. Thoughts expressed verbally are
very often edited in order to hide feelings and meaning from others
and from the self. When patients are asked to imagine a specific
situation, they do not usually know in advance what will be revealed.
Imagery has the capacity to break through the resistances employed
in verbal transactions.

Shorr has systematically organized over two thousand Imaginary
Situations into several categories. These include: General Imagery,
Spontaneous Imagery, Self-Image Imagery, Task Imagery, Body Imagery,
Sexual Imagery, Parental Imagery, Depth or Unconscious Imagery, and
many others. The limits of time in this workshop prevent us from
dealing with all of the categories today. However, a comprehensive
survey can be found in The Power of Human Imagination (Singer and
Pope, 1978).

It has been my experience that introducing Psycho-Imagination
Therapy to professionals is most effective when the theoretical
orientation, the practical applications, and the means of imple-
menting insights are dramatically demonstrated by personal experience. Just as we try to make the therapy session live by involving
both therapist and patient, I try to make the didactic session live
by involving the student in actual participation. Therefore, I am
going to let you do some of the imagery yourself. At times I will
let each of you report your imagery and then we will discuss the
category and some of the ways to utilize the images in the therapy
session. At other times I will deal with the material immediately
after it is reported. Since this is a workshop and our time is
limited, we will do very little in-depth focusing. In a sense
this is but a sampler or teaser for the material contained in
Shorr's books and that which is taught in his professional training
classes.

All you have to do is to relax, close your eyes, and just let
your imagery flow.

I want you to imagine two different animals. Give each
animal an adjective. Then have each animal say something to the other animal.*

---

*Sufficient time is allowed after giving each IS to permit
everyone to complete his/her imagery.

Has everyone finished? Let's start with Mary's image.

Mary: I saw a squirrel and a burro. The squirrel is furry and the burro is timid. I couldn't get the squirrel to say anything, but it seemed like it was sassy and fresh. I have squirrels in my yard, and I watch them all the time.

The burro didn't say anything; just looked with big eyes. I couldn't get them to speak to each other, but the squirrel was chattering and fresh. The burro liked to watch the squirrel, all the activity.

Pennee: You mean the burro envied the squirrel's ability to chatter and be sassy? Does that have any meaning for you?

Mary: I felt it did, but I didn't know if I was making the image happen because I envy people who can just go on and on.

Pennee: Are you timid like the burro?

Mary: In many ways, yes.

Pennee: Do you also chatter like the squirrel?

Mary: Sometimes.

Pennee: Maybe they are two aspects of yourself.

Mary: That's what came to mind, although maybe I was forcing the obvious.

Pennee: Even if you force or contrive the image, you are the producer, the director, the stage manager, the writer, and the actor of your own script--the movie in your head.* Even if you feel you are manufacturing the images, they are still coming from you. They are still a part of yourself.

Now let's hear another image.

Gina: I saw a baby deer and he had his eyes closed. And then I saw an animal. I don't know what it was, but it scared me. It was brown, sort of like a bear, but it wasn't a bear. I gave the adjective "peaceful" to the deer, and "frightening" to the other. The brown thing said to me, "I frighten you," and the

---

*Go See the Movie in Your Head (Shorr, 1977).

deer said, "I'm sleeping." I tried to get his eyes open
but he said, "I'm tired and I want to go to sleep."
When they talked to one another, the deer said, "You
frighten her, but you don't frighten me." And the brown
animal said, "I'm not interested in you, I'm interested
in her." After a while the brown animal changed as I
kept looking at him. He lost the whiskers and the horns
and all those frightening things.

Pennee: Does that relate to any kind of conflict
that's going on in your life now?

Gina: Yes, I guess so. Often when something is
bothering me and I face it, it isn't so frightening.

Pennee: Is that a characteristic mode of response
with things that frighten you?

Gina: Yes, but I still have anxiety. The anxiety
level stayed even though I stayed with it and tried to
look at it. I'd rather not deal with it here.

Pennee: Since this is a teaching session, we will
not pursue it.

In a therapeutic situation we could carry on the dialogue with the
animal and you. We could pinpoint the situation or relationship
that the bear symbolizes. Through dialogue a great deal of additional material and insight surfaces, not only the nature of the
conflict, but your style of approach in dealing with these things.
Also in the therapeutic setting, when we come across an anxiety-
producing situation, we can use several focusing approaches. For
instance, you can follow through and face up to the fear or anxiety
in order to learn it is not catastrophic. Or you may wish to redo
the image with a more successful outcome. That is sort of a
rehearsal for behavior so that you can experience success and perhaps carry it over into a life situation.

As you may have guessed, this is an example of a Dual Image.
We could have used two trees, or two anythings, but animals seem to
be most satisfactory, especially in introductory sessions. Many
times in therapy we suggest two of the same animal, dogs, for
example, and then look for the outstanding differences between them.

The Dual Images reveal conflicts. They may be interpersonal where the conflict is between yourself and another person.
They can also be intrapersonal when two parts of yourself are in
conflict. In the therapeutic session, Gina, I might also ask you
to give that menacing animal a name to see if you could relate it
to anyone that you know, or to a situation that is either current

or on-going. Usually the nature of the conflict becomes quite
clear and then it is possible to explore resolutions to the conflict. When the characteristic mode of response is neurotic, the
patient has the opportunity to recognize that it is unsatisfactory
and can look for other ways to handle conflicts.

Other Imaginary Situations in the Dual Imagery category lead
to exposure and investigation of specific kinds of conflicts. If,
for example, the therapist wanted to focus on the conflict between
the intellect and the emotions, the following IS could be suggested:
"Imagine an animal coming out of your head and an animal coming out
of your guts. (Pause) Imagine what happens when they walk down a
road together."

Now we will move on to a different category of imagery. "Imagine that there are two of you (pause) and one you is sitting on the
other you's lap. What do you see? What do you feel? What do you
do?"

     Pat: The lap one was all strong and solid and the
other side of me was frightened and holding on. The lap
side was holding the frightened one, but getting kind of
alienated, saying, "This is silly, you shouldn't be so
scared." The other was saying, "Hold me, I really need
you to hold me." So the lap side just held the other
really tightly and they felt better.

     Pennee: Do you sometimes have to remind yourself to
be nice to you?

     Pat: Yes.

     Rosanna: I saw a rocking chair and a very mother-
like figure dressed in a long flowing gown--sitting in
the chair and holding a very small infant. There wasn't
any dialogue, but there was a lot of stroking and caring
and rocking. It was very tactile and comforting and
calming.

     Edith: I was very much present in this room and
the two of me were dressed alike. At first I identified
with the one sitting on the chair holding the other.
First I noticed that she was heavy and then I said to
her, "You're heavy on me." And I began to think back to
the past week when I had been heavy on myself. Then I
identified with the one sitting on the lap and said,
"Yes, I have been heavy on you." They just kind of
carried on a conversation.

     Gina: I saw myself sitting on myself and at first

I didn't like it because I said,"Oh, God, you weigh so
much! I'm going to be all crippled from my own weight."
Then I said, "Well, that's you anyway." And the other
said, "Well, if you melt together it's the same person,
even if you are crippled." Then they kind of laughed at
each other, and then they melted together and became one.
I knew I was rejecting one at first, but that was wrong
and I didn't want to do that.

Mary: The one sitting on the lap was much bigger
than the one in the chair. The one in the chair really
didn't have any form. It was listing. The one sitting
on the lap kept laughing. I got up and pranced around
and said, "Come on, shape up." But the one in the chair
kept listing and it was like smoke and got bigger, but
it never did shape up.

Jack: I saw an older me sitting in an overstuffed
chair and very tired. Then I saw a younger me sitting
on my lap. I've seen that before. Then I switched them
--there was something I didn't like so I thought I would
switch them and had the older one sit on the younger
one's lap. That seemed to be some kind of positive
direction. What eventually happened was they kind of
melted together. And there was a me--probably my present day image, but there was a different quality about
it. I was sitting there and reading some journals and,
I guess, writing my own article that I should write.
And it was a movement in the direction I want to go.

Pennee: Several things have come out that are
expressive of this type of image. This falls into the
category of self-image imagery. When you are listening
to other people's imagery, never assume until you check
details with them. Some of you had images where both
were the same size and age. Others had images where one
was younger and one older. It is necessary for the
therapist to get as close an approximation of the
patient's images as possible.
    Pay attention, also, to the language--to the meta-
phors that provide clues to the world as the patient
sees it. Watch for statements such as: "Heavy on
myself," "Shape up. . ."

Gina: Lose weight.

Pennee: Right. These statements give clues to the
meaning of the images. Often the asides and "throw-
away" comments are as meaningful as the direct description of the image.

Edith: I noticed that for some of us the image was here-and-now; others saw the two persons.

Pennee: That goes along with my earlier statement, "Never assume." I have done it myself. When I image two me's I am always "in" one of the me's. I didn't realize until I listened to other people's image in workshops that people were often outside looking at the two of themselves.

*Jack: Sometimes that seems to be meaningful. The person is really stepping back. Sometimes it just seems to be a style of imaging. It does not necessarily mean they are distancing themselves. Some people are really involved in their imagery; others pull back and are really an observer.
This image had a great deal of meaning for me and it had something to do with when I looked in on another workshop yesterday.

Of course, that's not uncommon. Often imagery can change from time to time. You can do the same image a week from now or in six months and it may be precisely the same as you saw it today or it may be entirely different. This image seemed to reflect a current concern.

In a situation where a current concern is reflected in the image you can look for the relevance in the present, but do not overlook the opportunity to relate it to on-going concerns. For example, if you are stopped by a policeman shortly before doing imagery, you may get some very powerful authority figures in your imagery. This does not necessarily mean that you have an on-going, long-term problem with authority. You probably do have some, because this is a current concern; this is something that just happened and it comes through very strongly. If it is the only time you have images like that, then authority probably isn't a big problem. If, on the other hand, there is a series of authority images, then you may be reflecting a deeper, long-standing problem.

There is a congruity in imagery. One image alone will not reveal the total person, but a series of images dealing with various categories and over a period of time provide a glimpse at the internal consistency of the individual.

We have, at the Institute, devised two tests, the Shorr Imagery Test (SIT) and the Supplementary Shorr Imagery Test (SSIT), which

---

*Jack A. Connella, Ph.D., has been associated with the Institute for Psycho-Imagination Therapy since its inception.

provide a range of data that is truly astonishing. The tests are designed to give a conflict score that shows degree of internal conflict, and they can also be used for an in-depth personality assessment.

Gina: I am interested in the image of the child and the older woman.

Pennee: What did it mean to you, Rosanna?

Rosanna: Well, I related it very much to an image I had yesterday morning of myself as two people--a rabbit and a bird. And an on-going conflict in my life is a struggle between being very dependent and very free and loose. I have a tendency to be very, very hard on myself. The image that I just had was one of taking better care of myself and not punishing myself so hard. Starting to give myself some strokes and starting to caress myself. That is something I really need to do and I don't do that enough, so it was a very pleasant feedback to myself. Maybe I am starting to take care of myself. I may not have come to a resolution of the conflict, but I'm working on it in a positive way. The image has a lot in it for me, of nurturing. I'm very physically oriented and into the body-touching and kinesthetic kinds of things, and the feeling of being touched and rocked is very important to me.

Pennee: Was there also a component of allowing that dependent part to exist? Not just denying that child part?

Rosanna: Definitely. And it is also significant that there was no conversation. I would have expected the mother to do more talking because I tend to be very verbal, but what was important for me was that I was getting physical contact. That was a very significant way for me to receive love.
I have a question. When you have done an image before, or when you know the significance of what an image is supposed to reveal, does that interfere with imaging in the future?

Speaking from experience, I have found that it does not. I have done some of the images over a dozen times. Some of them are so firm, so right on target that they have never changed in the four or five years that I have been doing them. Others change through time to reflect changes in me.

It doesn't matter that you know the significance of the image.

It all comes from you and if you just let it flow, some of the
intuitive, unverbalized material arises. You can control it, but
even in therapy when we realize someone is trying to control it,
the content is much the same. It may be more abstract, but it is
still there. As long as there is a trusting, open relationship,
the same image can be done over and over again, and if the person
will just go with the imagery, the material will emerge. Foreknowl-
edge need not make a difference in the effectiveness of the imagery.

However, you must keep in mind that as your situation changes,
your images change to reflect the situation and your frame of mind.
The awareness that comes from what the images reveal is a step
toward the kind of change that is sought in therapy. The material
elicited by the images can change a person's perspective or suggest new ways of dealing with conflicts.

We often repeat images in therapy in order to point out
the dramatic changes that have taken place in the patient. Or we
may ask a patient to redo an image so that it has a better resolution. If an image has a negative or hopeless outcome or results
in peril to the patient, we may ask, "How else could you handle
that situation?" It is a form of rehearsal for living that can be
carried out in a safe setting.

Edith: Can you not also recreate this type of
image when you want to nurture yourself? That makes it
so rich.

Of course. You can always use your imagery in any way that
is satisfactory to you. Images that have strong positive meanings
for us can be recalled at any time to reinforce our position.

I would like to emphasize an especially important point.
These situations and categories require the theory in order to be
effective. We do not use laundry lists of images. One must have
a theory of personality development and of interpersonal relationships in order to use Psycho-Imagination Therapy. When the therapist understands the dynamics and the characteristic patterns of
behavior of the patient, then he/she can select images which will
probably reveal to the patient, as well as to himself, what is
going on within the person. I cannot stress too strongly the
importance of having a theory about the patient. Many of the images
used in initial sessions are designed to reveal to the therapist
these internal dynamics. As an example, we could start with:
"Imagine casting a fishing line into the water. What do you see
when you pull it out?" Or: "Imagine walking up to a fence. There
is a ladder leaning against it. Climb the ladder and look over the
fence. What do you see? What do you do? What do you feel?"

Psycho-Imagination Therapy revolves around two basic premises:

Do I make a difference to someone? Am I being acknowledged? Everyone needs to make a difference and to be acknowledged. And everyone develops strategies to achieve these needs. As therapists we
are trying to help the patient to see which strategies are effective and which are not. Of course, this is all based on interpersonal theory. Both Sullivan and Laing have expounded their
belief in the necessity to live in relationship to significant
others. We are constantly monitoring our behavior in terms of how
we see ourselves, how we see others, how we see others seeing us.
It all becomes involved and complex and is rarely thought out on
the conscious level, but it is going on all the time.

Now let's try something different: "Imagine climbing a flight
of 1,000 stairs to the top. What do you see? What do you feel?
What do you do?

Attila: I saw stairs like you saw in the old
movies--huge stairs and a lot of bright lights at the
top of them. I started climbing up and I was surprised
I was not getting tired. The lights beckoned and I was
looking forward to approach this bright top, but when I
got there I was disappointed because there was nothing
there. It was a flat surface and a mist around and
nothing there. So I climbed down.

Bill: I saw a fairly tight spiral staircase going
up and I had a hard time deciding what approach to use.
It seemed boring. I kept switching back and forth from
taking two steps at a time slowly, to making myself go
up very rapidly. I couldn't stay with one speed. About
half way up I saw the whole scene from a distance and I
sort of went into my body and I went on around and
finished and came up to a flat space. It was kind of
disappointing--not terribly, but I was wondering if
there'd be anything there, and there wasn't.

Edith: I saw the steps and they were mahogany and
they seemed to go almost into infinity. I found myself
standing and there was almost a compulsion to climb
them and I was waiting to see if I wanted to and I
found myself partly up the steps. Then I realized that
this was my life and I walked quite a way. Then I
realized that I had several more years to make it so I
didn't decide to continue. I just decided I was along
here about half way and I could take my time.

Rosanna: I had a similar feeling about the steps,
that they just went on, and I made the thousand steps
into about a million and I started to look up. I just
started to physically do it. I kept walking and going

up the stairs. I got really tired--huffing and puffing. My breath was going and my heart was beating and I said, "This is silly--I'm going to take a little rest." And then when I was ready, I went on again. That kept happening throughout the whole image. As I was getting higher and higher I was getting very hot and I was warm and there were clouds in the sky. I started gradually taking clothes off to lighten my load and change my perspective. I just kept going on and finally when I got to the top I did the whole "Rocky" thing. It was like a victory. I had met the challenge.

Gina: Well, I had a problem deciding which stairs. First I found myself at Cal State LA and I didn't like it so I changed it and somehow I was in the University of Naples. They are pink marble and reminded me of the war. The elevator could not be used. Somehow through the window I saw these beautiful mountains with stairs. But then I cheated because I bounced to the top. Then I decided, "This is cheating. Get down and do it." Then when I got half way I decided, "Who cares? At my age I'll never be able to climb a thousand stairs." So I bounced again and I found trees and greenery and it was nice.

Mary: I, too, got the Cal State stairs, but I soon left that. They turned into these mahogany stairs and I thought, "They are so brown." And I started climbing. I tend to count stairs and part of me said, "You're not going to count a thousand stairs. You've got to do something else while you are climbing." And I started climbing and the stairs kind of accordioned so they got narrower and steeper. And I still kept going. I wasn't compelled to count them, which was the best part of it. I didn't get to the top, but it didn't seem to matter.

Pat: I was really intimidated by all those stairs. I wondered how I could make it. I was worried about my breathing because I'm asthmatic and I was thinking I'd have to do the kind of breathing I learned to do and go up slowly. It was kind of a defeatist attitude. When I finally got to the top I just looked around and there was a very beautiful view of the mountains. I felt terrific. I was thinking, "Oh, I can't do this. This is ridiculous--I shouldn't be defeatist about this." It's very typical of the way I look at some big task, like writing something. I always think, "God, I can't do this."

Pennee: You just said the magic word--"task."
This is a task image. It is designed to say something
about your style of approach to tasks and problems.
Your images reflect many of the types of things encountered in this type of imagery. Also I might point out an
interesting omission. No one saw anyone else on the way
up the stairs. Each of you made the climb alone and
encountered no one along the way. I don't wish to imply
that everyone should or does see others on the way up.
But it is not uncommon to meet significant persons and
to have them join the climb or to be passed by, etc.

Your images did reveal some interesting information
about styles of approach, goal orientation, values, and
achievement motivation.

Attila, is there something in your life you have
been struggling to achieve that turned out not to be
quite as important as you anticipated?

Attila: Yes, but I was wondering more why I
didn't get tired. I was attracted to the bright lights
and just kept going and didn't get tired. I understand
that, but I don't understand the disappointment.

Pennee: Check it out in terms of what's going on
in your life. You may have a particular goal that is
bright and shiny but really doesn't mean much to you.

Attila: I am sure that the attractiveness of the
goal kept me from getting tired.

Bill: Mine fits very well with my strategy because
actually the only interesting thing was the staircase,
which was a tight attractive sort of thing. In life I
tend to look at things as working toward them is the
most important thing. So the staircase was important,
not where I ended.

Pennee: Is it characteristic of you to try out
several different approaches?

Bill: That's impatience. I'm very impatient. I
knew I couldn't make it to the top going as fast as I
could, so I kind of paced myself to something I could
make in the shortest period of time. And so I wasn't
tired when I reached the top.

Pennee: Some people never reach the top. It may
be because they don't care. Edith, you seemed more
interested in the journey than in the ultimate goal.
And Mary, you were more pleased with shedding the

compulsion to count than in reaching the top.

Some people don't reach the top because they can't
allow themselves to succeed. They get to the 999th and
can't go the last step or two because they fear success.

Mary: I think I didn't reach the top because
lately I've been too goal-oriented. Maybe a little lazy,
but I wanted to enjoy it along the way and I think maybe
that's something new. I was freed from the need to
count.

Edith: There was no big rush for me to reach the
top and that is typical of where I am right now. I
have some goals, but I'm more interested in the right
process.

Pennee: Gina, why is it cheating to bounce to the
top?

Gina: I was raised in that structure. I'm just
beginning to free myself. First I thought I'd better
do it the hard way. I worry if I don't do everything
just right, but I'm learning to be freer.

Pat: Does this image have anything to do with
physical problems? Do the task images always involve
physical exertion?

It is natural if you are concerned about your breathing to
have that appear in your imagery. Your physical, mental and emotional condition are important factors in how you approach tasks.
Most of the task imageries do involve physical activities because
achievement does usually require some physical movement. You
could have a mental task, such as a crossword puzzle, but our
images generally require physical effort of some kind.

If, in the therapy setting, a patient is disturbed by his
image; if he cannot achieve the top and he wants to; if he meets
what appear to be insurmountable obstacles, he can then try to redo
the image with a better conclusion. He can begin, in his imagery,
to experience success and learn to deal with it. He can also learn
to recognize other ways of approaching problems or tasks that will
not insure defeat.

Now, let's move on to still another category: Imagine
whispering something into your father's ear.

Edith: My father was sitting in a chair and I
reached over and whispered, "I appreciate your teaching me to be honest and truthful." He just reached out

and put his arm around me and said, "That's OK."

Pennee: Is that indicative of the kind of relationship you two have had?

Edith: Well, he could be receptive, but he wouldn't say much. He would just take it in and respond casually.

Pennee: Was it easy for you to say that to him?

Edith: Oh yes, I have said that before.

Rosanna: All I saw was this huge ear--it filled the whole room--and a very little teeny me. I was kind of sneaking up to the ear, very frightened, almost shaking. I was really contemplating what I would want to say if it was the only thing I could possibly say to my father. And finally I just whispered, "Hold me." And nothing happened.

Pennee: Did he ever hold you?

Rosanna: No, it just stopped there.

Pennee: Is that indicative of the kind of relationship you had with him?

Rosanna: Yeah.

Pennee: Did he hear you?

Rosanna: I don't know. I think the ear was so big and so plastic that he couldn't hear me.

Pennee: What did you have to do to make your father hear you?

Rosanna: The first thing that came to my mind was jump up and down and scream.

Pennee: Is that your usual style?

Rosanna: No, I don't think so.

Pat: I just immediately said, "I love you." I felt the need to reassure him and make sure that he knew because he died many years ago. I just said, "I love you and I wish you hadn't died. I have to accept that you have and I want you to know that." It was a real heavy feeling; I felt quite teary.

Gina: Do you mind if I pass?

Pennee: You don't need to share unless you want
to.

Mary: At first I was horrified, and then I ran
up and said, "Get lost!" And I kind of backed off and
then thought that wasn't very nice.

Pennee: One of the good things about imagery is
that it is private. You don't have to be nice. If
that's the way you feel, you can become aware of it and
say, "Well, it's OK to feel that way." It's a very
safe way to confront people that never listen to us, or
who have listened wrong, people who can't or won't hear
what we are saying.

Ruth: My father said, "I love you." And I
responded, "I love you, too. You taught me so many
wonderful things, but I wish you were stronger. I wish
you had stood up to people, particularly to mother."
He just looked at me and had tears in his eyes. I
couldn't continue any more.

This image brings up the dynamics between child and parent.
Of course it can also be done by whispering in the mother's ear.
In a group situation it is possible to have one person go around
and whisper something in each person's ear. In order to stimulate
interactions between group members, which are very often mirrors
of what goes on outside the group, we often ask people to go around
and whisper, or to give each person an adjective, or to make a
specified statement to each person.

With the whispering image we look for dynamics and heavy feelings. In a therapy situation, you, as therapists, can deal with
those feelings. The parent doesn't have to be there for the child
to say, "Get off my back," or to scream, "Please listen to me!"

By freeing oneself in the imagery, by confronting the parent
in the imagery, the patient can break some of the chains that hold
him where he is. He begins to realize that there is a person who
will never be anything but a gigantic ear, for instance.

Rosanna: I was just thinking about that. That
is something I have been working on for a long time.
Learning to communicate. Trying to get feelings back.
I've been working on that for maybe ten years. And I
was just thinking, "I was so small and that ear was so

big and plastic, maybe I will never get to him. Maybe
he cannot change. Maybe I have to stop trying to find
ways to make him change." I don't think I've ever
thought about that before.

Pennee: There is another way to resolve this.
That is to let him be who he is; the resolution is for
you. We can't make nice and everything works out
beautifully or the way we choose. But you can stop
spending ten years of energy trying to get someone to
listen who can't or won't. It can be very freeing for
you.

Rosanna: You're right because I think there isn't
anything I haven't tried.

Pennee: That was an example of a parental image.
There are many others that get at other aspects of the
relationship. I'd like you to try another now.
Imagine dancing with your mother. What do you see?
What do you feel? What do you do?

Pat: It was difficult to dance with her. She
was physically incapable of doing it. I kept feeling
like she's holding me back. I can dance so well by
myself, but with her I have to sort of slow myself
down and try to help her. So I did. I tried to help
her for a while and then I just said, "Fuck it." And
I just went off and danced by myself and felt great.
That's very much like what's happened with me and my
mother. I'm better off without her.

Gina: I lost my mother when I was seven years
old. So I had some trouble imagining dancing with her,
but first we were in our summer home and she didn't
want to dance. I remembered her as a very beautiful
woman and I put myself on her lap. From that I saw
myself as she used to put me to bed every night. She
used to read to me. I was on her lap and had a little
pink quilt around my legs. It felt good. Then I
remembered how I felt when I was a little girl and she
was dead and I used to think it was an injustice.

Pennee: The return of feelings from childhood is
quite common. That was a reminiscent image. They
often bring up incidents and feelings that we have
forgotten or repressed. Dancing is often a youthful
type of activity and often leads to reminiscences.

Rosanna: At first I thought, "I don't think I

can do this because my mother is real sick right now."
She has a neurological disease and her muscles are
wasting away. She can't even walk. I thought, "How
can she dance." Then I said, "Well, I'll just go with
it." So I closed my eyes. I did that kind of reminiscent thing, except it's not something we really did.
I just conjured up something we might have done. We
both were in very colorful clothing and we just
frolicked around and jumped around and were very playful. She was laughing and I was laughing. It was very
physical and we were really enjoying each other and the
moving. And then all of a sudden the image just
changed. I saw her wanting to move and not being able
to and me just sort of moving her around--her arms and
her legs. Then saying, "OK, you can't dance, but I'll
dance for you." And I danced for her.

Pennee: One of the processes that occurs in imagery is the dealing with reality and the practical
aspects of the situation. As the material surfaces,
we deal with physical realities, illness, death, etc.
We process the reality into the imagery.

Pat: I was dealing with the physical reality that
my mother can't dance, but the symbolic was even more
meaningful. It permeates every other aspect of our
relationship.

Mary: I was in my driveway at home and I was
dancing with my mother. But my mother is 83 so we were
just going around in a circle rather slowly. It was
interesting that we were at arm's length. Very distant and austere, in a crazy way. I started thinking
that that's sort of what I do in that relationship and
have for years. She seemed happy with it. She smiled
and looked very nice. I got some pleasure from pleasing her, but she chose the circle dance because she
wouldn't pay attention long enough to learn new steps.

Pat: You were most patient, because you slowed
down for your mother. I just chose to go off without
mine.

Mary: I was the oldest in one sense. There were
two batches of children and I was the oldest of the
young group.

Pennee: The oldest child, or the oldest daughter,
often is the one to accommodate to the mother.

Ruth: When I closed my eyes I was dancing with
somebody else. My mother came over and said, "Now you
dance with me." I couldn't see who the other person
was, whether it was a male or a female. I said, "Hmmm--
I have to" and I started dancing with my mother. I'm
taller than my mother and I started to lead her, but she
said, "That's not the way to dance." And I said, "I'm
just trying to show you. I know how to dance and you
don't." And she said, "That's not the way to dance."

I danced with her and I hated the whole thing, of
course, but I didn't stop. I just kept dancing. I
kept hating it and I kept dancing. Then my mother said,
"See, if you'd listen--see how nicely you dance." And
we weren't dancing nicely at all. We were tripping. I
was stepping on her and she was stepping on me. Finally
I couldn't go on.

Pennee: No wonder you wanted your Dad to stand up
to her in the other image.

This is a parental image that brings up many of the dynamics
between parents and children. You can, in the therapeutic situation, carry it to the next level. What other people in your life
do you deal with in the same fashion? We have a tendency to keep
these people in our lives and we surround ourselves with similar
people and perpetuate the same behavior and reactions.

You can, through this type of image, become aware of how you
deal with your parent characteristically. Then look around and
see if you are doing the same thing with others. For instance, if
all your life you have tried to please your mother, you may also
try always to please others. Group interactions often reveal these
dynamics. Your characteristic responses in a group may very
clearly reveal the strategies you developed to maintain your relationship with one or both parents, or with siblings.

Parental imagery helps also to reveal the patient's self
image. All of the images are capable of the same kind of effect,
but since the self image is so strongly influenced by the messages
received in the earliest years of life, the parents, or their surrogates, are certainly instrumental. From the time of birth the
significant others in a person's life begin to teach him/her how
to move, how to talk, how to think, what to wear, what do do, what
not to do. It is all part of the socialization process. But all
too often, the parent is imposing an identity on the child, an
identity that is "alien" to his/her nature. Conflict arises as the
child tries to conform to the identity conferred upon him/her. The
child begins to accept the alien identity and to deny his/her own
reality. Then it becomes necessary to develop coping strategies to
maintain his/her position vis-a-vis the significant persons in

his/her life.

All of this is, of course, part of the theoretical structure
of Psycho-Imagination Therapy which grows out of the work of Sullivan and Laing. It is a topic large enough to occupy several workshops, so I will suggest that you read Shorr's books for the complete exposition and application of these theories in therapy. I
do want to reiterate that much of what we do in Psycho-Imagination
Therapy revolves around helping the patient change a negative self-
image and in the process develop new effective strategies for coping with conflict.

In conclusion, I should like to emphasize a few of the vital
points of Psycho-Imagination Therapy. It is vitally important to
understand interpersonal theory and to have some picture of the
world as it is seen by the patient. The images are revelatory and
useful only in that context. A further understanding of the categories of imagery is necessary in order to tailor the therapeutic
interaction to the needs of the patient.

Once the therapist has some idea of the basic conflicts in
the patient's life, he/she can then use the imagery to reveal the
roots of the conflict and the strategies developed to maintain a
false position. At that point we use the focusing techniques to
help the patient deal with material he/she has become aware of.

We do not use just imagery. There are numerous other modalities explained in Shorr's books. However, I should like to point
out a particularly effective follow-up to an Imaginary Situation.
I mentioned earlier an image with a fishing line which can be used
in an initial session. (It is effective at any time in therapy.)
Whatever image is seen on the fishing line may have significance
to the patient, but its true import may not be clear. The next
step is for the patient to imagine he/she is that image--fish, old
shoe, tire, seaweed, etc.--and then finish the following sentences:

I feel_____.

The best adjective to describe me is_____.

I wish_____.

I must_____.

I secretly_____.

I need_____.

I will_____.

I fear_____.

Never refer to me as_____.

    The material elicited in this type of exchange provides an in-depth approach to the image and its meaning.

    The same stems can be used for any other image as well, and will provide additional material for discussion and focusing.

    Time prevents discussion or experiencing of other imagery categories. But I will conclude by offering a few examples of categories we have not had time for.

BODY IMAGERY:

    In what part of your body does your anger reside?

    Imagine a string coming from your gut. Pull on it. What do you see? What do you feel? What do you do?

DEPTH IMAGERY:

    Imagine a sealed can under water.

    Imagine reaching into a cave three times, each time reach in deeper.

SEXUAL IMAGERY:

    Imagine a woman (man) on a six-foot mound.

    Imagine escorting a group of male (female) prisoners to a building a mile away.

GENERAL IMAGERY:

    Imagine yourself in an area the shape of a circle. How do you feel? What do you see? What do you do? Can you leave the circle?

REMINISCENT IMAGERY:

    Imagine yourself in a classroom. What do you see? What do you feel? What do you do?

REFERENCES

Horney, K. *Our inner conflicts*. New York: Norton, 1945.

Horney, K. *Neurosis and human growth*. New York: Norton, 1950.

Laing, R. D. *Self and others*. Baltimore: Pelican Books, 1971.

Shorr, J. E. *Psycho-imagination therapy*. New York: Intercontinental Medical Book Corporation, 1972.

Shorr, J. E. *Psychotherapy through imagery*. New York: Intercontinental Medical Book Corporation, 1974.

Shorr, J. E. *Go see the movie in your head*. New York: Popular Library, 1977.

Singer, J. L., and Pope, K. S. *The power of human imagination*. New York: Plenum Press, 1978.

Sullivan, H. S. *The interpersonal theory of psychiatry*. New York: Norton, 1953.

MANAGING ANXIETY AND STRESS THROUGH

PSYCHO-IMAGERY AND BEHAVIOR THERAPY TECHNIQUES

Norma Lee K. Mittenthal, Ph.D.

Hillsborough Community College

Tampa, Florida

BACKGROUND

Anxiety is a pervasive problem in our society today as a
"crippling device" in blocking creative growth among children as
well as adults. The author has studied and employed eclectic behavioral approaches in the reduction of test anxiety, public speaking,
social anxieties, sexual anxieties, addictive habits, phobic fears,
and obsessive-compulsive traits.

There is no doubt that the psychotherapeutic interview itself
evokes emotional responses in many individuals. Sometimes the emotion is anxiety, but more often it is a mixture of hopeful expectation, confidence in the expert, and other positive emotions experienced in momentary imagery or in vivo (in real life) that are conditioned in the psycho-educational setting.

In behavior therapy, there are three methods of verbally-
induced imagery: (1) emotive imagery, (2) induced anger and fear,
and (3) direct suggestion. One of the most widely used of the
behavioral techniques today is Systematic Desensitization, also
called reciprocal inhibition or deconditioning, popularized and
refined by Joseph Wolpe in 1958. This technique breaks down neurotic anxiety response habits in piecemeal fashion. The essence
of systematic desensitization involves pairing relaxation with
imaginal representations of feared stimuli, beginning with the
weakest or least frightening imagery scene and gradually strengthening or increasing the complexity of the feared object. The individual is first trained in relaxation. Then an imagined hierarchy
is developed from the actual fear. Each scene in the hierarchy is
described while the individual is concomitantly relaxed; it is

presented repeatedly for increasing lengths of time until no more
anxiety is reported. Several variations of technique are used when
conventional desensitization cannot be carried out. For those
people who acquire some facility in relaxing, in vivo desensitization is used wherever exposure to graduated phobic stimuli is
possible.

SIGNIFICANCE

The stopping block to growth seems to be <u>anxiety</u>. Any time we
have to learn a new way to change and/or reorganize our behavior,
attitudes, and beliefs, the existence of anxiety is prevalent, for
it's risk-taking behavior that is feared. We don't know if we're
going to be accepted or rejected; thus, anxiety is the gap between
the now and the then. If we are in the now, there is minimal
anxiety, because there is an exciting flow and emergence of spontaneous activity, creativity, and sensory awareness.

PURPOSE FOR THE TRAINING AND
  USE OF IMAGINATION

Imagination is a function which in itself is to some extent
synthetic, since imagination can operate at several levels concur-
rently: those of sensation, feeling, thinking, and intuition. It
includes all the various types of imagination, such as visualiza-
tion--the evocation of visual images: auditory, gustatory, tactile,
kinesthetic, and olfactory imaginations. In particular, muscular
sensation is of utmost importance in the sensation of tension or
relaxation of the muscles in order for the successful execution of
the exercises of relaxation, and for acquiring muscular skill.

If a pair of scales is off balance, you have to add weight to
the lighter scale in order to restore the balance. This is what I
have attempted to do by combining the practical applications of
psycho-imagery and behavior therapy techniques to bring about sensory and insightful awareness followed by the deconditioning for
appropriate behavioral change for the individual.

The "imagination," in the precise sense of the function of
evoking and creating images, is one of the most important and
spontaneously active functions of the human psyche, both in its conscious and in its unconscious aspects or levels. Therefore, it is
necessary to regulate, develop, and utilize the imagination to the
optimum, as "every image has in itself a motor-drive." Additionally, "images and mental pictures tend to produce the physical conditions and the external acts corresponding to them."

The importance and value of imagery (visualization) is:
(1) for the individual to have a clear picture of the "ideal model"

...the self and/or event; (2) for the training of concentration; (3) to further develop use of the will; (4) for an incentive to creative imagination; and (5) to make effective use of symbolic visualization.

Most of our mentality consists of pictures and words. The unconscious has a greater affinity to pictures; the conscious mind to words. In order to achieve a good harmony between ego and unconscious, we should have the greatest possible control over our visualizations.

In Psycho-Imagination Therapy, Task Imagery (Shorr, 1974):

1. Involves one in a task or a way of doing something.

2. Reveals one's internal conflicts, style and manner of approach, defenses, and fears; doubts, need for power, lack of power, feelings of mastery.

3. Brings about awareness of how one performs jobs; how he/she relates to authority; and attitudes about various activities.

4. Serves as a vehicle for focusing on a changed self-concept in the "working through process" of the imaginary task.

5. Enables one to re-experience or redo the imagery in a manner that leads to a healthy conflict resolution.

6. Affords one the possibility of self-confrontation and attempting to change self-concept and behavior, as well as attitude regarding the world around him/her.

In conclusion, Psycho-Imagination:

1. Reveals a wide range of personality variables such as:

    a. Individual's personal world

    b. Relationships between self and others

    c. Self-image, body image, sexual attitudes

    d. Interpersonal relationships

    e. Internal and external factors influencing the individual.

2. Is a creative and positive value to enhancing relationships, situations, etc.

3. Is an aid to finding one's way--organic need for orientation to the surroundings.

4. Is an adaptive function to reorient old patterns of behavior to changed situations.

METHODS: PSYCHO-IMAGINATION THERAPY

Through my use of Task Imagery with individuals, I have observed their self-awareness, attitude change, and behavior change through insight they have gained. They have learned how to reinforce their courage to persevere and confront their problematic situation; how to enhance and increase control over themselves, as well as outside forces; how to reduce anxiety and tensions, and develop strength to extinguish--by not giving self permission to feel--guilt and shame. In other words, one must create order out of disorder. Task Imagery helps people draw on the power and energy that exists within every human being.

EXERCISE

Imagine climbing 1,000 steps to the top (Shorr, 1972). As you proceed up the stairs, do you meet other people? Do you get to the top? What happened on the way? What happened on the top? How do you feel about it?

Many indications of perseverance, achievement, and assertion will be revealed in this imagery. Also, this task imagery can show your characteristic styles of behavior, how you view yourself, and others, and can provide clues to possible conflicts within self.

If people are dissatisfied with their original response to any imagery, I ask them to reexperience it in a more creative, satisfying way immediately and again at a later time. This may be more rewarding and fulfilling, as motivation to change a painful state is vitally necessary.

Another powerful image in learning more about yourself is as follows:

Imagine building a bridge across a raging river which enables you to reach the other side. What kind of bridge did you build? How did you do it? Did you do it alone or with help? How deep was the river? How long was your bridge? Did you complete the task? Can you cross the completed bridge?

We live in a world of images. You should become very aware of them; explore them to know and understand their nature in order to

enable the image to reveal yourself to yourself. Imagery should be
used as a bridge from past to present for insightful understanding
of what must and can be changed for a more satisfying future.

Imagery can free creativity. Learning to be more creative in
imagery develops a deeper understanding of feelings, openness to
experience and acceptance; awareness of self and others, identification with others, awareness of richer available perceptual fields
and curiosity.

BEHAVIORAL METHODS: SYSTEMATIC DESENSITIZATION AND ITS VARIANTS

Systematic desensitization is a gradual deconditioning of
anxiety-evoking stimuli. A physiological state antagonistic to
anxiety is induced by means of muscle relaxation. The client is
then exposed to a weak anxiety-arousing stimulus for a few seconds.
If the exposure is repeated several times, the stimulus progressively loses its ability to evoke anxiety. Employing a counter-
acting emotion to overcome an undesirable emotional habit step by
step has a precedent in an age-old method. For example, if a child
fears going to bed in the dark, he/she is quite likely to become
reconciled to it by deconditioning events that may occur if he or
she listens to soft music, or hears a happy story with a parent/
caretaker while in the darkened room.

The autonomic effects that accompany deep relaxation are
greatly opposed to those characteristic of anxiety.

Yoga techniques lead to control of autonomic responses. I use
the breathing and exercise techniques as a means to break unadaptive
emotional habits, and focus attention solely on the breathing--
instructing the individual to imagine looking at him/herself breathing and exercising; thus, diverting attention away from the anxiety-
evoking stimuli. My studies indicate the considerable therapeutic
value and potentialities in Yoga as a means of relaxation and
calmness.

Implosive-Flooding Therapy, developed by T. G. Stampfl, is
employed by repeated presentations of the conditioned stimulus in
imagery, and is related to response prevention as a means of overcoming avoidance behavior.

Both Systematic Desensitization and Implosive Therapy expect
to reduce the client's fear by having him/her imagine the situations
that are frightening. They differ in that Systematic Desensitization has the client minimize anxiety during the imagery while
Implosive Therapy aims at maintaining the client's anxiety at an
intense level as the subject is "flooded" to exhaustion. He/she is

usually very drained and feels relaxed after having gone through so much stress and strain. Relaxation training is also used to extinguish any residual tension that might be present. Repetition of the same story occurs until boredom sets in and the fear is extinguished. People probably experience more reduction of their fears to the imaginal than to the actual stimuli, allowing them to better deal with feared stimuli in real life. In vivo desensitization will later be more effective with no aversive consequences.

Emotive imagery, mentioned earlier, is a procedure first described by Lazarus and Abramovitz (1962), in which hierarchical stimuli are presented to an individual in an imagery situation in which other elements evoke responses antagonistic to anxiety. These responses thus take the place of relaxation as the source of inhibition of anxiety. For example: the individual's hobby or favorite hero is used as the inhibitory source of relaxation when attempts at relaxation training have failed.

In vivo desensitization is used by exposing individuals in reality to feared situations to which they have been previously desensitized in imagination. For example, I have taken a 29-year old man on an airplane at the airport and employed systematic desensitization and relaxation training there in the plane. We later progressed to a moving plane, but increased the hierarchical incidences in imagery until the anxiety was no longer present. I repeated this procedure with him on an elevator and on an eighth floor balcony overlooking the ocean. His agoraphobic anxieties all lessened greatly--including test anxiety and public speaking-- enabling him to accept a job out of state that required him to periodically travel by air. Relaxation training is very important before progressing to another item in the hierarchy. The individual is asked to tense his/her muscles in four sets. First set: head, eyes, cheeks, forehead, tongue, jaws. Then instructed to control the sensation, focus attention on his/her tensing of those muscles, and when the tension reaches its peak, let go--go limp, and relax. Next focus attention on breathing deeply, evenly, rhythmically. Repeat breathing exercise twice more. Second set of muscle tension involves: tensing neck, chest, shoulders, upper arms, forearms, hands, fingers, upper back. Followed by deep breathing and relaxation of those muscles. Repeat breathing exercise twice more. Third set of muscle tension includes: tensing abdomen, stomach, lower back, spine, pelvic region, followed by relaxation of those muscles and deep breathing. Repeat breathing exercise twice more. Fourth set of muscle tension involves tensing thighs, calves, feet, toes, followed by deep breathing and concentration on that part until it felt free of muscular tension, and a state of quiet, calm, relaxation is experienced.

The method of relaxation taught is essentially that of Edmund Jacobson's (1938), as well as some of my own psychiatric dance

therapy techniques. The individual is also instructed to imagine
calming scenes on a beach, etc.

Now, the individual is ready to be instructed to imagine his/
her first anxiety-evoking scene. Thus, the technique of systematic
desensitization involves three separate sets of operations:

1. Training in deep muscle relaxation.

2. The construction of anxiety hierarchies.

3. Counterposing relaxation and anxiety-evoking stimuli from
the hierarchies.

Frequently, <u>assertive training</u> and role rehearsal are necessary variants of systematic desensitization to use with those experiencing low self-concept, social anxieties, rejection, and
agoraphobics.

Most recently, I have combined the use of psycho-imagery concomitantly with systematic desensitization to evoke self-awareness
other than the anxieties and conflicts already expressed. Relaxation training and assertion follow. I have observed individuals
overjoyed at the immediate insight in his/her exploration, discovery and creativity through psycho-imagery. The behavioral techniques merely decondition the reduction and/or extinction of anxiety
superimposed by the evocation of something calming and relaxing,
such as progressive muscle relaxation and/or a calming scene; reinforced self-assurance, and self-management into bringing about a
more aware, relaxed, sense of well-being in order for the individual
to experience closure, handle stress and internal conflicts, as
well as increase the capacity to change them effectively.

Fritz Pearls once said, "People have to grow by frustration--
by skillful frustration. Otherwise, they have no incentive to
develop their own means and ways of coping with the world. 'To
suffer one's death and to be reborn in not easy'" (Perls, 1969).
Hans Selye stated that "Stress is not necessarily bad for you. It
is the response of the body to <u>any</u> demand that is placed upon it"
(Selye, 1976).

I believe openness to experience and self-confrontation provide greater value and appreciation from the growth experience.

In Gestalt Therapy, as in Behavior Therapy and Psycho-
Imagination Therapy, we are working to promote the growth process
and develop the human potential. We're not talking about instant
sensory awareness, instant happiness, or instant cure. The growth
process is a process that takes time, effort, and energy. It is
necessary to fill in the holes in the personality to make the

person whole, and complete again, especially in today's period of
alienation, automation, and change.

REFERENCES

Assagioli, R. Psychosynthesis. New York: The Viking Press, 1961.
Hillman, J. Re-visioning psychology. New York: Harper and Row,
    1975.
Lazarus, A. A., and Abramovitz, A. The use of emotive imagery in
    the treatment of children's phobias. Journal of Mental Science,
    19 , 108, 191.
Paul, G. Insight vs. desensitization in psychotherapy. California:
    Stanford University Press, 1966.
Perls, F. S. Gestalt therapy verbation. New York: Bantam Books,
    1974.
Perls, F. S. Ego, hunger and aggression. New York: Vintage Books,
    1968.
Rosen, G. Don't be afraid. New York: Spectrum Books, 1976.
Selye, H. The stress of life. New York: McGraw-Hill, 1976.
Singer, J. L. Imagery and daydream techniques employed in psycho-
    therapy: some practical and theoretical implications. In
    C. Spielberger (Ed.), Current topics in clinical and community
    psychology. New York: Academic Press, 1971, Vol. 3.
Shorr, J. E. Go see the movie in your head. New York: Popular
    Library, 1977.
Shorr, J. E. Psycho-imagination therapy. New York: Interconti-
    nental Medical Book Corporation, 1972.
Shorr, J. E. Psychotherapy through imagery. New York: Inter-
    continental Medical Book Corporation, 1974.
Wolpe, J. The practice of behavior therapy. New York: Pergamon
    Press, Inc., 1973.
Wolpe, J. Psychotherapy by reciprocal inhibition. Stanford, Ca.:
    Stanford University Press, 1958.

III: MOVEMENT THERAPY AND ART THERAPY

CONTACTING BODILY-FELT EXPERIENCING IN PSYCHOTHERAPY

Erma Dosamantes-Alperson, Ph.D.

University of California

Los Angeles

Abstract: Experiential Movement Psychotherapy (which
integrates improvisational movement, imagery and verbalization in one process) facilitates bodily-felt level
experiencing in receptive and action modes. The bodily-
felt sense of ourselves provides us with direct feedback
concerning our feelings, needs and direction for future
action. How meaning may be attained through kinesthetic-
movement and through bodily-derived hypnogogic imagery
is discussed and demonstrated through clinical examples.

Gendlin (1973) defines bodily-felt experiencing as the concrete sense of being in one's body. This presentation will deal
with the importance of the bodily-felt level of experiencing in
psychotherapy. A form of therapy, Experiential Movement Psychotherapy, which uses body-movement as a medium to promote personal
growth and to synthesize nonverbal with verbal experiential modes,
will be described. Several body-movement concepts encompassed by
the approach will be presented and illustrated by clinical examples
from actual movement psychotherapy sessions.

EXPERIENTIAL MOVEMENT PSYCHOTHERAPY

Experiential Movement Psychotherapy is a form of psychotherapy
which seeks to integrate improvisational movement, imagery and verbalization through a single unified process (Dosamantes-Alperson,
1974a, 1974b, 1976). The process which emerges in this approach
seems analogous to that cited by Wallas (1926) in delineating the
stages of the creative process. There is an initial state of

223

imbalance (experienced by the client as a sense of dissatisfaction)
followed by an easing and relaxation of conscious controls which
lead the client to the direct contacting of nonverbal modes of
experiencing (i.e., the bodily-felt and the imaged). This is followed by a verification phase where a more conscious analytical
synthesis takes place. This cognitive phase paves the way for a
new-found state of equilibrium. The process moves in direction
from the implicit bodily-felt level to the explicit, rational verbal
level--from the inside-out.

When working with individual clients, the movement psychotherapist attends to how a client allows or inhibits the outward expression of incipient bodily movements, to how these felt-movements
interact with ongoing spontaneous images to reveal metaphoric meanings, to how these meanings are further articulated through words
and taken into action outside of the therapy situation. If working
within the context of a group, the movement psychotherapist additionally attends to how the individual client deals nonverbally
with interpersonal issues triggered while moving with others.

The movement psychotherapist (a psychotherapist trained in the
use of movement as a process for self-actualization and as a form
of communication rather than as a form of exercise or entertainment)
functions to provide the degree of structure which s/he feels is
needed by an individual or by group members to engage in improvisational movement without becoming overly inhibited, and as an
observer who intercedes in the movement process when the client is
unable to move. At such a time, s/he functions to help the client
move through the experience of being blocked. Each session allows
for spontaneous client verbalization to be expressed in association
to the nonverbal phase.

Since it appears that the meaning we obtain from nonverbal
experiencing is affected by the mode of consciousness through which
it is contacted, movement psychotherapists who are concerned with
their clients' integration of nonverbal with verbal experiencing or
with the relationship between intrapsychic and interpersonal events,
provide their clients with an opportunity to explore themselves
through movement in both receptive and action modes.

Deikman (1974, 1976) distinguishes between these two modes,
claiming that human beings function in terms of a bimodal consciousness which serves to organize perception and behavior. According
to him, in the receptive mode we function to let in sensory aspects
of the environment. Parasympathetic nervous activity and sensory-
perceptual activity predominate. Attention is focused inward on
internal events and base-line muscle tension is decreased. Para-
logical thought characterized by intuition and sensation assumes
prominence. By contrast, in the action mode, we function to manipulate or act upon the environment. Sympathetic nervous activity and

striate muscle activity predominate. Attention is maintained on
external events and base-line muscle tension is increased. If this
is so, it is reasonable to view effective, integrative psychological
functioning as a person's ability to regulate these modes of consciousness to suit the particular environmental situation, internal
or external.

EXPLORING BODILY-FELT EXPERIENCING
   IN THE RECEPTIVE MODE

     As a psychotherapist, I have found that if I wish my clients
to derive meaning from their internal nonverbal experiencing, they
need to contact and explore such experiencing nonverbally in the
receptive mode. The vigilant attention and discursive type of communication involved in verbal language are not conducive to the
processing of information derived from bodily-felt level experiencing (Langer, 1942; .Ornstein, 1972; Deikman, 1974). Isadora Duncan
made this same point more succinctly when she said, "If I could tell
you what it meant, there would be no point in dancing it" (Duncan,
cited in Bateson, 1972, p. 137).

     The emotional meaning inherent in incipient bodily movement
and the metaphoric significance found in visual imagery may be discovered directly by clients when they temporarily turn down the
verbal channel and tune in to the ongoing flow of sensations and
perceptions. When they allow themselves to feel, move and see their
experience, clients discover something about their style of approach
and also something about the significance of the content revealed.

     In order to facilitate my clients' exploration of their internal
nonverbal experiencing, which consists of physical sensations and
images, I find it necessary for them to assume a receptive state of
mind. This receptive state is achieved by clients when they lie
down, close their eyes and relax. The reclining posture appears to
promote a greater freedom and spontaneity of free-associative
material (Kroth, 1970), more vivid imagery (Morgan and Bakan, 1965),
and a greater number of memories and earlier ones than does the
sitting up position (Berdach and Bakan, 1967). The closing of one's
eyes has the effect of reducing input from external stimuli. Any
self-directed relaxation method (e.g., Jacobson's self-operations
control progressive relaxation technique) can be used to promote a
reduction in residual muscle tension.

Body-Focusing

     When clients are in a relaxed, inward-turned state of mind,
they are invited to engage in a sort of physical stock-taking which
I call "body-focusing." This is a direct attending to one's physical self which entails tuning in to:

The general sense of one's physical well-being

The ease of flow of one's breath

The degree of tension or effort present in one's body

The posture or bodily attitude one assumes during moments
of relative stillness

The feeling qualities which are triggered by internal
incipient body movements as these are given outward
obvious form

The feeling qualities experienced as one moves in relation
to other moving persons (if moving within the context of
a group)

The value of body-focusing in the receptive mode is that it
heightens the individual's "somatic perception." Jourard (1974)
used this term to refer to an individual's awareness of his or her
own bodily sensations at any given moment. He believed that any
reduction in somatic perception prevented the person from recognizing the effects of unduly stressful and devitalizing relationships
and from taking positive action for change. It has now been empirically demonstrated that body-focusing increases the ability of clients to detect and discriminate feelings (Dosamantes-Alperson and
Merrill, in press).

Incipient Body Movements

In the receptive mode, clients are able to follow the flow of
sensory experiences and incipient body movements. Rugg (1963)
defined these movements as motor attitudes which give rise to feelings. I refer to incipient body movements which occur in the receptive mode as "internal-intrapsychic movements." By drawing the
clients' attention to the experience of these movements and their
transformation into overt action, clients begin to sense feeling
and action as one. By tuning in to incipient body movement, clients
have the opportunity to track the flux of feelings which accompany
emergent sensory and imagery events.

Though internally experienced by the moving client, these movements are not readily detected by movement observers who track them
only visually because they are implicit and subtle. These movements
appear to signal an expectancy or intent of action on the part of
the mover. The overt or consummatory movement, which results when
incipient movements are given outward form, often reveals to the
mover something about his/her motivation or intent.

Body-self acceptance is increased through body-focusing and by attending to incipient body movements (Dosamantes-Alperson and Merrill, in press). The body-self concept refers to the attitudes an individual has towards his/her own body.

Given the subtlety of incipient body movements, it is unlikely that simple visual observation would be sufficient for the therapist to detect them. As a movement psychotherapist, I am able to make sense of my clients' kinesthetic responses because, while observing them in motion, I find myself recreating their movements in my own body, in the abbreviated and coded form of incipient movements. For instance, I follow the shifts in weight, effort, placement and direction without having to convert such movements into broader, overt ones. Through this kind of kinesthetic empathy, I am able to sense and respond to the clients' emotional state of the moment. By tracking these movements, I am able to provide the kinds of movement cues or structure which they might require in order to carry their experiential process forward.

How I use body-focusing and encourage the transformation of incipient to outward consummatory movement for the purpose of stimulating the associative process between physical and psychological experiencing will be illustrated through the following case.

Lorna, 38, heavy-set, intellectually-brilliant woman, sought movement psychotherapy because she found that whenever she attempted to dance spontaneously, she was moved to tears but could not explain why. She had some vague notion that a part of her was "untouched" and she wanted to find out more about this part of herself. What follows is a description of what ensued during her first movement psychotherapy session.

Following a brief verbal exchange in which she gave me her reasons for seeking this form of therapy, I asked her to look around the room and move to a place she thought she might be comfortable moving. She selected a place that was some distance from me and assumed a sitting position, facing away from me. I asked her to close her eyes and to focus on the flow of her breath, letting whatever thoughts she might be having to come and go without holding on to them. After a while, I suggested that she sense the pulse going on in her body and allow this pulse to be moved out in space without passing judgment on it. She moved for a while with her eyes closed. The movement which I could observe originated primarily in her upper torso. She led with her chest held forward and moved her upper torso in a circular pivotal fashion. By contrast to her active top-half, her lower torso remained perfectly still and appeared rooted to the floor.

She indicated that she was finished by automatically opening up her eyes. I asked her if she would like to share any associations she had to her movement experience. Her first verbal

association was that she felt that she moved in the studio in the
same way that she moved in the outside world. I asked her to
amplify what she meant. As she sought to explain further, she took
a deep breath, expanded her chest and placed both of her hands on
her hips in a confrontative or challenging posture. She explained
that the attitude she had just assumed represented the way that she
related to the world outside. She called it her "attitude to the
world at large."

I asked her how she would describe the feeling tone of this
posture and she responded with "angry" and "as though I'm saying
I'll show you." Then I asked her what she experienced below her
waist and she replied that she felt "nothing."

Then, almost as an afterthought, she wondered out loud if this
sense of no-feeling might have anything to do with her current lack
of sexual excitement?

Following these more immediate associations, she mentioned a
childhood memory which had been triggered while she was moving.
The memory was that of her father comparing her unfavorably to her
younger, prettier sister; berating her by calling her "big" and
"clumsy." As she spoke, she stuck out her tongue several times
(she was quite unaware of this action, though to me this unconscious
gesture seemed perfectly congruent with the feelings of resentment
she was expressing toward her father). She concluded her verbal
narrative of her childhood memory with a prophetic comment about her
existential condition; "It must have been then (referring to the
time of her childhood) that I must have decided to excel in the
world through my intellect rather than physical looks."

This session demonstrates how directly unconscious meanings
may be revealed when the clients' experiencing is approached initially in a receptive nonverbal bodily-felt way.

Releasing Bound-Affect

It is inevitable that when clients attend to their physical-
selves in the receptive mode, they will also contact areas of
chronic tension or blocked/frozen movement in their bodies. It
has been posited that such chronic tension is the result of psychic
conflict in which there has been a blocking of potential motor
action (Bull, 1951; Jacobson, 1938, 1970; Lowen, 1970, 1975;
Plutchick, 1954; Roskin-Berger, 1972; Reich, 1949; Rolf, 1977).
Persistent blocking of incipient body movements has been shown to
lead to tension in selective parts of the body (Bull, 1951;
Jacobson, 1967; Plutchick, 1954).

In Experiential Movement Psychotherapy, clients are encouraged
to focus on their experience of tension and to the varying degrees

discovered in different parts of their bodies (Dosamantes-Alperson, 1976). By learning how to release excessive residual muscle tension, clients simultaneously release the bound affect associated with chronic tension. The release of strong affect frequently triggers memories or psychological associations which have personal significance to the person.

How clients may contact such tension and explore the experiential effects of its release will be illustrated by the movement experience of a client participating in the early phases of an experiential movement psychotherapy group. Following a brief period of relaxation, group members moved through an open-ended but structured movement-imagery experience which included getting in touch with those parts of their bodies they experienced as most tense, then allowing a form or image to be developed from their experienced tension and assigning a name or label to it.

The phenomenological account of one of the group members to this movement-imagery experience is offered below.

Christine, 28, experienced a tightness in her intestines. The form she created was that of a large black, vile, oozy glob which became transformed into a tight fist. The fist became lodged on one side of her intestines. She was surprised that the name which spontaneously popped into her head was that of "Mother." She realized that she often experienced her guts tighten while relating to her mother. She attempted to extract the fist from her intestines but could not. As she tried to do so, she experienced an intense combination of rage and hurt. Finally, she attempted to expel her mother out by allowing her to pass through her anus. But, while she was able to move her mother from her guts to her bowels, she could not push her out of her anus. (Incidentally, this client complained of serious bouts with constipation; she often resorted to the administration of enemas as a means of relieving this problem.) The experience which Christine had led her to conclude that she was not yet ready to cast out the "bad" mother in her. She acknowledged that she needed to explore further the meaning of her relationship to her mother.

This case demonstrates how the release of tension may lead to the release of bound affect and correlate psychological associations. It also shows the psychogenic component involved in the formation of psychosomatic symptoms. The connection evidenced in this case between physical and psychological experiencing points to the need to work with physical and psychological structures simultaneously (Dosamantes-Alperson, 1974b, 1974c).

The Movement-Imagery Connection

By following the transformation of concrete physical

experiences into visual images, clients can discover the personal
context in which these physical and nonverbal experiences are
embedded. Such images frequently reveal personally meaningful content pertaining to unfinished problematic or conflict situations in
the client's life. The movement psychotherapist can assist the
transformation of the physical form to the visual symbol by first
helping clients discriminate the physical or bodily qualities they
experience and then encouraging them to allow an image to develop
which shares similar attributes to the physically experienced ones
(as was demonstrated in the case of Christine).

Images which occur while the person is in the receptive mode
(i.e., relaxed but conscious) are called hypnogogic images (Horowitz,
1970). These images are preconscious, preverbal visual symbols
characterized by changing thematic content, motion, vividness,
affect and relative autonomy (Kosbab, 1974). Clients who move while
focused on hypnogogic images appear to be hardly moving at all,
though in fact, they can be quite involved in the interaction
between physically-felt experiencing and emotionally-charged visual
symbols. By staying in touch with the evolving movement-image
interaction, clients can achieve new experiential associations
between current life experiences and past unfinished situations.
An example of how movement and hypnogogic imagery interact to bring
a personal conflict to conscious awareness and permit the therapist
to work through its current manifestations will be illustrated by
the following case.

Lorraine, 36, showed up to her movement psychotherapy session
seemingly distracted and complaining of feeling very tense all week
and of not being able to think of anything else but her upcoming
Graduate Entrance Exams. She feared that she would do miserably
and fail them. She tried lying down and relaxing but could not.
She fidgeted, twitched and complained of all sorts of aches, particularly an ache in her left leg which felt severely cramped.

I asked her to get in touch with what would not let her rest.
This suggestion gave rise to an image of her parents admonishing
her for "not keeping her place" and "making them feel inferior to
her." I asked her to imagine not staying in her place but of going
someplace. She imagined herself walking along a path which was
filled with fog all around. As she continued to walk along the
path she could see that there were stairs going up somewhere high.
She became aware that although she didn't know where the stairs
led and there did not appear to be any people around, she did have
a keen and concrete sense of her feet being firmly planted on the
ground even as she continued to climb the stairs. She seemed
quite pleased to be experiencing herself as "so grounded." With
this realization, the fog began to lift and she noticed that the
pain in her legs had vanished.

When she subsequently described her experience, she remarked
that while she could not see ahead to her future life because, in
fact, it was largely unknown to her, she did feel secure and confident that the path she had chosen was right for her. That, it
was right for her "to move up in the world" and to continue her
graduate studies.

Hypnogogic images possess several qualities which I find most
useful in my work as a movement psychotherapist. They possess a
motion component which embues them with a motion picture quality
(Shorr, 1974; Singer, 1974). Therefore, clients who can tune in to
incipient body movements and can move spontaneously, are able to
follow the thematic shifts which occur in their images with their
bodies. It is as though they were receiving continuous feedback
from their bodies while concomitantly watching the unfolding pictures in their minds' eye. Through the movement-imagery interaction, clients are able to obtain an appreciation for the flux and
intensity of feeling which accompanies their visually symbolized
experience.

In addition, hypnogogic images are often quite vivid and can,
therefore, provide clients with a sense of actually re-living significant past situations. Assagioli (1965), Desoille (1965), and
Leuner (1969) view such imagery as the direct voice of the unconscious. Because these images also appear to transcend time by making past, current and anticipated events simultaneously available
to the person, new solutions to personal conflicts are likely to
emerge while visualizing these images.

The value of "moving an image" rather than simply focusing on
an image without movement is that clients can take the visual experience into their bodies, allowing a physical identification to be
made between their internal sensations and the imagined situation.
They can empathize physically with all aspects of the image and
thereby gain an awareness of the felt-attitude they hold toward
each revealed experiential element.

Furthermore, "moving an image" serves to mediate between receptive and action modes, since the incipient body movements which
accompany hypnogogic images may be extended out in space and given
intentional and visible outward form.

EXPLORING BODILY-FELT EXPERIENCING
   IN THE ACTION MODE

When clients move in the action mode, they reveal how they
approach and deal with the external world of objects and people
(Ornstein, 1972; Deikman, 1974). The action mode appears to be
most effective when intentionally exploring the external world.

When clients move in this mode, a movement psychotherapist can observe them attending outward toward their external environment. They move with their eyes open and begin to explore the space around them, either alone or in relation to another in a group. Their movements are overt and readily detectable by trained movement observers. When trained movement observers use terms such as "an individual's movement style" or "a person's movement range," they generally are alluding to movements which are performed in the action mode. For this reason, movements performed in the action mode may be referred to as "external-interactional movements."

In order to facilitate clients' movement in the action mode, they need to be encouraged to move with their eyes open and to assume an exploratory attitude towards their environment of objects and people.

For most clients (particularly those who have not been formally trained as dancers) the prospect of moving through space rather than talking about their experience is a difficult one. This seems to be as true for the so-called well-adjusted clients as for the most regressed or mute ones. Consequently, most clients need to move through a desensitization or disinhibition movement phase before they will allow themselves to move less self-consciously in space. The movement psychotherapist can provide a safe movement environment by guiding clients through movement experiences which are impersonal or abstract, yet begin to get the person used to moving nonverbally through space (e.g., in a first group movement therapy session, the movement therapist might suggest that clients try using different parts of their bodies to take them across the room). This type of structure offers clients the opportunity to discover physical and movement aspects of themselves, while providing them with an opportunity to exercise a safe degree of self-direction.

As clients discover that they are not being judged by the therapist with respect to how well they move or for the types of movements which they do, they appear to become less self-critical and evaluative of themselves while moving. They are then able to begin to move with increased confidence and spontaneity. Once clients no longer feel inhibited while moving, they are able to turn their attention to how they move through space on any given day, and if moving within the context of a group, to how they engage others in nonverbal movement interactions.

Individual Movement Style

By moving extemporaneously in the action mode, clients gain a sense of which movements feel comfortable to them and hence are preferred by them, and which movements feel uncomfortable to them and therefore, are usually avoided. In this way, they are able to perceive something about their own unique movement preferences or about their own unique "movement style" and can begin to deliberately risk moving in new ways not previously attempted by them.

Interpersonal Movement Interactions

Through external-interactional movement, clients learn something about how they relate to others in a group. This is accomplished through the nonverbal dialogues which they have with others who are moving in the same space. As clients relate to the similarities and differences they perceive in others, they get in touch with what qualities they share in common with others and in what ways they differ. They discover how to mediate perceived nonverbal differences. Thus, a shy introverted person who initially is observed to move in a cautious, self-contained way will differ from an aggressive, extroverted individual who might move in an expansive, intrusive way. How these two personalities confront and mediate their nonverbal differences through movement becomes the focus of the movement session.

When clients realize that their nonverbal behavior parallels their verbal behavior in other social contexts outside of the movement therapy session, they are able to make use of their somatic percepts to guide their verbal interactions (i.e., there is an increased congruence between what they feel, how they act and what they say when they speak (Dosamantes-Alperson, 1977)).

The value of moving one's experience first before verbalizing it is that one can observe how one copes and protects one's self in relationships with others without the interference of a priori verbal scripts or plans. The words which flow from such nonverbal experiences then provide clients with an opportunity to clarify, verify and extend the meaning of their nonverbal experiences still further (Dosamantes-Alperson, 1974b).

How a movement psychotherapist provides a supportive milieu to encourage nonverbal self-exploration and relational insights within the context of a movement therapy group is demonstrated by the following example.

The session to be described took place during the eve of Halloween. One of the group members of an all women's movement therapy group took advantage of the occasion to show up to the group session dressed up as a witch. However, this was no ordinary witch. This "witch" had taken great pains to gray her hair, silver-paint her body, darken her front teeth, paint her nails a bright orange, drip theatrical blood down the side of her mouth, wear a long black silk gown and black cape, and even have a realistic-looking snake dangling from her shoulders.

Needless to say, the presence of this "witch" could not be

ignored or dismissed lightly by the group. Because the group
appeared to be stymied with respect to how to respond to this
"witch," and since it seemed to me that this woman needed to be
acknowledged by the group for that part of herself which the "witch"
character represented to her and which she had chosen to show to the
group, I encouraged her to move to the center of the group. I then
asked her to get in touch with what kind of witch she felt herself
to be by letting the spontaneous movements which emerged from her
tell her. She moved, using expansive, undulating movements, sometimes she moved seductively, and at other times she moved in a
menacing and assertive manner.

Once she was clear as to who she was as a "witch," I encouraged
her to relate to each member of the group as that "witch," moving
with one group member at a time. As she permitted herself to feel
her impact on others and theirs on her, she appeared to get in touch
with her own sense of power and control over them. The group members, in turn, responded to a particular aspect which she triggered
in them relative to the issue of power. Some allowed themselves to
be bewitched, letting themselves be overpowered by her and yielding
to her. Others rejected her attempts to overpower them by asserting
their own strength against hers. Still others converted the movement relationship into a sensual one. The discussion which followed
this bewitching movement experience brought out the issue of the
different meanings that "power" held for each of the women in the
group.

In conclusion, it appears that experiential movement psychotherapy (which is initially a bodily, nonverbal, inside-out approach
to psychotherapy) facilitates bodily-felt level experiencing in both
receptive and action modes. When clients engage in body-movement in
the receptive mode they gain direct contact with internal (intrapsychic) bodily-felt experiencing. Feeling reactivity, somatic perception, body-felt awareness and acceptance are increased through
body-focusing and by attending to incipient body-movements. Bound
affect may be released through the release of blocked/frozen movement and direct access to unconscious content and correlate feelings may be obtained by moving hypnogogic images. When moving in
the action mode clients have access to external (interpersonal)
bodily-felt experiencing. By moving in this mode, they can discover
their own unique movement style, as well as how they mediate perceived differences between themselves and others.

This total bodily-felt experiencing range may then be further
articulated and shared by clients through words. Thus, a synthesis
of the nonverbal with the verbal is accomplished in this form of
psychotherapy.

REFERENCES

Assagioli, R. Psycho-synthesis: a manual of principles and tech-
    niques. New York: Hobbs, Dorman, 1965.
Bateson, G. Steps to an ecology of mind. New York: Ballantine
    Books, 1972.
Berdach, E., and Bakan, P. Body position and free recall of early
    memories. Psychotherapy: Theory, Research and Practice,
    1967, 4, 101-102.
Bull, N. The attitude theory of emotion. New York: Coolidge
    Foundation Publishers, 1951.
Deikman, A. J. Bimodal consciousness. In R. E. Ornstein (Ed.),
    The nature of human consciousness. New York: Viking Press,
    1974.
Deikman, A. J. Bimodal consciousness and the mystic experience.
    In R. E. Ornstein (Ed.), Symposium on consciousness. New
    York: Viking Press, 1976.
Desoille, R. The directed daydream, Monograph No. 7. New York:
    Psychosynthesis Research Foundation, 1965.
Dosamantes-Alperson, E. Process for facilitating body-mind integra-
    tion. JSAS Catalog of Selected Documents in Psychology, 1974a,
    4(83) (Ms. No. 688).
Dosamantes-Alperson, E. Carrying experiencing forward through
    authentic body movement. Psychotherapy: Theory, Research and
    Practice, 1974b, 11, 211-214.
Dosamantes-Alperson, E. The creation of meaning through body move-
    ment. In A. I. Rabin (Ed.), Clinical Psychology: Issues of
    the Seventies. East Lansing: Michigan State University Press,
    1974c.
Dosamantes-Alperson, E. Experiential movement psychotherapy. Art
    Psychotherapy, 1976, 3, 1-5.
Dosamantes-Alperson, E. Nonverbal and verbal integration. In
    W. Anderson (Ed.), Therapy and the arts. New York: Harper
    and Row, 1977.
Dosamantes-Alperson, E., and Merrill, N. Growth effects of experi-
    ential movement psychotherapy. Psychotherapy: Theory,
    Research and Practice, in press.
Gendlin, E. T. Experiential psychotherapy. In R. Corsini (Ed.),
    Current Psychotherapies. Itasca, Illinois: Peacock, 1973.
Horowitz, M. J. Image formation and cognition. New York: Apple-
    ton-Century-Crofts, 1970.
Jacobson, E. Progressive relaxation. Chicago: University of
    Chicago Press, 1938.
Jacobson, E. Biology of emotions. Springfield, Illinois: Charles
    C. Thomas, 1967.
Jacobson, E. Modern treatment of tense patients. New York:
    Charles C. Thomas, 1970.
Jourard, S. M. Healthy personality. New York: Macmillan, 1974.
Kosbab, P. F. Imagery techniques in psychiatry. Archives of Gen-
    eral Psychiatry, 1974, 31, 283-290.

Kroth, J. A. The analytic couch and response to free association. _Psychotherapy: Theory, Research and Practice_, 1970, _7_, 206-208.

Langer, S. K. _Philosophy in a new key_. New York: The New American Library, 1942.

Leuner, H. Guided affective imagery (GAI): a method of intensive psychotherapy. _American Journal of Psychotherapy_, 1969, _23_, 4-22.

Lowen, A. The body in therapy. _American Dance Therapy Association Proceedings_, 1970, 1-9.

Lowen, A. _Bioenergetics_. New York: Penguin Books, 1975.

Morgan, R., and Bakan, P. Sensory deprivation hallucinations and other sleep behavior as a function of position, method of report and anxiety. _Perceptual and Motor Skills_, 1965, _20_, 19-25.

Ornstein, R. E. _The psychology of consciousness_. New York: Viking Press, 1972.

Plutchick, R. The role of muscular tension and maladjustment. _The Journal of General Psychology_, 1954, _50_, 45-62.

Reich, W. _Character analysis_. New York: Farrar, Straus and Giroux, 1949.

Rolf, I. P. _Rolfing: the integration of human structures_. Santa Monica: Dennis-Landman, 1977.

Roskin-Berger, M. Bodily experience and the expression of emotions. _American Dance Therapy Association Monograph No. 2_, 1972, 191-230.

Rugg, H. _Imagination_. New York: Harper and Row, 1963.

Shorr, J. E. _Psychotherapy through imagery_. New York: Intercontinental Medical Book Corp., 1974.

Singer, J. _Imagery and daydream methods in psychotherapy and behavior modification_. New York: Academic Press, 1974.

Wallas, G. _The art of thought_. New York: Harcourt, Brace, 1926.

IMAGINATION AND MOVEMENT THERAPY

Rose A. Dendinger, M.A.

Institute for Psycho-Imagination Therapy

Los Angeles, California 90048

AN EXPERIENTIAL SESSION PRESENTED
TO AASMI

The purpose of the session was to have people experience imagery through movement. What I have done in this paper is to select images from those given in the session, and give an explanation as to the intent and rationale for each image. The session was opened with some brief comments on the nature of the interaction between imagery and movement. Imagery flows out of movement and movement flows out of imagery. The body's motional usages of and emotional attitudes toward space, time, energy and rhythm can engender in the imagination deep images. The way we move within ourselves, gesture, posture, touch, or the way we move and are moved in relationship to another person contains the non-verbal movement history of our way of being in the world. This non-verbal history is inscribed in our very muscles and breathing. It is as if there is a retention of memory in the body, and movement can release this memory.

Movement also releases imagery through polarities of movement. Polar images easily come out of polarities of movement and are usually congruent with emotional responses. Some of the polar qualities in movement image include curved-angular, weak-strong, small-large, open-closed, active-passive, gather-scatter, living-dead. The following case study was presented to illustrate the dynamics of working with imagery and polarities. The patient had recently self-mutilated his eyes such that they had to be enucleated. Early in the course of movement therapy, the patient was asked to make the smallest movement he could. He gradually curled himself into a ball, and when asked to make a large movement, he slowly spiralled from the ground up. As he came up he said, "I'm growing, growing,

growing." The patient called this his "baby to man exercise." He
confided to me that it was comfortable to be in the ball, and that
it reminded him of being an infant, and that it was "scary to be
the man." This movement exercise became a metaphor for the growth
the patient experienced during his hospitalization.

After these brief comments on the nature of the interaction
between imagery and movement, I began the session with the movement
polarities of curved and angular in order to rouse people to move
and to help build a movement vocabulary out of which they could draw
in order to express themselves. I asked them to create curved,
rounded movements, first with their hands and arms, and then to
explore how many different ways curved and rounded movements could
be experienced in their body. Then they were asked to let their
movements' shape take them out into space. Curved and rounded movements produced qualities of motion such as graceful, fluid, sensu-
ous, and sustained. Sharp and angular movements produced different
movement qualities and feeling tones from curved and rounded movements: feet began to stamp, voices ejaculated sounds and words,
and the overall energy level increased. Bursts of movement ended
abruptly: slashes, jabs and strong movements filled the room.
While some people were totally involved in the exploration and
turned into themselves, others made eye contact and moved with each
other.

Working with polarities in movement, the body through its
imagination has the capacity to disclose conflicts, situations,
emotion, and action (movement). Attending to physical aspects of
movement, with its kinesthetic, proprioceptive, and tactile sensations, a person becomes more aware of himself and of internal
responses to others and the environment. The psychological aspects
of movement offer a myriad of opportunities for a person to explore
and vivify emotional states. Image in movement allows for a catharsis for the body which gives feeling and feedback.

After the exploration of moving in various ways with curved
and angular, this image was given: imagine one animal coming out
of the top of your head and one out of your guts. The animals are
walking down a road together. What do they see, feel and do? Have
the animals talk to one another. What happens? Make the shape of
one animal. How does it walk or move? You may choose to make
shapes to show the mood of your animal. Connect your shapes with
movement and move out into space. Time was given for the exploration of the second animal.

Moving in the image of an animal allows for individual movement
styles and psychological approaches. While some people stretched
their arms with fingers pointed upward, others held their arms in
close to their bodies with tight fists. Some leaped forward with
exultant expressions on their faces. Moving in the image of an

animal offered people a way to be less self-conscious and to become
completely involved in fantasy. Once involved, a movement story
usually unfolded on its own. Different feeling states come out of
different movement patterns. Being the animal and "moving" the
image gets a person more intensely involved with the animal. Pro-
jecting one's pathos onto the animal makes some people feel less
vulnerable to moving and expressing themselves.

The image of the two animals is in a category referred to as
"Dual Imagery," and is one of the many categories of imagery developed by Dr. Joseph Shorr (1974). I am concerned with how his
imagery-work can be integrated into movement therapy. The difference between the two animals reflects aspects of conflict within
the person or with others.

After the image of the two animals, people were asked to lie
down for relaxation. The relaxation method I used is based on
Dr. Edmund Jacobson's self-operations control progressive relaxation
technique which helps to reduce tension (1938). Not only is relaxation a way of lowering tension, but also it is equally important
for teaching a person to focus and concentrate on what is happening
internally and on the images that occur. When the body relaxes the
mind also relaxes and a person is more apt to enter deeper levels
of consciousness. In this relaxed state past memory and new images
provide psychological material for new meaning and reflection on
one's life.

In order to create a different level of intensity and experience in moving with imagery, I concluded the session by playing
African brass band music from Ghana, West Africa. The people were
first asked to feel the rhythm of the music in their bodies before
moving out into space. The following image was then given: you
are in Africa and the entire village, including a brass band, has
turned out to celebrate something you have accomplished or something
you wish to accomplish. You and the brass band are leading a pro-
cession around the village. Let the spirit of the music and image
move you. The image and sound of the brass band created a multi-
dimensional emotive mood which rhythmically transmitted the music
through the body. The power of positive suggestion in the image of
"having accomplished something" helped to redirect the mind and
body toward positive feelings and goals.

The mode of movement therapy that I was trained in works with
focusing on the inside-out for therapeutic "insight." The African-
inspired way of working is from the outside-in. The movement itself
does not bring insight, but it does change people's behavior and
then they feel better. Professor John Kennedy (1974) sees movement
as getting people going in certain patterns. When they move and
find out they can function, then the mind takes care of itself.

I took the privilege of presenting an image connected with Africa, for out of my experience as both a Movement Therapist and a Dance Ethnologist (I have spent four years in Ghana), I find that it enhances my effectiveness to look at another culture's dance to see what implications there are for movement therapy. The African image experience was given to illustrate that the outside environment can trigger an image (here, the use of brass band music, plus the image of being in an African village).

CONCLUSION

The session attempted to introduce people to the notion that images can be "moved." The images I selected to write on in this paper mainly work with polarities in movement and imagery. The intent of the "curved-angular" exercise was to have people experience opposite movement patterns which trigger different memory traces, images and feeling states.

The animal image gave people something concrete to work with, both on a psychological and movement level. The intent of the image was to reveal the contrasting differences between the two animals and to see if any conflict existed between them.

The African image was given to illustrate that images can come out of a suggested image, music, and out of the movement itself. Certain rhythms, postures, gestures, and movements will bring back an "image" of a past event or feeling state, or they can work with fantasies of the here-and-now or the projected future. Imagery, therefore, can either come out of the movement itself, or movement can come out of the imagery. There is an active sensory stimulation taking place, for the visual, tactile, auditory, and olfactory senses which may be activated in the creative process of imagery.

Movement Therapy is concerned finally with authentic movement that allows for the releasing of the emotional and intellectual (imagistic-mythic) unfolding of a movement (image) story.

REFERENCES

Dendinger, R. A., and Trop, J. L. Combined physical and psychiatric disability: a case study in movement therapy. _American Journal of Dance Therapy_, 1979, 3.

Dosamantes-Alperson, E. _Contacting bodily-felt experience in psychotherapy_, 1979. See paper published in this book.

Jacobson, E. _Progressive relaxation_. Chicago: University of Chicago Press, 1938.

Jacobson, E. _Biology of emotions_. Springfield, Illinois: Charles C. Thomas, 1967.

Kennedy, J. G. Cultural psychiatry. In J. J. Honigmann (Ed.),
    Handbook of social and cultural anthropology. Chicago: Rand
    McNally, 1974.
Shorr, J. E. Psychotherapy through imagery. New York: Interconti-
    nental Medical Book Corp., 1974.

CENTERING MOVEMENT AND THE VISUALIZATION

OF TRANSFORMATIONAL IMAGERY

Elisabeth Z. Danehy, Art Therapist

Charila-Delphi Foundation

San Francisco, California

THE CONCEPT

Body movement, experienced physically or imaginatively, plays a key role in the conscious awareness of inner images. In fact, physical movement can release the barriers to active, spontaneous participation in the visualization process that many individuals experience.

Centering movement that focuses on the inner sense of physical center, elongation of spine and release of tension, acts as a particularly effective catalyst for active visualization of deep level imagery. "Centering," in contrast to more active forms of movement, initiates a threshold state wherein conscious and unconscious meet in which "gesture as felt thought" (Rugg, 1963) triggers awareness of transformational or "healing" imagery. These images are experienced as spontaneous and powerful manifestations of the "Self" (Jung, 1956). Often they occur in the visualization as mandala or radial forms of light, accompanied by sound and other sensory data.

This creative threshold occurs between cerebral hemispheres as a light-altered state of consciousness, in which active visualization occurs kinaesthetically, not merely on a mental screen or picture. Because the centering movement (which incorporates aspects of T'ai Chi and the Alexander Method) places emphasis on body awareness and alert attention to inner sensory data, the experience is quite different from meditation, hypnosis, or other deep trance states. It can be described as contemplation, for the imagery is active and spontaneous, yet affords the individual freedom to change the viewpoint and the action.

The exercise, which is described fully in the second part of this paper, operates on a sequential continuum of movement ⟶ active visualization ⟶ art. The contemplative attention developed in the movement sequence encourages an attitude of relaxed, yet alert, attention throughout. The creative process experienced in the visualization makes significant life pictures available to the individual. The art process completes and concretizes the visualization, giving therapist and client an image to mark the essential aspects of the experience.

The three-part procedure creates a structure for relaxation and centering, active participation in life images, and conscious recognition of the creative choices available to the individual. The attention remains focused on creative activity, not on free-associational or tangential thought. It goes to the center of problem solving and self-healing, rather than working with mock-ups of incomplete or fantasy pictures and/or the rearrangement of old or habitual states of being.

MOVEMENT ⟶ VISUALIZATION ⟶ ART EXERCISE

The exercise can be varied in length and focus, in response to individual needs. Some individuals take more time to relax and release physical tension, while others begin active visualization soon after initial centering. The entire exercise is generally 1-1/2 hours in length.

Movement

1. Stand tall, with feet slightly apart. Eyes can be open or closed. Imagine that you are a puppet with your head hanging from a cord. You are the puppeteer, as well. Pull up on the cord, so that your head is high (not the chin), and your shoulders and spine hang down naturally.

2. Your feet are firmly grounded. Feel the contact they make with the floor by shifting your weight.

3. Send the energy, imaged as a beam of light, _up_ from your pelvis. There is a gradual lengthening of the spine, until your head begins to "float" up from the shoulders. Your body feels suspended. You can find "center" by moving back and forth or around slightly. There is a physical sensation of relaxation when the body finds its own natural "float."

4. The energy of your legs moves _down_ from the pelvis to your feet, grounding you. Feel this polarization of the energy moving down and up, and explore the movements you can make with it.

   5. Breathe deeply and slowly, letting the air go to the small
of your back and abdomen first. Continue relaxed deep, slow breathing until a natural rhythm develops.

   Imagine that a beautiful clear color enters your body with
each breath. It fills you up slowly from feet to head. With each
breath it brings calm energy. Each breath that goes out takes tox-
ins and tension with it. Your breath flushes your body, cleansing
it.

   6. Focus again on lengthening your spine, allowing head and
torso to float up on the energy, while legs move down. Let the
energy also move out your arms and to the fingertips.

   Let the hands glide up on this energy to whatever height feels
effortless, suspended. Allow them to move freely. They can
describe an inner rhythm with small or large movements, and can be
fast or slow. Nothing should be forced. See if the hands can
"feel" the energy which surrounds your body.

   The entire body may move freely toward the end of this exercise, or it may remain relatively stationary. The emphasis is on
authentic movement of the individual's inner sense. The movement
also flows directly into the visualization, which may begin whenever the eyes are closed.

Visualization

   1. Allow your attention to focus again on the color of your
breath. Continue to move the energy of the spine up and that of
the legs down.

   2. Close your eyes, if they are not already closed. Focus
on the patterns your hands and body make as they move. See them
as color designs.

   3. Focus upon any strong image which appears, letting your
body respond to it.

   4. Sit or lie down, so that your full attention moves to this
image. Let it move and change naturally. (Your spine should be
straight and relaxed.)

   5. Describe the active imagery as it occurs. (The therapist
may ask questions occasionally, such as, "Where are you now?")

   The events of the visualization are recorded by the therapist.
The role of the therapist as recorder/observer requires asking
questions which stimulate careful attention to sensory and affective
detail. At times, the therapist is called upon to intervene more

actively, when the client is stuck or frightened by the imagery.
Nevertheless, the responsibility for "moving" the images, confronting the dangers, or changing the point of view remains with the client. The individual psyche has its own answers, and if encouraged
to do so, the individual will discover them.

Art

1. Draw or paint a significant _image_ or _feeling_ which occurred
during the movement/visualization experience.

2. You may do more than one drawing or painting.

3. When you have completed the art product, tape it to the
wall.

The art products are discussed in terms of their relationship
to the movement/visualization exercise, their symbolic content, and
the feelings evoked. The client is given responsibility for interpreting and making choices about relationship to the life situation.
The therapist guides primarily through questions which focus attention to choices and details in the visualization which may have
been overlooked or forgotten.

RESULTS: THREE CASES

Recent work with individuals experiencing acute psychoses has
given some important insights on the movement/visualization/art
exercise, which had previously been applied only to non-psychotic
individuals. It became clear that the creative problem-solving
attitudes and the transformational imagery, which occurred in previous populations, appeared to a highly significant degree in the
behavior and art of these psychotic individuals as well.

Many caution that visualization modes are too dangerous for
psychotic clients (Hammer, 1967; Horowitz, 1970; Leuner, 1969).
However, the individuals in this study responded in a non-regressive
manner, expressed increasingly relaxed affect, and exhibited health-
ful changes in attitude about life situation. Where frightening
images appeared with potentially overwhelming affect, the fear was
overcome by Senoi Indian techniques (Stewart, 1969). The therapist
might suggest that the client could advance and confront the enemy,
and that this enemy had something of value to teach. In situations
producing extreme fear, the psyche could, nevertheless, be counted
upon to produce weapons, shields and other objects of power, equal
to the danger. In every case, danger, as well as anger, was relin-
quished by active participation in the imagery.

It was the hypothesis of this study that the movement sequence

would "center" the individual physically and emotionally and that
it would facilitate the active visualization of transformational
imagery. The following were evidenced by client responses, therapist and evaluators' observations:

1. Physical sense of centering during movement

2. Increase in body motility (Lowen, 1970)

3. Observable changes in affect

4. Images of spiraling energy or mandala-like motif in
visualizations and art

In each case, the imagery included a high number of healing or
transformational symbols, such as the mandala, spiral, or quadrated
circle, which Jung (1956, 1959) described as indicators of a self-
healing process within the psyche. Other images which appeared,
though less frequently, were the kingship and hero motifs, Great
Mother, and union of opposites, described by Perry (1974) as archetypes of the Self, which appear during a radical reorganization of
the psyche. This was corroborated by client responses to these
images as sources of power and healing energy, and as being numinous.

Three Cases

1. Michael drew a series of spiraling forms in the first two
sessions, which later became circles. In another session the circles became female faces. Later the circles became a self-image
of an idealized Self. On one occasion, the visualized image of
spiraling energy was so awe-inspiring, that he sat down in tears.
It took encouragement for Michael to put this on paper, yet it
became his favorite, a spiraling mandala as large as his arms could
reach.

The centering movement resulted in dramatic changes in body
motility, often followed by catharsis of angry and agitated feelings
about a generalized "others." Although he perceived the release of
this anger as healthy, he was unable to find clear messages in it
about himself. He was able to apply the principle of centering to
his everyday life by finding new places in which to feel relatively
uncrowded.

2. Larry was deeply depressed during each of the six sessions.
However, in his case, the cathartic effects of the centering movement were even more pronounced. The movement exercise relaxed him
initially, but soon focused his awareness on severe physical discomfort. Often his legs began to shake, his chest felt "squeezed in
a vice," his heart area was in excruciating pain and his throat was
constricted. These symptoms of distress preceded emotionally

charged visualizations. The pain, muscular rigidity, and trembling were discharged by taking an active role in the visualization experience.

Each visualization confronted feared or hated images from childhood, such as his abandonment at age four. Each hated image was accompanied by resolution images, seen as mandala-like objects such as a rise window, a four-square castle, a quadrant divided shield, and several symbols of rebirth of a new self as child and king.

On several occasions Larry described the visualization of a split in his brain (separating left and right hemispheres) from which a demon emerged. Upon his courageous confrontation of this hideous creature, a particularly bright yellow light, with every color of the spectrum spinning off of it, moved spontaneously through his body from toes to head, leaving him peaceful. While such images occurred well in advance of any noticeable changes in his depression, they seemed to give him some sense of hope that change could occur.

3. Chris was able to relax and center himself easily in every session. His movements were generally expansive, relaxed and unself-conscious.

In each session he experienced a central pulsating, star-like image, which moved through him and was accompanied by sound. His was a hero's quest, entering the Void, discovering power objects, spiritual sites and encountering spirit guides.

The hero's quest seems to have been crystallized during the fourth session. In it, Chris experienced a central light surrounding the Void. Out of this darkness a cross appeared, which was "brighter than sunlight," piercing in its intensity. While watching this brilliant image, he observed a bright blue light encircling it. This symbol constellation seemed very potent, very alive to him.

In the last session, a guide appeared, and Chris suddenly remembered him from his dreams. This figure indicated that there were too many unresolved aspects in his life, especially related to his work. He was then told to take no further journeys into the "Unknown" until he had begun to "clean up his messy life." Chris took this guidance seriously and acted upon it with a sense of commitment.

In all three individuals, there were dramatic encounters with inner conflict and resolution. In the two cases where an immense load of anger and resentment was repressed, the long-term effects of activating these images is not measureable. While the affect-images of the healing archetypes triggered corresponding changes in affect and body motility during each session, one can only speculate, at this point, about the effects of exposure to such deep-level images of wholeness.

At the least, each individual learned some ways of confronting unpleasant data and allowing intuition to provide alternatives. Further, the attitude of open, alert attention to emerging images may act as a subconscious learning program, providing a predisposition to look for new choices and alternatives to seemingly hopeless life situations.

Chris's encounter with his guide is similar to that of other normal subjects, who frequently experience very clear messages about life situations. The reaction to such information is variable in any population, yet it is seldom more realistically and acutely perceived, or more quickly acted upon, than in this case. The acceptance of responsibility for the images appears tantamount to significant change in life pattern for any individual. (It is not surprising that Chris is now working creatively and productively-- and doing volunteer counseling, as well.)

REFERENCES

Arguelles, J., and Arguelles, M. Mandala. Berkeley: Shambala Press, 1972.

Chace, M. Dance alone is not enough. Dance Magazine, 1964, 38, 46-47, 58.

Eliade, M. Birth and rebirth. New York: Harper and Row, 1958.

Gill, N., and Brennan, M. Hypnosis and related states. New York: International Universities Press, 1959.

Hammer, M. The directed daydream technique. Psychotherapy: Theory, Resident and Practicing, 1967, 4, 173-181.

Horowitz, M. Image formation and cognition. New York: Appleton-Century-Crofts, 1970.

Huang, A. Embrace tiger, return to mountain--the essence of T'ai Chi. Moab, Utah: Real People Press, 1973.

Jacobi, J. Complex/archetype/symbol in the psychology of C.G. Jung. Princeton: Princeton University Press, 1959.

Jung, C. G. Symbols of transformation. Princeton: Princeton University Press, 1956.

Jung, C. G. Mandala symbolism. Princeton: Princeton University Press, 1959.

Leuner, H. Guided affective imagery. American Journal Psychotherapy, 1969, 23, 4-22.

Lowen, A. The body in therapy. Fifth Annual Conference, American Dance Association. New York, 1970, 1-9.

Perry, J. The far side of madness. Englewood Cliffs, New Jersey: Prentice-Hall, 1974.

Rugg, H. <u>Imagination</u>. New York: Harper and Row, 1963.
Stewart, K. Dream theory in Malaya. <u>Altered States of Conscious-
    ness</u>. New York: John Wiley and Sons, 1969.

IV: GUIDED IMAGERY AND FANTASY

GUIDED IMAGERY: HEALING THROUGH THE MIND'S EYE

Dennis T. Jaffe, Ph.D.,* and David E. Bresler, Ph.D.**

*UCLA, Center for Health Enhancement, Education and
Research; co-director, Learning for Health.

**Adjunct Asst. Professor, Anesthesiology, Gnathology and
Occlusion; Psychology, UCLA; director of Pain Control,
UCLA Hospital and Clinics; executive director, Center
for Integral Medicine

The use of personal mental images to diagnose and modify bodily
processes is an ancient part of the healing tradition. The healer/
physician/shaman/priest has always utilized the latent power of the
imagination to alter the body, and many traditional health care
systems have focused on the amazing power of the mind to promote
the healing process (Beecher, 1955; Frank, 1975). With recent
demonstrations that the autonomic nervous system can be modified
through learning and various cognitive strategies, contemporary
health practitioners have also begun to explore the applications of
therapeutic guided imagery.

COMMUNICATING WITH THE BODY

Guided imagery is a method of communicating with autonomic
physiological processes which occur outside of conscious awareness.
This internal exchange of information can proceed in two directions.
First, information about subtle physiological processes can be
brought to conscious awareness as an aid to diagnosis. Second, the
power of the imagination can be recruited to promote specific physiological changes as an aid to therapy. Within limits yet to be
determined, the conscious mind, utilizing mental imagery, partici-
pates in both types of communication.

We have suggested that there are two fundamentally different
higher order languages utilized by the nervous system for internal

communication (Bresler, 1979). Verbal thoughts most directly access
the somatic nervous system, so if, for example, you wish to stand
up, all you need to do is think "stand up, now" and your voluntary
nervous system will coordinate the appropriate muscular activity.
On the other hand, the language of imagery directly accesses the
<u>autonomic nervous system</u> (ANS), which regulates breathing, the
heartbeat, blood chemistry, digestion, tissue regeneration and
repair, immune and inflammatory responses, and many other bodily
functions essential to life.

To illustrate the differing effects of verbal command and
imagery over "involuntary" functions, we often use the following
demonstration:

> First, using verbal language, order yourself to
> "manufacture and secrete saliva." By thinking about
> this command, see how much saliva you can generate. Most
> people produce a little, but not much, for the parts of
> the body that produce saliva do not respond well to ver-
> bal commands.
> Mental imagery represents a different approach to
> physiological change. Imagine that you have in your
> hand a big, yellow, juicy lemon. Visualize it in your
> mind's eye until you smell its fresh tartness. Then
> imagine taking a knife, and slicing into the lemon.
> Carefully cut out a thick, juicy section. Now, take a
> deep bite of your imaginary lemon and begin to sense
> that tart, sour lemon juice splashing in your mouth,
> saturating every taste bud of your tongue so fully that
> your lips and cheeks curl. Swirl it in your mouth for
> another 15 to 20 seconds, bathing every corner of your
> mouth with its acrid taste.

If you were able to paint the suggested picture vividly in
your mind's eye, the image probably produced substantial saliva-
tion, for the autonomic nervous system easily understands and
responds to the language of imagery. It is a short step to
hypothesize that other physiological functions, ones which are
directly concerned with the body's resistance to the disease process, can also be mobilized via imagery.

The need for a therapeutic approach to the use of mental imagery is evident when one notices that patients are always using
imagery to send messages to the body. These images can significantly affect the patient's progress in therapy, for in many cases,
the images transmitted are highly negative ones that inhibit the
healing process.

For example, many patients with chronic pain picture themselves as helpless, hopeless victims of an incurable illness. In

their mind's eye, they focus on thoughts like, "I hurt so much . . .
I am so limited by this pain (or disease) . . . I feel terrible
. . . No doctor can help me . . . This can only get worse . . ."
When the imagination is preoccupied by these negative pictures, the
autonomic nervous system is being told, in effect, "Prepare the
body to be helpless. Don't even bother mobilizing the immune and
inflammatory defenses that might facilitate healing. Just give
up." It's not surprising, then, that these patients often don't
get better, as these messages become a self-fulfilling prophecy.

Images seem to have a very limited effect on the body. No
matter what types of medical terminology are used to describe a
specific diagnosis, if a patient experiences his discomfort as "a
sizzling hot poker that is constantly being stabbed into my neck,"
or as "a lion gnawing on my back, tearing deeper into the nerves
with every bite," or as "wringing out the nerves like they re a
wet washcloth," then these are the ways it will be most fully
experienced.

A single mental picture, then, can be far more potent than a
dictionary of words. Thus, many clinicians have begun to use positive images to help their patients heal themselves. For example,
while sitting in a dentist's chair, a patient can be taught to
stop his gums from bleeding by creating a vivid image of it actually happening. Several dentists have reported that when they ask
their patients to imagine that freezing-cold ice was being applied
to their bleeding gums, the patients reported that the area soon
became numb. In addition, the blood vessels constricted, and the
bleeding stopped. In a similar way, the effectiveness of medica-
tion can often be enhanced through imagery. For example, if a
patient is taking antibiotics for an ear infection, he can be
taught to imagine that the blood vessels which nourish the ear are
becoming dilated. This may permit more blood--and a greater concentration of the antibiotic--to flow into the ear, thus hastening the
healing process.

There is no physical symptom or illness that is not affected
to some degree by the mind. Healing can thus be enhanced by positive and helpful images and expectations, and it can be hampered
and slowed by depression, hopelessness and fatigue. In our opinion,
the way a person uses his mind is a critical factor in the outcome
of therapy.

This is true whatever the cause of illness. For example, even
if a person is recovering from an operation after an accident, or
has an illness caused by some hereditary predisposition (with little stress-related or behavior-related etiology), he can still
speed up or slow down the recovery process by the use of mental
imagery. Thus, guided imagery represents an important adjunctive
technique for nearly all other forms of medical treatment.

THE DIAGNOSTIC USE OF IMAGERY

One of the most difficult aspects of medical diagnosis is an
accurate assessment of the patient's internal perceptions and expectations. Imagery can be most helpful in this regard, for it is a
highly evocative language that comprehensively conveys unconscious
attitudes and processes. As part of the diagnostic interview, a
patient can be asked to close his eyes, and to allow his mind to
present him with a picture that represents the experience of his
problem. The patient is then instructed to draw the picture that
came to mind as accurately as he possibly can.

These pictures can lead to important information not only
about the illness, but also about the patient's beliefs, hopes,
expectations and fears about his body, its ability to withstand the
illness, and the effectiveness of the recommended treatment. Many
patients have uncannily accurate intuitions about their illnesses,
and the imagery process can make these available to the diagnostician to add to other sources of information.

One of our hypertensive patients pictured himself crushed by
a huge vice. A woman drew her chronic bronchitis as a plug in her
chest blocking her breath. A man envisioned his added weight as
an inner tube keeping him afloat on a stormy sea. A woman's lymph
cancer became a termite invasion. The pictures offer a first
glimpse of the psychic reality which is associated with a symptom.
In symbolizing this reality through pictures, patients often open
psychological doors that permit them and their therapists to
explore the meaning of their symptoms in ways that were previously
unavailable.

Patients can also be asked to create a new and different image,
or something to be added to the original picture that would inspire
and promote the healing process. For example, a man with an ulcer,
pictured as a stomach being punctured with arrows, drew a heart,
and a pathway from it to his stomach. Discussing his picture, he
began to look at his lack of intimate relationships with others and
his denial of needs for companionship in his characterization of
himself as a "loner." He was lonely, and needed to open his heart
to others.

The imagery a patient chooses can be based on his knowledge of
the actual physiological processes through which the body combats
illness, or on a fanciful or symbolic representation of how it
might happen. For example, one cancer patient utilized the following image:

I'd begin to visualize my cancer--as I saw it in my mind's
eye. I'd make a game of it. The cancer would be a snake,
a wolverine, or some vicious animal. The cure--white,

husky dogs by the millions. It would be a confrontation
of good and evil. I'd envision the dogs grabbing the
cancer and shaking it, ripping it to shreds. The forces
of good would win. The cancer would shrink--from a big
snake to a little snake--and then disappear. Then the
white army of dogs would lick up the residue and clean
my abdominal cavity until it was spotless.

Several interesting observations concerning the relationship
between imagery and the prognosis of treatment have been described
by the Simontons (Simonton, Matthews-Simonton, and Creighton, 1978).
From the nature of the image a person selects, they can predict
with some accuracy how well that an individual will fare in treatment. The images thus seem to be important diagnostic indicators,
like Rorschach inkblots, about a patient's deep unconscious attitudes about himself and his illness.

The Simontons compare the patient's image of his body's power
vs. that of the cancer. The difference seems to indicate how the
real battle in the body will go. Generally, the side which is
stronger in the image prevails. If the cancer is pictured as a
dangerous animal, and the white cells are puffs of snow or cotton,
the prognosis is poor. As an example, they cite the image of ants.
People who spontaneously choose ants to represent their cancer seem
to do poorly, and the Simontons relate this to the real difficulty
in attempting to eradicate a plague of ants to the point where
every one is destroyed. In their residential treatment program,
the Simontons work with their patients' imagery to alter or modify
the images (as well as their attitudes) so that the cancer does, in
fact, lose the mental battle.

The Simontons were not the first to note that a person's
symbolic reality mirrors his physical disease. For example,
researcher Bruno Klopfer (1957) was almost unerringly able to predict from Rorschach responses which patients had slow or fast
growing tumors. Thus, the symbols a person chooses to represent
physical processes often present accurate, important diagnostic
information about the actual state of the body. The goal of the
diagnostician is to make this inner information clear, explicit and
relevant to the treatment process.

THERAPEUTIC USE OF IMAGERY

It is a short step from the diagnostic use of imagery to its
therapeutic application. If a patient presents a negative, helpless or hopeless picture of his illness or his body's potential for
overcoming it, helping him to see his situation more positively
through his mind's eye may have a significant salutory effect on
the response to treatment.

The most common therapeutic use of mental imagery is in the
induction of what is known as the "relaxation response." Relaxation is a well-known antidote to excessive daily stress that is
accompanied by chronic activation of the sympathetic nervous system. The relaxation state characterized by parasympathetic dominance, muscle relaxation, and slowed respiration is entered by the
induction of mental images that suggest physical regeneration and
deep rest. There are as many types of relaxation training as there
are over-the-counter medications, ranging from transcendental meditation to progressive relaxation, autogenic training, meditation,
and self-hypnosis, but they all seem to utilize the same basic
principles to initiate the relaxation response.

A person enters the relaxation state not by telling his body
to relax. Since the relaxation response is triggered by the ANS,
this verbal language would be ineffective. Indeed, the more one
tries to relax, the more the muscles tighten, and the less relaxed
one becomes. The relaxation response is attained by creating a
mental image of a scene, in which one is deeply relaxed, or by
suggesting via imagery certain changes in the body which simulate
the relaxation state. For example, repeating the phrase to oneself, "I am at peace," or simply paying attention to one's breathing, letting all other thoughts quietly slip away, are two ways to
initiate this state. We often ask patients simply to remember a
wonderful vacation spot where they were totally relaxed and at
peace. The memory stimulates the body to re-experience the relaxation response.

Attaining a state of bodily relaxation is a prerequisite for
all work with therapeutic guided imagery, for it provides inhibition of somatic muscle activity and verbal thoughts, allowing mental images to become dominant. The relaxation response can usually
be induced using any of the currently popular methods (White and
Fadiman, 1976; Bresler and Trubo, 1979), and for the minority of
patients who have difficulty in attaining this state, biofeedback
training may also be helpful.

Once a state of deep relaxation is entered, the patient is
then individually guided to create a picture in his mind's eye of
what he wishes his body to do. For the medically sophisticated or
the technically-minded, the image can be a precise representation
of the desired physiological change. For example, a person might
want the body to produce an extra supply of a particular enzyme or
to have the immune system inactivate a virus in the stomach. Many
people like to read medical texts to find out how their body might
aid in the healing process as preparation for creating their
therapeutic images.

But images can also be symbolic or fanciful. Several physicians who have used these methods feel that the healing image does

not have to be realistic for it to be effective. Thus, patients
who imagine little men with ray guns charging through the body kill-
ing an oozy green virus may achieve the same beneficial results.

An account of how mental imagery can be integrated into a
medical treatment program was given to us by a nurse born with a
hip deformity who learned to control her continual pain without
restricting her activities by a variety of methods.

She began by paying attention to the particular needs of various parts of her body, especially her hips and legs. When she felt
discomfort, she would ask her tight legs or muscles what she could
do to take care of them. "Massage us," or "Take a day off and
rest," they would reply through "a voice in her head." If she
needed to do something particularly difficult or especially active,
like a day of sailing, she would strike a bargain: "If you let me
do this without much pain, I will in return take special care to
rest you for the next two days. Is that all right?", she might
ask, and wait for an affirmative reply. By becoming intimately
aware of the needs of her hips and joints, and by catering to them,
she was able to enjoy 15 active, relatively pain-free, productive
years, until the total hip replacement operation was developed and
recommended to her.

She then began preparing for the difficult, highly experimental
procedure which was fraught with medical difficulties. Several
times a day, she imagined what her body needed to do. She told her
blood vessels not to rupture, and her immune system how to react.
She prepared her body for each step of the procedure over and over
in her mind's eye.

She also imaged the operation going perfectly well. She
imagined the surgeons being totally relaxed and their hands being
swift and sure. She imagined that they had had a relaxing weekend
and were refreshed and optimistic about her operation, scheduled
for a Monday morning. While her imaginings may not have had much
effect on the hospital personnel, it helped to calm her and increase
her optimism about the outcome. In effect, she prepared her whole
body, by way of imagery for the difficult process that was to come.

Even with all her preparation, however, a small complication
developed during the successful operation. One of the nerves in
her leg was damaged, leaving her with no feeling along part of the
leg. She was initially frustrated, but soon got to work. She
spent every moment she could imagining the nerve growing and becoming whole. Her physician said that it might grow a millimeter a
day, and that she had to grow it along her whole leg. She imagined
it going ever faster, and slowly, over months, normal sensations
did return. Her story demonstrates how imagery and relaxation can
become an integral part of traditional medicine, and perhaps

increase the chances of success in high-risk medical and surgical
procedures.

This account also illustrates another important therapeutic
use of imagery, namely, the use of positive future images to activate positive physical changes. Imagining a positive future outcome is an important technique for countering the initial negative
images, beliefs and expectations a patient may have. In essence,
it transforms a negative placebo effect (or nocebo) into a positive
one. Positive self-guided imagery also helps by giving the patient
something active and constructive to do, instead of telling him to
just sit and wait to heal or for the treatment to take effect.

The use of positive images to reinforce health has been an
integral part of many healing traditions. Around the turn of the
century, Emil Coué, a French pharmacist, initiated a clinic which
was modeled on the use of positive imagery as a method of attaining
maximum health. His famous phrase, which his patients repeated to
themselves several times a day, was the simple, "Every day, in
every way, I am becoming better and better." That basic suggestion,
combined with specific formulae for specific ailments, was aimed at
using imagery and suggestion to affect physiological responses.

Coué believed that imagining an outcome would do far more to
bring it about than willing, or forcing oneself, to do something.
Imagination was a gentle guide, taking the body in the direction of
its wanderings. Thus, when we expect to be ill or unable to recover
fully, the force of our imagination could help to bring that outcome
about.

By imagining the end point a person seeks--full health, some
specific career or life goal--without willing it or forcing oneself
to desire it, the mind is carried in that direction. This is
especially important when a person may be imagining or expecting a
negative outcome. The power of positive suggestion plants a seek
which redirects the mind--and through the mind and the body--toward
a positive goal. Using phrases and positive thoughts regularly as
part of a routine relaxation process is one of the best ways to
weaken the power of negative images.

In addition to creating healing images, we often ask our
patients to create a set of positive phrases that they tend to forget or feel they would like to remember, and to write them on a
card. They then place the card on their bathroom mirror, and try
to repeat the phrases to themselves from time to time during the
day. People create suggestions such as, "I can get the love I want
without having to eat," or "I will feel tremendous, vital, healthy,
and breathe freely each day that I do not smoke," or "I will treat
my body with love and respect."

Such messages help to counteract negative patterns that may
have been set inadvertently years before, and which subconsciously
set in motion negative physiological cycles which can culminate in
illness or cause health-destructive behavior. Many people also
find it helpful to add affirmative personal statements, letting
themselves know that they are worthy of being healthy, of being
loved, or of changing in a positive direction to reach some of
their life goals.

THE INNER ADVISER: A DIAGNOSTIC AND
  THERAPEUTIC USE OF IMAGERY

Clinicians like ourselves are experimenting with many creative
and highly experimental uses of mental imagery. One of the most
dramatic techniques we have used involves what is known as "the
inner adviser." This technique was popularized by Irving Oyle
(1976) and Mike Samuels (Samuels and Bennett, 1973), and is utilized
by many practitioners of integral medicine. By creating and interacting with an inner adviser, a person learns to gather important
information from their subconscious, and is able to feel comfortable
and familiar with parts of themselves that had previously been
inaccessible to conscious awareness.

A good illustration of this technique is the case of Julie,
whose life changed suddenly one afternoon. Until then, she had
been miserable and confused, and tormented by a grinding, throbbing
pain in her lower back that had persisted for nearly six years.
At its worst, the discomfort radiated into other parts of her body
as well--like razor-sharp bullets fired into her shoulders, chest
and buttocks. To aggravate things even further, her marriage had
collapsed, and she felt ravaged by the strain of raising her teen-
age sons by herself.

But one afternoon, during a period of relaxation, Julie learned
how to contact her inner adviser--an imaginary living creature--in
her subconscious mind. During Julie's first experience with this
technique, she imagined she was in a beautiful wooded forest, and
soon made contact with an imaginary hummingbird.

Doctor: What is the hummingbird's name?

Julie: Sam.

Doctor: Tell Sam you mean him no harm, that you
would just like to meet with him occasionally to talk
things over with him. Would that be OK?

Julie: He says he'd be willing to do that.

   Doctor: Good. Tell him you have brought some
honey and water for him today. And ask him if there is
any advice he'd like to give you in return.

   Julie: He says yes.

   Doctor: What does he want to tell you?

   Julie: He says he wants me to start liking myself
more and filling my life with more fun.

Later in the exercise, Julie was told to try the following
experiment:

   Doctor: Ask Sam, as a demonstration of his friend-
ship and good faith, if he is willing to take away your
pain right now, even for just a moment. . . . Will he
do that?

   Julie: Yes, he says he will.

Within seconds, Julie's pain was gone, and it stayed away for
several hours. Those sore and aching muscles that had plagued her
for so long were finally free of discomfort. Of course, Julie's
pain returned later that day. But by then, her disposition had
improved remarkably. For the first time in years, she realized
that it was <u>possible</u> for her to be pain-free.

In the ensuing weeks, she continued to communicate with her
adviser, who helped her to start thinking more positively about
her own future. After a few weeks, she was progressing very well
toward completely controlling her pain.

The advisers that people like Julie create are able to search
the inner recesses of the unconscious mind. The adviser can also
help change subconscious belief systems. Earlier, we noted that
patients may become imprisoned by their own inappropriate belief
systems. This happens not only on the conscious level, but subconsciously as well. So, if quite unknowingly, a patient envisions
himself as a hopeless, helpless victim of pain, it's essential for
him to become aware of that and to adopt a new belief system that
will facilitate healing. The adviser technique can help a person
become intimately connected with his subconscious mind and can tell
him how well he is incorporating new beliefs, new expectations and
new habits.

In the process, communication with the adviser also fosters a
"centering process," in which one's ability to observe the intuitive side becomes very sophisticated. Long after the immediate
physical problem has been resolved, sensitivity to the activities

of the subconscious mind will continue if contact with the adviser is maintained.

As clinicians, we have been surprised, not only by the immense value of guided imagery, but at how receptive most patients are to the technique. In retrospect, maybe this open-mindedness on the part of patients is not as amazing as we had originally thought. Guided imagery is basically just a way of talking to oneself, which is hardly a new concept.

People sometimes find themselves reacting to a particular event by saying, "Damn, I knew that was going to happen!" How did they know? Of course, it was the intuitive part of the mind--in essence, an inner adviser--that told them. The adviser is simply the imaginary embodiment in human or animal form, of subconscious intuitions and knowledge.

Getting in touch with an adviser is an extension of the imagery techniques we have already described. First, a person enters the relaxation state. Then, he imagines himself in a place where he feels perfectly calm, comfortable and at home. This is a special healing place where he will meet his adviser.

After spending a few moments enjoying and relaxing in this special place, he then sits back and waits for an adviser to appear. He is instructed to avoid trying to consciously create someone or something, but rather to let the spontaneous creativity and wisdom of the subconscious come up with an image which embodies a benevolent guide or adviser.

It is important to wait until their adviser appears in human, animal or other life form. The symbolic range is enormous, but each person creates an adviser in a form uniquely suited to his inner image of helpfulness. When the adviser arrives, the person is asked to greet it, and to begin the process of getting to know the adviser. This might include introducing himself, and learning the adviser's name. It might also include an exchange of gifts. Then, the process of dialogue and interaction begins. The person talks to the adviser, who answers either directly, or sometimes with metaphorical ambiguity or other indirect messages. People usually have the experience of receiving surprising or unexpected information from this inner oracle, and the information received is usually of critical importance to their healing process.

This seemingly silly process of creative imagination is a way to give concrete form and substance to subconscious feelings, attitudes and stored information. Patients are asked to talk regularly with their advisers, and as they practice this technique, they find that they can discover increasingly important sources of inner guidance.

Once a person has an adviser--whether it's a cat, a squirrel, a deer, or a dolphin--he can discuss anything that is on his mind-- or anything that the adviser might like to talk about. There are no limits, except that the dialogue should be kept totally honest on both sides. The adviser provides an endless number of insights --not only about a person's pain or illness, but about other aspects of his life as well.

In working with hundreds of patients using this guided imagery technique, we find that the adviser can be helpful in at least four distinct ways.

1. The adviser can provide advice on how to reduce stress and pain. When a patient needs pain relief or stress reduction, he can ask his adviser for suggestions. The adviser plays the role of an "imaginary doctor," as Samuels and Bennett (1973) note. We often ask patients to talk their physical problems over with this make- believe doctor, or adviser. For example, Sylvia, an ulcer victim with terrible stomach pains, described a meeting with Shorty, her adviser, and the surprising revelation she received:

> Shorty's sweet and darling, and the last time I talked
> with him, he said I needed to keep my pain for awhile
> longer so I'll continue working on myself. He said if
> I didn't have pain, I'd quit the relaxation exercise
> and become too anxious again. When I've learned to
> relax myself more consistently, he says the pain will
> go away.

2. The adviser can provide support and protection. One's adviser can supply encouragement for decisions on a course of action already decided upon sometimes with an enthusiasm not found in one's friends or family members. The adviser can also shield a person from danger by warning him--in advance--when he is about to do something that is not in his best interest. It is like having a personal oracle.

3. The adviser has the power to give total and complete symptomatic relief. One way the adviser can demonstrate his power is by providing total symptomatic relief for a few moments. Once a patient recognizes that the adviser's powers are, in essence, his own powers, then he begins to understand the enormous control he has over his body and his health.

4. The adviser can help discover the message behind symptoms. Because symptoms are a message that something is wrong, it is essential for a patient to identify that message if he wishes to completely overcome his problem. Often, the message has been repressed, and is not available to the conscious mind. But the adviser can help to uncover it in a gentle, loving, non-threatening

way. An adviser cannot only tell why a person's body hurts, but
also why his whole life hurts.

After a patient has developed a strong relationship with his
adviser, we recommend that he find other advisers as well. We
suggest that patients invite their advisers to bring mates or other
acquaintances to the next meeting. Some people use multi-advisers
to help resolve a particular conflict they may be experiencing.
Their two advisers can debate the issue, taking opposing viewpoints,
while the individual is able to objectively evaluate their respec-
tive positions.

Terry, a UCLA Pain Control Unit patient, was suffering from
chronic endometriosis (inflammation of the inner lining of the
uterus). She asked her first adviser, a dog named Max, to recruit
two other advisers to discuss her indiscriminant sexual activities,
which she thought might be contributing to her problem.

One of the new advisers was a rabbit named Rachel, who told
Terry, "You only live once, and life is very short. Why not make
it as sweet as you can? Have as many different sexual experiences
as possible, and don't worry about attachments. Just live loose
and free!"

The other adviser was a deer named Bambi, who argued, "You
have to respect yourself before others will respect you. Rather
than having a lot of meaningless experiences, save yourself for
the right person. It's quality, not quantity that's important."

Terry felt that she received some very helpful insights from
this debate. In a subsequent meeting with all three of her advisers, she decided she wanted to be more like the deer than the rabbit, and that while she still might occasionally allow herself to
be sexually free (like the rabbit), it would never again be a permanent lifestyle.

We feel that the advisers represent dialogues between different parts of one's nervous system. Although a patient may feel,
"I'm just talking to myself. How can that help me?", it's the
unique content and symbolism of the dialogue that is important.
We ask, "Why did only certain responses pop into your head? Why
did your adviser assume the name Roger? Why was he a frog? Why
did he tell you to love yourself more? All of these have relevance
and meaning to your life."

The use of inner advisers, healing imagery, positive suggestion,
relaxation training, and diagnostic imagery as part of medical practice represent a departure from the orthodox conception of the doctor's role, but is very much in keeping with the traditional conception and practice of the healer. Mental imagery mobilizes the

latent, inner powers of the person, which have immense potential to aid in the healing process and in the promotion of health. The techniques we have described are easy to teach and easy to learn, and have no negative side-effects, making them in many ways an ideal adjunct to any other type of therapy. It is our hope that health professionals from all disciplines will begin to utilize them to help their patients more effectively help themselves.

REFERENCES

Beecher, H. K. The powerful placebo. Journal of the American Medical Association, 1955, 151, 1602-1606.

Bresler, D. E. Free yourself from pain. New York: Simon & Schuster, 1979.

Bresler, D., and Trubo, R. Conditioned relaxation: the pause that refreshes. In J. Gordon, D. Jaffee, and D. Bressler (Eds.), Mind, body, health: towards an integral medicine (Monograph). Bethesda, Maryland: National Institute for Mental Health, 1980.

Cousins, N. The mysterious placebo. Saturday Review, October 1, 1977, 9-16.

Frank, J. The faith that heals. Johns Hopkins University Medical Journal, 1975, 137, 127-131.

Klopfer, B. Psychological variables in human cancer. Journal of Projective Techniques, 1957, 21, 337-339.

Oyle, I. Time, space and the mind. Millbrae, California: Celestial Arts, 1976.

Samuels, M., and Bennett, H. The well body book. New York: Random House/Bookworks, 1973.

Simonton, O. C., Matthews-Simonton, S., and Creighton, J. Getting well again. Los Angeles: Jeremy Tarcher, 1978.

White, J., and Fadiman, J. Relax. New York: Dell, 1976.

GUIDED FANTASY AS A PSYCHOTHERAPEUTIC INTERVENTION:

AN EXPERIMENTAL STUDY

Steven M. Blankman

Postdoctoral Fellow, Shasta County Mental Health Services

Redding, California

Guided-fantasy methods of psychotherapy, such as Desoille's (1966) directed daydream, Leuner's (1969, 1977, 1978) guided affective imagery, and Rochkind and Conn's (1973) guided fantasy encounter, have been described in many anecdotal and theoretical presentations (Garufi, 1977; Hammer, 1967, Johnsgard, 1969; Kosbab, 1974; Krojanker, 1966; Schutz, 1967; Van den Berg, 1962). These therapeutic methods are based on the assumption that important psychological conflicts, feelings, attitudes, and response tendencies of the therapy client can be elicited and represented in the form of a sequential, drama-like imaginal experience. Typically, the client assumes a relaxed state, and then the therapist suggests a fantasy setting, situation or symbol which serves as the starting point for the client's fantasy. The therapist facilitates the client's experiencing and reporting of the ongoing fantasy and may suggest images or courses of action the client can take in the fantasy.

The therapeutic processes and effects facilitated by guided fantasy have been the subject of more claims and speculation than systematic investigation. There have been a few outcome studies of guided affective imagery which demonstrated its efficacy in reducing psychometric measures of anxiety and other manifestations of neurotic and psychosomatic disorders (Leuner, 1978). Mitchell's (1974) phenomenological investigation of induced fantasy showed that experimental subjects participating in an artificial nonclinical context experienced rich cognitive and affective effects during fantasies prescribed by the experimenter. But little systematically-obtained information exists concerning the participants' experience and evaluation of guided fantasy in actual psychotherapy.

For therapists who do not ordinarily use guided fantasy as a

principal treatment modality, the question arises of the circumstances under which guided fantasy might be a viable or even a preferred method. Judgments of this sort might be made on the basis of
traditional psychodiagnostic criteria and other client characteristics (Kelly, 1972; Leuner, 1978; Van den Berg, 1962), or on the basis
of the client's actual performance during a trial guided fantasy.
The latter type of approach was suggested by Mitchell (1974) and also
seems warranted by the findings that in-therapy "state" measures of
imagery vividness were more highly associated with imaginal desensitization outcome than were pretherapy "trait" measures of imagery
abilities (Davis, McLemore, and London, 1970; Dyckman and Cowan,
1978; McLemore, 1972, 1976). Research is lacking, however, on both
"trait" and "state" variables which might be associated with the
therapeutic efficacy of guided fantasy. In addition to imagery
vividness, one aspect of guided fantasy which has been viewed as
important by proponents of the method (Desoille, 1966; Leuner,
1969; Rochkind and Conn, 1973) is the client's affective involvement in the guided fantasy. Could the therapist's judgment of the
client's involvement in a guided fantasy serve as an accurate index
of the therapeutic efficacy of the experience?

     In view of the paucity of research on these aspects of guided
fantasy, I conducted a study with the following objectives:

     1. To systematically obtain reports from psychotherapy clients
and therapists on the immediate effects, subsequent influences, and
therapeutic contributions of a single guided-fantasy session.

     2. To examine individual differences in responsiveness to
guided fantasy.

     3. To determine the influence on guided-fantasy effects of
the client's vividness of imagery and affective involvement during
the guided fantasy.

     4. To compare a guided-fantasy session with a comparable
session of conventional therapeutic encounter.

METHOD

Participants

     Thirteen adult outpatient psychotherapy clients, four males
and nine females, were selected by their therapists to participate
in the study. The mean age of the clients was 37 years, and their
diagnostic classifications included psychoneuroses, personality disorders, adjustment reactions, schizophrenia, and anorexia nervosa.
The clients had been in therapy with their present therapists for
an average of five months. The therapists were affiliated with

various agencies and private practices in San Diego County.

Design of the Study

The research procedures were incorporated into three of each client's regular therapy appointments, generally consecutive sessions. In one therapy session the client's regular therapist conducted a guided fantasy with the client, and in another therapy session (hereafter referred to as "conventional therapeutic encounter") the same therapist employed any non-guided-fantasy method of psychotherapy s/he deemed appropriate. The third session was an ordinary therapy session, but preceding it the client answered questionnaires for the study. To control for any possible effects from the sequence in which the two treatment procedures were administered, clients were randomly assigned to two different orders of treatment--seven clients receiving the guided fantasy first, then conventional therapeutic encounter; and eight clients receiving conventional therapeutic encounter first, then guided fantasy.

Instruments

Questionnaires were completed by the client immediately after the guided-fantasy and conventional-therapeutic-encounter session (the Immediate Post-Treatment(IPT) questionnaires), and just prior to the subsequent session after each of these research treatment sessions (the Subsequent Post-Treatment (SPT) questionnaires). These questionnaires, designed by the author for this study, assessed the clients' perceptions of the effects during and after the guided-fantasy and conventional-therapy sessions. Immediately after each of these two research treatment sessions, the therapist rated the client's affective involvement during the session using a five-point scale adapted from Bordin's free-association Involvement subscale (Kiesler, 1973). After the client had participated in both the guided-fantasy and conventional-therapeutic-encounter sessions, both the client and the therapist completed Final Questionnaires (FQ) to evaluate the guided-fantasy session and to compare it with the session of conventional therapeutic encounter.

Procedure[*]

Guided-fantasy session. At the therapist's option s/he and the client dealt with any matters that either wished to discuss prior to beginning the guided-fantasy procedure. Then the therapist suggested that the client assume a comfortable position, preferably

---

[*]For a more detailed description of the procedure, as well as copies of the preparatory materials given to the therapist participants, refer to Blankman (1979).

with eyes closed, and directed the client to follow the instructions from a 14-minute, tape-recorded muscle-relaxation procedure.
After the tape ended, the therapist instructed the client to imagine
being in a meadow and to describe it, and the therapist made comments to facilitate the client's engagement in, and present-tense
reporting of, an ongoing sequence of imagery and feelings. Then
the therapist instructed the client to visualize and describe the
appearance of a significant person in the client's present life or
in the past. The therapist encouraged the client to continue fantasizing and reporting the fantasy as it happened, and attempted to
enrich any encounter with the significant other by having the client attend to and report sensory details, feelings, dialogue and
the like. The therapists generally adopted a rather nondirective
approach to guiding the clients' fantasies, although some therapists
made general or minor suggestions of imagery or actions for the client to fantasy.

Conventional-therapeutic-encounter session. At the therapist's
option s/he and the client dealt with any matters that either wished
to discuss prior to beginning the experimental procedure. The
therapist then followed the same relaxation procedure with the client as described for the guided-fantasy session.

After the relaxation tape ended, the therapist told the client
to open his/her eyes and directed the client to talk about a relationship with a significant person in the client's present life or
in the past. The therapist then interacted with the client using
whatever approach the therapist chose, but not using guided fantasy.

In both the guided-fantasy and conventional-therapy sessions
the therapists used standard instructions to initiate the relaxation and therapeutic procedures. The therapists' adherence to the
standard procedures was verified through tape recordings of the
sessions.

RESULTS

Immediate Effects of the Guided-
Fantasy Session

Table 1 presents a quantitative summary of the clients'
responses to the Immediate Post-Treatment questionnaire items assessing immediate effects of the session. The IPT questionnaire items
consisted of forced-choice (yes/no) questions (e.g., item 9, "Did
the experience bring up any mood or emotions that you are still
feeling?") and seven-point rating scales for evaluating the intensity or significance of each effect that was assessed. The figures
given in Table 1 represent the percentage of clients who checked a
"yes" response to each question and the median and range of ratings

Table 1

Quantitative Data From the Immediate Post-Treatment Questionnaire (IPT)
Responses for Guided Fantasy (GF) and Conventional Therapeutic Encounter (CTE)

Questionnaire Item and Content	Percentage of clients giving positive responses		Range of ratings for positive responses		Median rating for positive responses	
	GF	CTE	GF	CTE	GF	CTE
4 Surprise	62	46	(There was no rating scale for IPT 4)		6	7
5 New knowledge or understanding	85	54	4-7	5-7	6	7
6 Feelings, sensations or bodily changes	85	69	4-7	3-7	7	6
7 Pleasant emotions*	100	69	2-7	4-7	6	7
8 Unpleasant emotions	62	62	3-7	4-7	5	5.5
9 Persisting moods or emotions	85	85	1-7	1-7	5	5
10 In-session attitude changes	69	54	6-7	2-7	7	6
11 Post-session attitude changes	54	46	4-7	6-7	6	7
12 New, unusual or difficult behaviors	31	31	4-7	4-7	6	6

*The sign test showed that a significantly higher percentage of clients gave positive responses on IPT 7 after the guided-fantasy session than after the conventional therapeutic encounter, N = 4, x = 0, p = .031.

among those clients. Inspection of Table 1 shows that for each
questionnaire item except 12, the majority of clients gave a "yes"
response after the guided-fantasy session, indicating that they had
experienced the corresponding effect. For six of the nine items
the proportion of such positive responses was higher for the guided-
fantasy treatment condition than for the conventional treatment
condition.

Subsequent Effects of the Guided-
Fantasy Session

In response to the Subsequent Post-Treatment questionnaire,
five clients indicated that they had thought about the guided-
fantasy session; two of these had shared material from the session
with others. Four clients described feelings which persisted or
developed after the session was over. Two clients reported subsequent visualization of the fantasy imagery, one describing his use
of the imagery to achieve mental relaxation. Two clients reported
little or no effects from the session.

Quantitative data for SPT item 2 is presented in Table 2. A
substantial majority of clients indicated that the guided-fantasy
session was influential with regard to the relationship with the
focal person. The effects on the clients' experience and behavior
in these relationships included increased "positive" (pleasant)
feelings and attitudes, deeper experiencing of unpleasant feelings,
self-questioning of attitudes, and increased assertiveness. In
comparison, the responses to the same questionnaire item for the
conventional-therapy session generally described changes in coping
methods and in understanding, with only one response indicating
greater affective experiencing.

Therapeutic Contributions of the
Guided-Fantasy Session

The clients' perspectives. Table 2 presents a quantitative
summary of the data on the helpfulness of the guided-fantasy and
conventional treatment conditions, as reported by the clients on
SPT item 3 and Final Questionnaire item 2. SPT item 3 read:

> How helpful/harmful would you rate your last session?
> (There followed the rating scale.) What was it about
> the session that made it helpful or harmful? How
> did it help or harm you?

The complete wording of FQ item 2 was:

> In retrospect, which of the two experiences has proven
> to be more helpful to you?
> ( ) the guided fantasy session ( ) the other session

Table 2

Quantitative Data From Subsequent Post-Treatment (SPT) and Final Questionnaire (FQ) Responses for Guided Fantasy (GF) and Conventional Therapeutic Encounter (CTE)

Questionnaire Item and Content	Percentage of Clients Giving Positive Responses*		Range of Ratings For All Responses		Median Rating For All Responses	
	GF	CTE	GF	CTE	GF	CTE
SPT 2 Influence behavior, attitudes, feelings, or relationships with person focused on**	77	58	–	–	–	–
Degree of influence***	–	–	1–7	1–7	5	4.5
SPT 3 How helpful/harmful	92	83	4–7	4–7	6	5
FQ 2 Which experience more helpful****	55	45	–	–	–	–

*One client terminated therapy prematurely without completing the SPT questionnaire for the conventional therapeutic encounter or the Final Questionnaire. Thus, n = 12 for FQ and conventional-therapeutic-encounter SPT data, n = 13 for guided-fantasy SPT data.

**, ****SPT item 2 and FQ item 2 were dichotomous-choice questions without rating scales.

***The "Degree of Influence" item on the SPT questionnaire was a rating scale following item 2 and did not have a dichotomous-choice (positive/negative) component.

What was it about the more helpful of the two that
made it a helpful experience? How did it help?

Table 2 shows that seven of the 13 clients designated the guided-
fantasy session as the more helpful session.

Qualitative analysis of the clients' descriptive responses to
SPT item 3 and FQ item 2, understood in the context of the other
questionnaire responses and the tape recordings of the sessions,
showed that the client-perceived helpful effects of the guided-
fantasy session could be classified under seven categories. The
following are the categories, in order of greatest frequency of client reports: increased awareness/understanding; relaxation;
enhanced mastery/self-concept; attitudinal change; influence on the
relationship with the focal person; stimulation of affect; and
increased motivation/problem confrontation.

As another approach to clarifying the nature of the therapeutic effects of the guided-fantasy sessions, Spearman rank correlations were calculated between the clients' ratings of guided-fantasy
helpfulness (SPT 3) and the clients' ratings on the nine guided-
fantasy IPT quantitative items (4-12). One statistically significant correlation was found, that between guided-fantasy helpfulness
(SPT 3) and self-reported attitude change during the session (IPT
10), r_s = .77, p < .01.

The therapists' perspectives. In the therapists' responses to
the Therapist Final Questionnaire, the attributes of guided fantasy
most frequently cited were its helpfulness in dealing with client
resistance and its capacity to bring up focal issues for therapy.
Otherwise, the therapists as a group reported the same types of
effects as the client group, although individual therapists often
differed from their clients with respect to the therapeutic contributions they emphasized.

Client Characteristics Affecting
  Guided Fantasy

The diagnostic classifications and sex of the clients appeared
to have some bearing on the impact of the guided-fantasy session.
As a group, the clients diagnosed anxiety-neurotic most consistently
rated the guided-fantasy session as more helpful than the session
of conventional therapeutic encounter. The two clients diagnosed
obsessive-compulsive differed from the other clients in that they
dwelled almost exclusively on relaxational effects in their
responses to the research questionnaires. The therapist of these
two clients, and the therapist of the anorexic client, suggested
that these clients' needs for control appeared to detract from the
efficacy of the guided fantasy in their sessions.

A tendency for male clients to rate the guided-fantasy session as less helpful than female clients rated it was statistically significant according to the Fisher exact probability test (Siegel, 1956), p = .05, two-tailed. There were no such significant sex differences for the client-rated helpfulness of the conventional-therapeutic-encounter session.

Imagery Vividness, Involvement, and Guided-Fantasy Effects

Application of the Mann-Whitney U test revealed no relationship between Imagery Vividness during the guided fantasy, measured on the seven-point scale developed by Betts (Richardson, 1969), and any of the effects of the guided-fantasy session, as assessed by the quantitative client-questionnaire items. This finding may be due to the skewed distribution of scores on Imagery Vividness: all the clients except one rated themselves in the top three points of the seven-point scale.

Using the therapists' ratings of the clients' Involvement during the guided fantasy, the Mann-Whitney U test showed that the more involved clients (those scoring at or above the median Involvement rating, n = 7) reported more significant attitudinal changes occurring immediately after the guided-fantasy session (IPT item 11) than did the less involved clients (n = 6), p < .01. Using the clients' ratings of their Involvement, the Mann-Whitney test showed no significant differences between the more involved group (n = 9) and the less involved group (n = 4). Using the averages of the therapist and client ratings, the U test showed that the more involved clients (n = 7) rated the unpleasant emotions they experienced during the guided-fantasy session as greater in "intensity or amount" (IPT item 8) than those reported by the less involved clients (n = 6), p < .01. As was the case for the Imagery Vividness self-ratings, the Involvement ratings were positively skewed, and this may have contributed to the small number of statistically significant findings.

Guided Fantasy vs Conventional Therapeutic Encounter

Analysis of the quantitative client questionnaire items showed that on all items most of the clients rated the strength of the guided-fantasy session effects as greater than or equal to the ratings of the conventional-therapeutic-encounter effects. Statistical comparisons of all the ratings on the questionnaire items for the two treatment conditions were conducted using the sign test (Siegel, 1956). The only statistically significant finding was that the clients scoring at or above the median score on Involvement, using the average of the therapist and client ratings (n = 7), reported having more significant attitudinal changes occur during the guided-fantasy session than during the conventional therapeutic encounter (Sign test, $\underline{N}$ = 5, $\underline{x}$ = 0, $\underline{p}$ = .031). In addition, there were repeated trends suggesting that the guided-fantasy session produced more somatic-affective changes (IPT item 6) and was rated more helpful by the client (SPT item 3) than the conventional therapeutic encounter, but these trends did not reach statistical significance.

As shown in Table 1, significantly more clients reported experiencing pleasant emotions (IPT item 7) during the guided-fantasy session than during the conventional therapeutic encounter (Sign test, $\underline{N}$ = 5, $\underline{x}$ = 0, $\underline{p}$ = .031). However, the self-ratings of the intensity or amount of pleasant emotions experienced were not significantly different for the two treatment conditions.

DISCUSSION

The reports of cognitive, affective, interpersonal and behavioral effects from the guided-fantasy sessions support the oneiro-therapists' claims of such comprehensive effects, and add to the body of research findings documenting these effects from various imagery procedures (Mitchell, 1974; Singer and Pope, 1978a). The finding that all but one of the clients in this sample rated the guided-fantasy session as helpful (SPT item 3) provides further evidence that a single guided fantasy can produce therapeutic benefits among clients whom their therapists have selected to engage in such an experience (Chestnut, 1971; Rochkind and Conn, 1973; Wilkins, 1976).

Therapeutic Contributions of Guided
    Imagery

The descriptive questionnaire responses by the clients and therapists and the significant correlation between in-session attitude change (IPT 10) and client ratings of helpfulness (SPT 3) for the guided-fantasy sessions point to the therapeutic importance of changes in what I have categorized as awareness/understanding, mastery/self-concept, and attitudes. These findings support the positions of those authors who consider such cognitive and conative effects to be major effective ingredients in imagery methods of therapy (Beck, 1970; Meichenbaum, 1978; Rochkind and Conn, 1973; Singer, 1974).

It has been proposed (Kazdin, 1978; Klinger, 1977; Meichenbaum, 1978; Singer, 1974) that the client's covert rehearsal of desired behaviors is a primary means by which imaginal therapeutic procedures promote behavioral change. In the present study a number of clients experienced guided fantasies which seemed to symbolically anticipate changes in their interpersonal relationships rather than to provide literal rehearsal of target behaviors. Leuner (1977) has reported

similar clinical cases. In the questionnaire responses of three
of the aforementioned clients in this study, cognitive-affective
experiences such as an increased impetus to change and become more
assertive, greater awareness of feelings, or a stronger sense of
mastery figured prominently. It may be that such covert self-
actualizing experiences, stimulated in one way or another by guided
fantasy, are more important to therapeutic change in at least some
cases than the particular imagined or overt events which elicited
them.

The therapists' questionnaire responses lended support to the
ubiquitous claim that imagery is especially useful for dealing with
resistance in therapy (Desoille, 1966; Leuner, 1978; Reyher and
Smeltzer, 1968; Scheidler, 1972; Singer and Pope, 1978b). The
therapists' reports that the guided fantasy helped to focus the
therapy on specific issues may reflect the concreteness and immedi-
acy of material presented imaginally as well as the structuring
effect provided by the use of a particular fantasy theme (Singer,
1974). The focusing effects of the guided fantasies exemplify the
informational and diagnostic value of imaginal expression:
clinically important material may appear in imagery which the client would be unwilling to disclose or even unable to represent in
conceptual, verbal conversation.

Client Characteristics Influencing

The findings on the effects of client differences suggest that
guided fantasy may be perceived as more helpful by female clients
diagnosed anxiety-neurotic than by male clients diagnosed obsessive-
compulsive. The sex differences, though statistically significant,
may be spurious because there were only four female clients, and
half of these were diagnosed obsessive-compulsive--a personality
type which both Leuner (1978) and Assagioli (1965) consider refrac-
tory to imagery procedures.

Involvement and Guided-Fantasy Effects

An important finding in this study was that the therapists'
ratings of the clients' involvement during the guided fantasy were
associated with the clients' ratings of the significance of attitudinal changes they experienced immediately after the therapy session. The therapist's Involvement rating was also a fair predictor
(p = .069) of the significance of any new knowledge or understanding gained during the session. Assuming the validity of the measures used, these findings indicate that the therapists could have
accurately used their assessments of the clients' overt affective
behaviors to infer the occurrence of therapeutically significant
covert changes--a valuable bit of information for a therapist to
have!

Guided Fantasy vs Conventional
  Therapeutic Encounter

The one statistically significant finding and numerous trends
in comparing the two treatment conditions can be interpreted to
mean that many clients found the guided-fantasy session more effective than the conventional-therapeutic-encounter session along
several, diverse dimensions and especially in facilitating attitudinal change. It is possible that most of these apparent differences
are due to chance variation rather than to actual differences
between the treatment conditions. However, the number and consistency of the nonsignificant trends suggest that a larger sample may
have shown significant treatment effects for at least some of these
variables.

Hopefully, this exploratory study has pointed to enough intriguing possibilities that it will stimulate further research and
clinical study of guided fantasy. Any of the areas touched upon
here are deserving of more intensive investigation using larger
samples, more refined measures, variations in procedure, and so on.
Worthwhile extensions of the present study might entail applying
similar methodologies to different guided-fantasy themes or perhaps
to a series of guided-fantasy sessions. The revival of research on
individual differences in imagery processes (Singer, 1974) has provided a number of variables which could be employed to study guided
fantasy. Further investigations of guided fantasy is likely to
enrich our understanding of fantasy and personality, and it could
advance both the practice and the scientific investigation of
psychotherapy.

REFERENCES

Assagioli, R. Psychosynthesis: a manual of principles and tech-
    niques. New York: Hobbs, Dorman, and Company, 1965.
Beck, A. T. Role of fantasies in psychotherapy and psychopathology.
    Journal of Nervous and Mental Disease, 1970, 150, 3-17.
Blankman, S. M. Guided fantasy as a psychotherapeutic experience:
    an experimental study. Unpublished doctoral dissertation,
    California School of Professional Psychology, San Diego, 1979.
Chestnut, W. J. Directed imagery: a means for dealing with
    patient defensiveness. Psychotherapy: Therapy, Research and
    Practice, 1971, 8, 325-327.
Davis, D., McLemore, C. W., and London, P. The role of visual
    imagery in desensitization. Behaviour Research and Therapy,
    1970, 8, 11-13.
Desoille, R. The directed daydream. New York: Psychosynthesis
    Research Foundation, 1966.

Dyckman, J. W., amd Cowan, P. A. Imaging vividness and the outcome
    of in vivo and imagined scene desensitization. Journal of
    Consulting and Clinical Psychology, 1978, 46, 1155-1156.
Garufi, B. Reflections on the 'rêve éveillé dirigé' method.
    Journal of Analytical Psychology, 1977, 22, 207-229.
Hammer, M. The directed daydream technique. Psychotherapy: Theory,
    Research and Practice, 1967, 4, 173-181.
Johnsgard, K. Symbol confrontation in a recurrent nightmare.
    Psychotherapy: Theory, Research and Practice, 1969, 6, 177-182.
Kazdin, A. E. Covert modeling: the therapeutic application of
    imagined rehearsal. In J. L. Singer and K. S. Pope (Eds.),
    The power of human imagination: new methods of psychotherapy.
    New York: Plenum Press, 1978.
Kelly, G. F. Guided fantasy as a counseling technique with youth.
    Journal of Counseling Psychology, 1972, 19, 355-361.
Kiesler, D. J. The process of psychotherapy. Chicago: Aldine,
    1973.
Klinger, E. The nature of fantasy and its clinical uses. Psycho-
    therapy: Theory, Research and Practice, 1977, 14, 223-231.
Kosbab, F. P. Imagery techniques in psychiatry. Archives of
    General Psychiatry, 1974, 31, 283-290.
Krojanker, R. J. Leuner's symbolic drama. American Journal of
    Hypnosis: Clinical, Experimental, Theoretical, 1966, 9, 56-61.
Leuner, H. Guided affective imagery (GAI): a method of intensive
    psychotherapy. American Journal of Psychotherapy, 1969, 23,
    4-22.
Leuner, H. Guided affective imagery: an account of its develop-
    ment. Journal of Mental Imagery, 1977, 1, 73-91.
Leuner, H. Basic principles and therapeutic efficacy of guided
    affective imagery (GAI). In J. L. Singer and K. S. Pope
    (Eds.), The power of human imagination: new methods in psycho-
    therapy. New York: Plenum Press, 1978.
McLemore, C. W. Imagery in desensitization. Behaviour Research
    and Therapy, 1972, 10, 51-57.
McLemore, C. W. Factorial validity of imagery measures. Behaviour
    Research and Therapy, 1976, 14, 399-408.
Meichenbaum, D. Why does using imagery in psychotherapy lead to
    change? In J. L. Singer and K. S. Pope (Eds.), The power of
    human imagination: New methods in psychotherapy. New York:
    Plenum Press, 1978.
Mitchell, E. C. Induced fantasy: a phenomenological study (Doc-
    toral dissertation, University of Tennessee, 1974). Disserta-
    tion Abstracts International, 1974, 35, 1056B. (University
    Microfilms No. 74-17, 727)
Reyher, J., and Smeltzer, W. Uncovering properties of visual imag-
    ery and verbal association: a comparative study. Journal of
    Abnormal Psychology, 1968, 73, 218-222.
Richardson, A. Mental imagery. New York: Springer, 1969.
Rochkind, M., and Conn, J. H. Guided fantasy encounter. American
    Journal of Psychotherapy, 1973, 27, 516-528.

Scheidler, T. Use of fantasy as a therapeutic agent in latency-age groups. Psychotherapy: Theory, Research and Practice, 1972, 9, 299-302.

Schutz, W. C. Joy: expanding human awareness. New York: Grove Press, 1967.

Siegel, S. Nonparametric statistics for the behavioral sciences. New York: McGraw-Hill, 1956.

Singer, J. L. Imagery and daydream methods in psychotherapy and behavioral modification. New York: Academic Press, 1974.

Singer, J. L., and Pope, K. S. (Eds.), The power of human imagination: new methods in psychotherapy. New York: Plenum Press, 1978a.

Singer, J. L., and Pope, K. S. The use of imagery and fantasy techniques in psychotherapy. In J. L. Singer and K. S. Pope (Eds.), The power of human imagination: new methods in psychotherapy. New York: Plenum Press, 1978b.

Van den Berg, J. H. An existential explanation of the guided daydream in psychotherapy. Review of Existential Psychology and Psychiatry, 1962, 2, 5-35.

Wilkins, W. Imagery-based decisions. Psychotherapy: Theory, Research and Practice, 1976, 13, 253-254.

GUIDED FANTASIES IN ELEMENTARY CLASSROOMS

Robert Rose, Ph.D.

Newmark Elementary School

San Bernardino, California

SOME PERSONAL RESULTS

In 1977-1978, my class of fifth and sixth graders showed average gains of 18 to 24 months in reading, language and math, as
measured by the CTBS. There are five major levels in the Raven's
Advanced Matrices Test, roughly equivalent to 130+ IQ, 120+, 90-110,
75-90, 75-. On this test, almost every child moved up one level.
This has never occurred with such dramatic differences in 10 years
of using the Matrices which I have found to be the most culture-
fair general indicator of intelligence.

In 1978-1979 I had class changes in October, and at the end of
February. Each time there were gains and losses totaling 8 to 16
children, making it difficult to create or continue the type of
growth patterns I'd managed with the other classes.

Every year during parent conferences, usually eight weeks
after school begins, I hear reports of gross behavior changes, such
as, "He's nicer to his sister," "She is sleeping better," "He has
fewer headaches," "She seems to be closer to her daddy now," "She
helps out with the housework without me naggin' at her all the
time."

There are many reasons for these changes. I have a holistic,
humanistic program of academic, affective, athletic, and aesthetic
activities to strongly encourage the development of each child's
potentials. In this article, I will focus on how the guided fantasies help accomplish these goals.

281

POSSIBLE REASONS FOR THE EFFECTIVENESS OR
LACK OF EFFECTIVENESS OF GUIDED FANTASIES

The first problem that would prevent effective creation of
fantasies is the teacher's belief system. Some teachers who cannot
or will not image are not convinced of its value. If the first
attempt fails they give up. This often occurs when people try to
incorporate a new idea into their lives and when they have little
invested in it and no assurance that it will work as advertised.

I have no doubt that the children will follow my directions
and they do. Except for a few. Any new group, pre-schoolers to
adults, deserve some explanation of why I am guiding them through
this experience. They need to know the things that may happen to
them.

Your brain has two sides and although one works with the
other, there are some things that one does better than
the other. In school you use the left side more for reading, writing, and math. This neglects your right side.
It doesn't get enough of a workout and makes your entire
brain less efficient. By having these guided fantasies,
your right brain gets the chance to exercise. This makes
your whole brain work better and you get smarter. After
I teach you how to do it you can get into fantasies by
yourself in your spare time or you can do them with me or
any other teacher.

I answer any questions and strongly emphasize that this is a
lesson as important as reading or science, and I expect, I demand,
their full cooperation. I seldom get it from every child, but the
few that act up I handle quickly and firmly before the silliness
gets contagious. After the first experience most of them are eager
for more and peer pressures disposes of most problems. Blindfolds
are a help in the beginning, or for continued use with the ones who
disrupt or disturb others. Isolation or separation also helps.

ANTICIPATING AND AVOIDING CONFLICTS WITH
OPPONENTS OF GUIDED FANTASIES

The parents can be a problem because of their misunderstandings
about what fantasies are and their dangers. Therefore, in the first
week of school I do two things. I send home a copy of my goals and
my projected program. Next, I have a meeting where I further
explain my total program and answer their questions. At this time
I suggest to those who are uncomfortable with my techniques or me
that they remove their children from my class. Each year I lose
one or two. A few times where a child was not removed at once it
caused great aggravation and trauma to the child caught between

allegiance to his parents and me, and it also made my life unneces-
sarily difficult.

One should have an agreement beforehand with the principal and
the receiving teachers with whom you may need to exchange students.
If you don't do this and don't conduct a parents' meeting, serious
problems may develop.

The important thing is to believe in the value of what you
want to do and then establish an openness and trust with the parents
and your fellow educators so that you can prevent problems or iron
them out as they occur.

Your colleagues can be for or against you. If they see the
innovation as a threat to their ways of working, they will cause
troubles with you, your class, the parents, or the administrators.
I've experienced all these troubles at one time or another because
of my innovations and my stupidity and stubbornness. It takes more
than merely being courteous or friendly with them; it means taking
the time to explain your purposes, finding what their objections
and fears are, and then increasing their knowledge and comfort
levels.

There are people who will remain unconvinced. Rather than
deplete your energies, accept the fact that they have a different
attitude which fits their belief system and which they see no reason to change. Respect it!

However, enlist the aid of your supporters physically and in
writing, and let your opponents know that you have the same right
to your beliefs and you intend to follow them.

As long as they have the opportunity to remove their children
from your class, and there are teachers who are willing to give
them what they believe is necessary, then they have no legal or
moral powers to prevent you from teaching your way.

Caution! Just because they don't have these powers does not
mean they are powerless or will leave you alone. They have the
power of constant harrassment and the power to frighten you out of
your resolve by the very strength of their fanaticism. Do NOT
underestimate them. It will take moral and physical courage as
well as intelligence to fight them. The results for you and the
children are well worth it!

The above is one reason why it's important that the principal
and your other supervisors need to know what you're doing and why.
Also, in these days of increasing numbers of law suits, your actions
could result in a law suit which could include them. The recent
court decision against the teaching of Transcendental Meditation in

schools is a case in point. This was based on the premise that TM
can be construed as bringing into the schools a religious dogma
which affects the separation of church and state. I needed to know
about that decision and be able to explain to the administrators
that my meditation training did not fall into this same category.
Still, they felt better after I called it Relaxation Training rather
than meditation. I was also asked to retitle my guided fantasies
to Imagination Training. These were not easy compromises for me
because I wanted to educate the public about these techniques and
spread their use. Yet, if my stance had concluded with my program
being stopped through legal maneuvers, then everyone would have lost.
So, I listen to and compromise with the powers that be. If euphe-
misms do the trick, then let them be. When enough people see the
validity of these techniques, they will create the public pressure
for their use. In the meantime, learn and keep accurate records of
your results.

Another frequent criticism of fantasy that you need to be aware
of is the implication of mind control. This is a fearful thing to
many people, especially since it is a reality of modern life.

Governments tell their populations what they want them to hear.
They filter the facts so that the truth is bent to fit the believed
needs of the society.

Advertising is mind control for business and economic reasons
which are rationalized as good for the country. Maybe it is, but
the fact remains that groups of highly skilled individuals create
new needs in people to buy things that are not necessities and may
even be dangerous to them.

Some of those who believe that fantasies are dangerous are the
same people who believe that traditional schooling is best for everyone. They believe that learning the basics, how to get a job, and
how to become a good citizen are the only reasons to provide free
schooling. They are unaware of how much mind control takes place
while these ideas are taught. They refuse to see straight rows of
chairs, lining up at the door, permission to get a drink or use of
the rest room, the no-talking and no-touching rules, specific times
for each subject, grade level books without consideration of individual needs of children as anything except efficient means of
getting the children to pay attention and learn better. They do
not understand that these controls develop a sense of conformity,
crush creativity and independent thought, and mold children to be
good consumers dependent on corporations and strong government.

Another criticism I've faced was, "Your children spend so much
time in fantasy that they cannot tell the difference between it and
reality!"

Completely reversed! My students have experienced the depths
of their inner worlds. They know how it feels in their minds and
bodies because I make it a point to make them aware of the difference between fantasy and reality. They do know the difference
between a casual, harmless daydream, a fantasy with a specific purpose in mind, and ordinary reality. What's more, they know when
and how to use their skills in fantasy to accomplish certain tasks
for themselves. At least, most of them do.

Through fantasies children learn to respect what goes on in
their minds, their friends' minds, to be unafraid of these experiences, and to be able to accept their individuality, creativity
and originality, as well as that of their friends. Love of learning and socialization that is responsive to individual growth usually accompanies these changes.

Therefore, it is not mind control, but mind release. This is
even more true if the fantasies are taught using both the direct
induction methods and the open-ended ones developed by Dr. Milton
Erickson. These begin with "as you are ready you MAY" type of
directions.

Sometimes, if you're having trouble convincing parents or
administrators of the validity and worth of fantasies, you may wish
to refer to the writings of practitioners. Dr. Beverly Galyean
has been and is involved with several exciting programs within
the Los Angeles School System. I have been using transpersonal
methods in San Bernardino, California, for many years, and my doctoral dissertation, Discipline, a Transpersonal Approach, explains
in detail the whys and how-to-do-it of many techniques. The Imagery
bulletin put out by the American Association for the Study of Mental
Imagery provides additional guidance, stimulation, and proof of the
effectiveness of guided fantasies to beef up your arguments.

Armed with information, convinced of the usefulness of these
methods, and having properly prepared all concerned, you are now
ready to embark your class on their first guided fantasy.

INDUCTION METHODS FOR GUIDED FANTASIES

The length and complexity of the induction depends on what you
want them to visualize and your conception of its purpose. All
types have worked and failed for me at different times. Some experimenters have found that no induction is necessary. They merely
begin by telling them what they want them to see and the subjects
reported seeing what they were told.

For the beginner I would suggest the following: 1) "Sit with
your feet together firmly on the floor. Place both hands quietly

on your desk with your palms down; 2) close your eyes and remain
perfectly still." You want to minimize the distractions from
others and within themselves.

See yourself, in your mind, getting up from your chair
and walking to the chalkboard. There is a piece of
colored chalk, whatever color you see is fine. Pick it
up and write or print your first name as large as you can
across the board. (Pause) Now, starting from the last
letter, erase your name, one letter at a time, backwards.

All these instructions are done in a pace rapid enough so that
they must respond by actively doing something at all times. This
effort prevents them from focusing on distracting stimuli and pre-
pares them for the next direction. Following these directions
occupies their thinking so that resistance is unthinkable. Also,
they're easy and fun to do.

Or, after 1) and 2), I'll say, "I'll count to five twice. With
each count you breathe in and out. The first five will be fast,
the next five slow. Ready! One, two, three . . ."

Or, after 1) and 2), "You're on a merry-go-round at Disneyland.
What are the colors of your horse? The one next to you?" Again,
you can see how easy it is to distract and occupy their thinking
to get them into it.

I like to vary my inductions, not only to fit my purposes better, but I have a low threshold for boredom. However, a case could
be made for using the same one every time. It develops a patterned
response to the procedure.

Before you begin any fantasy, you may also want to add this
protection. "If, at any time during the fantasy, you feel uncomfortable for any reason, you always have the right to stop it by
merely opening your eyes. You do not have the right to bother anyone else."

Remember, the purpose of the induction is to distract their
minds from ordinary reality, a generally left-brain function, and
to take them into nonordinary reality, usually a right-brain
function.

EXAMPLES OF GUIDED FANTASIES

Decimals

In addition of decimals it is important to always line
up the decimal points or dots. Whenever you see an

addition problem dealing with decimals, visualize each
decimal as a glowing, off and on, colored bead. See
them hanging in a straight line. Place them on your paper
in that line and the numbers will arrange themselves in
their proper columns. You may need to help put them into
their correct places. Then add.

Anatomy of Hearing

"You are a musical note, a high one. You are entering, bouncing into the meatus of my ear. You are entering my ear canal and
causing my ear drum called the tympanic membrane to move back and
forth at a rapid pace. You are . . ."

Building Confidence for Oral Reports

You've shown me your outline and your speech is well-
organized. You're going to tell the class what you did
to help your team win the baseball game. In each inning
you did something well and you're going to explain each
event. You're standing in front of the class, you're
comfortable, relaxed, very confident because you know
exactly what you did so you can say it clearly. You know
your classmates will listen respectfully because they
want the same respect and attention from you.

Technique for Handling Children's Conflicts

You are on the playground. You are angry at another
child. It may have happened today or a few days ago.
Feel your anger. Notice where it's located in your body.
Listen to what he's saying. Listen to what you're saying. Feel his anger. Suddenly I'm standing between the
two of you. I'm asking you to tell your side of the
story and reminding him to listen carefully. You're
telling your side. I'm now asking him to repeat what
you said so that we all agree on what you said. You
agree. Now, listen to his side. Repeat what you heard
him say. You have expressed both sides, listened to
both, now discuss some possible solutions that will
satisfy both of you, and make a compromise decision.

Obviously, this simplistic method is not going to work with all the
children all of the time, but it does give them a tool to slow down
their usual irrational responses.

Before I get into racial imagery, identification and conflicts,
I have them undergo fantasies in which they physically change into
Eskimos, Bushmen, Australian Aborigines, Navajos, and a Chinese

peasant. In each of these they have walked in the mocassins of that person for a time. From these experiences they are more easily brought into identifying with modern day problems. It is also useful for spotting the children with the most intense prejudices. I have observed that they are the ones who cannot change, cannot image themselves as members of different races. This form of prejudice is pointed out to them. Many of them admit stating that it is what their parents have taught them!

Within the context of your purpose you must determine the actual amount of time they should spend in a fantasy. The decimals fantasy could be seconds long, while the conflict resolution or the racial imagery ones might take a few to several minutes. You can determine this also by the level of activity of the children. As long as most of them are quiet and motionless, they are probably deep in the fantasy, or asleep! If they fall asleep I let them. They usually need it more than the fantasy, but it is often a form of resistance, although of the passive type. When you see them fidget, stretch, even open their eyes, then you know that they're coming out or you should bring them back. Be observant of their moods and you'll know when to terminate the experience. The open-ended fantasies that they complete without my specific guidance often last longer than those I direct step-by-step. They get into them so deeply that they do not want to come back.

Incidentally, don't be frightened if a child doesn't snap right back on occasion. I've had many children who fight coming out of a particularly delightful fantasy. Sometimes I let them stay until they return on their own or else I touch them gently and softly request that they come back. They do!

CLOSURE PROCEDURES

When you're ready to bring the class back to ordinary reality you may again choose to be very directive or nondirective.

"When I say so, take three deep breaths, stretch, and open your eyes. Ready! One, two, three," or "As you are ready to return take three deep breaths, stretch, and open your eyes," or even, "Open your eyes! Listen to my next direction."

I usually use the nondirective closure, but use the open your eyes closure for something like the decimals fantasy.

You may add, before you bring them back, the following phrase that will help get into the next fantasy more easily. "Next time we do a guided fantasy you will find it easier to relax, easier to get strong and clear images, and easier to ignore outside and inside distractions!"

MORE BENEFITS FROM GUIDED FANTASIES

Many of my student athletes rehearse their skills before going
to sleep, while riding in a car, or sometimes (unfortunately) in
class. Almost all of them have used fantasies to eradicate or alleviate the pain from some minor physical ailments, such as headaches,
stomach aches, leg cramps, and allergies. Several times during the
week at least one of the children can be seen lying on our wrestling
mat, relaxing, and ridding himself of a headache. The imagery that
has been most successful came from the Imagery Bulletin. I have
the child lie on the mat and see his head as a large cube of ice.
As the ice melts the pain gradually flows away as it changes into
water. With some children they need two cubes to completely rid
themselves of the pain. So far, it has worked every time, and,
more importantly, they use it at home on their own!

To demonstrate their concentration and involvement, I must tell
you that the mat is right next to the sink, and while the child is
getting rid of his headache, there is a constant stream of traffic
for drinks.

This is one indication that the guided fantasies teach them
that they have a lot of control and responsibility for what goes on
in their heads. This increases their self-confidence and allows
them a unique growth opportunity as they accept the responsibili-
ties for their actions. It doesn't just happen. I need to reinforce the learnings that take place as soon and as often as I see
them.

The fantasies stimulate their right-brain functioning and
logically gives them more access to their total brain potentials
as one side communicates and provides the other with more information. It has to make them more intelligent academically and
affectively.

Most educational theorists now believe that what we call play
is a major element in any learning that truly sticks in the mind.
Play is missing from too many classrooms. Yet, all the major
artists and scientists report that they "play" with ideas and concepts in fantasy before they get the "Aha!" Children also get the
"Aha!" from playing with ideas, concepts and materials. In a
guided fantasy you give them that opportunity, or, at least, you
legitimize their own abilities to fantasize, to use their sense of
playfulness.

Even if all that I've promised doesn't work for you, you'll
have a few minutes of absolute quiet each time you do it, and these
days, that ain't bad!

EYE AND IMAGE: EYE CONTACT AND GUIDED

IMAGERY IN PSYCHOTHERAPY

Patricia G. Webbink, Ph.D.

Psychotherapist

Brookmont, Maryland

Imagine that you are being watched by a huge eye! What is
your reaction to this image? Do you feel discomfort, fear, self-
consciousness? Or do you feel, perhaps, awe and reverence? Centuries ago, a large eye was worshipped as a sun god whose luminous
gaze communicated power and omniscience, while it also offered protection and comfort. Deities were portrayed as having one eye,
multiple eyes, or, as in Gnostic belief, a third eye; these gods
were alleged to be all-seeing and all-knowing. Eyes are so basic
and fundamental to human existence that the universal symbol of
the eye recurs in many cultures.

In many mythologies, the eye is portrayed as inspiring fear
and awe. For example, in the legend of Medusa, men were turned
into stone when they gazed upon her. The destructiveness of the
Cyclops' one eye was a powerful threat. The fearful properties of
the glance have been incorporated into the universal evil eye myth.
Literature from ancient Babylonia, Egypt and Rome abounds with
references to the menacing power of the evil eye. People could
cast spells on others with the evil eye by making a voluntary pact
with the devil. Even today, the evil eye myth is prevalent in many
parts of the world. However, the eye served not only as an instrument of fear, but also as a means of protection. The "almighty
eye" of the divine being was said to watch over the world. Amulets
and charms containing a large picture of an eye were made to ward
off evil spirits.

Throughout the ages, the eyes have had great symbolic impact
with many social, cultural and/or religious connotations attributed
to them. The eyes are associated with life itself, which is said
to begin when the eyes open and to end when they close. Primitive

beliefs about death aften involve the eyes, for instance, the notion that opening the eyes or kissing the eyelids will restore life. In some cultures, the eyes are the part of the body believed to live on after death.

One way to experience the power of the eyes is to think about your own eyes. How do you feel about them? When you close them, do you feel an increased sense of self or increased body awareness? According to popular belief, the very essence of the individual can be located in the eyes. Because our main contact with the world is visual, the eyes may stand for the entire self. It may not be a linguistic accident that in English the words "I" and "eye" are pronounced identically, or that in Greek they are spelled identically.

The two words, "I" and "eye," are said to be symbolically equated in dreams (Heaton, 1968). According to Freudian tradition, the eyes may represent either female or male genitalia. It has been suggested that since the sexual organs are taboo, emotion will be invested in another visible and highly valued organ of pleasure (Schlaegel, 1957). Perhaps the identification of the eyes with the self accounts for the imagery in literature in which the eyes are referred to as "smiling," "seizing," "holding," and "biting." Frequent allusions in literature portray the eyes as analogous to grasping hands or to a devouring mouth. A well-known example is Ben Johnson's request, "Drink to me only with thine eyes and I will pledge thee mine."

Not only are the eyes considered to be the "windows of the soul," but "mirrors of emotion," and a symbol of identity, but it has also been asserted that they are, more than any other feature of the body, indicative of personal qualities or character. After all, one does not imagine looking into another person's soul through the mouth, nose or ears (Katz, 1963). Thus, when two people turn these powerful features toward each other, something special happens--eye contact. Two people looking into one another's eyes is a type of looking behavior that, because of its special nature, is itself a significant phenomenon. Eye contact is both mutual and reciprocal and intimacy often occurs when both people encounter each other's eyes. But when one person looks at another, it is also possible to view the other as an object, an "it." One can look <u>at</u> the eyes of another without really making personal contact. Popular language illustrates this distinction: looking <u>at</u> one's face, but into one another's eyes.

It is worthwhile to note that the contact made with the eyes varies widely. Just as there are many ways in which one person can experience and respond to the touch of another (e.g., receiving a kiss coldly), so can eye contact range from blank stare to a deep gaze that penetrates the other's soul. For example, in an exercise done in a class, people were paired with their neighbors and asked

to make eye contact. A man was paired with a women who knew he was
dying. They held the contact for three minutes as instructed, but
the man restrained himself from expressing any emotion in his eyes,
while the woman's eyes filled with pain. The man's attempt to disguise his feelings revealed his fear of death. Sometimes an emotional block may be demonstrated by a look "through" the other person or a look "at" the other's eyes instead of into the other's
eyes.

The qualitative differences of eye contact can be easily demonstrated in a simple exercise similar to one developed by Virginia
Satir:

Photography--The group divides into dyads, who sit facing each
other. Instructions: a) open/close eyes; b) express emotion with
the eyes; c) put a barrier between you and your partner; d) lift
the barrier; e) touch hands with your partner; f) take a mental picture of your partner; g) close eyes, remember partner's face;
h) open eyes--whom does your partner remind you of? i) close eyes,
think of partner as other; and j) open eyes--take away projections
and see partner as partner.

(Look into your partner's eyes. What are you experiencing?
What are you feeling about yourself? What are you trying to hide
or communicate? How are you doing this? Do you feel comfortable
or awkward? Do you want to pull back, stare through the other person, become closer to the other person? Are your eyes moving,
blinking? If you look closely, do you see your reflection? Does
looking into this other person's eyes make you want to look more,
or look away? What are your desires or fears right now, and how
do they affect you? What do you notice when you look into this
person's eyes? Can you see your partner's fears or desires? Now
experience yourself and this other person at the same time. This
is eye contact.)

What I have been describing here are differences in the quality
of eye contact. These qualitative aspects of eye contact are perhaps the most fascinating and fruitful area of exploration, but in
the past they have been ignored to a large extent by academic and
clinical researchers who only recently have come to recognize eye
contact as the nonverbal behavior most worthy of extensive investigation. Elaborate eye communication patterns have been identified,
and one can now predict the amount and duration of eye contact on
the basis of such data as personality, status, sex, race, culture,
age, closeness of interpersonal relationships, and whether the
person is listening or talking. Interpersonal factors such as body
position, physical distance, amount of verbalization, topic of conversation, and emotional tone of the interaction also influence
eye contact.

Eye contact is an important process, as well as useful technique, in diagnosis and psychotherapy. The eyes may reveal many types of problems. The most common is decreased eye contact, which is found in autistic children, in depressed individuals, and in people who have severe problems with interpersonal relationships, commonly labeled as schizophrenic. Gaze aversion is one way of avoiding people and of reducing the stimulation that comes from interacting with them. Autistic children present some of the most dramatic examples of gaze aversion; they often adamantly avoid eye contact, even to the point of struggling to move their heads when held face-to-face with an adult.

Individuals labeled as depressed or "schizophrenic" also manifest abnormal eye behavior, most notably gaze aversion. This aversion is characteristic of an individual's avoidance of interpersonal relationships. Depressives may avoid mutual gaze because of feelings of guilt or shame. R. D. Laing (1960) reported that schizophrenics actively fear the gaze of another person and are especially vulnerable to feeling exposed by the looks of others. This fear he also observed among "paranoid schizophrenics" who feel eyes "looking at them" and dread being looked at directly, or who fear the destructive effect of a glance. Extremely fearful or paranoid people may fantasize that their glance, or that of others, possesses evil powers. To some of these individuals, a look can "kill" or make others "insane." A paranoid delusion may involve a fear of persecution by accusing or condemning eyes. An example is a woman in therapy who described her fear of "a shapeless figure looming in the darkness with crazy eyes. No matter where I go in the house it always watches me." At the opposite end of the spectrum are some highly distressed individuals who cherish the gaze and "grab" another's eyes in prolonged eye contact (Laing, 1960). The person with "devouring" eye contact may yearn for the protection and omnipotence of the other, or be expressing a wish to merge into the other's identity. For example, the person may feel, "I want to become you for I am nothing myself."

It is indeed a strange experience for a therapist to "relate" to an individual whose eyes seem constantly to grab hers/his, or with an autistic child who blankly stares away. Between these two extremes is a whole range of looking behavior exhibited by a variety of people who seek help. The eye contact between therapist and client is important in establishing, and then maintaining, the therapeutic relationship. As one client remarked, "The first thing I noticed about my therapist was her warm eyes." Eye contact, more than other nonverbal behaviors, lets the client know that the therapist is attending to her/him (Hammond, Hepworth and Smith, 1977). The therapist's eyes are superb vehicles for expressing warmth, acceptance, empathy, and respect for the client.

The behavior of the therapist, both verbal and nonverbal,

serves to communicate therapeutic attitudes to the client. Some
of these behaviors and attitudes will facilitate positive change in
the client. Carl Rogers (1957) identified three attitudes that are
characteristic of an intimate relationship and which are conducive
to positive therapeutic change. These attitudes--empathy, positive
regard and congruence--are fostered by eye contact. My own research
(1974) substantiated Rogers' statement. In my experiment, subjects
briefly experienced mutual gaze with a female confederate and then,
as compared with two other similar conditions, reported feeling
heightened empathy, greater willingness to reveal themselves, and
more positive feeling toward her.

Each of these therapeutic attitudes has been explored and
studied by a host of researchers. Common experience suggests that
eye contact and likeability are related, and experimenters have
confirmed the relationship (Mehrabian, 1967, 1968, 1969). The
positive feeling between client and therapist contributes to a
relationship that is warm, open and caring. Empathy, or the ability
to see the world through another's eyes (or perspective), also contributes to a good relationship. Empathy is found to be stronger
when mutual gaze takes place (Marks, 1971). The therapist's empathy
and positive regard may serve to increase the client's feeling of
self-worth, as well as a desire to engage in close interpersonal
relationships.

Congruence occurs when there is harmony between the feelings
within a person and the outward expression of them. People are
highly congruent during peak moments of emotional and physical
expression, such as when experiencing grief, anger, fear, or sexual
passion. Incongruence can often be seen in a contradiction between
the expression of the eyes and those of other parts of the face or
body. Sometimes the silent eye contact between client and therapist, between one client and another, or between a client and her/
his own eyes in a mirror will result in the client's discovery and
expression of emotions in an integrated way. One client reported:

> I thought I was angry at my therapist. I felt defiant,
> feisty, coiling my body in the chair opposite her,
> ready to attack. She told me she sensed very different
> feelings coming through my eyes, so she handed me a
> mirror. I looked into my own eyes and felt fear. I
> stared at myself until the fear flowed through my eyes
> to my forehead and mouth. It grew into a scream that
> filled my whole body until the tension was gone; my
> eyes grew softer; I relaxed, felt whole again, in
> touch with myself.

In psychotherapy, eye contact can be used by the therapist as
a gauge of the client's feelings of self-worth and as a measurement
of the client's progress. In my practice, I have seen many

children and adults who, when they entered therapy, had a great
deal of trouble making eye contact. As they worked through particular problems, they were better able to make eye contact. In one
case, after a child discovered he was angry at his mother, he began
to make eye contact for the first time. In another case, a person
who has had a slow recovery from a "nervous breakdown" began to
look at people again as she felt more confident and less frightened.

Eye contact serves as an intensifier of emotion, whether it is
positive or negative (Ellsworth and Carlsmith, 1968). This is
important in psychotherapy because often people need catharsis or a
way of expressing their emotions. If, for instance, one says, "I
love you," or "I hate you," the lack of eye contact may detract
from the expression. Its presence, however, may increase the
intensity of the statement. Profound communication between two
people, whether it exists between therapists and clients, close
friends or lovers, has been the subject of literature and song for
centuries. When people gaze into one another's eyes for a long
time, feelings are communicated which are difficult to verbalize.
Individuals feel relieved when they express the emotions they have
been frightened to reveal. It is these moments that can provide
a major source of healing within the therapeutic situation.

Although positive feeling and/or intimacy is probably a more
common vehicle for expression through the eyes, the person who
expresses anger and looks into the eyes of the other person will
probably experience greater intensity. The individual may find
that s/he is confronting other feelings and attitudes as well. For
instance, I have seen people who always looked away as they
expressed anger. When I encourage these clients to look at me and
express their anger, they find that their emotions are intensified.
But they also find themselves faced with other feelings, such as
closeness or the sadness of their own isolation. In one such case,
when a woman was timidly expressing anger, I asked her to look
into my eyes. As she did so, her eyes filled with tears as she
said, "I can't, I can't tell you." Then, as she became unfomfort-
able with the intimate gaze and lowered her head, I reached over
and held her. She cried for the first time in months of therapy.

There are many different techniques used to facilitate eye
contact. Several of them involve body work, such as bioenergetics,
Rolfing therapy and Reichian therapy, in which the client expresses
feelings through the body. In some cases massaging the muscular
tension around the eyes helps to release repressed feelings. Discussion of the client's eye contact behavior in the session is also
helpful for encouraging self-awareness. In one case, a man entered
therapy because he was unable to make eye contact in his public
speaking engagements. After discussing his problems and then con-
scientiously noting his eye contact throughout the day, he was able
to reverse the pattern. Another client, a woman with glaucoma,

discovered that her eye contact was quite poor because of her reluctance to confront her fears about blindness. As she became aware
of her fears, she stopped wearing glasses and found new joy in looking at people.

Several types of therapy use the eyes in facilitating awareness
and catharsis. In Gestalt therapy and psychodrama, a client may
uncover repressed incidents through role play involving eye contact.
In psychodrama, the client who makes eye contact with other "actors"
becomes more involved in the scene. The expression of intense
feelings may be facilitated in Gestalt therapy when the client is
asked to imagine that s/he is talking to someone and looking into
the eyes of the other person. In many cases, the person cries and
begins to feel "present" in the situation. The instruction to make
eye contact is one of the crucial factors in creating this intensity. Asking people to imagine that they are looking into the eyes
of someone who has died is extremely powerful. Recalling the eyes
of the person seems to make this imagined person come to life.
Clients often remember deathbed scenes vividly when asked to look
into the dying person's eyes.

A woman who frequently had unexplained crying spells was asked
in a session to imagine talking to her father on his deathbed. She
began sobbing as she recalled her last meeting with her father whom
she loved so much and who was paralyzed and helpless to speak except
with his eyes. "I look into your eyes, you who have always been so
strong and vibrant. Now you cannot move or speak. Your eyes cry
out to me to help and I can do nothing." In doing this exercise,
she realized that she had been burdened with this horrible memory,
and much of the sadness that she had "carried around" was directly
related to this incident. After she shared it with members of her
psychotherapy group, she felt as though a great weight had been
lifted from her.

The techniques of Gestalt therapy, bioenergetics, psychodrama
and Reichian therapy serve to intensify emotion, in much the same
way that eye contact does. Therefore, eye contact used simultaneously with these techniques can be a very powerful tool. If, for
example, a person is analyzing a dream with the psychoanalytic
technique of free association, s/he can intellectualize about
feelings more easily than if asked to imagine becoming part of the
dream, or to look into the eyes of the people in the dream.

Because of the interaction and feedback that a psychotherapy
group provides, the use of eye contact and exercises in a group can
be a valuable aid for the client's personal growth. Eye contact
can also serve as a barometer of feelings and attitudes in the
group. A therapist can encourage sensitivity among group members
by leading eye contact exercises in the safe environment of a group
(Blank, Gottsegan and Gottsegan, 1971). Many such exercises involve

mutual gaze in silence. This technique helps people to increase
their eye contact in everyday circumstances. People initially
experience discomfort and self-consciousness with these exercises,
which may cause them to giggle, talk, or avert their gaze. Eventually though, they become more comfortable with mutual gaze and discover an enrichment in their lives through it.

A common exercise begins with the leader's request that participants gaze intently into one another's eyes, perhaps that they
communicate specific emotions (e.g., fear, anger, love, concern).
The exercise can vary from one of self-expression or "express your
deepest feelings," to one of empathy or "experience the feelings of
your partner." In a variation of this technique, two people sit
and face one another about two feet apart. The first person intently
observes the second person and agrees that s/he will respond to the
second only when the second is communicating something through eye
contact, such as, "touch me," "get out of my sight," or "comfort
me."

At one meeting, two group members went through a series of nonverbal messages and discovered how their relationship and communication problems had been developing. One person was trying to send
the eye message "respect me." The other person waited a long time
without understanding the message. When the first person intensified the contact it felt like anger to the recipient, so she
responded with hostility. When the two of them talked afterwards,
they discovered that many times during the group session the second
person had felt suspicious of the first person's demands. In
reality, the first person was feeling unsure and was asking for
respect, though not expecting to receive it.

Because the eye has particular qualities and symbolic significance, focusing on the eyes of another person intensifies an already
powerful experience. One exercise involves two people sitting with
joined hands facing each other and engaging in silent "eye-alogue"
(Rosenberg, 1973). They look into each other's eyes trying to be
"present" to each other with their "whole beings." This is similar
to Tantric yoga, in which participants are instructed to maintain
eye contact for long periods of time. With practice, it is said
to "unite . . . the totality of the psychic energy of two people,
into one field, into one sphere of light. It can carry you and
your partner into physical and mental ecstasy" (Three H O
Foundation).

Eye contact does indeed play a significant role in the therapeutic process. Mutual gaze not only aids in establishing a warm,
supportive relationship, it also facilitates the communication of
therapeutic attitudes, which are conducive to positive change.
When used in combination with a variety of techniques, eye contact
can encourage awareness and growth in psychotherapy, or in other

types of group experience. One technique of considerable value is
Guided Imagery and Music. Developed by Helen Bonny, it involves
relaxation, music and guided imagery. In my own practice, I have
very successfully experimented with the use of eye contact, Gestalt
techniques, relaxation and music. Since each one of these methods
facilitates awareness, emotional discharge and increased intensity,
all three combined can be very powerful. During Guided Imagery and
Music sessions, asking the client to look into the eyes of an
imagined person can be most effective.

Following such a session, clients have described their experience variously as a healing force, deeply insightful, or a creative
exploration of their own psyches. Guided Imagery and Music involves
the use of music in reaching heightened, or non-ordinary, levels of
human consciousness. Music facilitates greater levels of emotional
intensity and understanding. It can evoke different emotions,
depending on the mood and situation. As Dr. Helen Bonny (1978)
describes it, "On a certain day in the life of a certain client,
relaxation and music is used to 'tune-in' to multiple layers of
ongoing, variously altered and expanded states of (her/his) inner
being" (p. 28).

Relaxation and concentration are necessary components for
entrance into a heightened state of consciousness. With a relaxed
body and a focused mind, the individual can begin induction to this
altered state. When awareness is enlarged and intensified, consciousness itself can seem to be multi-faceted and multi-dimensional.
Sometimes, even the music appears to acquire color, shape or motion
(Bonny and Savary, 1973).

The Guided Imagery and Music session may involve the intimate
unit of guide and experiencer, or there may be one facilitator for
a group of participants. The guide, through the use of voice and
suggestion, assists participants in relaxation. In a group, the
guide must provide an induction and a musical selection sufficiently general to help each member of the group. The guide's main
purpose is to provide supportive and directive reactions to the
client's imagery, which emphasizes her/his visual content and
deepens self-disclosure. Guides in a dyad serve as empathic reflec-
tors for the emotional experience of the "trippers."

Although the guide usually acts as a sounding board for the
client, occasionally a more directive use of suggestion and of imagery can be valuable. Gestalt techniques and eye contact have been
helpful for intensifying whatever emotions the participant is exploring. For example, a man whose children lived with his ex-wife, was
asked in a session to imagine looking into his son's eyes. The man
burst into tears. Imagining his son's eyes helped him to admit for
the first time how deeply he loved his children.

In another session, a woman's thoughts flowed to her long deceased grandmother of whom she had not thought for many years. The grandmother had had a stroke and "couldn't speak except through her eyes. She was telling me that she loved me, but I was not able to tell her how much I loved her. I was too young." The woman began to cry as she recalled "the eyes that I had forgotten, those beautiful eyes that reached out to me. I've never been able to accept her death."

Participants in a Guided Imagery and Music session report a variety of experiences, which must always be interpreted in context. Those people who experience a visual setting tend to respond to the details or events they note in their environment. Usually one mood predominates, though it may change with the scene or with a change in the musical selection. For some people, little imagery may appear or they experience colors and sensations without visual fantasy. Since emotional and kinesthetic responses can provide the basis of self-awareness, successful therapy does not require the presence of mental imagery (Bonny, 1978). Other participants relate a series of unrelated images, or alternatively, symbolic imagery that tells an insightful story.

The imagery that participants experience is as rich and varied as the music facilitating it. Participants often explore familiar or fantasy-like woodland, mountain or ocean scenes. They may "see" colors or geometric patterns or nothing at all, experiencing instead a quick succession of emotions or one predominant mood. It is a common experience to encounter resistance, many times in the form of images of a closed door or stepping into quicksand. Sometimes the imagery involves the separation of body parts. Whether this is perceived as fascinating or fearful depends on the client's context. A crucial element in this process, which distinguishes it from other techniques utilizing imagery, is that all comes from the client, who spontaneously reports her/his experiences as they happen. The guide or therapist only follows the client. An individual session usually lasts two or more hours. It is often intense and highly meaningful.

Now that I have explained the Guided Imagery and Music session, you can experience it yourself. In a typical session, the participant should remember three points. First, simply allow yourself to follow the music, without resistance. Second, act or react to any feeling, symbol or event that presents itself to you. Finally, allow the movement and feeling of the music to take you from one scene to another (Bonny, 1978). You might also keep in mind the aim of Guided Imagery and Music, which Dr. Bonny describes as a move "from confusion, to understanding, . . . to freedom of action, to decision and to inner control" (1978, p. 42).

GUIDED IMAGERY AND MUSIC/EYE
  CONTACT INTEGRATION

    1. Relaxation/induction by leader

    2. Instructions: go through your life; determine the
important people in your life; select one; relive; look into the
eyes of one of them.

        Imagine . . .

    (After you have relaxed, I may ask you to imagine that your
life is floating in front of you. See yourself as you are now,
see yourself as a young child, and see yourself in the future. As
you "live" these years floating in front of you, find yourself making contact with different people in your life from the past, the
present and the future. Look deeply into the eyes of these people,
talk to each one as you encounter her/him and see if you can make
your peace with that person. Notice the expression in the person's
eyes. What is the person trying to communicate? Tell this person
the most important things you have to say to her/him.)

    A discussion follows the group listening experience, which is
processed by the guide. Some of the questions asked include:
1) Did you have visual imagery? 2) Did your imagery include people,
events or nature scenes? 3) Did you see any colors while listening? If so, were they geometric designs, or were they associated
with nature? 4) Did the colors or scenes change with the musical
phrases? During this group discussion, only those aspects (such
as imagery, symbols, feelings and physical reactions) with which
the participant feels comfortable are shared.

REFERENCES

Blank, L., Gottsegen, G. B., and Gottsegen, M. G. Confrontation:
    encounters in self and interpersonal awareness. New York:
    Macmillan, 1971.
Bonny, H. Facilitating guided imagery and music sessions. Balti-
    more: ICM Books, 1978.
Bonny, H., and Savary, L. M. Music and your mind: listening with
    a new consciousness. New York: Harper & Row, 1973.
Ellsworth, P. C., and Carlsmith, J. M. Effects of eye contact and
    verbal contact on affective response to a dyadic interaction.
    Journal of Personality and Social Psychology, 1968, 10, 15-20.
Hammond, D. C., Hepworth, D. H., and Smith, V. G. Improving
    therapeutic communication. San Francisco: Jossey-Bass, 1977.
Heaton, J. M. The eye: phenomenology and psychology of function
    and disorder. London: Tavistock, 1968.

Katz, R. L. Empathy, its nature and uses. New York: The Free
    Press of Glencoe, 1963.
Laing, R. D. The divided self: a study of sanity and madness.
    New York: Quadrangle, 1960.
Marks, H. E. The relationship of eye contact to congruence and
    empathy. Dissertation Abstracts International, 1971, 32, 1219.
Mehrabian, A. Orientation behaviors and non-verbal attitude com-
    munication. Journal of Communication, 1967, 17, 324-332.
Mehrabian, A. Relationship of attitude to seated posture, orienta-
    tion, and distance. Journal of Personality and Social Psychol-
    ogy, 1968, 10, 26-33.
Mehrabian, A. Some referents and measures of non-verbal behavior.
    Behavior Research Methods and Instrumentation, 1969, 1, 203-207.
Rogers, C. R. The necessary and sufficient conditions of therapeu-
    tic personality change. Journal of Consulting Psychology,
    1957, 21, 95-103.
Rosenberg, J. L. Total orgasm. New York: Random House, 1973.
Schlaegel, T. F. Psychosomatic opthalmology. Baltimore: Williams
    & Wilkins, 1957.
THO Foundation. Some practical notes on tantric yoga. Toronto,
    Ontario: Centre for the Healing Arts, undated.
Webbink, P. G. Eye contact and intimacy. Unpublished doctoral
    dissertation, Duke University, 1974.

V: CLINICAL PERSPECTIVES AND REPORTS

THE EFFECT OF ROLE PLAYING UPON IMAGERY

Milton Wolpin, Ph.D.

Psychology Department

University of Southern California

INTRODUCTION

Recent Developments in Imagery

In the past 15 years there has been a vigorous growth of interest in imagery. Much of this work has been done by clinicians
utilizing imagery to modify all sorts of conditions and behaviors,
e.g., cancer, phobias, lack of assertiveness, and skin rashes. All
of that seems appropriate. It appears more and more that imagery
is an important process, and the way in which it functions has
marked implications for the way the human functions. At the same
time it does appear that the current thrust is consistent with a
behavioral orientation, i.e., the primary outcome that the majority
of investigators is concerned with is some kind of overt, visible
behavior, or readily observable physical condition; imagery remains
an independent variable to be manipulated to get a desirable outcome in the behavior, the dependent variable.

All this is well and good, except that it does seem time to
focus upon imagery for its own sake. We do image a great deal of
the time, and whether it is overt behavior or not, it is obviously
an ongoing experience of great consequence. It seems time to consider it as the dependent variable.

It is time to consider imagery as something important in its
own right. We need no longer be trapped in the behavioral mode.
We cherish our dreams, thoughts, wishes and fantasies. We are concerned beyond what we can say and do that is visible to others,
with the quality of our inner life. Recent work has focused on
teaching people to control their dreams, in part so as to have a

more satisfactory waking life. Images that come to us while we are
awake, while they may be of value in assisting us to change various
behaviors, are an integral meaningful part of our existence in their
own right; it would seem that were we to study imagery, and how it
varied under different conditions, it would help us to get more in
contact with ourselves and to develop a part of ourselves that might
lead us to having fuller, richer and more interesting "inner" lives.
It is with these thoughts in mind that the current research was
pursued.

On Modifying Imagery

Previous work by Wolpin and Kirsch (1974) suggests that some
procedures modify imagery and how important attributes of the imagery involved might be considered. In that study we were interested
in the images that accompany various muscle states, i.e., when one
is relaxed, tense, or in their "usual" state (of muscle tension).
On the basis of pilot studies and reports by various Ss attributes
of imagery were selected for the development of a scale. We eventually used 18 attributes of the imagery, e.g., "how vivid and clear"
it was, "how confident one felt." We found that on a number of
these dimensions there were significant differences in the imagery
experienced depending on the nature of the muscles while imaging.
While there did not seem to be any reliable differences, across
conditions with regard to how clear or vivid an image was, we found,
for example, that when one was relaxed one tended to visualize a
quiet, peaceful, calm ocean, but when one's muscles were tensed
the ocean was pictured as much more "stormy." These results are
intriguing, suggesting, in part, that in systematic desensitization,
for example, one may be changing the stimulus prior to changing the
response. The implications for the theoretical underpinning of systematic desensitization, as proposed by Wolpe (1960) seem clear.
Rather than reciprocal inhibition, one could hypothesize that one
was learning, as a function of changed muscle states during therapy,
to see the world in a new (and more peaceful) way.

There are obviously many ways of changing imagery besides
modifying muscle states. It is exciting to consider that one may
be able to do it readily and systematically.

In this study we chose to investigate the effect of role playing on imagery, hypothesizing that it (role playing) would significantly change imagery as measured by an open-ended interview and
the scale described above. The scale developed in that study was
utilized for the present one.

Role Playing

Role playing is employed in a number of therapeutic approaches,
e.g., psycho-drama, socio-drama, Gestalt therapy and assertiveness

training. It is an important component of assertiveness training,
where it is used effectively. The major question asked in this study
refers to the effect of this role-playing on imagery rather than upon
assertiveness. If, in fact, role playing changes not only overt
behavior but also the imagery we carry around with us, this could
obviously have substantial consequences for human functioning.

The author has had considerable experience with role playing,
as he has been utilizing assertiveness training, for both therapeutic and research purposes, for over 10 years. It is his impression
that it is a powerful tool for changing behavior. It is not uncommon
to see dramatic changes in the way one comports oneself (in a mock
situation) with a neighbor, friend, etc., after half an hour to an
hour of assertion training, with the emphasis on role playing. It
thus seemed quite logical to hypothesize that just as these are
striking behavioral changes occurring with role playing, that the
inner life might be changing as well. If it were changing, it would
be exciting to know that; and if it weren't, that seemed important
also.

With those considerations in mind, role playing was chosen to
give us further indications of possible ways to change imagery.

It was hypothesized that role playing would have a significant
effect on imagery, as measured by an open-ended interview and the
scale described above.

PROCEDURE

Subjects

There were a total of 14 Ss, eight women and six men; three
were graduate students, well acquainted with the author. Eleven
were undergraduates, one of whom had been assisting the author on
another project, and the rest friends of hers who volunteered to
participate in this project. She is an Armenian and so were five
of her friends, which has some consequences for the results.

It seems important to note that even though, in most instances,
that E and S were not acquainted, a fair degree of rapport was
established readily and that the overall situation seemed to be comfortable, if not satisfying and enjoyable for most Ss. This might
be due in part to the fact that Ss were referred by a friend, who
was in turn an assistant to the author. At the same time it appears
that these procedures are generally non-threatening; few if any of
the Ss needed much reassuring. These considerations might be important when devising future research; they suggest ways of gaining
access to exploring and possibly modifying imagery that does not
involve a great deal of stress.

Nature of Intervention

Each S was seen for about an hour, although several of the Ss were seen again, some three or four times; the results reported here are primarily for the first meeting only. Ss were seen individually.

Each S was informed this was a study on the relationship between assertiveness training and imagery, and was asked if there was something about which they would like to be a bit more assertive. Each S was able to describe, usually in a matter of a few minutes, a situation of some concern, e.g., getting money back that had been loaned to a friend, asking a friend to do something together over a week-end, asking a neighbor to turn down the volume on the radio. Subjects were also able to spell out, rather easily, precisely how they would like to handle the situation, i.e., what they would like to say and do.

Following a description of the desired behavior, Ss were requested to picture or imagine themselves, with eyes closed, for 30 seconds, engaging in the behavior of concern. The S and author then engaged in some role playing, as used in assertiveness training, for about 10 to 15 minutes, with the author playing the other person, then a reversal, i.e., playing the S, and once again playing the other person.

Immediately following the role playing, E and S sat down. Once again S was asked to close her/his eyes and imagine, for 30 seconds, engaging in the behavior of concern.

S was then asked to open his/her eyes and was interviewed. This was a non-structured, open-ended interview, asking S to compare the images in the first visualization with those in the second. The latter part of the interview specifically asked S to focus on the nature of the visual imagery, putting aside concerns about what was said and felt. (After 5 to 10 minutes, S was asked to estimate her/his SUDS (subjective units of discomfort) level for the first and second imagining.) Finally, S was given the 18 item questionnaire in which she/he compared the imaging the first time with that of the second time. Finally, Ss were asked if there was anything else about the experience they cared to report on.

There was little hesitation getting into the imagery, either at the beginning or at the end. Ss generally found it fairly easy to get into the role playing (even though on occasion there was some initial hesitation). They also found it meaningful to comment on their imagery and were able to give a considerable amount of detail without a lot of prompting.

In general, it might be said that rapport was typically established (sufficient for experimental purposes), without much difficulty and that the situation moved along fairly easily.

RESULTS

　　Although several Ss were seen more than once, the data reported on are analyzed statistically only for the first session with each S. Below are the results of the 18 item questionnaire.

Table 1

Imaging Scale and Significance Levels Comparing
Pre- and Post-Role-Playing Imaging Scores

Item	P
1. How relaxed you were	NS
2. How sure of yourself you were	.01
3. How good the solutions were	.01
4. How much you could concentrate and ignore everything else	.05
5. How attractive things were	NS
6. How safe you felt	.01
7. How friendly things seemed	NS
8. How much things seemed to be in their usual setting	NS
9. How vivid and clear things were	NS
10. How capable you felt of doing things	.01
11. How weird things seemed	NS
12. How much things were out of proportion	NS
13. How much you were part of the scene	.01
14. How rapidly things were going	NS
15. How detailed things were	NS
16. How active things were	NS
17. How loud sounds were	NS
18. How frightening things seemed	.05

As can be seen in Table 1 above, Ss tended when visualizing
the second time, as compared to the first, to feel more sure of
themselves, to achieve better solutions, to concentrate better, to
feel safer and more capable, to feel more a part of the scene and
to experience things as less frightening. On the "vivid and clear"
item "t" was 2.08 with 2.16 needed for significance at the .05 level.
The failure to reach significance on this item points up a weakness
of the scale.

The strong impression one received, during the open-ended interview, was that things were indeed much more clear, rich, detailed
and in proportion. What were pale shadows and barely and briefly
perceived figures and conversations were, from the impressions
received in the interviews, much more substantial the second time
as compared to the first. This was apparent in many of the reports.
On many of the items where non-significance is reported, the interviews suggest that S is not sure of the meaning of the item.

The self report data suggest that, to a large extent, the images
the second time parallel the role playing. Sometimes, however, it
went beyond that; though Ss did not practice yelling and screaming,
they sometimes imagined that. Also with Ss who were seen more than
once, other interesting changes occurred. One S went from screaming
and yelling, in imagery, to simply not taking the person very seriously and thus becoming very calm about the entire situation (again
not what occurred in the role playing). One S imagined (though did
not rehearse) screaming and yelling, and in a later session imagined
a fist-fight, an event that had actually occurred earlier in the
week when he noticed someone breaking into his friend's car.

While 11 out of 14 Ss reported a reduced SUDS level, the difference pre- and post-training, as measured by a "t" of 1.95, was
not significant. Two Ss reported a raise in anxiety of 10 and 15
points, but one S went from 20 to 100, on a scale of zero to 100,
in clear distinction to what happened to most of the others. He
was an Armenian student, as was one of the two others whose scores
increased. As he said in interview, "I'm not that kind of person,
yelling, shouting, making trouble, I'm amazed--I'm not that kind of
guy, to make trouble--seems like I don't know myself." This response
was to what went on in his imagery, not in role playing. Similar
reports were given by the other two Ss whose scores went up, indicating that for them the behavior they were rehearsing and for
imagining was not something they could readily accept in themselves.
At the same time, the S, whose score increased markedly, also said
that in the imaging the second time he was much more active and that
the outcome was better, although he was "getting into trouble."
One of the other Ss whose score went up, said that although he was
a bit more anxious, he was also more aroused and could go forward
with more anger and determination.

Ss were apparently in a state of transition, as a consequence of the role playing. The intriguing thing is that although for several Ss anxiety went up, they also reported liking their behavior better. One might speculate that when one helps one, through role playing and/or imagery, to face anxiety arousing situations that Ss can practice on fairly difficult anxiety arousing situations, and be able, though anxious, to feel good about what they accomplish. This would certainly be consistent with the work of Stampfl (1967). It is also important to note that Ss are probably, during imagery, getting into situations and behaviors they cannot completely control. As suggested above, some of the imagery may be foreign to themselves; "they are not that kind of person."

DISCUSSION

The results of this brief pilot study strongly suggest that role playing, as used in assertiveness training, has a marked impact on imagery. In general, the imagery experienced after role playing is evaluated in a "positive light," with strong suggestions that the imagery is more substantial and meaningful after role playing, as compared to before.

While to some extent imagery parallels behavior, it also seems to go beyond it. It is as though one sets a new direction for a person with role playing and the imagery proceeds apace--witness the screaming, yelling, fighting and indifference, none of which were rehearsed.

The consequences of this seem important. It would appear that behavior and imagery interact in a complex way, each giving impetus and direction to the other.

It would be interesting to study what happens to imagery after several sessions, how experiences from daily living get into the imagery (unsolicited) and how changes in imagery do and do not parallel later behaviors. One speculation would be that we would be more able to tolerate threatening and frightening imagery, the more we played with it.

It might be noted that with two Ss, whose later sessions were in situations that were easy and did not seem to require assertion training, the results obtained were similar to those involving difficult situations. This might be a consequence of reduction in minor levels of anxiety or just of repetition of this imagery.

Another intriguing question is what happens to imagery if one practices behaviors inconsistent with assertiveness, e.g., obsequiousness. More generally, it would seem worth exploring the effect of any behavior on imagery, e.g., running, jumping, smiling, being aggressive, passive, etc.

The way in which we talk to ourselves changes after various experiences, e.g., we say negative things to ourselves about ourselves after failure experiences and positive things after success experiences. It is likely that our imagery also changes in systematic ways. It is time to explore this.

A caution for assertiveness training is clearly indicated by the few Ss who seemed not quite ready to adopt new behaviors. The fortuitous use of Armenians who, at least in our culture, seem less ready to accept as appropriate assertiveness what Americans do, led to the highlighting of this issue.

It might also be noted that in post-role-playing imaging conversations, as indicated in the interview, though not picked up by the questionnaire, tended clearly to be far richer and involved than prior to the role playing.

If imagery is an important aspect of our ongoing experience, something we richly treasure for its value and own sake beyond the way in which it may be used in modifying overt behavior, it would seem we can look to changes in overt behavior as a vehicle for helping us change our inner experience.

REFERENCES

Stampfl, T. G. Implosive therapy, part I: the theory. In S. G. Armitage (Ed.), Behavior modification techniques and the treatment of emotional disorders. Michigan: V. A. Publications, 1967.

Stampfl, T. G., and Levis, D. J. Implosive therapy: the theory, the subhuman analogue, the strategy and the technique. Possible use of conditioning therapy with chronic schizophrenia. Battle Creek, Michigan: V. A. Publications, 1966.

Stampfl, T. G., and Levis, D. J. Essentials of implosive therapy: a learning theory based psychodynamic behavioral therapy. Journal of Abnormal Psychology, 1967, 72, 495-503.

Wolpe, J. Psychotherapy by reciprocal inhibition. Palo Alto, California: Stanford University Press, 1958.

Wolpin, M., and Kirsch, I. Visual imagery, various muscle states and desensitization procedures. Perceptual and Motor Skills, 1974, 39, 1143-1149.

EMOTIVE-RECONSTRUCTIVE THERAPY: A SHORT-TERM,

PSYCHOTHERAPEUTIC USE OF MENTAL IMAGERY

James K. Morrison, Ph.D.

Albany Medical College

Albany, New York

THEORETICAL ASSUMPTIONS AND
   THERAPEUTIC TECHNIQUES

Emotive-reconstructive therapy (ERT), a recently developed therapeutic modality (Morrison, in press (b); Morrison and Cometa, 1977), finds its theoretical roots in the cognitive theory of Kelly (1955), Piaget (1972), and Fiske and Maddi (1961). According to Kelly, each person constantly strives to understand and predict his or her experiences. Thus, ERT emphasizes the value of retracing early developmental experiences in order to apply the adult's more adequate construct system in better comprehending those experiences. Due to a child's simplistic way of understanding and coding life's experiences (Piaget, 1972), significant persons are often stereotyped (e.g., good mother, bad father), eventually leading to personally destructive relationships with others. A retrieval of images from childhood often helps adult clients to construe parents and others more adequately so that these clients are able then to understand and resolve current conflicts in their relationship.

In order to override a client's optimum level of arousal (Fiske and Maddi, 1961), and thus a client's resistance to retracing often very painful early experiences (e.g., death of a parent), mental imagery is used as the primary therapeutic technique. Because the client is usually not naturally skilled at using imagery in defending against the recall of painful events, that person finds it more difficult in therapy to keep from awareness those painful life-events which strongly influenced the development of personal problems. Although waking imagery is a natural function of our everyday life, as Shorr (1976) has so clearly illustrated, most clients do not think of such imagery as a tool with which to

313

probe their past and check on the adequacy of their perceptions and
judgments of others as well as themselves.

Family members are often unfamiliar with how they carry on,
generation after generation, the same dysfunctional roles (e.g.,
the martyr, the sick child, etc.) because of the similar way they
and their predecessors construe the world around them (Morrison,
1977). The way one construes the world is often learned within the
family system. By using imagery to recreate many of the sensorial
qualities (especially visual) of important, personality-damaging
events (e.g., death of a parent, rejection by a parent, severe
traumas, parental conflict), the therapist who uses ERT techniques
can frequently expose the client's simplistic way of understanding
those events. With the assistance of the therapist, the client
learns during such imagery recall to apply more sophisticated and
complex constructs to understand these events in personally more
satisfying ways. Such understanding tends to reduce anxiety and
depression.

An example will help to illustrate. In assisting a depressed
client in properly grieving (Morrison, 1978) the loss of his father
when the client was six years of age, the therapist asked the client
to close his eyes and to focus on all the images (sights, sounds,
smells, tastes, body movements) associated with the death, wake,
funeral and burial of his father. Such images rapidly led the client to unexpected expressions of feelings and, subsequently, new
constructs of himself and his father. Before this session the client never thought he cared for his father and that his father's
death had little or no effect on him. During therapy he sobbed
uncontrollably after he remembered the image of his father lying in
the casket at the funeral home. Knowing that he really did care
for his father made a great difference in his evaluation of himself
and the client's long depression began to subside.

Other techniques sometimes used in emotive-reconstructive
therapy are deep breathing exercises and role-playing. With some
clients, brief (20-30 seconds) periods of hyperventilation seem to
provoke important imagery and feelings; with others, a deep, relaxing form of breathing accomplishes the same end. Role playing is
used to help clients use more adequate constructs at the point when
they are experiencing strong feelings about a person whom they
report conflict. Occasionally, the therapist will attempt to speak
for those clients who, at least early in therapy, find role playing
too difficult.

SESSION FORMAT

Typically, the 45 minute sessions include an emotive and a
reconstructive phase. In the _emotive_ phase the focus is on the

eliciting of strong feelings about some person with whom the client has reported problems. This process is sometimes accomplished with guided imagery alone. Quite frequently, however, the ancillary techniques (deep breathing exercises, role playing) are also used.

In the reconstructive phase, now with eyes open, the client attempts to integrate what he or she has learned. Although the therapist will try to be of assistance in this process, the best insights seem to be those which the client gains with little or no help from the therapist. In the context of ERT, neither strong feeling catharsis with little insight nor insight gained without expression of feeling are considered of lasting value. The best insight is usually a by-product of experiencing psychological pain (e.g., feelings of rejection by a parent).

CONSUMER-ORIENTED APPROACH

Emotive-reconstructive therapy is grounded in a consumer-oriented approach to the client (Morrison, in press (a); Morrison, in press (c)). In the context of a consumer-oriented perspective, ERT therapists realize their responsibility to inform clients about therapy (e.g., risks involved, success rates determined by empirical research), and to protect the rights of those clients by various methods (e.g., problem definition contracting, client advisory boards, confidentiality contracts for group therapy, seminars with clients to refine theory and practice, etc.).

The responsibility of the client to participate actively in problem-solving is a focus of major importance. The dependency of the client on the therapist is discouraged since such "transference" is not considered a necessary factor in successful emotive-reconstructive therapy.

RESEARCH ON ERT

A numbef of empirical studies (e.g., Morrison, 1978; Morrison and Cometa, 1979) have indicated that ERT techniques are effective in inducing significant symptom reduction on the Psychotherapy Problem Checklist (a checklist of symptoms of anxiety and depression). Furthermore, these same studies demonstrated that ERT is an effective short-term therapy capable of producing significant symptom resolution in as few as five sessions. Research (Morrison, 1978) also indicates that ERT can induce a significant increase in clients' positive self-attributions (as measured by the Semantic Differential) within the standard 15 session sequence.

Some statistical data relevant to ERT may also shed some light on this form of therapy: (1) 41% of those who begin ERT complete

at least 15 sessions.   (2) Only 23% of those who finish 15 sessions
feel the need to continue with more sessions.   (3) The success rate
(determined by regularly administered self-report symptom check-
lists and measures of construct change) for those clients who complete at least 15 sessions is 96%.   (4) Among those clients who complete at least 15 sessions, 73% report a symptom reduction of <u>at
least</u> 50%.

A CASE STUDY

Susan, a 28-year-old woman who had returned to finish college,
asked for emotive-reconstructive therapy at the recommendation of
a friend.   Susan complained of depression, suicidal ideation, sleep
problems, constant headaches, a nervous stomach, and problems in
communicating with a boyfriend.   After one introductory session she
began ERT with the author.

Susan's third session gives us a glimpse into her problems, as
well as illustrating how a structured use of imagery can lead to
new insights, even early in the course of therapy.   A transcript of
the emotive phase of Susan's third session is offered, along with a
brief summary of the reconstructive phase.   The session illustrates
how retracing early, developmental experiences helps a client to
reconstrue her relationships in a new and more understandable way.

> Therapist: I want you to close your eyes and pic-
> ture yourself, at a young age, at the family dinner
> table.   I also want you to see the room you are in,
> smell and taste the food on the table, hear the clatter
> of plates and other sounds, and to feel like you are
> sitting on a chair and your feet don't touch the floor
> --and your head is not much above the top of the table.
> I also want you to begin breathing very deeply and
> relaxingly in the manner I showed you.   (After a pause.)
> Now I want you to tell me who sits where at the table.

> Client: (After a pause.)   I'm sitting across from
> my brother, Pat, who's sitting next to my sister.   Mom
> is on my right at one end of the table and she's sitting
> across from Dad.   My father's in business clothes but
> doesn't have a suitcoat on.   I'm in playclothes.   All the
> kids are in playclothes.   Mom has an apron on.

> Therapist: What kind of food is the family eating?

> Client: We have milk.   Mom and Dad are splitting
> a beer.   We're having pot roast, vegetables, boiled
> potatoes, gravy and cole slaw.   I don't like dinner time.
> We have to be careful not to spill things.   We have to

be careful how we eat. Poor Pat! I hope he doesn't do
anything wrong! Dad cuts the meat and gives it out.
Mom puts vegetables on the plates. It's okay now. We're
going to say grace now. Bless us, Oh Lord, and these
Thy gifts we are about to receive. God bless Grandma
and Grandpa. Amen. Now we're allowed to eat. We don't
talk too much. We have to be quiet now. Dad gets real
tired and likes it peaceful. I hope Pat doesn't spill
his milk. I feel real nervous. I don't want to eat
much but Dad yells if we don't each much. If I spill
my milk, Dad blames Mom for our manners. Oh God, I hope
Dad doesn't yell. It might be okay today. Now they
want to find out what happened at school. We're not
allowed to interrupt. My sister is real good at stuff.
I never talk too much. If I do real good in school
(client begins to whisper in a childlike voice), then
it's okay. But Dad doesn't want to know. I can go out
to play now. Mostly Dad talks to Mom about business.
Every night something happens. We try not to. I'm
just real afraid it'll happen again. My mother will
make him get out. I'm okay. I don't care. We always
spill the milk. Milk slips from my hand. I'm not careful enough. Not so bad for me. I should know better.
I'm older. I don't want Dad to yell at Mom. She takes
care of us all the time. (Client puts hands together
in a pleading gesture.) I say to myself, "Daddy, please
don't yell. I'm sick. Please don't yell."

Therapist: Tell your daddy out loud to stop
yelling.

Client: I can't. (She whispers.) He's mad now.

Therapist: Let me help you. Let me tell him to
stop yelling for you.

Client: Okay.

Therapist: Stop yelling! Stop it! (Words said in
a loud angry voice.)

Client: He stopped yelling. He says it's my fault.

Therapist: He almost sounds like he can't deal
with kids.

Client: He says he loves us. Now he won't talk
to me anymore. He doesn't listen to anybody. He's mad
now. He's going to yell at my mother now. Now it's
my fault. I wish it wasn't my fault. Why is he like

this? I'll talk to Pat outside the house. It's okay,
Pat. Daddy loves us. Mom says he does. It's okay.
I don't want you to cry. We'll learn. He doesn't yell
at Celia (sister). She can climb in his lap anytime.
I won't let anyone hurt you, Pat. Dad's okay now. I
want to go to my room now. I like it there. Quiet
there. No one yells up there. I can be like Peter Pan
up there.

Therapist: I want you to quickly see the years go
by since those events happened and to begin to focus on
the present again. (A short pause.) All right, you
can open your eyes now.

The emotive part of that session was now completed. During
the reconstructive phase, the therapist discussed with the client
the meaning of the many images and feelings which the client
recalled. The client said she was surprised that she felt so much
better in her own room and remembered how, when she was depressed
later in college, she would lock herself in a room for days.

The client was also surprised at how jealous she was of Celia,
her sister, during the session. She had not remembered her conflict
with her sister going back that far.

The client recalled how two years after the period covered in
the session the family stopped eating dinners together. Family members began to eat at different times, apparently to avoid family
tension. The client remarked that she had forgotten just how terrible dinners were when she was a child. The imagery of those
meals had triggered a great deal of anxiety, sadness, and anger.

In this session, her third, the client was beginning to trace
the roots of her conflict with men back to her feelings about her
father. She could now also understand that she tried to escape
from anger at her father by immersing herself in the "good girl"
role, as well as by withdrawing (e.g., to her room) when she came
close to feeling this anger.

The client's current feelings about her brother, Pat, with
whom she was still close, and Celia, with whom she was still distant, were illuminated by this early family scene. The client
could now see the roots of these relationships in family interaction. The session ended with the therapist commenting on how
family dinner scenes often reveal family dynamics.

After 15 sessions the client reported a dramatic reduction of
symptoms on the Psychotherapy Problem Checklist, as well as a significant increase of positive self-attributions on the Semantic
Differential. Her fear of leaving the area to go to an ivy-league

school disappeared, and she was able to attend this school successfully. In the year after therapy she reported her relationship with her father vastly improved. A 12-month follow-up confirmed the stability of all these results.

SUMMARY

Emotive-reconstructive therapy appears to be an effective form of therapy able to produce therapeutic effects within a relatively short span of time. The primary technique, that of mental imagery, is used principally to help clients trace the psychological roots of developmental experiences which they could not properly understand at the time they happened.

REFERENCES

Fiske, D., and Maddi, S. Functions of varied experience. Homewood, Illinois: Dorsey Press, 1961.

Kelly, G. The psychology of personal constructs (2 vols.). New York: Norton, 1955.

Morrison, J. K. The family heritage: dysfunctional constructs and roles. International Journal of Family Counseling, 1977, 5, 54-58.

Morrison, J. K. Successful grieving: changing personal constructs through mental imagery. Journal of Mental Imagery, 1978, 2, 63-68.

Morrison, J. K. A consumer-oriented approach to psychotherapy. Psychotherapy: Theory, Research and Practice, in press. (a)

Morrison, J. K. Emotive-reconstructive therapy: changing constructs by means of mental imagery. In A. A. Sheikh and J. T. Shaffer (Eds.), The potential of fantasy and imagination. New York: Brandon House, in press. (b)

Morrison, J. K. Client-psychotherapist seminars for refining theory and practice. Professional Psychology, in press. (c)

Morrison, J. K., and Cometa, M. S. Emotive-reconstructive psychotherapy: a short-term cognitive approach. American Journal of Psychotherapy, 1977, 31, 294-301.

Morrison, J. K., and Cometa, M. S. Emotive-reconstructive therapy and client problem resolution: periodic accountability to the consumer. In J. K. Morrison (Ed.), A consumer approach to community psychology. Chicago: Nelson-Hall, 1979.

Morrison, J. K., and Teta, D. C. Simplified use of the Semantic Differential to measure psychotherapy outcome. Journal of Clinical Psychology, 1978, 34, 751-753.

Piaget, J. Judgment and reasoning in the child. Totowa, New Jersey: Littlefield, Adams & Co., 1972.

Shorr, J. E. Dual imagery. Psychotherapy: Theory, Research and Practice, 1976, 13, 244-248.

THE INNER SOURCE* AND MEDITATIVE THERAPY**

Michael L. Emmons, Ph.D.

Private Practice and Co-director, Holof Center

San Luis Obispo, California

A NATURAL HELP WITHIN

There is inside each person a powerful source of knowledge, a self-contained system of help. This inner source is a natural, inherent, inborn process--a wisdom which some feel is God-directed and some feel is brain-directed. It has been given many names throughout the ages, the deep self, the over-self, the supercon-scious, the Buddha-nature, the higher self, the biological wisdom, the subliminal self, the God-within, the over-soul, the not-self, the Christ consciousness. I have added yet another name to the list, perhaps the least confining; I call it simply, "the Inner Source." The derivation of its power and the actual name given make no difference, because the Inner Source will work to help us what-ever we call it and wherever it comes from.

The tendency in the United States is to hypnotize the Inner Source, to biofeedback it, mind control it, seminar train it, guided imagery it, stimulate it with mantras, with music, with key phrases, with dance, with machines, with psychedelic drugs, with sensory isolation. The Inner Source is rarely allowed complete freedom of response. I do not deny that these other interventions are valuable. Nevertheless, when you are at the doorstep of wisdom, listen before

---

*From Michael L. Emmons, Ph.D., The Inner Source (San Luis Obispo, California: Impact Publishers, Inc., 1978.

**Due to the nature of the methods described here, no one should practice Meditative Therapy on oneself or others without first read-ing the book, The Inner Source.

321

you speak. There is an entirely <u>natural</u> way of getting in touch
with the Inner Source and it is best to let <u>it</u> decide how to proceed before deciding how it should be influenced. If we can learn
to trust the Inner Source, it will use a wide variety of systematic,
often intricate and beautiful, ways to help us.

MEDITATIVE THERAPY

     Meditative Therapy is an inner-directed, eyes-closed process,
in which the participant enters a naturally occurring altered state
of consciousness and allows an inner source to engage in a self-
unifying and self-healing process.

     The essence of Meditative Therapy relates closely to mindfulness-
insight methods of meditation as described by Daniel Goleman's book
presenting the works of the Vissudhimaga (1977). Mindfulness-insight
methods are contrasted in the Vissudhimaga with methods of meditative
concentration, examples of which are flourishing in the United States
today. Such methods as Transcendental Meditation (Bloomfield, 1975),
"Benson's Technique" (1976), and Carrington's Clinically Standardized
Meditation (1977) are all forms of the concentrative type of
meditation.

     Mindfulness-insight methods are traditionally less structured
than meditative concentration methods. Goleman states that mindfulness leads to insight by "continuing without lag." Continuing without lag seems to suggest that, after preliminary structured mindfulness methods, one advances to the stage of focusing on all impressions coming into awareness, passively accepting them, and allowing
the flow to continue. Examples of advanced mindfulness-insight
methods found in meditation literature are shikan-taza, a version
of Zazen meditation (Kapleau, 1967), vipassana, a practice of
Tibetan Buddhism (Trungpa, 1973) (Deatherage, 1975), self-
remembering of Gurdjieff (Walker, 1969), and Krishnamurti's self-
knowledge (1960).

     Meditative Therapy also has roots in several current psycho-
therapeutic approaches: Jung's Active Imagination (1958), Frederking's Deep Relaxation With Free Ideation (1949), Kitselman's
E-Therapy (1950), and Schultz and Luthe's Autogenic Abreaction
(1969). Each of these basically adheres to the non-directive conditions of the natural way of the Meditative Therapy process. To
engage in Meditative Therapy one lies down, closes the eyes, and
describes <u>visual images</u>, <u>bodily responses</u>, and <u>thoughts</u>. The participant and the therapist are to patiently allow the Inner Source
to do what it needs to do to help, without interruption or interference and without subsequent interpretation. The Inner Source
is allowed to begin and end sessions on its own.

This natural way of approaching an individual's inner workings is largely de-emphasized in the United States in favor of synthetic psychotherapeutic methods, such as Freud's Free Association (1924), LSD-assisted therapy (Grof, 1975), and Janov's Primal Therapy (1970). Synthetic methods tend to interfere with the natural workings of the Inner Source either before, during, or after sessions.

THE THERAPEUTIC AND CREATIVE
GOALS OF THE INNER SOURCE

Content analyses of Meditative Therapy transcripts reveal that the Inner Source presents a wide variety of mental, physical, and spiritual data if allowed its full realm of response. I have chosen the term psychophysiospiritulogical to depict this tripartite function. In the adjoining chart, a graphic characterization of the psychophysiospiritulogical workings of the Inner Source is presented. These aspects of the three realms of human inner response are hypothesized to be potentially available to manifest in each person. If the Inner Source were allowed to work regularly over time, the full range of responses would come forth.

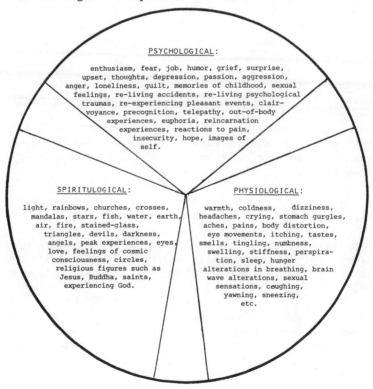

PSYCHOLOGICAL:

enthusiasm, fear, job, humor, grief, surprise, upset, thoughts, depression, passion, aggression, anger, loneliness, guilt, memories of childhood, sexual feelings, re-living accidents, re-living psychological traumas, re-experiencing pleasant events, clairvoyance, precognition, telepathy, out-of-body experiences, euphoria, reincarnation experiences, reactions to pain, insecurity, hope, images of self.

SPIRITULOGICAL:

light, rainbows, churches, crosses, mandalas, stars, fish, water, earth, air, fire, stained-glass, triangles, devils, darkness, angels, peak experiences, eyes, love, feelings of cosmic consciousness, circles, religious figures such as Jesus, Buddha, saints, experiencing God.

PHYSIOLOGICAL:

warmth, coldness, dizziness, headaches, crying, stomach gurgles, aches, pains, body distortion, eye movements, itching, tastes, smells, tingling, numbness, swelling, stiffness, perspiration, sleep, hunger alterations in breathing, brain wave alterations, sexual sensations, coughing, yawning, sneezing, etc.

A PSYCHOPHYSIOSPIRITULOGICAL CHART OF INNER SPACE

The Inner Source has an overall goal of leading one to higher
and higher levels of mental-physical-spiritual good or actualiza-
tion. Synthesizing this global goal into component parts, two basic
goals can be derived: a Therapeutic or Healing Goal, and a Creative
Goal. The therapeutic process takes place more frequently in Meditative Therapy and focuses on helping the individual overcome difficulties through:

1. Discharging: Experiencing momentary visual images, bodily
reactions, thoughts, feelings.

Examples: Seeing colors and patterns; experiencing smells;
twitching; feeling cold; feeling anxious; visualizing people, places,
events.

2. Extended Discharging: Experiencing longer sequences of
visual images, bodily reactions, thoughts, and feelings, but without
abreactive intensity.

3. Reinforcement: Gaining a rewarding psychological, physical, or spiritual feeling during the Meditative Therapy process.

Examples: Seeing a beautiful or relaxing scene; feeling deeply
relaxed; feeling exhilarated; experiencing a humorous incident;
having a "peak" experience.

4. Understanding: Realizing the causes of one's difficulties,
gaining insights; arriving at solutions to confusing problem areas.

Examples: Connecting the therapy experience with a past physical injury or mental upset; coming to new conclusions about one's
upbringing; gaining personal answers about the meaning of life
and/or how to live.

5. Abreaction: Reliving or re-experiencing various portions
of disturbing or traumatic events.

Examples: Reliving psychological and/or physical mistreatment
by a parent; reliving physically and/or psychologically disturbing
physical events such as auto accidents, childhood illnesses, major
injuries.

The creative goal focuses on experiences, often having spiritual and/or parapsychological overtones, which seem designed to
awaken new levels of awareness and/or to develop new dimensions of
one's being. The ultimate meaning of these experiences is often
not readily attainable. This aspect of the Inner Source comes
through:

1. New Experience: Contacting a new dimension of life or of

one's being not previously experienced. The person is usually
"struck by" or amazed at the experience and it leaves a lasting
impression.

   Examples: Having a "peak" experience, an intense religious
experience, an out-of-body experience, a "reincarnation" experience.

   An analysis of 423 individual Meditative Therapy sessions of
100 (54 female, 46 male) university counseling center and private
practice clients demonstrated the following percentages of occurrence for each of the above categories:

	Category	Percentage Occurrence
1.	Discharging	100%
2.	Extended Discharging	95%
3.	Reinforcement	75%
4.	Understanding	71%
5.	Abreaction	20%
6.	New Experience	13%

   The abreaction sequences and the new experience sequences of
Meditative Therapy are often the most striking. An example from
two categories follows:

Abreactive Sequence

   A 28-year-old woman in her first session revisits her past
relationship with her father.

   Now I feel sad, not like striking at him, just feel sad.
   I've not done anything, but he doesn't seem to like me.
   No matter how hard I try it's never enough. But I can
   do well in school, but it doesn't matter. Daddy--I like
   school (tears). That's not enough--school's not enough
   (sobbing). Makes me feel angry, he won't tell me why,
   he won't tell me how to fix it. I just wish you'd tell
   me why you don't like me (sobbing). I've always tried
   to do what you wanted, but it's never been--oh, oh, my
   head feels better. Oh, I feel so hot and sweaty. If
   he would just tell me why, I'd feel better. I just
   can't bear not knowing why you don't like me.

New Experience Sequence

A 35-year-old college professor in his sixth session.

I'm beginning to feel myself sort of drop into a deeper
sense of relaxation--a feeling of letting go, almost
like falling. That feels very good just to let everything go. I notice that my breathing is very weak or
shallow, but I don't need any more. Very good feeling
just to breathe very little. I can't even feel my heart
beating (seven-minute silence)--(outwardly, it appeared
as if he might have fallen asleep). I feel like I'm
sort of detached. For a short time I didn't have any
real sense of where I was or what time it was. I saw a
fish, very large, sort of lying on its side. It was on
the beach, a pleasant feeling about it. I saw a very
docile black and white dog. Very large dog with a thin
face like an Afghan. A calm, very friendly dog, not
asleep, but resting. Then I got such a feeling of being
detached. Like I could go anywhere I wanted to go--sort
of leave my body behind, just because I wanted to, and
free myself of all physical limits and just be anywhere
I wanted to be. And I sort of went somewhere--not sure
where I went. I couldn't tell you how long. No sense
of time or physical place. Just before that I was very
aware of my breathing in that I couldn't feel myself
breathing. Not sure that I was breathing. When I came
back from wherever I went I was a little startled and a
little disappointed to come back. I feel so good about
it that I would like to go back again. It's sort of
like tapping a new resource that I've known was there
for a long time, but I was kind of out of touch with.
Now the fingers on my hands and the back of my neck feel
very thick. It's a good feeling. Now my eyelids feel
that way. Now it feels a little uncomfortable, like a,
like the need to move (opens eyes, moves hands and feet).
I guess that's it.

At this point I made sure that he was done. He replied that
he felt fine and then stated:

That feeling of being able to just transcend the physical and go anywhere I want to was really an exhilarat-
ing feeling. And it wasn't like dreaming, it was a
real feeling. But it was sort of like I just tapped it,
discovered it, didn't really use it.

When he returned one week later he stated that he had thought about
the experience all week long and it left him with a feeling that he
could do anything; literally, not in a figurative sense.

MEDITATIVE THERAPY OUTCOMES

The Inner Source utilizes various combinations of its components (Discharging, Extended Discharging, Reinforcement, etc.), to
produce concrete behavioral changes in the participant. Working
with a university counseling center and private practice population
suffering from neurotic disorders has produced the following range
of potential results:

1. Relief from psychosomatic complaints.

2. Resolution of childhood conflicts.

3. Regulation of sleeping patterns.

4. Increased ability to relax.

5. Lessening of tension and anxiety.

6. Reduction of habitual fear responses.

7. Greater self-confidence.

8. Decreased physical pain.

9. Closer alignment to a spiritual core,

10. More frequent recollection of dreams.

11. Increased tendency toward inner direction.

12. More satisfying interpersonal relationships.

The reason that these results are given only as likely outcomes is because each person has his or her own unique set of outcomes, depending upon what areas of one's life may need help. If
one is presently sleeping well, the Inner Source will not need to
regulate that area of life; if one doesn't have much physical pain,
it will not need to work in that area. Some have had little childhood conflict, some already feel very close to a spiritual source.
Some may have no need to relax more deeply. The Inner Source knows
where each person's life is in need of attention and will seek to
help in those areas.

The Inner Source has the capability of producing exciting and
lasting outcomes in a relatively short period of time.

Jack was a 26-year-old Viet Nam veteran who was referred to me
because he was suffering from recurring emotional upset in relation
to a war experience which took place some three years before. In

his words:

> I was a platoon leader in Viet Nam. During one mission,
> I sent a man out in front of me and he was killed. While
> he died I watched him bleed, but because of enemy fire I
> couldn't save him. After I found out that he was dead--
> I went crazy. I tried to "charge" but someone was on
> top of me and prevented it.

Although Jack knew rationally that he could have done nothing to
save the man, feelings of self-doubting guilt continued to haunt him.
At some point prior to his discharge, he did consult a military
psychiatrist, but was unable to gain much relief.

His present behavior was to cry, hyperventilate, and become
emotionally upset when various stimuli which reminded him of the
experience confronted him. In addition, he reported other difficulties which he maintained were with him prior to the Viet Nam
experience, but had been worsened as a result of the trauma. He
would experience a large amount of anxiety before tests, he avoided
giving speeches, and he was shy with people. Jack also reported
physical symptoms of stomach trouble and periodic twitches in his
body. Under stress he would experience palpitations and bowel disturbances.

His initial two 1½-hour Meditative Therapy sessions were
uneventful in relation to his main presenting complaint. During
the third session, after about 45 minutes, he became frustrated and
stated he felt we were getting nowhere, that the therapy wasn't
working. I mildly intervened by asking if his Inner Source could
give some hint as to what was blocking progress. Jack then saw two
scenes in succession. First, he was standing someplace with a
blanket entangling his head and arms. He was flailing his arms
trying to get it off. Second, he was underneath a dark cloud bank
which entirely blocked the sun, but at the same time, he knew it
was clear and sunny up above. I asked him if he knew what was
blocking out the sunlight and he said, "Yes, I know." When I
replied, "What is it?", he was instantaneously crying, yelling, and
writhing, vividly re-experiencing the event that had haunted him
for three years. This lasted for two or three minutes and perhaps
wasn't much different from drug-induced war neuroses experiences
most have read about or seen depicted in the movies. What transpired next, however, was particularly exciting. In his own words:

> Oh wow! It's like this huge blob of energy, just
> working its way down my body. I can actually feel it,
> it's going down my left leg now! Oh wow! It's unbeliev-
> able. Oh, I just feel so good!
> It's--how could there be so much--must be tons of
> energy! Now it's starting again, more is sapping out!

It's just amazing! I'm just so happy, it's just amazing!
Now there's another vibrating, really fast oscilla-
tion, my face and scalp are tingling! Arms and fingers
too!
It's all so clear, it's like all this fantastic
energy attacking my heart, my stomach, it's so amazing!
Still a great big charge in my legs.
It's like a dam that just broke comes pouring out!

After 20 or 30 minutes of this energy-draining experience, he
opened his eyes, we chatted for awhile, then the session ended.
When he returned one week later, he reported that he had felt
ecstatically relieved of his burden. Life seemed beautiful again.
His draining had continued on and off during the week, but not as
dramatically as during the actual session. We decided not to continue the therapy, but to wait another week and see how he felt.
He returned and we tried Meditative Therapy for about 15 minutes,
but he terminated it because he felt it was not needed. That was
the last I saw of him.

Approximately six months later, I sent him a follow-up evaluation. Results showed that he felt his main difficulty, recurrence
of the traumatic Viet Nam experience, was Very Much Improved (the
highest category on the scale), as was his general nervous condition and his pre-test anxiety. His avoidance of speeches was in
the Much Improved category, and his shyness and twitches showed
Average Improvement. He reported Little or No Improvement in his
stomach trouble and his bowel disturbances and palpitations under
stress.

Lynne, a woman of 40, came to see me with a wide variety of
mental and physical problems. She had experienced a traumatic history, which included an extremely difficult childhood, a series of
near-death auto accidents, and her own divorce and subsequent
attempted suicide. Prior to seeing me, she had been in therapy
for two years. Upon returning for her second Meditative Therapy
session, following a first session of 90 minutes duration a week
before, she reported the following experience. "While driving down
the road four days after the session, I hear a voice in my head
say, 'You aren't alone anymore.'" She said it was a religious
experience to her and was very real and very peaceful. She had not
felt alone since the experience. One year later, Lynne still felt
the experience was a very significant, life-changing one for her.

Susan was 34 when she came to see me. Three years before, she
had undergone surgery for Raynaud's disease, a disease of the sympathetic nervous system. The operation involved severing certain
nerves. During Susan's first session, 42 minutes after the start,
she started sobbing and wringing her hands, then reported:

My hands are sweating. That's funny because I'm not
supposed to have any sweaty hands because of the operation. My hands have been dry for three years and now
they actually feel sweaty. There's perspiration on my
lips. These are things I haven't felt for a long time.

Six months following this session, Susan stated that her perspiration response in the hands and lips had not returned on a regular
basis, but had happened a few more times. She had undergone a total
of five Meditative Therapy sessions and did report that her migraine
headaches were gone, that she no longer felt as pressured as she
used to, that she had much less tightness in her eyes, and that she
no longer felt a tense urgency about her school and home life.

One may find what happened to these three individuals difficult to believe or to understand, especially considering that the
events took place in such a short period of time. Not all results
are as dramatic or happen as fast as those of Jack, Lynne, and Susan,
but the Inner Source does not lack for profound experiences and outcomes. The experiences given here are only a glimpse of the range
of response inherent in each person.

THERAPIST FACILITATION SUGGESTED

I believe that clients should have an average of five to ten
therapist facilitated Meditative Therapy sessions prior to starting
self-Meditative Therapy. These intensive experiences can be
frightening and even dangerous for some people until their progress
has reached a certain point, especially if a trained therapist is
not present. The support of a professional therapist is essential
to "monitor" the initial stages of getting in touch with this
power, and to help the individual to develop an independent capacity to allow the Inner Source to work. There have been reports
that simple concentrative meditation methods have produced disas-
trous results in some cases.

ROLE OF THE THERAPIST IN
  MEDITATIVE THERAPY

The therapist is very important in Meditative Therapy, despite
the non-directive nature of the process, and the curative leader-
ship of the Inner Source. Specifically, the therapist is responsible for: (1) selecting clients; (2) introducing and instructing
clients in the processes of Meditative Therapy; (3) answering questions which the client may have; (4) prompting the client to continuously describe what is taking place; (5) reminding the client
to be patient and not to interfere with the process; (6) handling
fears and resistances; (7) making sure that the individual allows

the session to finish properly; (8) assigning homework; (9) being
available between sessions as needed; (10) following up after Meditative Therapy is completed. Each of these areas will now be dealt
with in greater depth.

Selection of Clients

It is my belief that <u>each individual</u> should have the opportunity to observe the workings of his or her Inner Source. After
contacting the Inner Source, the client may decide not to continue.
There are certain clients who will choose not to participate in
Meditative Therapy after hearing a basic explanation. I respect
this decision and attempt to help the best I can with other
approaches. There are also clients with whom I decide not to begin
Meditative Therapy until other methods are employed. I recently
analyzed my choice of therapeutic approach for my 25 most recent
clients. The group included 17 counseling center and eight private
practice clients; there were 16 females and nine males. Meditative
Therapy was my choice for 20 clients; assertion training was chosen
for three, and client-centered for the remaining two. Of the five
with whom I did not begin with Meditative Therapy, I subsequently
utilized it with two.

Interestingly, Luthe elects to use Autogenic Abreaction in
less than 15% of his cases. It is my observation that the Inner
Source begins its work with each person on his/her own level in a
very wise, step by step manner. I feel that it is desirable for
each person to be allowed to choose whether or not to get in touch
with the Inner Source at some point in therapy based on actual
experience if possible.

Introducing the Client to
Meditative Therapy

Clients who agree to participate in Meditative Therapy would
be given a general introduction to the therapy. An example of the
form such an introduction might take is given below:

Today I would like to explain about a new approach which
I feel might be helpful to you. It works on the assumption that each of us has inside a source or intelligence
that knows everything about us and knows what to do to
help. This Inner Source seems to be very wise and capable of doing anything to set you free, so to speak, or
to get you going toward your full potential.

At this point I will usually say, "How does that sound?" or
"Do you have any questions?" Individual clients will either say
that it sounds OK and want to know what to do to start, or they
will have some questions. Questions should be answered honestly,

but in a general manner because of the individual differences in
response each person has to the therapy. For example, to the question, "How does it work?" I might answer as follows:

> Well, it works by having you visualize with your eyes
> closed such things as colors or patterns or events from
> the past that have bothered you. The human system seems
> to store pain that hasn't been completely dealt with from
> bad experiences. If it gets a chance to release the
> pain, it will. Sometimes your Inner Source will do this
> by recreating pain or by having your body jerk or twitch
> or cry. So the therapy can be upsetting at times.

At this point I may offer some examples of what other clients have
gone through, but I am always quick to point out that each case is
different and there is no way to predict precisely what will happen
to them.

Explaining about Meditative Therapy a week before you plan to
start permits arrangement of an appointment time of at least 1½
hours for the first session. You never know how long a particular
client's session will last until you become used to how that particular Inner Source functions. Sessions may last anywhere from
20 minutes to over two hours, so it is best to have an extra half-
hour if it is needed.

If the client has no questions at the initial MT session, the
therapist should explain how to proceed. It is helpful to give an
additional statement about ending the session by saying something
like, "As you proceed in the session today, be sure that you pay
attention to when your Inner Source wants to finish. It will usually let you know when it is done for the day." By sensitizing the
client to this fact, you will lessen the chances of missing when
the Inner Source is finished. With more experience, you will usually be able to tell when the session is finished, but it is, of
course, best that the client learn to figure it out. Sometimes I
forget to mention this factor before the sessions begins, and so
will interject it at an opportune time during the session.

The essential things for the client to do are: (1) lie back,
close the eyes; (2) watch patiently; and (3) describe continuously
what is being experienced; and allow the Inner Source to do what it
wants to do to help. I usually remind the client not to interfere
with the Inner Source, but simply to trust in what it wants to do.
It seems to be very wise; more so than the client or the therapist.

One other factor to be mentioned to the client at the end of
the first session concerns a possible build-up of anxiety or pressure just prior to the next session. The Inner Source will often
begin preparing in advance material to be released. The build-up

can take many forms, including dislike of the therapist, so it is vital that the therapist mention the possibility of the pre-session build-up.

Answering Client Questions

Most client questions come during the initial minutes of the first, and possibly the second session. These questions relate primarily to whether or not the client is doing the therapy "correctly." Below are several actual questions, followed by my responses, taken from Meditative Therapy transcripts.

Questions	Responses
"Am I just supposed to experience it or what?"	"Yes, and just describe what is happening."
"Whatever I feel, I say?"	"Yes."
"Should I just start telling you?"	"Yes."
"Should I report what I am thinking about?"	"Yes."
"I'm not sure where to start, right now I'm aware of my body functioning."	"Just describe it."

It is a good idea to reassure and reinforce client questions to encourage continued description of what is happening. The following examples from actual sessions suggest how the therapist might respond in the early stages of Meditative Therapy.

Client Description	Therapist Response
"My stomach's becoming tight."	"OK"
"My face doesn't feel so hot, it's cooled off, but I get this blue. It comes and goes."	"Mhm." "How does the rest of your body feel?"
"I feel like waiting, waiting, waiting in the fog."	"Mhm."
"Just noises, tense, colors, different patterns."	"Just describe those."

| "Not really much in the way of colors, just flows, no set pattern." | "Keep watching and describing." |

Once the therapist feels confident that the person is proceeding well, this minimal amount of direction may be dropped. Knowing what types of process events to watch for, the therapist can determine whether or not the therapy is progressing as it should. While there are wide variations in client response, there are certain types of events which indicate that the therapy is proceeding in the direction planned by the Inner Source. These signs along the way may be of either a physical or psychological nature. When the client experiences bodily reactions, such as feelings of falling, tingling, heaviness or lightness, pain or discomfort, there is a good chance that the therapy is working correctly. If one reports seeing lights, colors, patterns, or objects such as clouds, or houses, or events from the past, these mental or visual signs usually indicate that the therapy is going as it should. Inner directed thought patterns are also a good sign to watch for, but it should be determined that the person is not consciously deciding to think of certain areas, but simply allowing the Inner Source to prompt one's thinking.

Prompting the Client to Describe
What is Taking Place

Another duty of the therapist is to keep the client verbalizing. This doesn't mean that one must describe continuously, but if there are long pauses and the individual does not appear to be asleep, it is useful to ask what is taking place, If there are events taking place and the person is not describing--emphasize continual description. Also, the effort to describe verbally the experience may sensitize the client to the importance of seemingly "trivial" occurrences (body feelings, random thoughts).

Emphasis on Patient and
Non-Interference

The therapist is to remind the client to be patient and not to interfere with the therapeutic process. It is best for both to trust what the Inner Source wishes to do. Examples of how the therapist might handle this are given below.

Client Statement	Therapist Response
"Now I feel shaky inside, I feel like crying."	"Yes, just let it happen."

"Now I have a feeling of
wanting things to happen,
though I know I shouldn't
want to force it."

"Right, just be patient. It
works very subtly at times, so
let it do what it wants to
do."

"What if I don't see
anything?"

"That's OK; there may be
periods where you won't, just
let it do anything it wants."

"I feel real small, but
puffy sometimes--I don't
like the way I feel."

"Just try to let it happen
anyway."

Handling Fears and Resistances

The therapist must be able to handle the fears and resistances
of the client, which are often related to the examples in the preceding section, because the client at times will have a tendency
to fear or resist the therapeutic process when it gets to be uncomfortable. Luthe (1973), in writing about Autogenic Abreaction, presents a thorough and systematic analysis of resistance. He devotes
87 pages to this very important subject and his treatment of the
topic goes beyond any, including those found in psychoanalytic
sources. The material is essential reading for anyone planning to
do Meditative Therapy. Luthe divides resistance into five broad
categories: (1) Antagonizing Forms of Resistance, (2) Facilitating
Forms of Resistance, (3) Essential Forms of Resistance, (4) Indirect
Psychophysiologic Resistance; and (5) Resistance and Autogenic
Abreaction at Home.

I feel that most resistances in Meditative Therapy are based
on fears of various kinds. For most people, resistance in psychotherapy seems to be characterized as an underhanded way of "beating
the therapist at his own game," or an unconscious desire to destroy
one's chances of getting well, and so on. I have observed that
clients don't "cooperate" because they are afraid. They have some
very real reason why they are unwilling to proceed.

There are five readily apparent fears which may come up before,
during, or after Meditative Therapy: (1) Fears of Self-Disclosure;
(2) Fears of "Deep" Mental Illness; (3) Fears of Pain and Discomfort; (4) Fears of Losing Control; and (5) Fears that the Therapy
is not working properly.

During the actual process of Meditative Therapy there are bound
to occur what Luthe calls "side-effects" to the therapy: such
things as crying, various aches and pains, psychological discomfort.
Because these are not pleasant and are sometimes a little scary,
some clients decide to "shut off" the unwanted reaction. That is,
they decide that they will not cry any more, they will refuse to

feel dizzy any longer, they won't deal with the topic of sex because
it is disgusting.

My approach in these cases is again to encourage trust in the
clients' Inner Source. It has a very good reason for each experience, no matter how painful, and so it is best to follow what it
presents.

Allowing the Meditative Therapy
  Session to Finish Properly

Remember that the Inner Source is able to start a session on
its own without any "inducements," such as special breathing techniques or drugs. The Inner Source is also quite capable of finish-
ing a session on its own without any special emphasis by the therapist or the client. It is a good idea for the therapist to point
out to the client just prior to the first session that the Inner
Source starts and stops on its own, and suggest he/she watch closely
and follow its promptings. We can never predict precisely when a
session will end, but the Inner Source usually makes it quite clear
that the session is done for the day.

It is crucial that the Inner Source be allowed to finish on its
own without interruption by the therapist or the client. Most of
the dangers of Meditative Therapy center around not allowing the
Inner Source to do what it wants to do. Not allowing a proper finish is probably the most vital concern in this regard. I have had
to learn this the hard way by having made mistakes. I hope to spare
you the same mistakes by sharing mine. The most prominent example
occurred in my early use of the therapy when I failed to allow the
Inner Source to adequately finish a young woman's first session.
Shortly after the session she fainted and in falling suffered a
hairline fracture of the jaw. (Subsequently, it was also discovered
that she had a very low blood sugar condition.) I, as the therapist,
should not have allowed her to leave the office until I was absolutely certain she was OK. I have also had other cases where individuals, after leaving the office, have had to sit down and regain
their balance due to feeling dizzy or faint. In one instance, the
person was driving on the freeway and had to pull over. In another
case, the individual slightly bumped another car in the parking
lot. Needless to say, I am extremely cautious now and make very
sure that each client is finished, clear-headed, and can walk
straight before I allow him or her to leave the office.

After the first session is completed, be very careful to check
with the client to find out his or her reaction to the therapy, to
provide appropriate encouragement or reassurance if the process is
working correctly, or to find out what needs to be changed to help
it work correctly. Typically, the client will either know that the
process is working and accept it, or will ask a question such as,

"How is this going to help me?" At this point it is good to point
out some of the signs which indicate that the therapy is working
properly or to explain some of the theory relating to how the
therapy works. I usually give my impression of how the therapy
appears to be working and ask for patience for a few sessions in
order to see what the results will be in relationship to feelings
and to the presenting complaints. If I get the feeling that the
individual really does not wish to proceed, I shift to another
therapy.

Assigning Homework in Meditative Therapy

I stress that clients undergoing the therapy engage in some
form of extra session work. The source of these tasks once again
is W. Luthe's work in Autogenic Abreaction (1970). Luthe feels,
and I have come to agree, that homework exercises can greatly facilitate one's understanding of therapy and therapeutic progress and that
they also serve as a necessary safety valve when one is experiencing
between-session side effects.

Luthe describes six basic homework exercises. The first centers around his requirement that the client undergoing Autogenic
Therapy audio-tape-record his or her sessions. His suggestion is
that as soon as possible after returning home from a session, one
should transcribe word for word the entire session. In cases where
a complete transcription is impossible, one should at least make out
a summary of the material. The second homework task is to reread
the transcription of the session out loud twice per day. This is
vital according to Luthe, in cases where the individual is experiencing a great many between-session reactions, such as crying
easily, various aches and pains, sleep disturbances. By reading
the session content over and over out loud, one is able to further
facilitate overcoming disturbing material.

My experience with having clients reread session material out
loud over and over again is that it produces variable emotional
reactions depending upon what took place in the actual session.
Some will feel little emotional reaction during the session and
later when rereading, whereas others find high initial emotions
being triggered quite easily once again. Some will gain little
insight into their material, whereas others feel that they have
gained new understandings by reading the material out loud several
times.

The third suggestion deriving from Autogenic Abreaction
research is that one should write out what is termed a thematic
commentary. By analyzing and writing about what the Inner Source
is trying to do to help, and what the presented material has to do
with the past and the present, the individual greatly facilitates

progress. Luthe indicates that this particular procedure is needed
more when the session content is less clear-cut. There are times
when the content is rather abstract or symbolic so that more time
is needed in order to figure out the meaning. When the content
meaning is very obvious, little analytic commentary is required.

Drawings of pertinent Autogenic Abreaction session material is
Luthe's fourth assignment. His main interest is for the individual
to prepare sketches which represent details or the patterns of
images which have been presented in therapy. Although I have not
required this exercise as such, I have had clients spontaneously
draw things. One of my clients recently was confronted with "the
devil" in one of his sessions and it so intrigued him that he drew
a picture of the image. Others have drawn patterns of light,
machines, or flying saucers. Certain individuals with artistic
abilities may come up with new ideas on how to initiate or complete
a project.

Luthe believes that the four suggestions given above most
closely follow what the brain is attempting to do in order to heal
the person. In addition to these tasks, Luthe recommends that one
keep practicing the Autogenic Standard Exercises, making sure to
keep progress notes, and that one make notes on dreams. Luthe indicates that the brain may repeat dreams or parts of dreams in order
to facilitate its journey in Autogenic Abreaction. Also, dreams may
bring up new material which has not been dealt with in one's sessions. Moreover, Luthe is quick to point out that there is no time
spent in Autogenic Therapy on interpreting dreams as such.

Luthe may suggest that a client seek out more information about
a past event, such as an accident or childhood event. In my work I
have found clients doing this spontaneously out of curiosity. For
example, after one session in which a young woman spent a great deal
of time re-experiencing an old house she used to live in, she made
a special trip in order to check out some specific details given in
the inner journey. Another client who had relived a birth experience in therapy checked out the details of the birth with his mother
the next time he saw her. The two experiences matched up quite
closely even though he claimed to have not previously known the
details.

Keeping a day-by-day journal of reactions to the Meditative
Therapy experience, in addition to rereading session transcripts out
loud, is the primary homework assignment I employ. The content of
the journal has many possibilities:

1.   Summarizing the session in one's own words.

2.   Writing down the central topics dealt with.

3. Noting bodily reactions, psychological-emotional reactions, spiritual reactions.

4. Recording experiences or feelings that occur while rereading the transcript aloud.

5. Attempting to figure out what the Inner Source is trying to do to help.

6. Noting changes during the week that seem to be a result of the session.

7. Keeping questions or comments one would like to discuss with the therapist.

8. Recording dreams one has experienced that seem related to the therapy.

9. Keeping drawings one has made of the session content.

10. Writing down overall thoughts and feelings about what is taking place.

The idea is for the individual to keep an account of the total reaction to Meditative Therapy. Obviously, one will need to gear the intensity of such recording to the amount of time available and to one's interest in helping oneself.

Despite these suggestions for homework, one should be reminded to be careful about interpreting Meditative Therapy material within any one system, such as Freudian, Jungian, or behavioral. One ought not place any limits on the Inner Source by burdening it with one particular view of what it is trying to do to help. The major changes in Meditative Therapy take place <u>without</u> any interpretation, and often without any insight into causes by the individual <u>or</u> by the therapists.

Availability of the Therapist Between
Meditative Therapy Sessions

Between Meditative Therapy sessions the therapist should be available to answer any questions which the client may have and to handle any needed emergency treatment. It is helpful to give the client the therapist's office and home telephone numbers, and, in instances where the therapist will be out of town, the phone number of another therapist who is knowledgeable about Meditative Therapy. At the completion of the first session the therapist should explain to the client that there is a possibility that reactions of various kinds may occur between sessions. The therapist may say, "Let me give you my phone numbers now in case you need to call me during

the week. Call me if <u>anything</u> happens. Perhaps nothing will happen, but if something bothers or upsets you, make sure you call me.
Once the Inner Source begins helping you, it will often continue to
do so during the week between sessions. If you should happen to
get physically sick,call me. Or if something else concerns you,
just call me and we can talk about it."

Only a small percentage of clients actually call the therapist
between sessions. The calls I have personally received usually
center around psychologically upsetting feelings and/or reactions.
Reactions which clients have reported include these: "I was watching The Waltons and started crying, sad to hysterical, back and
forth. I felt like I was crying for a lot of things." "I've been
getting flashes of things I hadn't realized before and also crying
spells. I haven't cried for years, even after my auto accident
where I had my brain injury." "Two peculiar things have occurred
that have never happened to me before. Just the tip of my penis
has been itching all day and also itching on my behind. And there
is a big red welt on my behind, which has been there since the last
session." "I've been feeling depressed and my stomach has been
upset. I've not been myself." "My thumb was really painful, I
couldn't concentrate because of it. Also, my lower back hurt a lot
for two days. I've had kidney problems several times in the past.
I've also noticed that my legs have not hurt for the first time,
for as long as I can remember, when there are severe weather
changes."

When I receive a call from a client who is concerned about a
between-sessions reaction, I first check out how serious the reaction is in order to decide whether or not the person should come
in for an emergency session. If the person is feeling out of control or overwhelmed, I invite him or her to come in as soon as
possible.

Whatever else I do, when someone calls, I do make sure that he
or she understands that there is no reason to become unduly alarmed
because the Inner Source is simply trying to help. The reactions
are normal and natural, and, as during the therapy, it is best to
simply be patient and allow the reactions to work themselves out.
My purpose is to offer reassurance that these reactions are understandable, acceptable, and helpful. Generally, a discussion of
this type is enough to hold the person over until the next regular
session, but it is good to be cautious if there are any doubts and
to schedule an immediate appointment when needed.

The Follow-Up of the Therapist After
Meditative Therapy

At some point it becomes apparent that the client is ready to
discontinue Meditative Therapy with the therapist. Although this

decision should be made jointly, I try to encourage the individual to undergo a minimum of five therapist-facilitated sessions. Whenever the decision is made to discontinue, the individual should be encouraged to continue Meditative Therapy on his or her own, or to at least practice some form of relaxation or meditation once formal sessions with the therapist are terminated. I also encourage clients to keep up other skills gained from therapy, such as following an adequate diet, exercising regularly, or being assertive.

Ideally, the therapist should also conduct a follow-up of the outcomes of all Meditative Therapy clients. Invaluable information about the workings of the Inner Source and the effectiveness of Meditative Therapy can be gained with appropriate follow-up measures. Moreover, such follow-up is consistent with the therapist's ethical responsibility to assess client progress in some systematic way. If the follow-up process becomes too time-consuming or expensive, at a minimum a random sample follow-up could be conducted to assess the effectiveness of therapy.

In any event, the therapist should be available for clients who wish to initiate follow-up contacts at some time after therapy is complete.

MEDITATIVE THERAPY IS NOT A
CURE-ALL

Meditative Therapy is a powerful way of helping individuals in the stride toward full development as persons, but as with any singular approach, it is not a panacea. It is best when Meditative Therapy is used as a component part of an holistic approach, treating the whole person.

REFERENCES

Benson, H. The relaxation response. New York: Avon Books, 1976.

Bloomfield, H. TM (Transcendental Meditation). New York: Delacorte Press, 1975.

Carrington, P. Freedom in meditation. New York: Anchor/Doubleday, 1977.

Deatherage, G. The clinical use of 'mindfulness' meditation techniques in short-term psychotherapy. Journal of Transpersonal Psychology, 1975, 7(2), 133-143.

Frederking, W. Deep relaxation with free ideation. Psyche, 1949, 2, 211.

Freud, S. A general introduction to psychoanalysis. New York: Washington Square Press, 1952. (Originally published, 1924.)

Goleman, D. The varieties of the meditative experience. New York: E. P. Dutton, 1977.

Grof, S. <u>Realms of the human unconscious</u>. New York: The Viking
    Press (as Esalen Book), 1975.
Janov, A. <u>The primal scream</u>. New York: G. P. Putnam's Sons, 1970.
Jung, C. G. The psychological aspects of the kore. In <u>The collected
    works of C. G. Jung</u>. New York: Bollingen Foundation, Series
    XX, Vol. 9, Part 1, 1958, pp. 190-193.
Jung, C. G. Psychology and religion. In <u>The collected works of
    C. G. Jung</u>. New York: Bollingen Foundation, Series XX, Vol.
    11, 1958, p. 496.
Kapleau, P. <u>The three pillars of zen</u>. Boston: Beacon Press, 1967.
Kitselman, A. L. <u>E-therapy</u>. La Jolla, California: Institute of
    Integration, 1950.
Krishnamurti, J. <u>Commentaries on living</u> (third series), D. Rajago-
    pal (Ed.). Wheaton, Illinois: The Theosophical Publishing
    House, 1960.
Luthe, W. (Ed.). <u>Autogenic therapy, Vol. I: autogenic methods</u>,
    by Schultz, J., and Luthe, W. New York: Grune and Stratton,
    Inc., 1969 (b).
Luthe, W. (Ed.). <u>Autogenic therapy, Vol. II: medical applications</u>,
    by Schultz, J., and Luthe, W. New York: Grune and Stratton,
    Inc., 1969 (c).
Luthe, W. (Ed.). <u>Autogenic therapy, Vol. III: applications in
    psychotherapy</u>, by Schultz, J., and Luthe, W. New York: Grune
    and Stratton, Inc., 1969 (d).
Luthe, W. (Ed.). <u>Autogenic therapy, Vol. IV: research and theory</u>,
    by Luthe, W. New York: Grune and Stratton, Inc., 1970 (a).
Luthe, W. (Ed.). <u>Autogenic therapy, Vol. V: dynamics of autogenic
    neutralization</u>, by Luthe, W. New York: Grune and Stratton,
    Inc., 1970 (b).
Luthe, W. (Ed.). <u>Autogenic therapy, Vol. VI: treatment with auto-
    genic neutralization</u>, by Luthe, W. New York: Grune and
    Stratton, Inc., 1973.
Schultz, J. H. <u>Das autogene training</u>. Leipzig: G. Thieme Verlag,
    1932.
Trungpa, C. <u>Cutting through spiritual materialism</u>. Berkeley,
    California: Shambhala Publications, Inc., 1973.
Walker, K. A. <u>A study of Gurdjieff's teaching</u>. London: Jonathan
    Cape, 1969.

IMAGERY: A METAPHOR FOR HEALTH

IN THREE CANCER PATIENTS

Patricia L. Musick, Ph.D., ATR

School of Human Sciences and Humanities
University of Houston at Clear Lake City
Houston, Texas

The use of imagery to promote healing and improved mental
states in cancer patients has been studied extensively in recent
years, providing strong evidence that individuals can use their own
creative images to produce positive treatment of the psychological
and physical effects of this devastating disease. For example, the
interactions of mind and body have been examined by Simonton and
Simonton in an attempt to increase host resistance to the invasion
of cancer cells by mobilizing the patient's imagery to fight malig-
nancy. Patients are told to visualize their disease, their treatment and their own immune system acting upon the cancer.

The Simontons report a high incidence of improved physical and
emotional health in their clients. Three case studies, an adult
male with cancer of the left hemisphere of the brain, a male child
with terminal leukemia, and an adult male with advanced melanoma,
offer support for the Simontons' assumptions. In addition, these
cases provide an opportunity to examine the importance of individual
differences in the use of imagery as a therapeutic intervention.
From them we learn that the therapist-clinician who utilizes imagis-
tic techniques must be especially sensitive to the need the imagery
is fulfilling in the individual patient, and cognizant of the ways
in which imagery will vary as a function of differences in personality, disease and environmental variables.

The person described in the first case study is a 52-year-old
male, John, who suffered two serious illnesses within one year.
First, he was treated by surgery and radiation for a malignant
tumor in the Wiernecke's area of the left lobe, which produced considerable loss of speech and conceptual reasoning. Seven months

343

after surgery he was treated for demyelinization of the spine which
resulted in partial paraplegia. As a former coach and athlete he
found it far more difficult to cope with the loss of control of his
body than to deal with the effects of the tumor upon his brain. He
had a great deal of repressed anger and accompanying depression
which he was not able to express verbally. He had, however, used
visualization-meditation techniques since the onset of the disease
and so he agreed to depict his thoughts and feelings in drawings.
The goal of the imagery therapy was to expand his modes of expression. It was hoped that the act of generating his images into
physical forms would lessen his feelings of frustration and helplessness.

In selecting imagery as a part of John's treatment program,
the therapist took into account his disinclination for verbal psychotherapy, and his desire not to reveal himself. Such a technique was
particularly indicated for this patient because it made use of the
healthy right hemisphere abilities to create visual, spatial information, rather than concentrating on the damaged verbal capacities
of the left hemisphere. Images provided a means of expressing his
pent-up emotional states in a non-threatening manner. Interpretation was not a part of the therapeutic program. The emphasis was
on abreaction, the freeing of psychic energies and the development
of emotional strength through release of tension. Because familiarity and continuity are extremely important to the brain damaged
person, the therapist utilized a technique with which John was
familiar. As a football coach he had taught his players to visualize success in the game, to form a mental picture of some scene
that would be attendant on winning the game. During the early
stages of his illness John had used imagery to produce the calm and
strength he needed to get through the endless hospitalizations.
During the latter stages of the illness, he produced his images on
paper in order to externalize his frustrated emotional needs.

John used his own version of the Simontons' technique. Three
times a day he meditated and visualized his body fighting the cancer that had attacked the left hemisphere of his brain. He formed
mental images representing the tumor and cells of his body. These
images were then externalized by means of drawing them with felt
tip pens on paper. John's early drawings were characterized by a
confusion of lines and scribbled circles. Soon, however, specific
forms began to appear and reappear: a figure composed of two con-
centric circles which he used to represent cells, the tumor or his
spinal column, and long linear forms which he called worms or
nerves.

During this time John began physical therapy treatments three
times a week. He was in a wheelchair about 90% of the time, but
he was beginning to regain some strength in the lower part of his
body. As he noticed physical improvement, the imagery of his

drawings began to change. He began to deal with more recognizable
objects usually expressing some symbol for strength, such as an
elephant with a tumor and worms and cells, but who was standing
strongly and walking along on four legs.

In an attempt to examine the extent to which the drawings were
an index of physical change, a Q-Sort was given to eight graduate
students in art therapy. They were told to rank order the drawings
on a dimension of increased physical strength. Nothing was suggested to the raters about how physical strength might be manifested
in terms of visual art. There was significant agreement among the
raters on the early and late drawings (1 and 2, 6 and 7), in contrast to the middle three which were more difficult to sort. As
John continued to improve, both he and his therapist agreed that
drawing images provided him with a new and badly needed mode of
expression which allowed him to communicate more effectively with
himself and others, and that those images did, indeed, reflect the
progress of his physical rehabilitation.

The second case study is a beautiful six-year old child with
touseled golden hair, large eyes, a cynical smile and a body thinned
by cancer's appetite. He is full of defense. It is almost impossible for him or his fear-ridden mother to cry, but he hurts and he
is afraid. The therapist hoped to engage him in drawing images,
but as the child-patient, patiently explained, "I can't draw." He
agreed to a "dream trip," a fantasy journey to a special place.
The induction for this patient consists of deep breathing and relaxation instructions. As his body becomes lighter, he images himself
as a little cloud in the sky, floating along gently, to and fro,
until he is directly above a special place. There he descends,
drifting slowly downward until he lands. The patient describes,
verbally painting his images of the special place. There is sunshine and it feels warm. There is a soft breeze blowing gently and
he can feel it upon his face. He can hear the birdsong, smell the
flowers. There is a pond with fish and a mallard duck. It is a
nice place to be, he feels good there, and safe. And the therapist
reminds him when he is back in the room, he can go there any time--
when he is having a chemotherapy treatment, or getting an IV, or
when he is angry, tired or sad.

For this patient, imagery is a way to cope with pain, fear,
sadness. He is only a small child but the therapist recognized his
need to be a strong man. He goes with his special images but preferably alone. They provide him with a bridge to an unknown vision.
He cannot draw, he cannot speak about it, but he can visualize his
need.

The third patient is Bob, a 46-year old male who suffers from
malignant melanoma, contacted when he was 31, resulting in the loss
of his right eye. Bob has exceeded the medical predictions by

quantum leaps. He is a tall, large, muscular man, independent and
self-determined, who has consistently refused all of the traditional
forms of therapy.

Two years ago the melanoma reappeared in his right lung, his
left clavical, and in the lymph nodes at the base of his skull. Bob
was offered chemotherapy as the treatment of choice. He was told
that he would be in the hospital 120 days during the year, that he
would live 6-12 months without treatment, and six months to three
years with it. There was a one in three chance for success. He
was confused by all he heard and the monumentality of the decision.
He did not fully comprehend and he asked his sister, who is a nurse,
to explain "all those big words" to him. He observed the patients
who were on chemotherapy treatment and perceived them as "walking
zombies." He read about the side effects. He didn't care about
losing his hair, but the nausea, vomiting, and fatigue did not seem
to be the way he wanted to spend his time. He enjoyed sexual activity, was a fully alive person at that moment, and desired to remain
so until the last possible second. He read the consent form for chemotherapy treatment and then told the doctor it was not for him.
Despite the doctor's arguments, Bob was determined to live life in
his own way. He would live with, or die with, his decision. There
would be no treatment--with few exceptions. He agreed to immuno-
therapy once a month to build his immune system, and decided to
take massive doses of vitamins, and eat apricot pits--a source of
laetril.

In September of 1977 he was hospitalized with pleurisy, and
the doctors told him the growth in the tumor indicated that he
probably had four months to live. He was determined to live at
least for a year. He was going to "show them." He went through
the stages of dying described by Kubler-Ross, anger, self-pity,
withdrawal. In April, 1978, when he found himself still alive, he
decided to take a trip through the Western United States. He
stepped on a bus, scared, but by the time he had his first beer in
Albuquerque and a second in Arizona, and was still alive, he decided
to fight. From then on he decided to live without being "next to
death." He came back to Galveston and started to attend church,
where he met the woman he will marry next month. He retired from
a steady job to do pick-up types of work which he enjoys, and which
leave him the freedom to do other important things, like talking
long hours with good friends. One of these was a psychiatrist who
discussed the Simontons' work and asked him if he would be interested in trying such a therapy. At first Bob was reluctant. It
sounded like hypnosis to him and he had some sort of mental block
about hypnosis. Finally he agreed to give imagery a try.

Bob believes that only HE can fight his cancer, only the
mobilization of his tremendous will, using his physical and mental
powers can keep him going. He finds it very difficult to lean on

others or to seek outside help. His therapist quickly learned that
the dominant image which he would use in his fight was a tiny homun-
culus of "himself" inside himself," a miniature recreation of his
own outer being.

Bob takes control of the session once the induction has been
accomplished by the therapist. He allows the therapist to guide
him to the relaxed state, but once he has located the inner image
of himself, he controls the exercise until instructed to return to
the room. Bob's cancer is suspended from the ceiling of a long,
dark corridor. It hangs in mid-air, a black, meat-like mass full
of pores. It is frightening. It fills the tunnel. He could barely
squeeze by it but he is afraid of what he will find on the other
side. He attacks the cancer with his bare hands and knocks big
chunks off to the floor. He shovels these down the drain and they
leave his body as waste. He is exhausted by the effort. His body
twitches and perspiration and tears blend on his bearded face. He
leans on a shovel and surveys the tiny dent he has made in the
tumor. Although remaining independent, Bob has admitted a helper
to his battle. His dog, who recently died, has come to help him
and Bob allows his image to stay and guard the tumor. Daily the
cancer image grows a little smaller, as monthly the x-rays attest
to zero growth.

For imagery to be effective with this patient, it was crucial
for the therapist to abandon any pre-determined "recipes" and allow
the client to create and determine his own unique imagery. One of
the important aspects in his treatment is the therapist's willingness to allow the patient to make a decision for life or death with
which she may not be in agreement (such as the decision to refuse
all medical treatment). It is crucial here to allow the patient
the integrity to deal with his disease in his own way. Imagery,
for this man, appears to be the most effective way to deal with his
emotional states, for it gives him, rather than an outside agent,
control of his disease.

Summary: Three case studies describe patients with terminal
illness who use imagery as a metaphorical statement about their
physical and emotional states. Each individual represents a different set of problems with which to cope; functions of their personalities, disease and their environment. For each the process
of imaging helps to produce emotional stability and some physical
comfort. An essential element of this outcome was that the therapist recognize and treat the unique situation of each patient.

THE SANDTRAY: GROUP TECHNIQUES

Russell Bader, M.S.W.,* and Revel Miller, Ph.D.**

*Private Practice; **California School of Professional
Psychology

Fresno, California

The purpose of this paper is to describe a non-directive,
dramatic, projective technique used to elicit mental imagery--the
sandtray. Although originally associated with individual psychotherapy, it has recently been used in group therapy with adolescents
and adults (Miller, 1979; Mizushima, 1971-1972).

MATERIALS

The sandtray materials include a sandtray and a collection of
figures or toy miniatures (Miller, 1979). The sandtray is a free-
standing box with 3-1/2 inches of sand that stands about 30 inches
off the ground, and measures approximately 3 x 20 x 29 inches.
The accompanying figures are representative of anything found in
the world or within one's fantasies, and may be placed into the
following broad categories: people, animals, housing, transporta-
tion, scenery, natural forms, and miscellaneous. Collections range
from 250 to 1,500 items, and average about 600. Pieces may be made
of wood, metal, plastic, rubber, and clay, and vary in size from
one to 10 inches. These collections are personally made or acquired
by therapists who include items deemed symbolically useful in facilitating projection. Each sandtray collection is unique and is
reflective of the therapist's own personality. Therapists must
select objects which they may find personally repelling to ensure a
rich variety. All these assorted items are placed on shelves near
the sandtray where they are easily accessible and visible to the
clients.

BRIEF HISTORICAL OVERVIEW

Lowenfeld (1931, 1938, 1939, 1950; Bowyer, 1970) is the formal
originator of the Lowenfeld World Technique and began her work in
England in the late 1920's. She devised this apparatus as one
method of play therapy to allow children to express themselves, to
work through psychic conflicts, and to experiment with feelings and
new situations. It also provided her with a concrete means to
observe and record this therapeutic process. Lowenfeld employed
this symbolic approach with children because she believed that they
had not yet developed language skills, and that this apparatus
would allow them to "speak" their inner world.

Buhler, an American psychologist, visited Lowenfeld's clinic
in 1934 (Lowenfeld, 1939) and saw great potential in this technique
for the creation of a standardized diagnostic tool. Buhler (1941,
1951a, 1951b, 1952) created the Toy World Test in an attempt to
facilitate diagnostic evaluation by differentiating between normal
and abnormal children and adults. Inconclusive attempts to standard-
ize this device were made by other researchers (Bolgar and Fischer,
1940, 1947; Fischer, 1950a, 1950b; Kamp and Kessler, 1970; Lumry,
1951; Michael and Buhler, 1945; Ucko, 1967). A major controversy
evolved as one camp used the sandtray as a therapeutic tool while
the others employed it as a diagnostic test. The diagnostic
approach was never well substantiated on a statistical basis as a
valid means to differentiate between and among diagnostic categories
(Miller, 1979).

Meanwhile, in the late 1950's and 1960's, Kalff (1966, 1971),
a Swiss Jungian analyst, nurtured and developed the sandtray and
successfully incorporated it into the Jungian psychotherapeutic
approach, calling it "Sandplay." Kalff's major concern was to
provide her child and adult patients with the "free and protected
space" in which they could feel secure and then grow and develop
psychologically. Others of this therapeutic persuasion (Aite,
1977, 1978; Dundas, 1978; Reed, 1975; Sandu, 1978; Stewart, 1977;
Sullwold, 1971) have written about this method as a means to elicit
unconscious material. The Jungian methods of association, amplifi-
cation, and objectification are incorporated into the sandtray
administration, as they are used in dream analysis and active
imagination.

THEORY

At present, most persons using the sandtray are Jungians.
Traditionally, Jungians court the unconscious for its oracular and
healing powers. They possess a comprehensive theory of the unconscious which holds that the unconscious is the repository of contents, both personal and trans-personal, which, under some

circumstances, i.e., dreams, visions, imaginings, may erupt into
consciousness. This process may help to regulate the attitude of
consciousness. It is hypothesized that unconscious contents are
transmitted in symbolic form. When one interprets and understands
this symbolism, new directions and energy can be gained. Like the
dream, the sandtray is a method for gaining access to unconscious
material. The principal mechanism of the method is the projection
of unconscious, symbolized contents onto concrete objects, and the
reciprocal stimulation of the unconscious by the objects. In
dealing with the symbols thus externalized, all functions of consciousness (feeling, thinking, sensation, and intuition) may be
brought into play. The symbols may be manipulated, and associations adduced. Objects are juxtaposed, removed, and replaced as
the arrangement is contemplated.

SANDTRAY WITH GROUPS

     Group work in the sandtray allows individuals the opportunity
to share their inner world with others, and to expose aspects of
themselves without being persuaded or intimidated. We are currently using two approaches to group work in the sandtray which we
call Logos and Eros. A description of each follows.

THE LOGOS APPROACH

     The sandtray was experimentally introduced in group therapy
when, in an attempt to get two members to understand a conflict
between themselves, each was asked to choose objects that represented the other person. Oddly enough, both persons chose objects
for one another which they later recognized as being parts of
themselves. For example, A chose a cactus for B, and B chose a
barking dog for A. When queried, A said that B stabbed her every
time she spoke to her. Later, however, she recognized that she
felt very vulnerable and self-protective in B's presence. Her
defense was to prickle B with her spines. B reported at first
that A growled and snarled when she came near her, but later saw
in herself the same snarling dog, quick to alarm and defense, and
ready to snap and bite. Thus, both persons became aware of mutual
defensiveness and resistance, and no longer saw the other as exclusively at fault. They then went on to discuss relevant associations. This experience pointed to the fact that objects employed
to concretize projections could be a source of knowledge in the
world microcosm that a group constructs.

     This pleasant discovery led to the first group approach, which
is called the "logos" or knowledge approach. This concrete approach
stresses coming to know and own one's projections and associations.
It is necessary that participants take responsibility for the

projections they share. Also, it is the free choice of each individual to accept or reject all or parts of the meanings being attributed to his or her sandtray picture. Subsequently, it is the task of each individual to attempt to find the meaning in his or her own projections. As Jung (1972) said, "All the contents of our unconscious are constantly being projected into our surroundings" (p. 264). Retrieving these projections and taking full responsibility for them unlocks unconscious contents and associations, and leads to awareness of one's self.

In utilizing this technique, we instruct individuals to begin by choosing one to three objects that seem to represent themselves and to place these objects in the sandtray. They are asked to note and to write down their feelings and thoughts about others' arrangements. Then each participant voluntarily explains and associates to the objects he or she has chosen. The other group members are then asked to share their projections and associations, always trying to discover what is unconscious within them. The process terminates when each participant has fully dealt with his or her objects and the group's projections.

EROS TECHNIQUE

The second technique we use is called Eros, which refers to the process or relating. In this group activity, one selects symbols to represent oneself and one becomes that symbol. When other group members are engaged in the same act, many symbols interact and interrelate.

The exercise begins as the group leader asks the participants to feel the sand with their hands and to add water to it if they wish to change the texture. We feel this mixing of water and earth by many hands has positive consequences which stimulate memories and affects. We believe it activates the unconscious in the same way that similar ceremonies have been used traditionally to initiate other group rituals. This also aids in creating a spontaneous community of trust and cooperation.

Participants are then asked to choose a few objects that either attract them or have personal meaning for them. These items are then placed into the sandtray. We ask the chooser to become the object and to be its voice and mover. The individual may begin with words such as these:

Well, I'm this old house here. My porch is falling off, and I have holes in my roof. But people can come and see what I am and look down into me to see what's going on. I could be a new house and get fixed up, but I'm real comfortable here, being what you see.

Another participant who is a laughing dinosaur comes to the old house, and looks into the roof and says, "Yea, looks mighty homey in there. Guess I'll stay here and watch what goes on."

We observe a course of development in the drama. At first, some participants may be quite timid, but soon they shed their concerns for appearances. As they are increasingly drawn into the experience, they generate more active participation. We make no attempts to interpret this rich material, and simply encourage people to play freely. During the course of this experience, participants may change their selected objects, discarding some and adding others. This development may signal some personal experiment or breakthrough.

ROLE OF THE THERAPIST

The role of therapists in group sandtray work is threefold. First, they are responsible for providing the materials and introducing them to the group. Second, therapists are non-judgmental leaders whose supportive and stable presence "contains" the process by offering their clients protection and an environment of freedom and security. Finally, therapists are responsible for setting the group tone and for placing limits on the interactions when necessary. In essence, they are acting as an ethical model for their clients to follow. At times the therapist is called upon to provoke and to stimulate activity while using the experience as a mini-laboratory where observations are made.

CONCLUSION

This group sandtray activity becomes a cooperative enterprise as risks are taken and as individuals experiment with roles, conflicts, and self-perceptions. It facilitates sharing, interacting, and reaching out to others in a novel and playful manner. As new information is processed, it enriches an individual's personal identity. This group experience aids participants in exploring and discovering themselves within the collective, a goal which is essential to the individuation process.

REFERENCES

Aite, P. Communication through imagination. The Annual of Italian Analytical Psychologists, 1977, 1, 105-129.
Aite, P. Ego and image: some observations on the theme of "Sand Play." Journal of Analytical Psychology, 1978, 23, 332-338.
Bolgar, H., and Fischer, L. The toy test: a psychodiagnostic method. Psychological Bulletin, 1940, 34, 517-518.

Bolgar, H., and Fisher, L. K. Personality projection in the World
    Test. American Journal of Orthopsychiatry, 1947, 17, 117-128.
Bowyer, L. R. The Lowenfeld world technique. Oxford and London:
    Pergamon, 1970.
Buhler, C. Symbolic action in children. Transactions of the New
    York Academy of Sciences, 1941, 17, 63-68.
Buhler, C. The World Test. Journal of Child Psychiatry, 1951(a),
    2, 2-3.
Buhler, C. The World Test: a projective technique. Journal of
    Child Psychiatry, 1951(b), 2, 4-23.
Buhler, C. National differences in the "World Test" projective
    patterns. Journal of Projective Techniques, 1952, 16, 42-55.
Dundas, E. Symbols come alive in the sand, 1978. (Available from
    author, Santa Cruz, California.)
Fischer, L. K. A new psychological tool in function: preliminary
    clinical experience with the Bolgar-Fischer World Test.
    American Journal of Orthopsychiatry, 1950(a), 20, 281-292.
Fischer, L. K. The World Test. In W. Wolff (Ed.), Projective and
    expressive methods of personality investigation. New York:
    Greene & Stratton, Inc., 1950(b).
Jung, C. G. Structure and dynamics of the psyche, Vol. 8, Collected
    Works. Princeton, New Jersey: Princeton University Press,
    1972.
Kalff, D. The archetype as a healing factor. International Journal
    of Psychology in the Orient, 1966, 9, 177-184.
Kalff, D. Sandplay. San Francisco: Browser Press, 1971.
Kamp, L. N. J., and Kessler, E. S. World Test developmental aspects
    of a play technique. Journal of Child Psychology and Psychi-
    atry and Allied Disciplines, 1970, 11, 81-108.
Lowenfeld, M. A new approach to the problem of psychoneurosis in
    childhood. British Journal of Medical Psychology, 1931, 11,
    194-205.
Lowenfeld, M. The theory and use of play in psychotherapy of child-
    hood. Journal of Mental Science, 1938, 84, 1057-1058.
Lowenfeld, M. The world pictures of children: a method of record-
    ing and studying them. British Journal of Medical Psychology,
    1939, 18, 65-101.
Lowenfeld, M. The nature and use of the Lowenfeld world technique
    with children and adults. Journal of Psychology, 1950, 30,
    325-331.
Lumry, C. K. Study of World Test characteristics as a basis for
    discriminating between various clinical categories. Journal
    of Child Psychiatry, 1951, 2, 24-35.
Michael, J. C., and Buhler, C. Experience with personality testing
    in a neuropsychiatric department of a public general hospital.
    Disease of the Nervous System, 1945, 6, 205-211.
Miller, R. The investigation of a psychotherapeutic tool for
    adults: the sandtray. Unpublished doctoral dissertation,
    California School of Professional Psychology, Fresno, 1979.

Mizushima, K. Art therapies in Japan. Interpersonal Development,
     1971-1972, 2, 213-221.
Reed, J. P. Sand magic. New Mexico: J. P. R. Publishers, 1975.
Sandu, M. Feminine psyche: an initial investigation of archetypal
     constellations as projected in sandplay. Unpublished master's
     thesis, United States International University, 1978.
Stewart, L. Sand play therapy: Jungian technique. In B. B.
     Wolman (Ed.), International encyclopedia of psychiatry, psy-
     chology, psychoanalysis and neurology. New York: Van Nostrand
     Reinhold Co., 1977.
Sullwold, E. Eagle eye, the well-tended tree: essays into the
     spirit of our time. (Jung Foundation), Putnam, 1971.
Ucko, L. E. Early stress experiences mirrored in "world" play test
     at five years. Human Development, 1967, 10, 107-127.

EXPERIENTIAL RECALL OF COMA IMAGERY

Virginia Johnson, Ed.D.

Los Angeles, California

Coma imagery is coded into memory during an altered state which is assessed neurologically on the basis of responses known to be impaired in the deeply unconscious patient. Such factors as context-awareness, time-binding, predictability, sensorimotor perception, information-processing, cognitive memory, assessment and interpretation, communication, and voluntary behavior are only a few of the CNS activities adversely affected by coma. Motor responses may be absent, or nearly so; muscle tone rigid or flaccid; eye movements and pupillary reactions are abnormal or may not occur at all; breathing may be shallow or labored, or stop altogether, requiring emergency procedures; and the patient does not respond appropriately to attempts to communicate verbally with him (Cartlidge, 1979).

Nevertheless, at the same time that these unfamiliar body sensations are being experienced, environmental inputs may be simultaneously conditioned. In other words, incapacity to respond to stimuli in an expected way does not therefore limit mnemonic recording of those inputs at some level of consciousness (Oakley, (1979). Simultaneous conditioning continues to occur in the comatose patient, but is subject to amnesia. The problem in obtaining recall of amnestic experiences is not because memory storage is unavailable, but because retrieval is state-dependent (Whitty and Zangwill, 1977). The retrograde amnesia characteristic of coma effectively interrupts the usual processes of conscious association unless the conditional state is reinstituted.

Tulving states as an "encoding specificity principle" that the memory trace itself determines the retrieval conditions under which the stimulus event can be recovered (Tulving, 1977). This "encoding specificity" operates in all learning, including state-dependent inputs during altered states, so that when conditions are most similar, retrieval is facilitated. This means in effect that the state of consciousness experienced during coma must be reconstructed to precipitate memory of comatose experiences. If it is accepted that there is a state-specifity, then recovery of state-dependent experiences will reflect the prior state of consciousness and its concomitant imagery.

To conscious awareness, the not-imagery of deep unconsciousness is experienced as an engram of error. The person strives to push aside lapses into blankness as if he were struggling against being taken over by an "alien" presence. Since conditional experiences in comatose states are not reality-contexted, the spontaneous precipitation of symptoms which are a function of such memories may be anxiety-producing or even terrifying. Reinforcement then continues to contribute to further misinformation in feedback systems (Jonas, 1973; Miller and Dworkin, 1969).

Since all life processes are vulnerable to state-dependent experiences, any system in the body may be subject to malfunction because of feedback from cryptomnesic memories. When functional symptoms occur in what we think of as bodily processes, such disorders are labelled psychosomatic; when those neural pathways are affected which have to do with mental activity, the usual term is psychopathology; either may be the final common pathway of prior dissociative experiences during coma. This functional relationship between coma imagery and psychiatric syndromes suggests a useful therapeutic model.

Fischer (1971) points out that amnesia is a constant between sleep or other altered states and alert/awake states of experience, so that we are subject in a sense of "multiple existences" by going from waking state to waking state, without contexting the intervening altered states. Bourguignon studied 488 societies as to their rituals involving dissociational states, and concluded that such states reflect a "universal human capacity" (Bourguignon, 1970). Nevertheless, it is the loss of continuity and context which may bring about disturbed mental states and psychosomatic symptoms. The human continuum of consciousness states ranges from hyperactivity or "transcendental" experiences to deep coma and clinical death; and from the first altered state, probably in the embryonic period, to those common to the adult (Tart, 1972; Zinberg, 1977). It is the spectrum of nonalert/noncognitive states with which we are concerned, and most especially with the deeper states of unconsciousness which are diagnosed as coma.

Evidence from experiential recall of comatose and other altered states of consciousness (ASC) indicates that specificity of conditional experiences in these states can be traced in later functional

syndromes, both mental and physical. Such findings have been presented by the present author in a series of papers on various
aspects of the clinical information from over 25,000 sessions of
detailed state-dependent recalls reflecting a wide range of imagery
(Johnson, 1969, 1973, 1974, 1977). Among patients with psychiatric
histories, dissociative responses characterize most of the more
severe disorders, and the hypothesis is suggested here that these
syndromes reflect conditional coma-state imagery, and are in fact
a function of the learning of such imagery.

Bowers, for example, is explicit that acute psychotic experience reflects past and present elements "portrayed through the permissive mechanism of an altered state of consciousness" (Bowers,
1974), in which patients

> recognize an altered way of experiencing themselves,
> others, and the world . . . psychotic consciousness
> represents the experiential pole of an altered pattern
> of central nervous functioning. (Bowers, 1974, pp.
> 212-213)

Thus, in terms of altered state theory, schizophrenia is represented
by a neuropsychological learning model based on the imagery of a
specific pre-morbid comatose experience (Johnson, 1972).

Clinically, coma most frequently is brought about by trauma,
especially head injury; by drugs or anesthetics, whether medically
administered or from drug abuse; or from various "medical" causes,
such as hypoxia, cardiac arrest, hepatic failure, stroke, diabetes,
meningitis, and so on.

Diagnosis of irreversible coma has reference only to the direction of process, the death vector; an aspect of coma which is not
relevant to the present discussion. Under special circumstance,
however, a "death" state may be sustained for varying periods of
time, followed by recovery of cerebral function, presumably the
deepest state of unconsciousness which man can experience and live
to record it in his memory. Our sophisticated procedures now make
possible many more such experiences than previously was possible,
so that the state-dependent not-imagery of cerebral silence may
have increasing significance for our culture. Most authorities
now are of the opinion that patients who survive near-fatal episodes of coma do have impressions of that state (Grof, 1975).

Perhaps the most frequently induced comatose state is brought
about by drugs or anesthetics, and the conditional experience then
is characterized by their effects (Colpaert and Rosecrans, 1978;
Weingartner and Murphy, 1977). The "unconditional" stimulus is
this drug effect; while other variables in the environment can
become "conditioned" to it by simultaneous association.

During anesthetic coma neurophysiological events reflecting a
wide range of function are affected and all of these responses can
be learned without conscious awareness (Miller, 1969). This is
the basis for the retrieval of visceral imagery during coma.
Patients also hear and see during an operation, even though they
are not in pain.

The hospitalized comatose patient is very likely to require
some form of life support system, and may thus be subjected to a
variety of emergency measures such as airways, intravenous drips,
heart-lung machines, and possibly a sojourn in the beeping-clicking-
rustling acute ward. Any of these stimuli can become conditional
when associated with the comatose state, and can reflect in later
behavior dependent on coma imagery. Nevertheless, at least 25
million operations a year are performed in the United States, many
of them on children, all of which add to the cryptomnesic engrams
which are a state-dependent function of anesthetic coma.

Cheek uses what he calls "ideomotor questioning" as a hypnotic
technique to recover anesthetic experiences, on the theory that
since the "surgical memory is incorporated below the conscious
level, the involuntary musculature is most closely related." He
emphasizes absence of reasoning faculty and context in deep anesthesia, resulting in a literal and childlike response to input
stimuli, especially reflected in the tendency to assume self-
referrents (Cheek, 1964, 1966; Cheek and LeCron, 1968).

Bunker cautions that

In the clinical situation, it is apparent that some
patients do remember operating room events, and there
are a good many published reports of awareness during
anesthesia and surgery. . . . we must pay attention to
the danger of conversation during light anesthesia, and
particularly to its emotional content. (Bunker, 1972)

The following dialogue is an excerpt from OR conversation overhead by a patient during a prostatectomy:

He has a history of skull fractures, and I think
we'd better airway him. . . . You can go ahead now.
Oh! Here we are--the groin area doesn't look bad--
I thought it would be worse.
You don't think he needed the surgery?
Oh--he would have had trouble eventually, if we
didn't operate.
His blood pressure is dropping--give him a little
oxygen. You better hurry.
Let's take a good look around first. Let's not
rush it. . . .

He's doing better. If he'd keep on with that low
BP he could have died on us.
　　　Here's the tissue report, Doctor. It's benign.
　　　That's good--he's a nice guy, and I'd hate to have
to be the one to tell him it was malignant.
　　　Well, you can relax now, Doctor. We did it, and
did it all right.
　　　How about the airway? I think it's stuck in his
throat--there's construction.
　　　Oh no! That's all I need! Uh huh! I'll ease it
up gently. It will tear a little, but not much. A
little problem getting it around the arch--we'll just
wait until those spasms ease up. Oops! We did it!
　　　What's that? That was a groan if I ever heard one--
After you got the airway out!
　　　God! I'd almost say he's conscious, but he's too
deep--it's impossible.
　　　Well, I need some coffee after this one.

Since many lesser drugs induce coma or at least altered states,
the theory of state-specificity and state-bound imagery applies to
their effects as well. Sedative drugs and anesthetics which
induced coma were known to the Greek and Roman physicians;
Paracelsus made potions of wine and poppy juice; and Mero's surgeon
Dioscorides used mandragora root to lessen pain.

The wines and beers themselves were early found to be
of comfort in an agony, and to them many herbs were
added by the priestly surgeons everywhere; the lotus,
lettuce, mandrake, poppy, dock, the henbane, hemlock,
hellobore and hemp, berbena, primrose, myrrh and
frankincense, the deadly nightshade, garlic, bhang,
datura, mulberry and rue--and half around the world,
where men learned also--kava, mescal, coca, and tobacco,
these and many more kept secret, unidentified, comprise
the ancient anodynes. (Leake, 1978)

Many of these medications are used today, while barbiturates
and other sleeping pills, as well as mood-altering psychotropics,
are dispensed by the millions. One of the most common and widely
used (and abused) neurochemicals in our society is, of course,
ethyl alcohol, which clearly results in state dependent effects in
both animals and man.

A second major cause of comatose states is injury to the head,
and the severe concussion syndrome is characterized by prolonged
coma and its accompanying amnesia (Russell, 1971). Symptoms may
follow head injury after long intervals, including anxiety, mental
confusion, muscle tension, insomnia, nightmares, sexual difficulties,
outbursts of temper, movement disorders, or fatigue (posttraumatic

neurosis).

Many violent criminals have a history of brain damage which
was accompanied by altered states, reflecting a learned "dyscontrol
syndrome," which is often a function of coma imagery (Mark and
Ervin, 1970). For example, mass murderer

> (Hickok) . . . had a serious head injury with concussion
> and several hours of unconsciousness in 1950. . . . He
> says he has had blackout spells, periods of amnesia, and
> headaches ever since that time, and a major portion of
> his antisocial behavior has occurred since that time.
> Smith shows definite signs of severe mental illness . . .
> there was historical evidence of altered states of con-
> sciousness, frequently in connection with the outbursts
> of violence. Two of the four men studied reported severe
> dissociative trance-like states during which violent and
> bizzare behavior was seen, while the other two reported
> less severe, and perhaps less well-organized, amnesiac
> episodes. During moments of actual violence, they often
> felt separated or isolated from themselves, as if they
> were watching someone else. . . . Also seen in the his-
> torical background of all cases was the occurrence of
> extreme parental violence during childhood. (Italics
> mine) (Capote, 1965, pp. 292-303)

Studies of other murderers reflected similar findings, and
studies of teenagers arrested for crimes of violence indicate a
high percentage of "blackouts" and dissociative behavior.

As to coma states during medical emergencies, nonspecific
stressor reactions can be learned by the body during traumatic
shock, while high fever is often accompanied by comatose states and
delirium. Febrile imagery usually differs from drug or trauma coma
in that there may be stimulation, the distortions of delirium, and
fast, confusing visual imagery. The memory of "being hot and fever-
ish" is nearly always recalled.

Many persons experience a comatose state from the impact of
electric shock, accidentally or as a therapy. Neurophysiological
responses to shock have common patterns, including disruption of
neural pathways, abnormal heart rhythms, muscular jerking, and
neurochemical changes, and there is predictable loss of memory and
thought disorganization. The present author reported that recovery
of state-dependent electroshock experiences consistently involved
involuntary muscular spasms characteristic of those in the original
experience, so that recovery of electroshock imagery is mediated
primarily by the neuromuscular system (Johnson, 1970).

Coma-inducing behaviors not usually considered as such are the various practices to achieve "highs," which may induce a state approximating coma by means of nondrug/nontrauma methods (Rosenfeld, 1973; Conway, 1978). For example, there are similarities between the behavior observed in members of the drug culture, and those who join evangelistic cults. State-dependent retrieval is involved in deprogramming (Edwards, 1979).

Techniques for state-dependent retrieval include the use of hallucinogens; hypnosis; meditation; experiential recall; electrosurgical stimulation of the brain (Penfield and Roberts, 1959); sleep deprivation; dream control; conditional stimuli known to have ASC input associations, and so on. The basic process is the same, searching for the appropriate state as the preliminary requirement for access to cryptomnesic information.

In interviews directed toward obtaining recall of ASC such as those reported here, the subject usually lies flat on his back on a couch (Berbach and Bakan, 1967), with a mask over his eyes to minimize external visual stimulation (see Figure 1). However, any position in which he can concentrate will do. Hands and arms are "positioned" in response to involuntary tensions. Reporting is descriptive, in terms of any experiencing of which the subject may become aware. Frequently, an unconscious state will predominate. The memories of coma are time-bound--it has a beginning, a middle, and an end, sequentially, like any other experience. Retrieval of comatose states first tends to precipitate sequences in a recovery period, then scenes leading to the loss of consciousness, then the seconds or minutes or hours of acute ASC.

Most often in the original experience, there may be a fast descent into coma, followed by a gradual awakening, and an even more gradual return of memory, sometimes over weeks, months, or even years. We are thus also talking about imagery sequences associated with these experiences over long periods.

While the experience may be reported in sequence and in great detail, neither during the recall nor afterwards is cognitive memory activated in the usual sense. The subject is aware of what he is reporting, and "knows" he has reported certain impressions; but at no time is there a reaction, "I remember," nor does the recalled experience become integrated into memory in any conscious sense. The memory remains state-dependent.

Knowledge of characteristic responses under various ASC conditions frequently enables the observer to identify the state of the subject, and to establish a reasonable expectancy with respect to behavior during the sessions. For example, a person in a deep state of coma may have the eyes rolled back or fixated, and the usual visual focus is lacking. No clear scene will be reported in that phase of the recall, because there are none. The field may

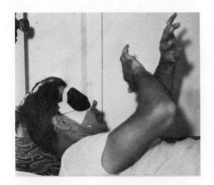
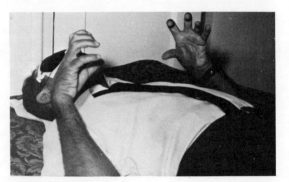
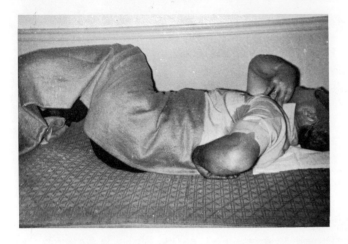
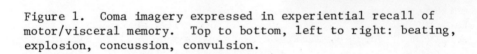

Figure 1. Coma imagery expressed in experiential recall of motor/visceral memory. Top to bottom, left to right: beating, explosion, concussion, convulsion.

be black or grey, but that is about all that is reported, and it is
on this the subject is asked to concentrate. In delirium or certain
drugged states (e.g., morphia), fast-moving or drifting visuals are
often reported. In this case, the visuals as such are not particularly significant, and concentration on the state of experience
itself is what should be emphasized. Verbal cues also may establish context, and especially sequence.

If a past event is characterized only by motor responses, the
recall will be enacted in terms of movement; whatever sensory
impressions were experienced will be reported as such, but without
the contexting characteristic of alert/awake responses. Any or all
of the recognized bodily sensations may be part of the experience,
such as pain, heat, cold, nausea, breathing changes, abdominal pressures, sweating, throat constriction, and so on, often reported as
"symptoms."

Auditory input and therefore memory of sounds is not impaired
by most altered states, even during deep coma, and can establish
feedback. Verbal input is information processed, not only by
sound, but by the orderly progression of language structure, and
voice changes, which will often be imitated precisely in experiential recall, and appear to be processed verbatim.

The nonverbal-nonvocal auditory recall during coma may be difficult to define, but subjects often can identify "pure tone"
ranges accurately, and can state the direction, volume, and rhythm
of the sounds. In some cases the "sound" appears to be intra-
organismic, as, for example, "cricket" sounds which were due to a
brain injury:

> I hear the "crickets" in a curved arch, like fog, in an
> even pattern, the arch is like brain halves. There is
> no order to my thinking. There's a mish-mash of sound--
> a mottled effect. I'm not aware. A chill--my whole
> skeletal structure is defined. I'm maybe 15. The back
> of my head hurts--aches--a plane right through it,
> which almost extends to the sides of my face.

Listening to "silence" is useful until some other auditory perceptions develop.

Visual experiences are similar to imagery reported while conscious, as was already mentioned, except for the predominance of
grey or black steady-states over long periods.

To summarize, then, what characterizes coma imagery as distinct
from the cognitive imagery of alert/awake mental processes? Most
significant is the fact that ASC imagery, because of amnesia, is
state-dependent and non-contexted, which means that retrieval of

coma imagery is therefore also state-dependent. Experiential recall
of experiences of coma is not an exercise in directed fantasy, but
descriptive reporting of subjective observations while maintaining
an alternate state of consciousness.

As to the content of experiential recalls of comatose states,
sensory information is similar to that from cognitive memory, with
the exception that visceral and motor responses tend to be dominant
(see Figure 1). Some coma states are accompanied by intense neurological (involuntary) responses in the muscular system, as, for
example, recall of delirium, depressed skull fracture, and the
gran mal seizures of epilepsy. Visuals are apt to be grey or black,
and auditory input includes verbatim language uninterrupted by any
verbal response from the patient.

Lastly, while the statement appears simplistic, coma states
when recalled are characterized by unconsciousness itself--the true
experience of not-imagery. There may be many hours spent in
retrieval of this comatose state, as is illustrated by the excerpts
from ASC recalls.

Experiential recall of altered consciousness is described in
many ways.

My eyes don't exist. There is no awareness of my head
but the ringing. I'm stuck-blocked--there is nothing
to hear--I can't hear. I'm insensible.

Another patient likened deep coma to being in a cavern:

These are sand filled caverns, so cold and deep that the
winds from nowhere never sleep, caverns measureless to
man, so that its depths cannot be perceived. . . . A
cave where the river leaves ten thousand hidden shores,
but can only flow in silence. A cave where water drips
from yesteryear into tomorrow, and murmurs this is for
me, but the echo that comes back says it was a depth
deeper than one's mind can conceive and yet shallow
enough to perceive one's thoughts; a dark black hole so
vast that one can exist without being. I need nothing
but my emptiness, and your thoughts cannot pierce my
solitude.

More usually, the experiential recall of deep unconsciousness
is involved with bodily sensations, illustrated by the following:

I am going to sleep or dropping off under anesthesia.
Heartbeat less heavy but still feel the beat on face
surface, lips, back of eyes in temple. Skin crawling
sensation like when tense or nervous. Suddenly a clear

eye's in the visual, then it fades out. More weight pressure in the back of my head, and it is as if trying to
push my chin down toward the chest. Hands and legs slowly
going numb. My whole body from the shoulders down is
terribly heavy and feels as if completely immobile, then a
light drifting sensation. Flashing patterns in left eye,
pitch black to paper white, with jagged zigzagging lines.
I don't know where I am. Some kind of high-domed ceiling,
web structure, glass, turning, as if I'm looking straight
up. Distorted shadows of persons, like I'm seeing them
through a big glass dome. Visual dark to dark gray, and
there is something going on in it. A tremendous amount
of pressure on the base of the skull that gives me a headache to both temples. I see a face upside down. A bright
light coming into right eye, then like a head comes
between it and me. I see this as if with eyes closed.
Heartbeat is picking up.
      (After six months)
      Hyperventilating has diminished, and tension head-
aches minimal. Not as irritable. Have taken over an
administrative job. If I get tense I talk more slowly, and
it doesn't get out of hand.
      Hands no longer go to full numbness, and the "skull
cap" effect is dissipating. The heart palpitations are
only occasional and mild. Not getting the flushing
response.
      My heart goes "pitter-patter" but it's only annoying
now and doesn't bother me. I know when I'm tense and I
back off. I still work at home on getting the feelings.

The memory of an altered state may last several decades, and
perhaps for life. This patient had a hidden memory of a time 40
years before in early childhood, when she was very ill, and a
religious teacher was praying over her in a ritual of exorcism.

I think spinning, spinning, it's circular, but I don't
seem to be it. I'm dizzy, and it's unpleasant. It's like
a game. I'm in a world of my own, of black and white
lines and I'm being drawn further into it. The voice is
saying: "Soon you'll be drawn into it, and into another
world of pretty flowers and blue skies, but you will have
to go by yourself, I have to stay on this side, so I can
bring you back again. You will only think nice thoughts."
It's a land where no one cries, and no one lies, where
everyone is happy and good. (I am conscious, but my
whole brain is blanked out. I really can't think, and my
head is full of cotton.) The thought comes to me "brain
abscess."

Typical ASC Recalls Over a
  Period of Six Months

     2/13 ASC. Everything around me is silent. It is
completely dark. Intermittent tightening and loosening
of muscles across my back. My hands are cold and numb.
I have a vague impression of snow, but I can't see it.

     2/20 ASC. There are three levels of consciousness.
At one time it was as if the outer area of the brain was
dead or numb. Vague, shadowy figures. Pain in the
lower abdomen, pressure at the base of my skull. There
is something white over me. A round spot between the
shoulder blades like a heart beat.

     3/27 ASC. There are some visual flashes, and a deep
"bone" pressure over nose and face. Each time I go a
little deeper, but my body and mind use everything to stop
me. I haven't felt panic or fear in over a year. There
is pain over the bridge of my nose, then sharp pain in
waves up to my eyes and head.

     4/23 ASC. It's like looking up through an odd open-
ing. Two arms reach down. There are vague faces, distorted, as if masked.

     4/30 ASC. No movement. The silence is a "total
blank."

     5/7 ASC. Vague, swirly, repeated black waves. An
impression of "not being able to get back under," as if
in water.

     6/4 ASC. In and out levels again. Different waves
create different levels of sensation, some visual and in
color. Words: What did you tell them? I was "aware"
the whole time.

     6/11 ASC. I seemed to go deeper. I had a flash of
uneasiness--something is going to happen. A spatter of
little oblong objects.

     6/18 ASC. In and out feelings. A circle of light.
The feeling of breathing stoppage.

     6/25 ASC. Numbness of hands. Occasional vague "form-
less" visuals. Flashes of a clear black and white scene
were accompanied by stimulation of entire body in waves.
Some distorted faces.

     6/29 ASC. When cutoff comes, it's black nothingness.
Waking is like coming out of a morass, and I don't function well.

     7/13 ASC. The visual was practically a total blank
except once a cedar chest.

     7/20 ASC. Nausea and pressure, a tight jaw and
throat. No visual except a vague face, followed by waves
of gray or black. In and out feeling. Hands and arms
were numb at times.

Hypnotic or trance states are recovered as state-dependent memories, often with very vivid imagery, as Figure 2 and the chanted words indicate.

Figure 2

I hear (American) Indian chanting, rapid bursts of talking and more chanting. It's a woman, arms wide, bending over me.
Your chest is like a stone and you cannot move. (She chants between the words.) You are as a stone, you cannot see. (My visual was grey, but then turned black. My body is very rigid, the head shaking from side to side to side in bursts.) You are as rigid as a stone. He will not remember, only his spirit will know. His spirit and the spirit of the rocks and stones. (The lady is leaning over me and passing her hands in a circular motion overhead, the circles gradually getting smaller. She made me to go sleep this way.) You are as limp as a rope. (Now I have turned into a pile of rope, I'm getting very hot, and I'm on fire. They are burning the hair off my head and arms, and it is as if my whole body is on fire. The fire has gone out and now turned into a tree and then a river.) I am a deer

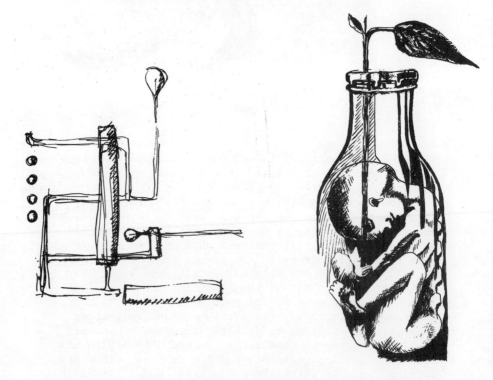

Figure 3. Visceral impressions at or during birth.

that's been captured and tied up--I am a great bird.
(Hands move slowly like wings.) I'm a great storm,
and I turn to black. (Hands form clouds in motion.)
My fingers are a train, and I feel the cold. Flowers
are all over and around me, now the flowers are all
gone, replaced with snow. (I feel very scared and would
like to stop the interview. She's going to scream at me
very loud. I have a headache. She put a hand on my chest,
and drew around it--the hand print is going to grow and
cover my body. I am going to be deep in the other world,
and she says she will be with me. Then I hear another
voice say: "It's a bunch of hogwash," and someone else
says, "Well, it works." I think it's my aunt and uncle
talking. I feel very strange.)

Retrieval of auditory comments during coma experienced at
three months by patient 30 years of age at time it was recalled.
(See Figure 3.) This same subject spent many hours recovering
perinatal memories, during which the mother was oversedated and the
unborn infant was also comatose.

(My head feels irritable, I don't see well, like
I'm floating around in a dream sequence. The darkness
is inside my head, frontal part. I see two men--doctors
maybe?)
--must be brain damage. There's blood all over her
head--gaping wounds.
(They're trying to repair the damage. I can feel
them picking at my brain.) What a mess! I hate this
kind of surgery!
How old do you think she is? 3½ months?
About that.
Isn't it hard for her to be restrained and attached
to all that stuff?
We gave her drugs to calm her down. (He has things
all over me--a wire in my head.)
When you gonna take this kid off this stuff?
Pretty soon--she had brain surgery.
I feel very disconnected and faint. I'm not getting
enough oxygen, because there is some covering over my
face. I really feel like a little baby. My brain feels
"mushy.")
What in hell's the matter with her? What kind of an
asshole would have pulled this bandage off her? Goddamned
incompetents!
Don't yell at me! I didn't do anything.
Shut up, nurse. Get me scissors, tape, and bandage.
I'm going to have to sew her up again. Damn! I'm going
somewhere else to finish my residency. I'd like to find
out which of those apes it was. The whole top of her head

is a mess!

Doctor! Keep your voice down!

(There's a black mass in my brain, maybe from the ether while they patch me up.) Look at that blood caked in there.

I hate to see a messed up wound--and in the brain, too.

(This drug they gave me gives me a weird feeling.)

Why in hell isn't that child in pediatrics?

Nobody had time to take her down.

(I feel I'm glued to the bed. I think I was getting spastic, that's why they strapped me. Once in a while I can see a distorted hand. I have always gestured in a "spastic" manner.)

(I know it's light in the ward, but I can barely see in my own little dark cave.)

(They're digging around in my head again. Makes me very tense.) ASC

Look at the scar tissue on this baby's head. It's impeding growth of cells.

Well--don't go too deep there, or you'll strike the speech centers. Must have been some wound. (I can see part of what they're doing. There's a mirror.)

(Must have had a drug--funny lines and blackness in my brain.)

Well that baby better be better or I'll report you for malpractice. She could suffer brain damage.

Yes---well--102 temp.--not so good.

Get her into a vaporized room, keep the penicillin coming, keep her head cool. Boost up the IV feedings, a drip if necessary, vitamins and glucose. Poor little tyke.

REFERENCES

Berbach, E., and Bakan, P. Body position and the free recall of early memories. Psychotherapy, August, 1967, 4(3), 101-102.

Bourguignon, E. Hallucination and trance: an anthropologist's perspective. In W. Keup (Ed.), Origin and mechanisms of hallucinations. New York: Plenum Press, 1970.

Bowers, M. B., Jr. Retreat from sanity. New York: Human Sciences Press, 1974.

Bunker, J. P. The anesthesiologist and the surgeon. Boston: Little, Brown and Co., 1972.

Capote, T. In cold blood. New York: Random House, 1965.

Cartlidge, N. E. F. Clinical aspects of coma--the assessment of acute brain failure. TINS, May, 1979, 126-130.

Cheek, D. B. Surgical memory and reaction to careless conversation. American Journal of Clinical Hypnosis, January, 1964, 6, 237-240.

Cheek, D. B. The meaning of continued hearing under general chemo-anesthesia. _American Journal of Clinical Hypnosis_, 1966, 8, 275-280.

Cheek, D. B., and LeCron, L. M. _Clinical hypnotherapy_. New York: Grune and Stratton, 1968.

Colpaert, F. R., and Rosecrans, J. A. _Stimulus properties of drugs: ten years of progress_. New York: Elsevier/North-Holland Biomedical Press, 1978.

Conway, F., and Siegelman, J. _Snapping_. New York: Lippincott, 1978.

Edwards, C. _Crazy for God_. Englewood Cliffs, New Jersey: Prentice-Hall, Inc., 1979.

Fischer, R. A cartography of the ecstatic and mediative states. _Science_, November 26, 1971, 4012, 897-904.

Grof, S. _Realms of the human unconscious_. New York: The Viking Press, 1975.

Johnson, V. _The medical significance of conditional experiences in semiconscious or unconscious states_. Paper presented at the Academy of Psychosomatic Medicine, Scottsdale, Arizona, 1969.

Johnson, V. A clinical assessment of the conditional effects of electroshock. In N. L. Wulfsohn, and A. Sances, Jr. (Eds.), _The nervous system and electric currents_. New York: Plenum Press, 1970.

Johnson, V. The schizexperience: a learning and feedback model for schizophrenia and schizoid process. _Society for Neuroscience_, 1972.

Johnson, V. Clinical evidence of neurobehavioral responses conditioned during experiences in altered states of consciousness. _Society for Neuroscience_, 1973.

Johnson, V. Reconstructive memory in human subjects observed as neuromuscular behavior patterns: a clinical model. _Society for Neuroscience_, 1974.

Johnson, V. Symposium: deconditioning altered states of consciousness and traumatic experiences. _Association for Advancement of Behavior Therapy_, 1977.

Jonas, G. _Visceral learning_. New York: Viking Press, 1973.

Leake, C. D. Letheon: the cadenced story of anesthesia. _Science_, February 24, 1978, 857-860.

Mark, V. H., and Ervin, F. R. _Violence and the brain_. New York: Harper Medical Department, 1970.

Miller, N. E. Learning of visceral and glandular responses. _Science_, January 31, 1969, 163, 434-445.

Miller, N. E., and Dworkin, B. R. Effects of learning on visceral functions--biofeedback. _New England Journal of Medicine_, 269, 1274-1278.

Oakley, D. A. Neocortex and learning. _TINS_, June, 1979, 149-152.

Penfield, W., and Roberts, L. _Speech and brain mechanisms_. London: Oxford University Press, 1959.

Rosenfeld, E. _The book of highs_. New York: Quadrangle/The New York Times Book Co., 1973.

Russell, W. R. The traumatic amnesias. London: Oxford University
     Press, 1971.
Tart, C. T. States of consciousness and state-specific sciences.
     Science, June 16, 1972, 176.
Tulving, E. Context effects in the storage and retrieval of
     information in man. Psychopharmacology Bulletin, February,
     1977, 67-68.
Weingartner, H., and Murphy, D. L. Effects of drug states and
     clinical phenomena on the storage and retrieval of information
     in man. Psychopharmacology Bulletin, February, 1977, 66-67.
Whitty, C. W. M., and Zangwill, O. L. (Eds.), The pathology of
     forgetting. London: Butterworths, 1977.
Zinberg, N. E. (Ed.), Alternate states of consciousness. New
     York: Free Press, 1977.

"JANE":   CASE STUDY OF A RAPE VICTIM

REHABILITATED BY ART THERAPY

Dee Spring, M.A., A.T.R.

H.E.R.E. Rape Crisis Clinic

Placentia, California

IMPRESSIONS AND OBSERVATIONS

When I first encountered Jane, she was experiencing marked distress and was difficult to work with since she attributed all of
her discomfort to others via blame. This included her ex-husband,
her children, her mother, her family, the welfare system, environmental influences and circumstances. Her motivation for change
appeared high. Through her intellectualization and game playing,
however, her willingness to surrender control was low (Perls, 1969).

Jane appeared to have an inner personality which controlled,
intervened and exacerbated her difficulties. I called this her
"subpersonality." She constantly referred to this as "it" which
seemed to be the responsible party for everything. Perls (1969)
makes reference to the "it" as a substitution of "I"; a denial of
the reality of self. The subpersonality seemed to be tremendously
conditioned by old patterns and habitual ways of thinking, acting
and feeling. The "it," she stated, seemed to possess tremendous
strength and always caused failure. She had intense inner conflict
and spoke of suicide or insanity as being ways to ease the pain and
frustration. She contended, however, that she did not have the
energy nor fortitude to plan and execute suicide; or should insti-
tutionalization occur, there would be no one to look after her
mother. Jane did a great deal of fantasizing about how it should
be, rather than accepting what is.

Jane appeared to have a fairly high intellectual potential but
was unable at this time to function adequately in her daily life
due to her emotional involvement. Her energy to accomplish was
low; she had no goals; she appeared helpless to change her life;

she was afraid of herself and others and angry at "them." She
spoke of the constant battle between "it" and "them." She expected
to be laughed at and accused, trusted no one and expected the worst
to occur. She was negative about herself, her appearance and her
world; there was no good anywhere.

Jane seemed to take everything in until she was ready to overflow and then spew it all out. In addition, her guilt was disabling
to the point that she had given up directing energies outward to
bring about changes that would enable her to have an environment
she enjoyed or one that satisfied her needs. She felt she was
"dumb" and "stupid"; uncapable of providing for herself and signifi-
cent others adequately. She felt she always encountered insurmountable obstacles and felt frustrated, depressed, punished and confused; there was no way to win, so why try; she just gave up.

Superimposed on the mountain of difficulties already noted,
Jane had a stuttering problem which alerted me to the possibility
of multiple rapes in her history. At this time, such had not been
ascertained. This added to the difficulty in working with Jane
since she had such a need for incessant chatter. The constant chatter with no particular focus made me very nervous and I was amazed
how many hours this could go on if allowed to run its course. Her
denial of self and reality through this facade of intellectual gar-
bate created tensions in the beginning and made progress slow.
The verbalization was a part of the self-defeating properties which
added momentum to her escapism. When she wasn't talking, she was
sleeping. There wasn't much in between. When she was sleeping,
she was experiencing frightening dreams and nightmares.

HISTORY

At age five, Jane had four younger brothers and sisters whom
she was expected to look after. When she made a mistake with them,
she was chastised with, "You should have known better." She had
at one time convinced one brother, who caused her a great deal of
stress, to eat almost a whole bottle of aspirin. She felt this
might alleviate her frustration in trying to cope with problems
he created and her incapability to maintain.

She recalled an incident around age six which reinforced her
feelings of helplessness and fear. Her mother and a cousin took
her out in a rubber raft while at the beach. This incident is
related in her own words from her written dialogue. This dialogue
came after she looked at her drawings.

Through my series on "External Realities and Responsibili-
ties," I remembered an incident of my being helpless and
terrified out of my mind. I was in a rubber raft. My

mom and her cousin took me out in the ocean. I was terrified. I couldn't swim. I wanted out, but the water was
there. They were laughing and teasing me. I was terrified! I wanted out and there was no place to go--just
water, all around and the bottom of the boat was soft and
squishy. I couldn't do anything. I was afraid and they
thought it was funny. I was so scared, I couldn't stand
it and I couldn't help it. They wouldn't take me back to
the shallow water. I was alone in the boat; they were in
the water at the side. They were propelling the boat and
taking me in it. I couldn't do anything about it. I
wanted out, I was afraid and probably mad as hell.

Beginning at age eight, she encountered sexual molestation from
her father's friend and an older cousin who frequented the home.
This same action was perpetuated by an uncle around age 11. Proto-
col was for her to kiss this uncle as a greeting when she encountered
him. During this period, she was apparently raped with forced oral
and anal sex by the older cousin, but has to date not been able to
approximate the exact time, due to her own amnesia of the incident.
Through art therapy, parts of the incident have emerged. Each of
these instances made her quite nauseated physically. Also during
this time, there was a male friend whom she played "doctor" with,
as most children do. Later on in high school, however, this childhood friend took delight in recalling and relating the various
incidents to mutual friends. Jane experienced acute and severe
embarrassment which was reinforced by imagery of the other sexual
molestations that had occurred in her family.

During her high school years and following the above incidents,
she learned of widespread homosexuality in the female population of
her family. She had a boyish appearance and preferred jeans
and shorts to dresses, she was accused of being a part of this population. This elicited more embarrassment and intensified her feelings of contamination, helplessness, fear and guilt which had been
occurring since age five.

Jane remembers little of her high school days, except that she
was an achiever and quite active in extra-curricular activities.
She cooked for eight, every day after school, and cared for the
family while her mother worked. Her father was much older than her
friend's fathers, and had retired. She stated she was her father's
favorite and they talked a lot. Her friends teased her because her
father was "so Old." She felt comfortable with him and had a close
relationship which appears to be the only close male relationship
Jane has encountered for any period of time. When he died, some
years later, she felt very denied and alone.

Jane married at the age of 18, immediately following high
school. She had taken a college prep course, but felt she was "too

dumb" to attend college. To get married and have a family was
expected; therefore, it was easier to assume this role.

Immediately after the marriage, the sense of independence
acquired in high school, disappeared. She realized that she had
received no prior sexual education other than abuse and was shocked
when this entered the picture. She realized she had no understanding of being a wife. She found books which theorized on submission
and passivity. Since books had been Jane's support system, she
believed this was the correct role, so she adopted it. The marriage quickly took on the theme of "Master and Slave." Her repetitive pattern of internalization was constantly being reinforced.
She felt guilty and blamed herself for every failure whether hers
or his. Everything was her fault. She felt helpless to control
her environment or her life.

When she was pregnant with her first son, she was both aston-
ished and frightened. She had difficulty accepting the pregnancy
or that she would be a mother. Fortunately, experiences earlier
in her life, when she was in charge of four younger brothers and
sisters, were a valuable asset, especially when the second baby came
less than two years after the first. Once again, she was overwhelmed with helplessness and fear; felt out of control.

When the second baby was six months old, her husband began an
affair with another woman. Since Jane had by this time totally
adopted the conditioned reflex of passivity and learned helplessness, she did nothing when Doc, her husband, came in, cleaned up
and told her he was going out with Suzanne. After he left, she
would put the babies to bed and sit by the window in the dark,
until she fell asleep waiting for his return. This behavior was
repeated over a long period of time.

When Doc began gambling and drinking, Jane repeated the pattern and waited by the window. She learned she was pregnant again.
She had a difficult pregnancy. The baby was born, but died before
she left the hospital. She felt she could do nothing right. Again,
she felt helpless, hurt and very much alone.

Later on, when Doc abused her sexually and physically, she was
hurt, embarrassed, ashamed and angry. She didn't want anyone to
know. The growing debts and lack of money from the gambling and
drinking compounded the situation. Her sense of helplessness, fear,
humiliation and dumbness mounted.

Excessive inner turmoil and conflict was taking place, intensified by the arrival of the third baby. When this baby was still
in the bassinette, Jane was raped by a man who had broken into the
house while she and the three children slept. The rapist disappeared through the window when Doc returned to the home. Doc

accused Jane of having a lover. He blamed her for the rape and she
accepted the blame. The intensity of helplessness, embarrassment,
guilt and fear was acutely magnified at this point. Once again,
the internalization process. The senss of contamination and anger
which had manifested since age eight was also intensified and added
to the already over-burdened coping mechanisms. Jane felt she was
a total failure by this time and indeed felt it was "all my fault."
The environment and others were to blame for her lack of success in
anything. She felt "dumb and stupid" that she had no control. She
thought she should know what to do.

When Doc suddenly left Jane at age 25, with three small children, all the old patterns and feelings were reinforced. He had
gambled away all the money. Unknowingly, Jane had circulated bad
checks. She was arrested and faced jail on a charge she couldn't
understand. Jane stated, "I was left holding the bag, and an empty
one at that." At this point, she had no money, no family support
and no job skills. She asked herself, her now famous question,
"What to do? I don't know what to do. I need help." This statement has appeared repetitiously throughout her dialogue, both written, drawn and spoken, for the past 13 months. It is just recently
that she has begun to realize that her patterns are reversible.

After she realized that Doc was "really gone" and did not
intend to help or return, she tried to find a job. She finally
derived from her job search that she had no job skills. She had
never worked. However, after much searching, she acquired a job
at a lunch counter in a variety store which paid her less than the
baby sitter cost. She learned she could be subsidized by welfare.
For her, the embarrassment was overwhelming. She became a welfare
recipient and now blamed her lack of success on the system. Her
dependency on the system was because of her "dumb stupidity," she
stated.

Through her determination over the next several years, she
learned the waitress trade very well, and through several experiences, she finally managed a fairly good job. All of the hardship
took its toll, however, and she sought psychiatric care for a year.
No power was assigned to the sexual molestation or abuse during the
psychiatric treatment, nor was the rape evaluated as having any
significance to the conflicts. She left therapy little improved
with a lot of tranquilizers.

At the end of this time, she saw an ad at a junior college
concerning licensed vocational nursing. She felt this might enable
her to provide better for her children. She took the exam required
and passed it. When the head of the department called her in for
an interview and told her she had scored too high to be in this
field, she could not understand what was happening since she had
thoroughly convinced herself she was "dumb and stupid." She felt

this was another defeat--another failure. "It" did it, she stated,
and would take no credit for passing the test too high. The
instructor suggested that she enroll in the R.N. program. Since
she had conditioned herself to be submissive and take orders, she
did enroll in the R.N. program.

Following her graduation from the nursing program, and naturally much denial to acquire this education, she went to work at a
hospital as a nurse. She felt her life situation would now improve.

The second rape occurred at this time, and her pattern was
further reinforced. Her mother had a stroke. Her family felt she
was the logical one to take care of the invalid mother, since she
was now a nurse. Until the present time, Jane cares for her mother,
totally independent of help from her family members.

By the time the above had occurred, Jane felt she had to leave
the environment in which she lived. She moved her family, took a
new job, but found it impossible to continue as a nurse. Her excuse
was: a nurse's income was not sufficient to provide for an invalid
mother and three children. She did not like to work. She reen-
countered the welfare system since she believed she could make more
money on welfare. This was Jane's situation when she came to me.
At this time, she had been entrapped in her own prison for two
years with two teenagers, a grade school child, an invalid mother
and a dog.

EVALUATION OF JANE'S CASE

Jane's rape incident put her in the normal position of rape
victims who often develop "learned helplessness." If they are
left to believe that they have no control over their environment,
they fall prey to self-defeating behavior. A victim must be
guided to understand that her own actions control reinforcement.
In other words, if they continue to believe that their environment
is such that the same type of thing will occur again and again,
they give up and let "it" happen. Jane fell into this trap at
an early age and experienced exaggerated reinforcement of her
beliefs. The rapes convinced her of the process.

Knowing this about rape victims and through my observations of
Jane, I called on Perls' theories of the "dummy" complex, retroflection and introjection since Jane appeared to fall into these
patterns.

Relative to Perls' "Dummy Complex," Jane has throughout her
life dummified several objects, a teddy bear and boots at an early
age, later it became intellectual garbage and a verbal facade. As

an adult, all of these fetishes culminated into her "it" which she
has just barely begun to dismiss.

Each time Jane gets to a point where she can confront such
action by herself, she manages to impress herself by contriving a
way to dummify herself in order to continue her self-defeating patterns. She feels danger at this point and throughout her dialogue,
she repeatedly draws and speaks of being very sleepy and tired.
This has been a repetitive solution to her personal denial of her
own reality. Perls (1951) makes mention of the fact that such persons "feel sleepy or drowsy, whenever they perceive the 'danger' of
provocation in any situation." Jane began this pattern when she
waited by the window for Doc's return.

Jane fits Perls' description of the perfect dummy "which all
obsessional and paranoid characters are looking for." Her relationship with me, as the therapist, could continue for years because of
her own ability to sabotage her success. Her continued lack of
success, even though she appeared to work very hard, would, in her
mind, keep our relationship status quo, because of her need for
"technical advice" on how to use the tools she had been given and
the tools that she had designed for herself.

After almost three months of spewing out material, we were
ready to begin focusing work with art materials. Jane was terrified and I knew it would be another trauma since decisions were
extremely difficult for her. The entire issue caused her to fluc-
tuate from aggressiveness to kindness, from withdrawal to a need
for contact, from agonizing fear to trust. She was overwhelmed
with the idea of failure, imprisoned by feelings of helplessness
and relayed painful contradictions in her daily existence as to
whether she wished to continue with "this project of learning
experiences." She floundered, and faced with decision, she experienced moments of extreme difficulty and anxiety. Even though academically intelligent and adroit, she was illogical, flighty, sometimes unreasonable and egocentric at times, and still haunted by
persecution nightmares. She did not want to set goals or focus on
accomplishments; she had a desire to escape from daily obligations.

Jane wanted to hang-on and she contrived ways to do this by
playing "dumb and stupid." She told me she could not possibly do
all "these things" without my assistance. She expected me to continue to give without her having to do anything to achieve a new
position in her life. She was willing to "just let it happen."
She contrived all kinds of ways to get attention from me. She
played all kinds of games to consume my time and pretended to be
working extra hard. In reality, it was only a way of hanging-on
while she continued the same old patterns. She stopped directing
energies outward and complained that there was no way to control
her environment. Everything was done to her and she had no control

over anything. She felt I was punishing her because she was dumb
and stupid. She knew she was not worth my attention and became
very jealous of other clients and students with whom I worked. In
order to avoid the pain, she would retreat, only to come back at
the scheduled time with all kinds of plans which she never followed
through on nor talked about a second time.

I knew my value as a therapist was to guide her in a transition from a self-concept which had developed from frustration, self-
defeating behavior, self-denial and rejection to one of self-worth
built on trust. I had a strong belief that the art experience
would be conducive to her growth in self-esteem, learning and
adjustment.

PARTICIPATION IN ART THERAPY

Jane was placed in a group with five other participants, plus
an appointed time weekly for private work with me. I was apprehen-
sive about her participation in the group since she emphatically
and repeatedly told me she was terrified. She had been in groups
(her family) all her life and hated it. She stated that she could
not draw or paint or "do any of that stuff," although she had been
doing such exercises for months. However, she came to the group
and participated. Not only did she participate, she stated, "I
don't understand, but I really like it; it fascinates me." I was
relieved and felt two important parts of the therapeutic process
had been established: trust and change.

Jane's first group art experience was entitled, "I See Myself
As . . . ." She stated she saw herself as "alone."

There are people above and people below. It looks like,
with a little effort, I would not have to be separated
and uninvolved. I don't know what the colors mean, but
I do relate to the facts that a lot of things are happening around me, but I am not involved.

"My Road of Life," done after three and one-half months of art
therapy, brought out a lot of Jane's history. Prior to this time,
she could not remember much of her childhood, teen years or parts
at the end of her marriage. Such historical information continued
to erupt as she progressed with visual dialogue.

Following the drawing of the first "Road to Life," Jane experienced the first eruption of child sexual molestation through her
feelings of contamination associated with the break-up of her
marriage.

The activity of "My Road of Life" was repeated several times

throughout her therapy. After seven months, she stated, "I feel a
coming together, but I'm still confused now." The drawings were
more integrated as were the colors; so was Jane.

After 10 months of art therapy, her drawings clearly depicted
where Jane was in her emotional development. She was able to evaluate her own changes and stated:

> I am on my road of life and at an intersection. There
> are different ways to go. I see two ways I don't want
> to go; one takes too long and one looks like oblivion,
> so I have two roads to choose from.

Her drawings of "My Parts" provoked discussion which caused
Jane to become cognizant of the sexual abuse as a child. She could
not identify to what extent at this time. The drawings made her
aware that her depression was grey symbolized by a penis-shaped
figure. She could not identify the meaning of a large, black wedge,
nor a vaginal-shaped figure. She was bothered by the drawings and
later had a violent dream which included weapons and tremendous
feelings of separation, fear, desire to escape, rejection and being
out of control.

As her awareness enabled her to accept and communicate more
of her inner feelings verbally, she became more afraid of what was
happening emotionally. One month following these drawings, she
experienced extreme distress. We worked for several hours and my
suspicions about multiple rapes was confirmed as she painfully drew
her series entitled, "Rape." Following this artistic expression
and the sharing of the associated feelings, Jane was able to cry
for the first time since she had been in therapy. She was able to
express the devastating feelings of helplessness and terrorizing
fear that had been internalized for so many years. Repetition of
the gesture of throwing her arms in the air, present at my first
encounter with her and which appeared in many of her drawings, was
strongly prevalent.

The series entitled, "Rape," proved to be a turning point for
Jane. When she was free to project her blocked impulses and
repressed feelings onto the media, visually see and verbalize about
these, she was tremendously relieved. Following the catharsis,
she crawled under a table, curled up in a fetal position and slept.
When she awoke several hours later, she was refreshed, energized
and exhibited her feelings of accomplishment. This was a different
kind of sleeping from her previous escape from fear and frustration.

Emotional change happened rapidly following this experience.
Two weeks following her series on "Rape," she participated in an
artistic expression entitled, "New Birth." Her own statement about
what transpired during this series is important to the drawings.

I don't know too much about what's going on. Emotionally, I feel somewhat relieved, but physically, I seem
to have lost the nausea and constriction in my throat;
my jaws are tight. I have a tremendous amount of tension
across my shoulders and down my upper arms. I feel like
I'm going to have a baby. I have pain in my lower abdomen, a hard knot the size of a fist. I have a tremendous
urge to bear down vaginally, which I'm doing rhythmically.
I feel a stretching at the pubic bone and I have mild pain
extending from the groin down both legs. Feels good to
bear down, don't have to control it. I am moaning and
groaning. It hurts! I want it to be over, it hurts!
I'm tired. I hurt, legs ache. It's done.

Following her "New Birth" series which she completed in a new
medium, Jane felt she had a new identity. She worked in her new
medium of colored pencils which she had not used before to complete
her drawings of "This is Me, Mary Jane." The change in how Jane
perceived herself after 10 months of art therapy was quite obvious.
In her first drawing she was a void with others around her. She
had no identity. "This is Me, Mary Jane," has identity, form,
color, movement and rhythm.

Following this dramatic period of self-awareness, more directed
work has begun in order for Jane to learn to focus her attention and
zero in on her reality.

She began to focus more on handling one thing at a time by
using the suggestion of a basket which she was to put in a conspicu-
ous place with small strips of paper nearby. Each time she had a
thought about something she needed to work on or things she wanted
to change, she was to write it on a strip of paper and drop it in
the basket. Periodically, she was to take out one and work on it.
This proved to be an excellent tool for Jane and kept her out of
such complexity of conflicts.

In her private sessions, she was able to shed light on her
present feelings by identifying feelings of the past, when and how
they occurred. Through her visual dialogue, she was pleased with
herself when she made connections for herself. She felt a sense of
accomplishment which was new for her. She realized this could be
addictive and enjoyable.

The next major undertaking was working with Jane's growing
dependency on the therapist. It was time for Jane to accept and
integrate disassociated parts of herself and learn what was truly
hers. It was time for her to acquire a selective and critical attitude toward what was offered and develop the ability to "bite off"
and "chew" her own experience so she could feel good about herself.
It was time for the weaning process to take place. It seemed very

proper to begin the weaning process now, approximately nine months
following her first visit to the Centre. When I thought about this,
I thought how "coincidental." Nine months is the natural time for
babies to be born. Jane had a new identity, the pain of birth was
over and she had survived. She had suckled at the breast (depended
on the therapist) and was still dependent on her environment. Now
she was at a point of shifting to self-support; this naturally con-
stituted weaning.

This weaning process was quite upsetting to Jane and she felt
very hurt and rejected by me, as I began slowly to put more tools
in her hands to use on her own.

She many times behaved like a child, whining and accusing,
withdrawing, getting angry and throwing temper tantrums through her
art, as well as physically. Perls discusses the "gulping down"
process which is what Jane had done in the art therapy sessions,
much as she had done all her life. Now being put in a position to
think and act on her own, she reacted with, "I don't understand,
this is all foreign to me. You, like all the others, just want to
hurt and reject me."

During the weaning process, Jane could feel herself slipping
into her old patterns and was struggling. She did not want to give
up what she had attained.

She drew her "Support System" and described it as follows:

My support is a tree trunk which is ugly and grotesque.
The tree trunk is a face, the body (leaves) of the tree
is a ludicrous, gaudy, unfitting, unbecoming hat, turban
style. The whole thing is ludicrous. The hat is too
gaudy and flamboyant; the face grotesque. The lights on
the tree are my pain, the candy and gifts are the good
things in life I deny myself because I don't deserve
them. The lines through the body are how I cut myself
off from success and others.
    The bird's nest with the two eyes is me, just peek-
ing out and the hole in the trunk has a night light in
it for the squirrel so he won't have to be in the dark, a
way to light his dark retreat.
    A support system is the life-giving part, but my
support is not providing that for me. I need a new support system.

She was having dreams of no one helping her. She kept saying
that she needed a plan, then made a flamboyant plan, but never followed it through to completion. More repetition of her life's patterns. She saw ladders in her dreams and drew some, stating they
were her desire to rise up in the world. She came across the

realization that she sapped others of their energies in order to
fulfill her needs of dependency, verify and perpetuate her game of
"dumbness and stupidity." She took in all she could get as quickly
as she could. When she felt the need, she would "spew it all out,"
or it would overflow. At this time, she became aware that she did
"it" to herself without the aid of others. By her constancy of
living in the past, she continually convinced herself that "everything will fail, so why bother?"

Insight and understanding began to erupt quickly for Jane at
this time and she felt out of control, did not know what to do, and
pressured for "technical assistance." Through her dreams, visual
dialogue and verbalizations, she realized she had a concern about
homosexuality which frightened her since she was just beginning to
accept and enjoy her sexuality. She expressed a desire for a stable
and healthy sexual relationship with a male counterpart.

Her fears of mental illness erupted, as well as the fear of
more violence in her life. She wanted neither of these. She
realized she still had work to do on the rapes and that these events
had devastatingly altered her life, plus added to her feelings of
helplessness, sense of contamination, guilt and anger levels. She
realized she imaged herself as an innocent bystander and her environment controlled her. She was beginning to understand that she had
the power to be self-supportive rather than environmentally supported, but "it's hard work and takes my energy," she stated.

Many dreams and drawings showed how she was trapped, but
inflicted this position on herself by saying, "I didn't do anything,
'it' just happened."

> I am trapped and contained in a circle. I keep mov-
> ing, but it is always in a circle. I have complete free-
> dom as long as it is in my circle. My circle has depres-
> sion leading to frustration and anger and self-hate, self-
> destruction and depression.
> I am the circle I created. I am a good circle because
> I have no beginning and no end. All my parts are over-
> lapped and dependent. All links are as strong as each
> other, no weak links. Each link has just as much power
> to destroy me as any other. Do you remember the "Big
> Depression"? Where you ended up taking the Librium?
> Do you remember the God-awful feeling of knowing you'd
> wake up the next day--so depressed you couldn't even
> stand the thought of living another day? Sleep to
> escape, escape to sleep--some life quality--ignoring your
> capacity to learn, feel, share, love. You had all that,
> yet chose to be depressed.

Material continued to pour forth. She remembered how ashamed and embarrassed she was about still wetting the bed at age 11 and how things were taken away from her because of the smell, her teddy bear, her blanket, her beloved boots. She equated this with the weaning process. I had taken me away from her. She had no control of these things (her environment). "It" was done to her.

She continued to experience a lot of dreams, especially about toilets. She heard herself saying, "I would like to sit back and let somebody else do the work. I am afraid of success, I don't want responsibility. I am comfortable with my self-pity and knowing, I can't. . . . This is a secure place to be." One of her dreams showed a barn so old it had holes in it. She laughed when she said, "Yep, my patterns are so old they have holes in them." Dreams also included a lot of black people which makes no connection for her yet; a lot of cars, trucks and vehicles, usually with others driving. She experiences a lot of dreams about all different types of rapes, which recalled the fact that she began stuttering after the first rape, when reporting it to the police. Through this she realized she had been raped by her older cousin as a child. She was able then to realize that she had been raped three times, as well as molested as a child by her father's friend and her uncle.

Through her visual dialogue and confrontations with herself, she realized that she really liked and felt comfortable with playing "poor me"; that she indeed held onto her anger and that her physical pains were a cover-up for the emotional pains she had not dealt with yet. Her self-defeating patterns had paid off for her and the pattern became self-rewarding. She continued these patterns adding to her maladjustive behavior.

After this period of "pouring out," as I called it, she began to bring about very positive therapeutic change, although she was still resisting the weaning process, using all kinds of tricks to get my attention and "get the milk flowing" freely again. This included the breaking of her ankle and being completely incapacitated for two months.

Next came her series on "Obstacles." She stated that she felt the meaning of this series was like so many of her dreams where she started down a street which looked perfect, but when she tried to go back, there were always obstacles in the way and she had to keep going; she could not complete her trip; she became diverted and had to start somewhere else. She gave another example of a dream about obstacles and her self-defeating game with herself. She had on a beautiful blue party dress which was torn underneath. Her attention was called to the dragging part. She stated it didn't matter. The person warned her about the possibility of tripping, but she continued on her way, refusing to take responsibility for the possibility of self-inflicted pain of a fall.

As she continued through her basket of "Things to Work On,"

she touched on her "Anger for Her Ex-husband," but ever so slightly for the first time.

It is interesting to observe that the series that followed the "Anger for Ex-husband," was entitled, "Guilt Because I'm a Girl." This indeed opened up some blocked channels for more intense work.

At the end of 13 months, I felt Jane's visual dialogue and feelings of her progress can best be summed up in her own words as to her most recent realizations about her insight and understanding of herself.

> I am afraid to finish when it's something I like or enjoy doing, because that's the end, no more and I am sorry that it's done, probably because I don't have the good feeling of doing it anymore--it's lost--gone forever. So I attempt to "hang on to it" by not finishing it and I know it's there and I can finish it any time (to get the good feeling), but I see that's not the way it goes. Actually, what happens is that I leave it, it's not done, can't be used, or in a hurry-up situation, gets finished in less than good circumstances. I feel bad, either way and no success factor either.
> I guess I have felt thousands of times the feelings of not having anything "good" to look forward to; so I hang on to something I know feels good.
> I feel, too, that if I finish it in an adequate manner and in plenty of time, that it might show how dumb I am; that I really couldn't do it, so by putting it off to the last minute, I have an excuse for why it's not done right or well, etc.
> I think, too, that I don't finish stuff because I just plain don't want to, don't like it, etc. I don't see anything neurotic in that. What I do see is my not knowing which is which. I had not thought of the difference until now. Both, however, end up in bad feelings, which I don't need any more of.
> My own intervention can be to attack the stuff I don't like to do and do it because it has to be done and HATE every minute I'm doing it. Then on the stuff I like to do, do it, enjoy the minutes I'm doing it and finish it so I can feel good and know that since I've kind of set goals, that there are things I can move on to that indeed will at least be of benefit to me and also some I can enjoy doing.

There has been much change for Jane in many areas. She still has a lot of work to be accomplished to reach the awareness levels and behavioral changes she is striving to attain. When I look back at her first visit and then compare that to where she has progressed

currently, it is difficult not to acknowledge the therapeutic change
that has transpired. Her own recognition that she can alleviate her
own physical symptoms of nausea and headaches by "emptying" her
internal garbage through her own specially designed visual dialogue,
makes it safe to ascertain that the therapeutic use of art has
indeed been used to advantage to rehabilitate a rape victim who has
many complex and compounded components of her personality, these
being disorganized for a long period of time. Most of her life's
production has been circumjacent to her self-defeating behavior and
her own self-punishment. For years, she has been at war with herself, constructing her own fortification surrounding her besieged
place; a circumvallation of inner torture and denial of her own
power as a person in process.

SUMMARY

This study has presented how art therapy has benefited a 38-
year old rape victim who suffered from retroflection, introjection,
and the "dummy complex": who bordered on schizophrenia, developed
against the background of some family pathology and three incidents
of violent rape. The art therapy technique provided for expressions of conflictual feelings which might have gone unnoticed until
such time as Jane might have entered a psychiatric hospital under
the disguise of a more acute problem. Since Jane used her verbal
facade to fortify her system of defense, art expression facilitated
important confrontations and aided her in recognizing some of her
authentic feelings. In addition, art therapy offered much needed
release of blocked impulses which had incapacitated her for years.

She has just begun to see through some of her most crippling
defenses and the importance of a realistic and tangible future.
She has begun to play a role in the present with the belief that
it is possible to enjoy her own personality integration and has
shown that "there is an inextricable relationship" between her and
her developing art (Kreitler, 1972).

REFERENCES

Arieti, S. Creativity, the magic synthesis. New York: Basic
    Books, 1976.
Arnheim, R. Art and visual perception. Berkeley: University of
    California Press, 1974.
Arnheim, R. Visual thinking. Berkeley: University of California
    Press, 1969.
Birren, F. Color preference as a clue to personality. Art Psycho-
    therapy, April, 1973, 1(1), 13-16.
Dax, C. E. Experimental studies in psychiatric art. London: Faber
    and Faber Limited, 1953.

Gantt, L., and Schmal, M. S. Art therapy, a bibliography. Rockville, Maryland: National Institute of Mental Health, 1974.

Jakab, I., ed. Psychiatry and art, proceedings of the 4th International Colloquium on Psychopathology of Expression, Washington, D.C., 1966. Basel and New York: S. Karger, 1969.

Keyes, M. F. The inward journey: art as psychotherapy for you. Mellbraw, California: Celestial Arts, 1974.

Kiell, N. Psychiatry and psychology in the visual arts and aesthetics: a bibliography. Madison, Wisconsin: University of Wisconsin Press, 1965.

Kramer, E. Art as therapy with children. New York: Schocken Books, 1971.

Kramer, E. Art therapy in a children's community. Springfield, Ill.: Charles C. Thomas, 1958.

Kreitler, Hans and Shulamith. Psychology of the arts. Durham, N.C.: Duke University Press, 1972.

Kwiatkowska, H. Family art therapy: experiments with a new technique. Bulletin of Art Therapy, 1967, 1(3), 3-15.

Meares, A. Shapes of sanity. Springfield, Ill.: Charles C. Thomas, 1960.

Naumburg, M. Dynamically oriented art therapy. New York: Grune and Stratton, 1966.

Naumburg, M. Art therapy: its scope and function. In the clinical application of projective drawings, E. F. Hammer, et al. Springfield, Ill.: Charles C. Thomas, 1958.

Rhyne, J. Gestalt art experience. Monterey, CA.: Brooks-Cole, 1973.

Rhyne, J. Orientations in art experience. In humanistic perspectives: current trends in psychology. Monterey, CA., 1977.

Robbins, A., and Sibley, L. B. Creative art therapy. New York: Brunner/Mazel, 1976.

Spring, D. Art therapy: a treatment modality for rape victims. Placentia, CA.: H.E.R.E. Rape Crisis Clinic, 1978.

Ulman, E., and Dachinger, P. Art therapy in theory and practice. New York: Schocken Books, 1975.

Zinkers, J. Creative Gestalt art therapy. New York: Brunner/Mazel, 1976.

CONTRIBUTORS

Erma Dosamantes-Alperson, Ph.D.,
    D.T.R.
Head, Graduate Dance-Movement
    Therapy Program
U.C.L.A.
405 Hilgard Avenue
Los Angeles, California 90024

Russell Bader, M.S.W.
844 North Van Ness
Fresno, California 93728

Paul Bakan, Ph.D.
Psychology Department
Simon Fraser University
Burnaby, B.C.
Canada V5A 1S6

John Battista, M.D.
Department of Psychiatry
University of California, Davis
Davis, California 95616

Steven Blankman, Ph.D.
Shasta County Mental Health
    Services
2750 Eureka Way
Redding, California 96001

Louis Breger, Ph.D.
Department of Humanities
California Institute of
    Technology
Pasadena, California 91125

David Bresler, Ph.D.
1515 Palisades Drive
Pacific Palisades,
    California 90272

Elizabeth Z. Danehy
Charila Delphi Foundation
San Francisco, California

Rose A. Dendinger, M.A.
Institute for Psycho-Imagination
    Therapy
580 South San Vicente Boulevard
Los Angeles, California 90048

Michael Emmons, Ph.D.
2510 Rodman Drive
Los Osos, California 93402

Eugene Gendlin, Ph.D.
School of Human Development
University of Chicago
5848 University Ave.
Chicago, Illinois 60637

Dennis T. Jaffe, Ph.D.
Learning for Health
1314 Westwood Boulevard
Suite 107
Los Angeles, California 90024

Virginia Johnson, Ed.D.
1416 Westwood Boulevard
Los Angeles, California 90024

Eric Klinger, Ph.D.
Division of Social Sciences
University of Minnesota
Morris, Minnesota 56267

Revel Miller, Ph.D.
California School for
    Professional Psychology
1350 M Street
Fresno, California 93721

Norma Lee K. Mittenthal, Ph.D.
1301 South First Street
Jacksonville Beach, Florida 32250

Clifford Morgan, Ph.D.
Department of Counselor Education
University of New Mexico
Albuquerque, New Mexico 87113

James K. Morrison, Ph.D.
678 Troy-Schenectady Road
Latham, New York 12110

Patricia Musick, Ph.D.
Associate Professor
School of Sciences and Humanities
University of Houston at Clear
   Lake City
2700 Bay Area Boulevard
Houston, Texas 77058

George Oliver, Ph.D.
Newton Center for Clinical
   Hypnosis
11340 West Olympic Boulevard
Suite 350
Los Angeles, California 90064

Joseph Reyher, Ph.D.
Department of Psychology
17 Snyder Hall
Michigan State University
East Lansing, Michigan 48824

Pennee Robin, MFCC
IPIT - Shorr Clinic
111 North LaCienga Boulevard
Beverly Hills, California 90211

Robert Rose, Ph.D.
6677 Suzanne Lane
San Bernardino, California 92404

Edward Joseph Shoben, Jr., Ph.D.
Clinical and Consulting
   Psychologist
1287 Avocada Terrace
Pasadena, California 91104

Joseph E. Shorr, Ph.D.
Institute for Psycho-Imagination
   Therapy
580 South San Vicente Boulevard
Los Angeles, California 90048

Gail E. Sobel, M.A.
IPIT - Shorr Clinic
111 North LaCienga Boulevard
Beverly Hills, California 90211

Dolores G. Spring, M.A., A.T.R.
Director of Psychological
   Services
516 North Placentia Avenue
Placentia, California 92670

David Tansey, Ph.D.
7670 Opportunity Road, Suite 165
San Diego, California 92111

Dan Tomasulo, Ph.D.
Instructor, Human Behavior
Brookdale Community College
Newman Springs Road
Lincroft, New Jersey 07738

Bernard Virshup, M.D.
4900 Dunman Avenue
Woodland Hills, California 91364

Evelyn Virshup, A.T.R.
4900 Dunman Avenue
Woodland Hills, California 91364

Patricia G. Webbink, Ph.D.
6033 Broad Street
Brookmont, Maryland 20016

Milton Wolpin, Ph.D.
Psychology Department
University of Southern California
734 West Adams Boulevard
Los Angeles, California 90291

Robert Zanger, M.A.
Newton Center for Clinical
   Hypnosis
11340 West Olympic Boulevard
Suite 350
Los Angeles, California 90064

INDEX